Cyber Zen

Cyber Zen ethnographically explores Buddhist practices in the online virtual world of Second Life. Does typing at a keyboard and moving avatars around the screen, however, count as real Buddhism? If authentic practices must mimic the actual world, then Second Life Buddhism does not. In fact, a critical investigation reveals that online Buddhist practices have at best only a family resemblance to canonical Asian traditions and owe much of their methods to the late twentieth-century field of cybernetics. If, however, they are judged existentially, by how they enable users to respond to the suffering generated by living in a highly mediated consumer society, then Second Life Buddhism consists of authentic spiritual practices.

Cyber Zen explores how Second Life Buddhist enthusiasts form communities, identities, locations, and practices that are both products of and authentic responses to contemporary Network Consumer Society. Gregory Price Grieve illustrates that to some extent all religion has always been virtual and gives a glimpse of possible future alternative forms of religion.

Gregory Price Grieve is Professor and Head of the Department of Religious Studies at the University of North Carolina at Greensboro. He researches and teaches at the intersection of digital media, Buddhism, and the theories and methods for the study of religion.

Media, Religion and Culture
Edited by Stewart M. Hoover, Jolyon Mitchell and David Morgan

Media, Religion and Culture is an exciting series which analyzes the role of media in the history of contemporary practice of religious belief. Books in this series explore the importance of a variety of media in religious practice and highlight the significance of the culture, social and religious setting of such media.

Cyber Zen

Imagining Authentic Buddhist
Identity, Community, and Practices
in the Virtual World of Second Life

Gregory Price Grieve

Routledge
Taylor & Francis Group

LONDON AND NEW YORK

First published 2017
by Routledge
2 Park Square, Milton Park, Abingdon, Oxon OX14 4RN

and by Routledge
711 Third Avenue, New York, NY 10017

Routledge is an imprint of the Taylor & Francis Group, an informa business

British Library Cataloguing in Publication Data
A catalogue record for this book is available from the British Library

Library of Congress Cataloging in Publication Data
A catalog record for this book has been requested

ISBN: 978-0-415-62871-6 (hbk)
ISBN: 978-0-415-62873-0 (pbk)
ISBN: 978-1-315-64585-8 (ebk)

Typeset in Bembo
by Apex CoVantage, LLC

For Fred Young

"We are but whirlpools in a river of ever-flowing water. We are not stuff that abides, but patterns that perpetuate themselves."

Norbert Wiener

"Philosophy is ending in the present age. It has found its place in the scientific attitude. . . . [T]he fundamental characteristic of this scientific attitude is its cybernetic, that is, techno-logical character."

Martin Heidegger

Contents

     and the cybernetic steersman   175

     Conclusion – Mind the gap: Screens, ontologies, and
     the far shore   194

     Appendix 1 – Cyber Zen*'s theoretical tool box*   215
     Appendix 2 – *Second Life terms*   224
     Appendix 3 – *Buddhist technical terms*   230
     Bibliography   233
     Index   251

Figures

Tables

Acknowledgments

Second Life happens when you are making other plans. I find it hard to believe that what started as a curiosity and a simple click of a mouse became almost a decade-long quest, out of which *Cyber Zen* emerged. Throughout my investigation, I have been blessed with an expansive network of good friends, excellent colleagues, and rigorous critics who have helped refine and shape the final product. First and foremost, none of this would have been possible without my *inworld* friends and informants. There were real people behind the avatars who showed me that Second Life was not just a game but also an important part of people's lives and indicated that researchers should not so much investigate but rather learn from and even be changed by those with whom they interact. For reasons of privacy, I leave them unnamed, but they know who they are. _/!_.

Next I need to thank the ethnographers who composed the Cardean Virtual Research Team and conducted much of the initial research. They started out as students but along the way became invaluable colleagues: a warm thanks to Rebecca Davis, Sabrina Epps, Kevin Heston, Jayme Mallindine, and Anna Michelle Lampley. Beyond my research team, a debt of gratitude goes to my cohort of fellow researchers and friends who helped create the field of digital religion. They are a truly interdisciplinary and international group of scholars: Rabia Gregory, Shanny Luft, Kerstin Radde-Antweiler, Vit Sisler, Daniel Veidlinger, Michael Waltemathe, and Xenia Zeiler, to name just a few. Also a special thanks to the fellow media and religion travelers Lynn Schofield Clark, Nabil Echchaibi, and Sarah McFarland Taylor. Jeff Wilson was also key in helping me see the significance of the work at an early and crucial juncture. The book only exists because of my interactions with my intellectual brother and sister, or at least close cousins, Chris Helland and Heidi Campbell. Lastly, I want to thank the trailblazers in the study of media and religion. Without the research and institutions this trinity built, the field of digital religion would not exist: a special thanks to Clark Stewart Hoover, David Morgan, and Angela Zito.

Many of the ideas in these chapters were presented at meetings and conferences at the American Academy of Religion; International Society for Media, Religion and Culture; the International Academy for the Study of Religion and

Digital Games; New York University's Center for Religion and Media; and the University of Colorado, Boulder's Center for Media, Religion, and Culture. I want to thank the members and officers of these organizations for the work they do to keep the field vibrant. Time and financial support for work on this manuscript were provided by the University of North Carolina at Greensboro. I especially want to thank Dean Timothy Johnston, who has navigated the College of Arts and Sciences through some difficult times. I would also like to thank the Center for Religion and Media at New York University, the Asian Research Institute at the National University of Singapore, and the Center for Contemplative Mind in Society. Finally I want to thank the members of my department, who have been gracious with their time and ideas. I want to thank especially Derek Krueger who gave me the courage to be virtual and Ben Ramsey whose conversation has given invaluable feedback over the years. Finally, I would like to thank Gene Rogers, who has always been able to see the importance of my project when even I had trouble seeing the significance for the details.

Most of all, however, this work would not have been possible without my family. Thanks to my sisters and father. My wife, Sarah, is simply amazing; I only need to talk with her to have my work made larger and more beautiful. And she has passed this along to our son Grey. In acknowledgements, one sees the author apologizing to his or her children. Grey would have none of that and often asked about what he called "the Buddha game." Much of the book was researched and written with a cat on my lap or a dog at my feet – a special thanks to Haku, Claribel, Sprite, and Baby Kitty. Last, but not least, I want to thank Matthew Butwinski, who asked almost every day, "Is the book done yet?"

Introduction

Digital Dharma: Authenticity, cybernetic entanglement, and silent spiritual media practices

"An unexamined Second Life is not worth living."
Resident Human Riddle (Second Life *profile*)

Cyber Zen ethnographically studies Zen Buddhist practice in a virtual world. The *event* that triggered the investigation occurred at 9:30 P.M., on December 23, 2007, when I found myself sitting in full lotus position, meditating next to a bear by the name of BodhiDharma Rosebud (Figure I.1).[1] Obviously this event did not take place in *real life* but rather in Second Life, a three-dimensional, immersive, interactive virtual world housed in cyberspace and accessed via the Internet.[2] Through on-screen representations, called *avatars*, millions of Second Life *Residents* explored the virtual world, communicating and socializing with one another, as well as creating, selling, and purchasing virtual goods. During the time of my research in the late 2000s, Second Life differed from other *MMORPGs* (massively multiplayer online role-playing games) because the content – buildings, *objects*, and even bodies – was created by users rather than by game designers. For instance, on June 7, 2010, the resident Fae Eden was asked what she did on Second Life, she explained, "I meet *friends* and interact, *roleplay*, shop, *build*, and tune my avatar."

Unexpectedly, my research team found that religious practices, particularly Buddhism, had a significant presence in this virtual world. In hindsight, finding religion online is actually not surprising. Wherever people go, religion seems to follow, and the spread of digital media corresponded to a growth in online practice. As early as 2004, a Pew survey reported that 64 percent of Americans with Internet access had used the medium for religious reasons.[3] Almost a decade earlier, on December 16, 1996, the *Time* magazine article "Finding God on the Web" stated, "Like schools, like businesses, like governments, like nearly everyone, it seems, religious groups are rushing online, setting up church home pages, broadcasting dogma and establishing theological newsgroups, bulletin boards and chat rooms." Intriguingly, digital *Dharma*, more than other religious practices, flourishes online.[4] As spelled out below, digital Dharma describes Buddhist teachings spread through computer-mediated communication.[5] There is no doubt that during the time of my research, the vast majority of digital

Figure I.1 Gregory Price Grieve's research avatar Clint Clavenham at convert Zen Buddhist Second Life location.

(Second Life snapshot by G.P. Grieve).

Dharma consisted of websites that merely offered information. Still, there was a sizable presence of Buddhists in Second Life who practiced "online religion," which the Canadian sociologist Chris Helland defines as locations "where people could act with unrestricted freedom and a high level of interactivity."[6] Second Life's online religion enabled users not only to gather information but also, as epitomized by BodhiDharma's online meditation, to engage in ritual and other types of digitally mediated religious practices.

While at first an informant, BodhiDharma became a guide and eventually a friend whose personal knowledge of people and the community made this book possible. With his and other residents' assistance, *Cyber Zen* analyzes Second Life's Zen Buddhist community from November 2007 to October 2011, concentrating on the year 2008 and the region known as the Hoben Mountain Zen Retreat.[7] In June of 2008, when my research team engaged in a full-scale survey, the Second Life's Zen community consisted of five *groups* that had 3,756 members and five regions and held approximately seventy-five events a week. Like the event that BodhiDharma invited me to, and what became the central focus of my research, 87.1 percent of events consisted of silent online meditation. During my research, Hoben was the largest of the Buddhist groups, which had a community of around 1,500 members: approximately 300 who were active, fourteen who were *meditation leaders*, and four who were the *owners*. The Hoben community described themselves on their website "as a nondenominational

Buddhist practice site dedicated to bringing Buddha-dharma to a virtual world. . . . the seeds of Dharma are spreading in Second Life!"

Often labeled Western, nightstand, or "convert Buddhism," as explored in chapter two, such popular forms like those at Hoben focused on several facets of the Buddhist tradition: the therapeutic, the nonhierarchical, the nonviolent, the ecological, and most importantly, the meditative.[8] For the most part, convert Buddhists live in the West – North America, Europe, and other parts of the developed world – but can also be found in many of the cosmopolitan centers of developing nations.[9] Hoben was Anglophone and mostly attracted members from North America, England, Australia, and New Zealand. Hoben's central philosophy was that they were not trained teachers but rather guides for practitioners along the path of practice. Most Second Life Zen adherents approached their practice very seriously and were conscious of Buddhism's legacy, and of how Zen had been introduced to the West, and consciously and mindfully strove to translate Buddhist practices into Second Life. As Hoben's founder, Cassius Lawndale, said in a conversation on July 1, 2009, "we are a real Buddhist community in a virtual world."

Screens

Cyber Zen theoretically focuses on how people tactically employ religious media to act upon and transform their everyday life. "Tactically" describes people's agency that operates from outside the bases of established authority, is used by more marginalized individuals, and by necessity is more flexible and innovative. Media practices consist of such activities as reading a book, watching television and film, and listening to the radio, as well as screening a computer, smartphone, or another digital device.[10] Media practices do not merely transmit information but rather perform embodied social activities that users execute with varying degrees of regularity, dexterity, and flair. "Media" here does not mean "the media," as in the diversified communication corporations that influence and even control the dissemination of information, although they obviously influence the message. Instead, media practice indicates "mediation," a term that indicates how different media, such as print, broadcast, and digital, are not neutral conveyers of information but rather play a fundamental role in producing the message. Media practices emerge from a relationship between possible human action, on one hand, and systems of communication, on the other, and describe how social beings, with diverse motives and intentions, tactically use the technologies of communication at hand to make and transform the realities in which they live. This is not a mysterious process. All media practices utilize the material substratum and code that enables communication through the spreading of differences and can be any material object: a word, image, sound, smell, act, object, or even a set of pixels on the screen.[11]

Cyber Zen focuses on the media practice of "screening," which describes how users engage with their digital devices through a flat digital visual interface. Screening as the main form of digital media practice can be traced at least as far back as the SWAC (Standards Western Automatic Computer) console of 1950

and was very much on the mind of 1970 computer hackers with such moni-
tors as the VT-100. As the American pioneer of digital technology Ted Nelson's
1974 *Computer Lib/Dream Machine* says, "If computers are the wave of the future,
Displays are the surfboards."[12] Between 2008 and 2011, when I conducted my
research, the screens of digital devices afforded Second Life and other virtual
worlds, as well as almost all types of digital media practices. Users rarely pay
attention to screens. Screens are such an integral part of contemporary digital
media practice it is hard to imagine life without them. Users stare at them so
often that they look right through them and hardly see the screen. As the media
historian Erkki Huhtamo notes, "how often do users of smartphones think about
the curious shifts of perception between nothing less than ontological realms that
take place when they move their gaze from the screen to other humans, to the
surrounding landscape, to another screen, and back again, in rapid succession?"[13]

As described in the pages that follow, as an integral part of Network Consumer Society, screens do not merely transmit information but generate desire.
Network Consumer Society defines late capitalistic forms of consumer-driven
corporate free market economy that are intertwined with digital media practices. Here I borrow the Buddhist term *tṛṣṇā*, often translated as "desire," but
which literally means "thirst" and defines an unquenchable craving that is the
ultimate cause of suffering, anxiety, and dissatisfaction. Desire immerses users
in their screens, but because desires are fleeting and ultimately unsatisfactory,
screening never seems to satisfy but leaves users uncertain and anxious.

While on a conventional level Second Life may be imagined as a world that
residents create and inhabit, ultimately, like all digital artifacts, Second Life consists
of programmable bits displayed across a screen that are used for symbol manipulation. As described in chapter one, because it is a digital media practice, screening
differs from analog media practices because it does not merely represent the world
but creates simulacra, which are not simply copies but become a truth in their own
right. "What is essential" about simulacra, writes the French philosopher Gilles
Deleuze, "is that we find in these systems no *prior identity*, no *internal resemblance*."[14]
As the French theorist Jean Baudrillard writes, this "inaugurates the era of simulacra and simulation, in which there is no longer a God to recognize his own."[15]
The screen marks the boundary between the actual and these digital copies, and
through it users emerge from, interface with, and are sutured to digital virtual
worlds. In digital communication, suturing refers to the process by which the
fabric of the actual world is sewn together with computer worlds.[16] If done well,
in virtual world practices users do not even notice the seams. They are invisible.

Why did BodhiDharma go online?

Between 2008 and 2011, I would friend BodhiDharma Rosebud and many
other Second Life Buddhist residents. Each had a purpose, a driving need,
want, ambition, vulnerability, or goal that drew them inworld. A typical

online silent meditation event attracted around twenty practitioners, who ran the gamut from those dressed in Zen monastic garb to those who looked like they should be out clubbing, elves, *submissives*, and *tinies,* animals that resembled nothing more than animated stuffed toys. On my right was Cassius Lawndale, the founder of Hoben, an Internet designer, talented *builder*, and knowledgeable lay practitioner, whose path inworld had taken the classic route from *griefer* to the leadership position he maintained because of his design skills. Cassius had a passion for spreading the Buddha's Dharma using this virtual new world but often seemed vulnerable because he ruminated about failing. A few rows up sat Human Riddle, who reported to be a famous mindfulness expert in New Zealand and was often at odds with Cassius. Human's ambition was to refine and publicize his practice but keep hidden his own agoraphobia in real life. Behind me was Algama GossipGirl, a submissive who came to Second Life to explore her sexuality but ended up leading education classes. She felt shame at her *edge play* and would talk about feeling unworthy of love. Leading the meditation was Georgina Florida, who had a stunning avatar. Many suspected her of being a male in real life, a point that would become an issue during a governing crisis. While giving of her time and self, because she seemed afraid to reveal herself, she would never completely open up to the community. In front of me, sitting on one of the cushions made especially for tinies, was Twinkle MoonLight, whose smaller-than-normal avatar was a cute hedgehog. In real life, Twinkle was disabled and used Second Life as her chief form of socializing, and she would become one of the main performers at the Hoben's Friday night campfire concerts. Behind me, smiling at each other, were Tai Buckinghamshire and Venomfangx Bardfield – a pair that had just recently become *partnered* and who would rise to leadership positions in the community. They had found romantic love. A few rows distant was the visionary, Mystic Moon; the often angry and *drama*-creating Rasa Vibration; a very classically trained scholar of Theravada Buddhism, Buddha Hat; the Zen pagan, Ashley Lee; the skeptic, Boon Thinker; and the entrepreneurial Zeus Ides.

Cyber Zen may be no substitute for the traditional community, identity, locations, and practices that networked consumerism has dissolved in the actual world. Yet practitioners used Second Life as a social workaround for creating innovative contemporary spirituality. As I illustrate in chapters three, four, five, and six, Second Life Zen adherents "poach" both popular and canonical Buddhist sources to create innovative groups, fashion residents, build places, and engage in religious events.[17] What congealed this group of residents into a community were spiritual media practices. BodhiDharma was deeply influenced by sixties counterculture, was well read in Eastern philosophy, and in his own playful manner desired an intense and authentic spiritual experience. As he said to me in one of our early conversations on January 10, 2008, "my goal is to wake up. All the rest is extra."

Digital Dharma

Digital Dharma is the Buddhism that users encounter on the screen. Because over the last twenty-five hundred years Buddhism has created techniques to address the suffering caused by desire, as *Cyber Zen* details, it proves particularly apt at resolving user's disease. At Hoben, digital Dharma consisted of mindful media practice, which describes the material systems by which people communicate ultimate reality and thus generate the moral economy of a lived religious world. As detailed in chapter two, derived from the Buddhist notion of *smṛti*, for convert Zen practitioners, mindfulness refers to the nonjudgmental focus on the emotions and thoughts as occurring in the present moment. Mindful media practices were spiritual for adherents, not because they communicated faith in a divine being, but rather because they were techniques for experiencing the empty (*śūnyatā*) nature of existence. For most practitioners, the spiritual goal of Zen practice was ethical. Most adherents stated that because it allowed one to sense the interconnected nature of the world, online Buddhist practice lessened the suffering created by contemporary society by affording personal therapy and generating compassion for others.

In early June 2008, after a late-night online meditation at Hoben, the community leader Georgina Florida privately instant messaged me: "do you wonder why so many Buddhists (Monastics, Dharma teachers) are playing a game called Second Life?" I was taken back for a moment, because while I had attended many meditation sessions that she had led, she had never spoken to me at all and truthfully had all but ignored me. While she had accepted my *friend request* when I first joined the group, I still figured she did not approve of my research. Feeling nervous, like I was being scolded by an elementary school teacher, I answered in public chat, "that is the question that brought me here." Differing from the chaotic communication of most Second Life residents, Georgina's conversation style was slow, as if she was carefully composing and thinking over each line of text. When I was just about to resend the message, Georgina answered, "well there are many reasons but the most obvious one is that most of us Buddhists realized quite quickly that this is a 'great mechanism' for spreading the Dharma."

Dharma is a key concept for many religions – Hinduism, Buddhism, Sikhism, and Jainism, which originated in South Asia – and is derived from the Sanskrit root √*dhṛ*, which means "to hold, maintain, and support."[18] For many at Hoben, as a Buddhist practitioner responded on July 20, to my 2010 Second Life Survey (*n*=108), "The Dharma is both the teachings of Buddha and the characteristics of those teachings, i.e. the Four Noble Truths, the Noble Eightfold Path, the Three Marks of Existence, and other guidelines that Buddha gave us." As another practitioner responded to the survey on August 6, Dharma tends to hold three meanings: "the great teaching, the truth, [and] the way the universe functions." Teaching usually described, as another respondent reported on September 4, 2010, "a 'manual' to the path of salvation [which are] Buddha's words to end suffering." Truth tended to indicate notions of mindfulness. One practitioner responded on July 8 to the question of "what is Dharma?" with "life as it is," and another on July 7 simply said, "Joy." The workings of the universe reflected the concept of the Buddha-nature (*tathāgatagarbha*) and were conceived in two ways: first, as a respondent said on July 7, "that unseen Presence which unifies, guards, directs, and guides all existence and all experience," and, second, as another reported on July 20, "all dharmas are interrelated and spring from matter and time but are ultimately empty."

My study focused on how Second Life practitioners translated Buddhist Dharma into the virtual world. An obviously translated media practice, for instance, is the *gasshō* emoticon, "_/!_," which reflects the real-life Buddhist gesture of pressing palms together as an act of piety. In one of my first conversations with him, in December 2007, BodhiDharma Rosebud said: "the Dharma is still sorta of evolving. . . . India, China, Japan . . . the little 'gassho' emoticon is used a lot _/!_ to translate Zen into Second Life." One of the last group messages I received *inworld*, in November 2011, was a group instant message from the resident Human Riddle: "Meditation @ 1 PM SLT, Hoben will be holding 30 minutes of silent meditation. Please join us!_/!_." Typed into public chat, or instant messaged, Second Life Buddhist residents used the _/!_ as a way both of greeting each other, showing thankfulness, and also of marking communications as having particular reverence, such as at the beginning and end of a group meditation.

Digital Dharma consists of material and public media practices. On Second Life, digital Dharma included not just information, such as written texts and videos, but also media practices that communicated objects and events. As described in more detail in chapter five, objects are virtual items created by residents using Second Life's building tools. A few weeks after my encounter with BodhiDharma, my avatar *rezzed* (materialized) and I was standing next to the Buddhist builder Mystic Moon and his partner Fael Eden. In real life, Fael was a Finnish art student whose intricate and hauntingly beautiful avatar played otherworldly music on a flute. On Mystic's back was a spinning *dharmachakra*, or dharma wheel. After I had praised its design, Mystic said in chat, "it was the first thing I built in Second Life. It represents the Eight Fold Path." Fael privately instant messaged me, "and the Buddha's teachings in the world. It's cool isn't it?"

Interdependent with objects were Second Life events. As described in chapter six, events at Hoben included *campfire concerts*, dharma and book discussions, dharma talks and interviews, and more rarely weddings and memorials. By far the most prevalent and significant practice, however, was silent online meditation, which describes a media practice in which users rested their avatars for twenty to thirty minutes on virtual cushions while they meditated in real life in front of their computer screens. For the vast majority of Hoben community members, silent online meditation was seen as the central focus of their digital Dharma. As a survey respondent wrote on July 8, 2010, "It takes Practice to understand and engage in Dharma." Dharma was not perceived by practitioners to involve faith in supernatural beings. As another respondent said on July 7, Dharma "doesn't matter who wrote it, or when, or where. The core teachings are what matter and they do serve to improve the quality of life. They are rational, testable and effective."

As investigated in the pages that follow, digital Dharma afforded being mindful of the world and oneself as "empty" (śūnyatā). For adherents, emptiness was reported not as a sui generis static void standing behind the veil of the illusion. There was no Great Emptiness out there somewhere to be found. Instead, as the resident Human Riddle stated, "emptiness is right here, right now." Emptiness indicated the mindful perception that reality has no static intrinsic essence and is constituted by networks of codependent human and nonhuman elements. Online practice was significant for practitioners because it relieved the suffering of living in a highly mediated consumer society and offered up alternative possibilities for emergent communities, identities, locations, and spiritual practices.

Spirituality

Dharma is usually translated into English as "religion," a term that undergirds this research but bends under the weight of the topic. As used in *Cyber Zen*'s analysis, the category of religion describes the media practices by which Second Life groups engaged with what they perceived as "ultimate reality," those ontological models that included both the content of what is ultimately real and what is not but also the larger cultural matrix that shapes the abstract idea of reality itself. By giving a face to a group's ultimate reality, religious practice engages their authentic desires – those deeper existential needs that arise from the very social condition of being human. My research team's use of the term, however, was often at odds with most Second Life Buddhist practitioners, who often understood "religion" as being opposed to "spirituality." Frequently, Buddhist practitioners used "religion" to indicate oppressive forms of organized institutions that they perceived as having lost their authentic search for divine expression, while "spirituality" was used to designate a deeply personal, existential, unique anti-institutional focus on personal exploration and spontaneity. In what follows, I attempt to stay as close as possible to Second Life Buddhist emic or insider use of the terms. I use "religion" to describe institutions and "spirituality" to describe the media practices by which users report personal engagement with Buddhist Dharma. To be clear, *Cyber Zen* argues for an essential definition neither for religion nor for spirituality. Rather, my aim is to investigate, explain, and analyze how the categories were used and lived in the virtual world. Spirituality and religion did not just happen in people's minds but rather by necessity as observable media practices that played out as a web of communication across the screen.[19]

At Hoben, spirituality was not ideological false consciousness. Rather, spiritual media practices screened a user's desire, creating moral economies that played a part in producing a user's lived reality. Spiritual media practices enabled residents and groups to engage authentically with what they perceived as their ultimate reality, which at Hoben usually engaged notions of suffering. Many residents stressed that the point of Buddhist practice was not to locate a dogmatic "religious truth" but to end suffering. The Buddhist gardener Ashley Lee's *profile* read, "Pain is inevitable. Suffering arises from grasping and Desire. Follow the path and be free of suffering [capitalization in original]." Adherents reported that suffering was caused by a nonmindful view of the world in which people clung to perceived lacks. The meditation note card "Stillness Speaks" goes on to describe desire as "the need to add something to yourself in order to be yourself more fully. All fear is the fear of losing something and thereby becoming diminished and being less." Many wide-ranging examples, often from outside classical Buddhist sources, were given to support this claim. For instance, the "Stillness Speaks" note card mixed Buddhist thought with quotes by the popular teacher Eckhart Tolle to argue that "most people's lives are run by desire and fear." Third, spirituality at Hoben served as a support for people's everyday life by offering what was felt to be ultimately lacking. From a convert Buddhist perspective, users are always already alienated in the actual world.

As reflected in the account of Gautama Buddha and the "Four Sights," many Buddhist residents saw existential suffering arising not out of any particular lack but out of the very existential human conditions of old age, sickness, and death. As a note card given to me by the resident Dubhshlaine Gustafson, titled "The First Noble Truth" and attributed to the Tibetan Buddhist lama Gelek Rimpoche, read, "We have so much dissatisfaction in our lives. We are dissatisfied with our achievements and with everything else. This dissatisfaction really brings pain into our lives, in addition to the usual pain and misery of sickness and aging."[20] For many, however, the statement from *The Wheel of Law* (Dhammacakkappavattana *Sūtra*) "that all life is suffering" appeared, as the resident Algama GossipGirl declared, "a little too *drama*-queenish." Rather than some overwhelming anguish, residents described suffering as a subtle, barely discernible, quality of unease. As a meditation note card, handed out on April 9, 2009, titled "The Mind That Suffers" and attributed to the Buddhist author Phillip Moffitt, reads,

> How often in your adult life have you experienced the queasiness and unease that come from a sense of meaninglessness in your life? Think of all those occasions when you felt as though you were wasting your life, or sleepwalking through it, or not living from your deepest, most heartfelt sense of yourself.[21]

Silent spiritual media practices

Cyber Zen theorizes Second Life's digital Dharma as a spiritual media practice by which residents communicate their ultimate reality so as to create moral economies that address the suffering in their lives. As the core of Buddhism, "suffering" is usually indicated as *duḥkha*, which literally means being stuck but is usually translated into English as 'anxiety,' 'stress,' 'unsatisfactoriness,' or 'dis-ease.' As I investigate below, the difficulty the study encountered is that Second Life Zen was a silent media practice. How can one analyze what is not there? I contend silence is not simply the absence of information. Silence's significance is produced by media practices that have different connotations, depending on their cultural context and media environment. I asked the Hoben leader Georgina Florida to expand on how Second Life helped spread the Dharma. She answered, "Many are thirsting for knowledge (contact) and are in isolation; this provides a *sangha* [community] and teachings for them. Also the community here in Second Life accepts people who do not fit the standard mold." After a long pause, she added, "most of all it helps to be aware of silence."

Silence appears at first an extremely obvious form of communication, or lack of communication, but its analysis brings out that it is a very strange thing, abounding in spiritual subtleties and theological niceties. I asked BodhiDharma Rosebud directly the night I first met him and a frustrating number of nights afterwards why he practiced online, but he never actually answered. Kind and wise, BodhiDharma frequently seemed absentminded, because in real life he was a barista and had to be AFK (away from keyboard) so he could pull espresso for his customers. Also, he relished his trickster character and enjoyed nothing more than answering questions with further riddles. On January 15, 2007, I asked him, "Why did you come to Second Life?" to which he answered, "the oak tree in the courtyard. Yesssssss." BodhiDharma's insistence on remaining silent about his practice proved to be a general pattern in the community's communication. For most practitioners, to talk about Zen was to miss the point of practicing it. As a July 7, 2008, meditation note card read, "If you must insist on words, then Zen is an elephant copulating with a flea."

Silence is not simply an absence of sound that somehow exists outside of lan-guage, nor does silence have a universal meaning that conveys the same signifi-cance in different social settings. Silence in an elevator has different meanings from silence next to a grave. *Cyber Zen* argues that silence is produced from specific media practices that have different connotations depending on their cultural context. Accordingly, to understand silence, researchers cannot simply record a lack of content but need to contextualize it in a media environment. When I asked Georgina what silence meant, I felt like I could feel her sigh, and then she wrote simply "being mindful." When I asked her to describe mindful-ness, rather than answering directly, she sent me a note card titled, "Meditation, Simple Breathing," and then logged off. The note card informed me to "follow your breath, in and out."

The problem of unreality

I had met BodhiDharma Rosebud the day before at a *sandbox*, a region in the virtual world where residents can rez virtual objects, unpack *boxes* filled with purchases, and experiment creating their own inworld content. At the time I was only six days old, still just a struggling *noobie* concerned mostly with acquiring the basic skills needed to survive my second life. The virtual world was still new to me and dominated by a chaotic mix of perceptions, feelings, and wants. I had not sought him out and had no intention at that time to study Buddhism in Second Life. BodhiDharma had grabbed my attention because his avatar was not the typical, young and beautiful, often highly sexualized, idealized convention common to the virtual world. He was not in bear form but was fashioned as an almost hunched-over, elderly, solemn-looking human, with a bald head and large Gandhi-like spectacles, dressed in full black Zen Buddhist robes. As discussed in chapter four, I asked him about his Buddhist robes, which led to an hour and a half long conversation. I told him that I taught Religion Studies at a North Carolina state university, about my own long but often lagging meditation practice, and that I had been fascinated by computer worlds since I played the digital game *Colossal Cave Adventure* as a child.[22] I learned that he had been using Second Life for a just under a year, was in his early sixties, lived in a small town in Alaska, and in real life was the only Buddhist practitioner for hundreds of miles. About forty minutes into the conversation, to prove that he was from Alaska he playfully changed into his bear form.

My conversation with BodhiDharma begged for an interrogation that promised to illuminate the voices and agency of online spiritual practitioners, and the role of religion in contemporary popular culture. When I looked for analysis of digital Dharma, however, I found sources sadly lacking. Rather than approaching Second Life and convert Buddhism as a media practice that many adherents find intellectually pleasurable and spiritually satisfying, digital Dharma and other forms of online spiritual practice seemed to exist in the mass media and academic imagination as a conundrum to be solved, as a phenomenon to be explained away rather than analyzed and understood. The usual way to handle virtual world religious practice is to question its reality. As a May 2007 *NBC Nightly News* segment, "Religion Online and in Second Life," asks, "Is this real religion? Can there be a church if you do not have flesh and blood interaction?"[23] A 2007 *Los Angeles Times* article, "It's Easter: Shall We Gather at the Desktops?" maintained that believers on Second Life should find more enriching ways to spend Easter Sunday than typing out commands to make their avatars pray.[24]

On the surface, the question of reality seems to address physicality. Yet all religious media practices, except for small groups of cohabiting worshipers, and perhaps even these, are mediated.[25] Even face-to-face interaction requires speech and bodily gestures that depend upon systems of communication that require material signs and humanly evolved semiotic code. Moreover, religious mediation is not simply a contemporary phenomenon and can be found in Early Christian use of epistles and in the Buddhist circulation of scripture and images. The difficulty with declaring online religious practice unreal, however, is that whether one likes it or not, people are using Second Life and other digital media for religious practice, religious communities do exist in virtual worlds, and residents do perceive the platform as an authentic place of worship. Telling online practitioners that what they practice is unreal is like telling a bumblebee that it cannot fly. Instead, under the guise of "reality," what is being expressed is a moral objection to online religion, spiritual practices that are practiced primarily on digital media.[26] The objection is not that these media practices do not exist, but that they should not be happening. One cannot deny that virtual digital media practitioners engage in something they are calling religion, and these practices exist as part of a lived material reality. The screens on which users type, click, and tap are as materially existent as any place of worship or any book of scripture.

Screened religion is often reduced to simulacrum. Yet, like a magician's sleight of hand, the question of reality camouflages the iconoclast's ethical doubt about the proper use of media for religious practice behind an inquiry of physical presence. The problem of unreality arises because popular digital religious media practices often poach for spiritual reasons contemporary popular images and concepts drawn from sources that elites find troubling.[27] Scholars of religion would question the authenticity neither of canonical scripture nor of premodern and non-Western groups and in fact often go out of their way to be respectful of the beliefs of others. For many scholars, however, popular religious practices exist in an academic uncanny valley because these popular forms of spirituality look almost, but not quite, legitimate.[28] Second, popular spirituality has always been suspect, yet digital media accelerate cultural poaching because, unlike analog forms, their procession of simulacra affords endless copies.[29] Screening differs from previous media practices because it does not merely represent the original source but rather displays copies that become a reality in their own right.[30] Because they are substitutions that replace the original, these digital simulacra are "hyper-real," to borrow a phrase from the French cultural theorist Jean Baudrillard.[31] Like Aaron and the Golden Calf, photographs, and margarine, the moral danger is that the unwashed masses will come to prefer the humanly constructed imitation to the genuine original. Yet, there is no natural reason that the original ought to be more authentic than the copy. Questioning the reality of online religious practice is a form of iconoclasm, the rejection or destruction of religious images as heretical.[32]

Digital Dharma critics frequently assume that digital religion is inherently alienating because as a simulacrum it robs users of their humanity and connection to reality.[33] As my research illustrates, however, such alienation did not hold for most Second Life residents, who often found the creativity and alternative roles opened up by the virtual world to be liberating.[34] Rather than being victims seduced by alienating media practices, many Second Life users found digital media to be empowering and a central part of their spirituality. In an interview from June 23, 2009, the tiny Hoben community member, Twinkle MoonLight, who was often in the shape of a hedgehog, told me, "I thought I was here for fun and games," but my time on Second Life has "turned out to be a spiritual journey which has changed me in ways I could not imagine." I asked her "how?" "This might be a fantasy world, but fantasy and spirituality can mix together in wonderful ways."

Rather than signifying any content, accusations of unreality are a way of explaining away digital Dharma that marginalizes and trivializes practices religiously significant to the people who actually adhere to them. Scholars of religion need not be caretakers of digital religion, but they should walk in the shoes or at least type on the keyboards of those who practice it. Buddhist practitioners have long journeyed to a wide variety of what they perceived as spiritual destinations. No one can deny that with the onset of digital media, many types of media practices, while only tethered to the actual world, are often coded as Buddhist. Rather than a matter of fact, the question of "reality" asserts a value, or rather, a particular hierarchy of values. By proclaiming online practice as "unreal," critics silence adherents without having to actually engage with them. The proclamation of something as unreal is a rhetorical strategy that protects critics' own view of reality from the abnormal and threatening, which transgresses the cultural hierarchies that critics have a vested interest in maintaining.

Network consumer virtual orientalism

As theorized in chapter one and described in chapter two, often "unreality" hides the accusation that digital Dharma is a form of Network Consumer virtual Orientalism.[35] As the English Buddhologist Richard King writes in "Spirituality and the Privatization of Asian Wisdom Traditions," often "historically rich and complex traditions are exploited by a selective re-packaging of the tradition, which is then sold as the 'real thing.'"[36] In a similar fashion, the Slovenian cultural critic Slavoj Žižek perceives "Western Buddhists" as a threat because they embody the spirit of Network Consumer Society.[37] He argues that convert Buddhism is the new opium of the people, "the imaginary supplement to terrestrial misery." Particularly, "the 'Western Buddhist' meditative stance is arguably the most efficient way for us to fully participate in capitalist dynamics while retaining the appearance of mental sanity."[38] For better or worse, the critics' rejection of reality is actually a moral objection that accuses online practices of being inauthentic because they are popular simulacra, unsatisfactory consumer digital forgeries. Critics' objections usually include one of two accusations: either digital Dharma is a contemporary orientalist practice or it is a product of Network Consumer Society. Orientalism describes the network of media practices employed by European culture to divide the globe into two unequal halves, "East" and "West," and employs this epistemological framework to dominate non-European people and places.[39]

Because it untethers Dharma from a referent, digital media often accelerate convert Buddhism's perceived inadequacies. The scholar of religion Jane Iwamura argues, in *Virtual Orientalism: Asian Religions and American Popular Culture,* that orientalism did not disappear in the postcolonial period starting after World War II. The new American orientalism just became more covert than its European predecessors, operating through a network of popular mass media that displays "Asia" in print, broadcast, and now online. In the contemporary American version, which Iwamura describes as "virtual orientalism," actual people and Asian phenomena become even more detached from their representations and "within this hyperreal environment, orientalized stereotypes begin to take on their own reality and justify their own truths."[40]

To be clear, Asian lives matter. *Cyber Zen* denies neither that convert Buddhism is an ideological symptom of Network Consumer Society nor that its practices are a popular form of orientalism. I contend that digital Dharma is both a symptom of and response to the suffering generated by a Network Consumer life and that a romanticized fantasy about Asia plays a key role in these practices. For many convert Buddhists, Asia remains deeply embedded in clichéd and shorthand forms in their practice, which often takes on a manifest destiny that overwrites and dislodges Asian American practices as well as continues racist stereotypes.[41]

I do, however, counter the notion that digital Dharma's practices are unreal. Although virtual and mostly performed by middle-class white adherents, these are actual people engaging in actual religious practices that obviously fill a craving for those who use them. Scholars may disagree about digital Dharma on moral grounds, yet such critics should not throw out the baby with the bath water. There is an increasing number of actual human beings behind the keyboards whose religious practices deserve to be fairly investigated and understood. One does not need to be an advocate, yet the investigation does require an alternative approach to Second Life residents, and convert Buddhist practitioners more generally, which does not posit them as isolated social misfits, unknowing orientalists, or mindless consumers. Behind the exotic media stereotypes, which are often uncritically perpetuated by academics, lies a largely unexamined territory of popular forms of authentic spirituality. In fact, I contend that the most effective means to counter convert Buddhist shortcomings is not to posit a transhistorical, self-identical Dharma that has moved from one culture to another, unchanged through the vicissitudes of time.[42] Rather, I argue that convert Buddhism needs be decentered and provincialized, illustrating that its form of practice, while real and authentic for those who use it, is just one of the many actors on the world stage.[43]

Authenticity

To analyze Second Life Buddhist media practices, we need to reframe the problem of "unreality" as a question of "authenticity."[44] Most in the Hoben community, and this included BodhiDharma Rosebud, saw Second Life Buddhism not as a final remedy but as a contemporary "workaround" and would answer the question of authenticity with a qualified yes. A "workaround" is a computer science term describing a temporary fix and suggests that a final answer is still needed. While often not elegant, frequently workarounds are creative solutions that rethink the problem in innovative ways. As Cassius Lawndale said in an interview from June 2009, "I am torn in my own feelings about the platform. On the one hand I find I enjoy it and that I've made some good friends, but at some level it also feels destructive and a bit contrived or senseless. Kind of like everything here is fluff!" In an interview from May 21, 2009, I asked the Hoben practitioner Ashley Lee why she practiced in Second Life. She answered, "to be awake, like the Buddha." I asked her if "her understanding changed between real life and Second Life?" There was a long pause, and then she replied, "It's more or less the same. Although it might be harder than in real life." Other adherents actually thought that Second Life intensified their practice. As the practitioner Nanda Westland said in conversation on June 21, 2009, "I think here the limitations of keyboard and screen help by limiting our awareness and help to be mindful. We therefore get to focus on less intense complexities, and sometimes get to know ourselves better as a result."

If authenticity refers to fidelity to an original source, then a meditating online bear has at best only a family resemblance to canonical Asian sources.[45] A fidelity notion of authenticity models religious communication on a "transmission theory" that reduces media practices to broadcasting content. In such a case, authentic religious communication can only be that which filters out the background noise so as to most accurately reproduce an original informational source.[46] Formed from a metaphor of transportation, in the transmission model communication imparts, sends, and transmits information to others like water in a pipe or, better yet, like commodities along a factory's conveyer belt. The transmission theory of authenticity was active at Hoben, and one can find that leaders, particularly Cassius Lawndale, made numerous attempts to develop official links with real-life Zen centers. As he said in an interview from September 23, 2009, "our goal is to integrate as many aspects of real life teachings and practice into Second Life – including streaming audio talks, live discussions, meditation, temple building (virtual preservation, if you will)." Cassius was concerned that Buddhism on Second Life was "not transparent enough for people who have no real idea about Buddhism." He maintained that the "focus should be more on information that takes away the usual false views, like that Buddha is a god, and whatnot."

The problem with a fidelity model of authenticity is that there has never been an original Buddhist source. Because all traditions are humanly constructed, ultimately the original Buddhism eludes any empirical search. As the Buddhologist David McMahan reminds us, in *The Making of Buddhist Modernism*, there has never been a "pure" Buddhism; even the canonical Asian traditions are a "hybrid of what were already hybrid."[47] As is true of all living religions, while its practitioners strive to retain a perceived connection with the origins of a tradition, Buddhism has never been fixed or static but instead has continued to evolve and adapt to changing attitudes and circumstances. Buddhism has been modified and translated into new cultures wherever it has spread, and it is not surprising that post–World War II America has altered and crafted a unique form of Zen for a specific set of social needs. "Or, put another way," as Bernard Faure writes, in *Unmasking Buddhism*, "Buddhism is not an essence in itself, it is something Buddhists do."[48]

Cybernetic entanglement

Buddhist Dharma's centers are as plural and diverse as its margins, and Buddhist practices emerge differently depending on the historic context and media landscape. Often assumed to be either shallowly postmodern or deeply archaic, the genealogy of convert Buddhism exists in a middle realm, having only constituted a coherent web of practices since the end of World War II. Throughout its history, as Buddhism spread to new lands, it has been shaped by the cultures it encountered, finding indigenous systems to translate its practices to the local desires. In postwar America, I argue that convert Buddhism became entangled with cybernetics, the scientific study of systems, particularly feedback loops. In particular, *Cyber Zen* illustrates how convert Zen has used cybernetic procedures to translate Buddhist concepts into popular culture. In the postwar period, cybernetics viewed the world as systems that contained individuals, societies, and ecosystems and was deeply influential in the creation of computers and digital media. The term "cybernetics" was popularized in 1948 by the American mathematician and philosopher Norbert Wiener in his seminal work *Cybernetics: Or the Control of and Communication of Animal and Machine*. Wiener forged "cybernetics" from the Greek *kybernetes* (steersmen) and defines it as "the entire field of control and communication theory, whether in the machine or animal."[49] Principally, as I trace in chapter two, convert Zen has a genealogy leading from late 1940s cybernetic thought through Alan Watts, the Beats, California's sixties counterculture, the work of Robert Pirsig and, finally, to the 1980s corporate poaching of the concept of mindfulness.

As America became the postwar consumer nation, cybernetics offered a frame on which Buddhist concepts and practices were hung and offered a way for practitioners to be in the consumer economy but perceive themselves to be outside of it. As hostilities ended in World War II, cybernetics promised not just a new science, but as the American engineer and head of the United States Office of Scientific Research, Vannevar Bush, wrote in *As We May Think*, an entire "new relationship between thinking man and the sum of our knowledge."[50] In *Cybernetics*, Norbert Wiener argued that cybernetics differed from hard empirical sciences because the focus was not on material form but rather on networks of organization, patterns, and communication made up of users and machines. Such systems can be rain forests, the nervous system, brain and sense organs, and the relationship between mechanical-electrical communication networks such as computers and their users. "In this view," as the postmodern literary critic Katherine

Hayle writes in *How We Became Posthuman*, "a universal informational code underlies the structure of matter, energy, spacetime – indeed, of everything that exists."[51]

Key to cybernetics' entanglement with Buddhism is the spiritualization of the Greek concept of *kybernetes*, "steersman, governor, pilot, or rudder," and its use to translate the concepts of no-self (*anātman*), delusion (*avidyā*), and mindfulness. As I suggest in the pages that follow, the self-aware steersman becomes the model for the mindful Buddhist practitioner sitting on his or her meditation cushion. The contemporary usage of "cybernetics" stems from the mid-twentieth century but can be traced back to Plato's *The Alcibiades*, where it signifies "the study of self-governance."[52] As the cybernetic theorist Stafford Beer writes in "Cybernetics and the Knowledge of God," "Now a man is himself part of a large system, namely the universe, which is . . . in control."[53] Rather than being outside the system, in cybernetic thought the self-aware agent is conceived as an integral part of it and as actually constituted by the system. In *Cybernetics*, Wiener describes how humans are part of a link of information systems, "in what we shall from now on call the chain of feedback."[54] Cybernetics was not just a scientific theory but comprised an ontological view of how the world worked, a model of reality that pictured the world as a set of self-generating systems governed by a mindful steersman who regulated the operation. The classic example is the heating system of a house. The resident, who feels cold, turns up the thermostat, which then changes the state of the furnace. After a while the steersman may start to feel overly warm and turns the thermostat down, which then again changes the state of the system (Figure I.2).

To be clear, *Cyber Zen* does not reduce postwar American Buddhism to cybernetic thought (or vice versa for that matter), but rather suggests in a complex feedback loop that cybernetic pragmatic procedural ontology was used to translate Buddhist terms into popular American culture, and this folded back and influenced how cybernetic practices were understood. I call this process "social entanglement." As I argue in chapter two, epistemologically "entanglement"

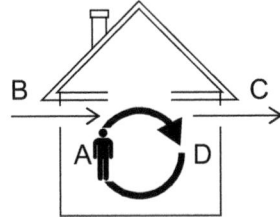

Figure I.2 Cybernetic system compared with house with thermostat. (A) Steersman sets the temperature, which is (B) affected by input from environment and (C) output to environment but is regulated by (D) the thermostat.

has links to Buddhism and digital media. I poach the concept of entanglement, however, from quantum physics, where it is used to describe pairs of particles that interact in ways such that the state of each particle cannot be described independently – instead, each must be described as part of the system as a whole.[55] In entangled systems, the behavior of the two is different from the juxtaposition of the behaviors of each considered alone.

An existential approach to spiritual authenticity

As described above, if authenticity is approached as fidelity to canonical Asian sources, then Second Life Zen has at best a family resemblance. On the other hand, however, if authenticity refers to a cultural model of media practices that allow users to existentially explore and create alternative identities and communities in relation to what they perceive as divine, then the virtual world can be considered authentic.[56] In such a case, much online Buddhist practice, to borrow a phrase from the scholar of comparative religion David Chidester, proves an "authentic fake."[57] "Existential" describes media practices that allow the acting, feeling, living person to build meaningful realities.[58] A cultural theory of communication perceives lived reality as jointly constituted over time by people through media practices and authenticity as how effective media practices are at affording the existential construction and maintenance of these livable worlds.[59] A cultural model of communication does not filter out change as noise but theorizes authentic religious world construction as a dialectic between tradition and innovation. An existential approach to authenticity explores how adherents frequently adopt, integrate, and adapt media practices in particular ways so that they fit more cohesively with the moral life and expectations of the communities with which they are affiliated.[60]

In Second Life, such pragmatic existential workaround notions of authenticity were often coded as "spirituality." Frequently dressed up in Eastern clothing, Second Life spirituality repeatedly reflected popularized versions of existentialist philosophy, which holds that philosophy begins with the human subject, not just logical thought, but the acting, feeling living person. As the Danish philosopher and theologian Søren Kierkegaard suggests, authenticity lies in the power of each of us to "become what one is."[61] As the German cultural critic Erich Fromm writes in *Escape from Freedom*, people are authentic when they are "free and not alone," "critical and yet not filled with doubts."[62] In such a case, authenticity arises when people realize their true selves in a spontaneity that counters the compulsive activity of the automaton. It is through authentic lives that people shoulder the burden of being truly and fully human. As Fromm maintains, only if one "has become transparent to [oneself], and only if the different spheres of life have reached fundamental integration, is spontaneous activity possible."[63]

The existential approach to authenticity undergirded most of Second Life's religious media practices and relied on a cultural model of communication.

In a cultural model of communication, media practices do not simply transmit information but communicate through the play between the affordance of material sign systems and the agency of users as well as the historical, social, and cultural context of their use.[64] From an existential standpoint, authenticity does not just describe received fidelity to tradition but also indicates a morality that results from authentic living. Spiritual existential authenticity describes how people and groups act in accordance with desires, motives, ideals, or beliefs that express, as the resident Ashley Lee said, "who they really are." For many Buddhist residents, Second Life practice is authentic exactly because it is beneficial to their lives. "The Point" as BodhiDharma Rosebud said in an early interview "is not what some old fart in India said or did not say. It is to wake up and end suffering." Consider for, instance, a note card handed to me before a meditation event titled "Suicide Solution" and excerpted from the Buddhist author Noah Levine's *Dharma Punx*: "Nothing I have been doing has worked, and there is nowhere else to turn, so I guess this is my best bet. The meditations do seem to help a little, at least a few seconds here and there; when I am able to focus on my breath I feel better and forget that I'm locked up."[65]

Scope of the study

In order to understand what digital Dharma, is, does, and means in a developed contemporary networked society, *Cyber Zen* uses an ethnographic method to explore the intersection of digital media, Buddhism, and popular culture. As described in the chapter on method, a virtual ethnography's effectiveness emerges from the everyday nitty-gritty spadework of exploration, which does not just answer known unknowns but uncovers unknown unknowns. The scope of *Cyber Zen* developed not from what I had calculated or hypothesized about before entering the field but emerged out of thickly described emic categories gleaned from participant observation of Second Life's convert Zen Buddhism. I logged onto Second Life interested in identity and community but ultimately came away with an understanding of the spiritual reasons why Hoben's residents, such as BodhiDharma Rosebud, found digital Dharma not only possible but also desirable.

The volume's first two chapters lay out the context of the study. The first chapter explores the media practices that produce the virtual world of Second Life. If one leans back from the keyboard when using Second Life, it is not immediately clear how the pixels on the screen are any different from other types of "digital media" enabled by the culture of Digital Utopianism. To analyze how the flat pixels are transformed into a three-dimensional virtual world, the study refracts an analysis through Second Life's tag line, "Your World, Your Imagination." I argue that "World" indicates digital screening practices indebted to the history of the concept of cyberspace. "Imagination" describes the platform's creative software tools that use digital media affordances to enable resident fantasies. The "your" displays the tension between Network

Consumer Society's promise of unlimited imagination and alienating limitations of its actual media practices. The significance of the chapter is that it demystifies virtual worlds and illustrates that their immersive qualities are the outcome of specific and historically contextualized media practices.

As mentioned above, the volume's second chapter describes convert Zen Buddhism on Second Life as a practice-oriented spirituality. The problem I encountered was that the media practices were silent and thus difficult to analyze. Using a sign titled "Understanding the Path of Practice," which hung in Hoben's meditation hall, the chapter makes two claims. First, I straightforwardly theorize Second Life convert Zen as spiritual practices that enable residents to engage authentically with what they perceive as divine and thereby generate a moral economy that emerges from and engages with what they feel as ultimately significant in their lives. Second, I maintain that convert Zen flourishes on Second Life because, like virtual worlds, it has its historic roots in postwar American cybernetics. I trace convert Zen from the cybernetic thought of the late 1940s through to its poaching by corporate consumerism in the late 1980s. What is at stake is the ability to understand convert Zen as an existentially authentic media practice and not reduce it to Network Consumer ideology or a popular form of orientalism.

The body of this volume, chapters three through six, employs key terms from Second Life's search engine to detail the media practices from which Second Life Zen emerged. Chapter three analyzes "groups," which are the most basic and stable Second Life social unit. The chapter makes two claims. First, it argues that the communal sentiment created by silent online meditation afforded authentic community. Second, it maintains that the groups formed are best understood as "cloud communities," a term that refers to online digital groups that meet primarily online and usually are governed through network authority. Network authority rises from consensual media interactions consisting of peer-to-peer egalitarian social ties that mimic "cybernetic management," a term that describes a networked, entrepreneurial, noncentralized conception of personal interrelationships whose organizational style can be traced back to 1920 and Bell Laboratories.

Chapter four investigates "people," a Second Life search category for residents, a term developed by the virtual world's corporate owners, Linden Lab, to describe users. Frequently, discussions of online identity either frame it as an alienating dystopia or as a utopic place of endless identity play. Focusing on how free virtual monk robes fashion gender, the chapter takes a middle path and argues that residents are cybersocial beings that are activated in the virtual world by the feedback between "user" and "avatar." The chapter contends that the robes at Hoben liberated female avatars both politically and spiritually. On a political level, the robes allowed female avatars to fashion online identities that traversed Second Life's intense heteronormativity, media practices that divide people into complementary genders and assert heterosexuality as normative. On a spiritual level, by affording an experience of the empty nature of gender, the robes enabled a glimpse of the empty nature of the lived world more generally.

Chapter five studies "place," a term that refers to the regions that constitute Second Life's land. Using building tools that are part of Second Life viewer software, residents can create almost any environment they imagine. I argue that Hoben residents transformed the raw abstract potential of cyberspace into a place because virtual bodies interacted with virtual objects that afforded immersion and social relationships. Understanding how Zen practitioners built an existentially authentic spiritual place is significant because Second Life allowed the screening of convert Buddhist imagination. Many Second Life Buddhist practitioners wanted a virtual place that did not merely copy the actual world, but as the resident Mystic Moon declared, was "better than real life." I argue that Hoben's spiritual *builds* were "third places," which refers to social locations that are liminal alternatives between work and home, which in contemporary society are composed of a hybrid mix of everyday media practices and real-life locations.

The final category, "events," indicates performances and other types of religious practice, such as silent meditation. The chapter contends that Hoben's main spiritual events consisted of online meditation that communicated silence through ritualized procedural media practices that disrupted typical practices and engaged these gaps with the group's perception of the ultimate reality. To make sense of the silence of online mediation events, the chapter makes three arguments. First, the chapter asserts that online silent meditation is a media practice dependent upon both on- and offline bodies that are bridged by virtual meditation cushions. Second, the chapter argues that online silent meditation is a ritualized procedural process, which, by doing "nothing," connotes mindfulness. Finally, the chapter suggests that Hoben's contemporary practice of online silent meditation, while it has a family resemblance to the Buddhist concept of ānāpānasmṛti (mindfulness of breathing) and is informed by Protestant rejection of ritual and celebration of inner experience, has since the 1950s been entangled with the cybernetic conception of the "steersman" (*kybernētēs*).

The book's conclusion examines the ontological conditions that made cyber Zen not only possible but desirable. Spiritual screening media practices operate both as a surface onto which to project a group's ultimate concern and also as a filter that polices a group's moral world. Such screening is not only a matter of epistemology but ultimately of ethics. The conclusion argues that to understand Hoben's silence, researchers need to analyze the gaps in the virtual world's media practices. In actuality, Second Life consists of a flat screen of pixels that users manipulate through digital media practices. By making the process conspicuous, Second Life's gaps, its stutters and interruptions, reveal how these media practices employ desire to transmute the screen into something fantasized as both almost and also more real than the actual world. I contend that the ultimate significance of Hoben's silent practice lies neither in the virtual nor in the actual but in the gap produced between the two. To understand what cyber Zen means to practitioners, I investigate these gaps in Second Life's media practices so as to map Second Life's Zen community's understanding of ultimate reality itself.

Conclusion

At the end of our conversation at the sandbox, BodhiDharma Rosebud invited me to come to sit silent meditation with what he called the other "Zennies." He must have sensed my skepticism, because he added, "some of [Second Life practice] is kinda goofy . . . But it has potential. It is still evolving." There is no doubt that too many online practices such as silent meditation are trivial at best and maybe even harmful because they distract users from real-life practice. As Network Consumer Society simulacra, and having at best only a family resemblance to canonical Asian practices, a nagging suspicion remains that there must be more authentic ways to practice Buddhism than typing on a keyboard sitting in front of a screen. The problem, however, as seen by BodhiDharma's invitation to meditate online, is that whether critics like it or not, people are using digital media for Buddhist practice. As the chapters below describe, Buddhist adherents are forming communities, finding identities, building locations, and holding events online. BodhiDharma *poofed,* or suddenly teleported away. He soon sent me an instant message with a *teleportation* invite. Because I did not know BodhiDharma at the time, and because I had learned that accepting such invites could often lead to weird encounters, I hesitated. Finally, taking a chance, I clicked the invite. I – or really my research avatar Clint Clavenham – materialized at Hoben. By looking at the map I could tell that a number of residents were already at the nearby zendo (meditation hall). In front of me stood a wooden building, through the glass door of which I could see a long wooden altar with incense, candles, flowers, and a large statue of Shakyamuni Buddha. I pushed through the door and found rows of meditation cushions (*zafus*) that were laid out in semicircular lines. BodhiDharma greeted me with a *gasshō*, a gesture of palms together and fingers pointing upwards in prayer position, which is represented both by avatar gesture and also by the emoticon "_/!_."

   Cyber Zen investigates my time in Second Life. What is at stake is the radical position that users of digital media do not stop being human when they log on and that in contemporary popular culture religion plays a key role in determining people's humanity.[66] Often in religious studies, popular everyday human life goes unexamined, and the essence of being human is assumed to exist only in canonical scripture. Yet ignoring digital popular culture camouflages under our collective noses the very contemporary practices that offer the resources to afford our humanity.[67] Often digital Dharma consists of temporary workarounds, which are fragile because once they are gone they leave no traces. In real life, lost cultures at least leave archeological remains; in Second Life, when a region is abandoned all that is left is a blank screen. As a type of "salvage ethnography," *Cyber Zen* recorded these emerging digital cultures before they were discarded like an unreadable floppy disk.[68]

Salvaging these fragile human creations was significant, because Second Life Zen Buddhist practice expands our understanding of the relationship between religion and what it means to be human in the past, present, and future. Cyber Zen illuminates the past because it shows that the creation of virtual worlds has always been a key aspect of religion. Cyberspace is only different in degree from earlier media. In fact, digital media did not create virtual worlds: people and communities have always to some extent been virtual, and religion has been the social arena where people have worked out many of their virtual realities. Indeed, religion in Second Life is only possible because the platform reworks the virtuality of that which has already characterized much of what it means to practice religion.

Because popular digital media practices reveal contemporary religiosity, Second Life also displays what it means to be human in the developed world of the late 2000s. My research team's time in Second Life recorded a moment of transition, in which the old traditions were dissolving into pixels, and it was not clear what types of practice users were going to negotiate to replace it. Just as the print and broadcast communications caused a profound transformation of society, the emergence of virtual worlds and other digital media has brought about profound renovations in everyday life. Yet virtual worlds are not simply reflections, which one sees looking straight on. While often hyped as the coming of brave new worlds, virtual cyberspaces do not imagine future utopias but rather afford slightly askew ways of living in the contemporary actual world. In other words, the forms of religion being practiced online shape religious practice that are not really exotic, or even unique, examples, but very prosaic instances of broader cultural shifts occurring in contemporary religious practice.

While fragile, virtual worlds also allow fascinating glimpses of the future. As almost pure imagination, virtual worlds reflect different groups' desires and allow religious practitioners to project a coherent spiritual fantasy. Whether creating neolithic cave art, a medieval cathedral, or a video game, humans are creatures that have always imagined virtual worlds because they are the animals that imagine alternate futures and arrangements. "Virtual" does not take a position about real or unreal but distinguishes a third thing, something powerful that differs from the ordinary everyday. The word "virtual," from a Latin word for power (*virtus*), identifies these powerful alternatives. The alternative visions imagined in virtual worlds fascinate users not because they are unreal but because they make users aware of alternative possible identities, of other possible worlds, and of the limitless intersecting stories of the actual world. While often playful and even whimsical, Second Life Zen practitioners were very serious about using the new digital media to explore alternative spiritual templates. Such alternative imaginings are at the heart of American religion. As Laurence Moore argues, in *Religious Outsiders and the Making of Americans*, while it is often assumed that the character of American religion was formed from mainstream Protestant unity and dominance, it was actually alternative groups whose dynamic role shaped not only American religious identities but also American identity more generally.[69]

Ultimately beyond what they display about popular spirituality, virtual worlds are fascinating because they call into question reality itself. It is often assumed that a shared reality holds our commonsensical ground. Virtual worlds make one question: To what extent does reality as a phenomenon exist unmediated and to what extent do media practices determine people's experience of it? One strains to imagine a world without reality. Yet what Second Life's spirituality illustrates is that reality does not exist objectively but rather emerges from media practices. By mediating between the "inside" of cyberspace and the "outside" of the actual world for many groups, screens also negotiate between everyday existence and the divine and indicate that the relationship between the virtual and actual often depends on how a group imagines the distinction between the profane and divine. In such a case, scholars should not question the reality of the virtual and actual but rather investigate the ontologies that make possible these realities, the history out of which these realities emerged, and the type of ethical human beings that they produce.

Notes

1 Unless stated otherwise, the names of Second Life residents and regions are pseudonyms (see Luciano Paccagnella, "Getting the Seats of Your Pants Dirty: Strategies for Ethnographic Research on Virtual Communities," *Journal of Computer Mediated Communication* 3, no. 1 [1997], 2–17). This choice was difficult because I desired to give credit to the individuals who became not just subjects but friends and without whom the study would have been impossible. However, to err on the side of protecting individuals' privacy, when information was collected through participant observation, interviews, or surveys, or if there was the possibility that public sources could be tied to a conversant, I have used pseudonyms. Also, sometimes to obscure a resident's identity and protect sensitive information, I take the liberty of changing details or of combining details from more than one resident. Taking a Hippocratic oath, I attempted to stay as close to the material as possible without causing harm. In a few cases, if the sources are publicly available, I use actual names so as to give the individual credit. According to the Georgia Institute of Technology's "Ethical Guidelines for Research Online," Second Life fits the definition of "public domain," that is, one may freely quote and analyze online information without consent if it is officially, publicly archived and no password is required for archive access (see Amy Bruckman, "Ethical Guidelines for Research Online," www.cc.gatech.edu/~asb/ethics [2002; accessed August 22, 2013]). Furthermore, "Ethical Decision-Making and Internet Research: Recommendations from the AOIR Ethics Working Committee" defines virtual spaces such as Second Life as chat rooms, which can be treated as public spaces (see Annette Markham and Elizabeth Buchanan, http://aoir.org/reports/ethics2.pdf [2012; accessed August 22, 2013]).
2 Like any social space, Second Life has many emic terms that I have treated as foreign words by leaving them untranslated. My goal is to convey the meaning of the terms but to leave an aura of foreignness about them so that they convey a sense of being inworld (see Charles L. Briggs, *Learning How to Ask: A Sociolinguistic Appraisal of the Role of the*

Interview in Social Science Research [Cambridge: Cambridge University Press, 1986]). All "foreign" words are italicized in their first use in each chapter and are also defined in the book's glossary. *Foreign* refers to emic terms used by the Second Life Hoben community. These include terms that may have "native" meanings in English but that have slightly different meanings from those of the actual world in Second Life. It also includes Japanese and Sanskrit terms used by the community that may not have the same significance as they do in Asian settings. For consistency, I use Sanskrit transliterations for Buddhist technical terms as much as possible.

3 Pew Research Center, "64% of Online Americans Have Used the Internet for Religious or Spiritual Purposes," www.pewinternet.org/2004/04/07/64-of-online-americans-have-used-the-internet-for-religious-or-spiritual-purposes/ (accessed November 3, 2015).

4 Daniel Veidlinger, *From Indra's Net to Internet: Communication, Technology and the Evolution of Buddhism*. Working paper. California State University, Chico (2015).

5 Following the Buddhist community of Hoben's conventions, I capitalize "Dharma" to indicate Buddhist teachings and use lowercase "dharma" to refer to the phenomenological factors that constitute everyday reality (saṃsāra).

6 Christopher Helland, "Online Religion as Lived Religion: Methodological Issues in the Study of Religious Participation on the Internet," *Online – Heidelberg Journal of Religions on the Internet* 1, no. 1 (2005), www.ub.uni-heidelberg.de/archiv/5823 (accessed November 3, 2015). See also Christopher Helland, "Religion Online/Online Religion and Virtual Communitas," in *Religion on the Internet: Research Prospects and Promises*, ed. Jeffery K. Hadden and Douglas E. Cowan (London: JAI Press/Elsevier, 2000), 205–24.

7 Places as well as practitioners are pseudonyms.

8 See Charles Prebish, *American Buddhism* (North Scituate, MA: Duxbury Press, 1979); Charles Prebish, *Luminous Passage: The Practice of and Study of Buddhism in America* (Berkley, CA: University of California Press, 1999); Thomas Tweed, *The American Encounter with Buddhism: 1844–1912* (Chapel Hill, NC: University of North Carolina Press, 1992).

9 It is now very common in Buddhist literature to find the expression "Western Buddhism"; I do not perceive "the West" as a homogeneous whole, which provides similar sociopolitical, cultural, and legal settings in the various countries considered. On the contrary, I use the term in a pragmatic way, to denote non-Asian industrialized nation-states where Buddhist teachings and practices, Buddhist people and ideas, have become established outside of traditional Asian spaces and locations.

10 Because of the quickly changing media environment of contemporary society, and the work that emergent learning entails, media practices are much more conspicuous now than they were in the recent past. See Espen Aarseth, *Cybertext: Perspectives on Ergodic Literature* (Baltimore: John Hopkins University Press, 1997); Heidi Campbell, *When Religion Meets New Media* (London: Routledge, 2010).

11 Gregory Price Grieve, *Retheorizing Religion in Nepal* (New York: Palgrave Macmillan, 2006); Gregory Price Grieve, "Studying Religion in Digital Gaming: A Critical Review of an Emerging Field," *Online – Heidelberg Journal of Religions on the Internet* 5, no. 1 (2014), www.online.uni-hd.de/ (accessed November 3, 2015).

12 Theodor Nelson, *Computer Lib: You Can and Must Understand Computers Now/Dream Machines: New Freedoms through Computer Screens – A Minority Report* (Chicago: Hugo Book Service, 1974). The Nelson book has two front covers and can be read forward and backward. See the flipside, *Dream Machine*, 22.

13 Erkki Huhtamo, "Screen Tests: Why Do We Need an Archaeology of the Screen," *Cinema Journal* 51, no. 2 (2012): 144–48.

14 Gilles Deleuze, *Difference and Repetition* (New York: Columbia University Press, 1994), 299.

15 Jean Baudrillard, *Simulacra and Simulation* (Ann Arbor, MI: University of Michigan Press, 1994), 6.

16 See Kaja Silverman, *The Subject of Semiotics* (New York: Oxford University Press, 1983). In medical terms, sutures stitch over wounds. In psychoanalytic theory, sutures account for how subjects emerge from discourse. Suture describes that moment when the subject finds herself inserted into a symbolic world because it describes the covering over of the psychic wounding that occurs when individual desires and needs are necessarily repressed by social codes and symbols. As Kaja Silverman explains in relation to cinema, "This sleight-of-hand involves attributing to a character within the fiction qualities which in fact belong to the machinery of enunciation: the ability to generate narrative, the omnipotence and coercive gaze, the castrating authority of the law" (Silverman, 232). In Buddhism a sutra is a collection of teachings. The term literally describes a thread that holds things together and is derived from the verbal root √*siv-*, meaning 'to sew.' Sutra probably described texts written on palm leaves and sewn together with a thread.

17 Like poachers, Second Life practitioners draw from materials not √siv completely of their making, media already at hand in their cultural environment, resources that they make work for them. Poaching, as the French theorist Michel de Certeau describes, is a process of reading texts that raids the elite preserve. Poachers "move across lands belonging to someone else, like nomads poaching their way across fields they did not write" (see Michel de Certeau, *The Practice of Everyday Life* [Berkeley: University of California Press, 1984], 174).

18 "Monier-Williams Sanskrit-English Dictionary, 1899," www.sanskrit-lexicon.uni-koeln. de/scans/MWScan/2014/web/webtc/indexcaller.php (accessed November 3, 2015).

19 I take a middle path between the historians of religion Mircea Eliade and J. Z. Smith. I argue that "religion" is not an essential, unique category. I also argue that the category of religion does not emerge solely from the scholar's imagination. Instead, while a social construction, it is not totally under the rational theorizing of the academic. Religion emerges from a dialogue between the scholar's outsider etic theorizing and insider etic everyday use. For Eliade's notion of the sacred, see *The Sacred and the Profane: The Nature of Religion* (New York: Harvest/HBJ Publishers, 1957); for his method of comparison see *Patterns in Comparative Religion* (London: Sheed and Ward, 1949); for his concept of history see *Cosmos and History: The Myth of the Eternal Return* (Princeton, NJ: Princeton University Press, 1954). See also J. Z. Smith, *Imaging Religion: From Babylon to Jonestown* (Chicago: University of Chicago Press, 1982). In Smith's seminal work, he argues that religion is solely the creation of the scholar's imagination and posits three conditions for its use: (1) a mastery of both primary and secondary materials; (2) an example that is used to display an important theory or fundamental question; and (3) a method for explicitly relating the theory to the example.

20 See Gelek Rimpoche, *The Four Noble Truths* (Jewel Heart Publication), www.jewelheart. org/digital-dharma/four-noble-truths-transcript/ (accessed November 3, 2015); *Tibetan Buddhism 48 First Noble Truth from the Four Points* (Jewel Heart Channel), YouTube Video, 13:27, www.youtube.com/watch?v=PG8LSJmUVGU (accessed November 3, 2015).

21 "Recognizing the Suffering in Your Own Life – Chapter 4," Dharma Wisdom, http://dharmawisdom.org/books-phillip-moffitt/dancing-life/excerpt-dancing-life#sthash. kfvAx7H6.dpuf (accessed November 3, 2015).

22 "Colossal Cave Adventure: The Original Text-Based Adventure Game," www.amc.com/shows/halt-and-catch-fire/colossal-cave-adventure/landing (accessed November 3, 2015).

23 *NBC Nightly News – Religion Online in Second Life*, YouTube Video, 2:26, posted by Zach Gilliam, May 22, 2007, www.youtube.com/watch?v=1-BGQKaKi18 (accessed November 3, 2015).

24 Stephanie Simon, "It's Easter; Shall We Gather at the Desktops? Virtual Houses of Worship Await You Online in Second Life," *Los Angeles Times,* April 8, 2007, http://articles. latimes.com/2007/apr/08/nation/na-virtual8 (accessed August 28, 2008).

25 Gregory Price Grieve, "Imagining a Virtual Religious Community: Neo-pagans on the Internet," *Chicago Anthropology Exchange* 7 (1995): 98–132; Benedict Anderson, *Imagined Communities: Reflections on the Origin and Spread of Nationalism* (New York: Verso, 1983).

26 Helland, "Online Religion as Lived Religion." See also Helland, "Religion Online/ Online Religion and Virtual Communitas."

27 Henry Jenkins, "*Star Trek* Rerun, Reread, Rewritten: Fan Writing as Textual Poaching," *Critical Studies in Mass Communication* 5, no. 2 (1988): 85–107.

28 Masahiro Mori, "The Uncanny Valley," *Energy* 7, no. 4 (1970): 33–35; Norri Kageki, "An Uncanny Mind: Masahiro Mori on the Uncanny Valley and Beyond," *IEEE Spectrum*, June 12, 2012, http://spectrum.ieee.org/automaton/robotics/humanoids/an-uncanny-mind-masahiro-mori-on-the-uncanny-valley (accessed November 3, 2015).

29 John Frow, "Michel de Certeau and the Practice of Representation," *Cultural Studies* 5, no. 1 (1991): 52–60.

30 Deleuze, 87.

31 Baudrillard, 256.

32 Gregory Price Grieve, "Symbol, Idol and *Murti:* Hindu God-images and the Politics of Mediation," *Culture, Theory and Critique* 44, no. 3 (2003): 57–72.

33 Academics also tend to reduce convert Buddhism to an ideological symptom of Network Consumer Society. The work of the philosopher and cultural critic Slavoj Žižek, for instance, detests both cyberspace and convert Buddhists. In "Cyberspace, or, the Unbearable Closure of Being," Žižek sees virtual worlds as the clearest symptom of Network Consumer Society's transformation from the modernist culture of calculation to the postmodernist culture of simulation. He frets that digital media robs us of our humanity and connection to reality and argues that cybernetic simulation forecloses the difference between reality and artifice because that leads to a decentered self and a plurality of self-identities without a coordinating center (see Slavoj Žižek, "Cyberspace, or, the Unbearable Closure of Being," in *The Plague of Fantasies* [London: Verso, 1997]: 127–59).

34 In the mid-2000s as I conducted my research, religious leaders of mainstream groups with a well-built brick and mortar presence tried for the most part to ignore virtual worlds and online religious practice. Yet the growing popularity of digital religious practice, especially among younger users, often forced them to respond. On June 5, 2011, His Holiness Pope Benedict released "Truth, Proclamation and Authenticity of Life in the Digital Age" and argued "new technologies are not only changing the way we communicate, but communication itself." He goes on to proclaim, "the Gospel demands to be incarnated in the real world and linked to the real faces of our brothers and sisters, those with whom we share our daily lives. Direct human relations always remain fundamental for the transmission of the faith!" Pope Benedict XVI, "Truth, Proclamation and Authenticity of Life in the Digital Age" (Vatican: the Holy See), for the 45th World Communications Day, June 5, 2011, http://w2.vatican.va/content/benedict-xvi/en/messages/communications/documents/hf_ben-xvi_mes_20110124_45th-world-communications-day.html (accessed November 3, 2015).

35 Jane Naomi Iwamura, *Virtual Orientalism: Asian Religions and American Popular Culture* (Oxford: Oxford University Press, 2011). Cf. Vincanne Admas, *Tigers of the Snow and Other Virtual Sherpas* (Princeton, NJ: Princeton University Press, 1995).

36 Richard King, "Spirituality and the Privatisation of Asian Wisdom Traditions," in *Selling Spirituality the Silent Takeover of Religion*, ed. Jeremy Carrette and Richard King (London: Routledge, 2005), 87–123.

37 *The Buddhist Ethic and the Spirit of Global Capitalism*, European Graduate School Video Lectures, YouTube Video, 1:09:56, October 2, 2012, www.youtube.com/watch?v=qkTUQYxEUjs (accessed November 3, 2015).

38 *The Buddhist Ethic and the Spirit of Global Capitalism*.

39 Edward Said, *Orientalism* (New York: Vintage, 1979).

40 Iwamura, 8.

41 Jane Naomi Iwamura argues, in *Virtual Orientalism: Asian Religion and Popular Culture*, that Eastern traditions have become a convenient symbol for alternative spiritualties and modes of being. She shows that, although there has been an increase in popular engagement with Asian traditions, the virtual form makes stereotypical constructions of the spiritual East obdurate and especially difficult to challenge. As the blogger Justin Chin argues in "Attack of the White Buddhists," while many non-Heritage Buddhists embrace Eastern traditions, they keep at arm's distance the "violence and bigotry directed toward Asian Americans" (*Mongrel: Essays, Diatribes, + Pranks* [New York: St. Martin's Griffin, 1999], 113–19). Often American convert Buddhism is envisioned as a type of manifest destiny, in which the old world can only find its full potential in the new world. For instance, in a 1991 editorial by the founder of the convert Buddhist magazine *Tricycle*, Helen Tworkov writes, "The spokespeople for Buddhism in America have been, almost exclusively, educated members of the white middle class. Meanwhile, even with varying statistics, Asian-American Buddhists number at least one million, but so far they have not figured prominently in the development of something called American Buddhism." (Helen Tworkov, "Many Is More," *Tricycle* 1, no. 2 [1999], www.tricycle. com/new-buddhism/buddhism/many-more [accessed November 3, 2015]). That is, as Charles Prebish writes, "What is often implied, according to Asian American critics, is that Buddhism becomes truly American, only when white Americans become seriously involved" (Prebish, *Luminous Passage*, 57).

42 A blanket accusation of Network Consumer virtual orientalism obscures, however, what actually occurs and leads toward the search for a transhistorical, self-identical Dharma that has moved from one culture to another, unchanged through the vicissitudes of time. The search for a real Buddhism leads to the search for an "original," "primitive," or "pure" form of Buddhism that cannot help but be orientalist, because the location of any universal conception of Buddhism always seems to be the libraries of Europe and in all cases its truth is contrasted over and against the many ways contemporary cultures actually manifest everyday lived practice (see David Lopez, *Curators of the Buddha: The Study of Buddhism under Colonialism* [Chicago: University of Chicago Press, 1995a], 6–7).

43 Dipesh Chakrabarty, *Provincializing Europe: Postcolonial Thought and Historical Difference* (Princeton, NJ: Princeton University Press, 2000).

44 See Theodor Adorno, *The Jargon of Authenticity* (Evanston, IL: Northwestern University Press, 1973).

45 Stephen Addiss, Stanley Lombardo, and Judith Roitman, eds., *Zen: Traditional Documents from China, Korea, and Japan* (Cambridge, MA: Hackett Publishing Company, 2008); Carl Bielefeldt, trans., *Dōgen's Manuals of Zen Meditation* (Berkeley, CA: University of California Press, 1988); Robert E. Buswell, *The Zen Monastic Experience* (Princeton, NJ: Princeton University Press, 1992); Morten Schlütter, *How Zen Became Zen: The Dispute over Enlightenment and the Formation of Chan Buddhism during the Song Dynasty China* (Honolulu: University of Hawai'i Press, 2008); Philip Yampolsky, trans., *The Platform Sutra of the Sixth Patriarch* (New York: Columbia University Press, 1996); Jason Ānanda Josephson, "When Buddhism Became a 'Religion': Religion and Superstition in the Writings of Inoue Enryō," *Japanese Journal of Religious Studies* 33, no. 1 (2006): 143–68.

46 Claude Shannon, "A Mathematical Theory of Communication. Part I," *Bell Systems Technical Journal* 27 (1948): 379–423; Claude Shannon and Warren Weaver, *A Mathematical Model of Communication* (Urbana, IL: University of Illinois Press, 1949).

47 David McMahan, *The Making of Buddhist Modernism* (Oxford: Oxford University Press, 2008), 19.

48 Bernard Faure, *Unmasking Buddhism* (New York: Blackwell, 2007); cf. Bernard Faure, *The Rhetoric of Immediacy: A Cultural Critique of Chan/Zen Buddhism* (Princeton, NJ: Princeton

University Press, 1991); Bernard Faure, *Chan Insights and Oversights: An Epistemological Critique of the Chan Tradition* (Princeton, NJ: Princeton University Press, 1993); Bernard Faure, *Double Exposure: Cutting across Buddhist and Western Discourses*, trans. Janet Lloyd (Stanford: Stanford University Press, 2004).

49 Norbert Wiener, *Cybernetics, or Control and Communication in the Animal and the Machine* (New York: Technology Press, 1948).

50 Vannevar Bush, "As We May Think," *Atlantic* (1945), www.theatlantic.com/magazine/print/1969/12/as-we-may-think/3881/ (accessed January 24, 2014).

51 Katherine Hayles, *How We Became Posthuman: Virtual Bodies in Cybernetics, Literature, and Informatics* (Chicago: University of Chicago Press, 1999), 11.

52 Nicholas Denyer, "Introduction," in *Alcibiades*, by Plato, ed. Nicholas Denyer (Cambridge: Cambridge University Press, 2001), 1–26; Charles Young, "Plato and Computer Dating," in *Plato: Critical Assessments. Volume 1: General Issues of Interpretation*, ed. Nicholas D. Smith (London: Routledge, 1998), 29–49.

53 Stafford Beer, "Cybernetics and the Knowledge of God," *The Month* 34 (1965): 292.

54 Wiener, 96.

55 Erwin Schrödinger and M. Born, "Discussion of Probability Relations between Separated Systems," *Mathematical Proceedings of the Cambridge Philosophical Society* 31, no. 4 (1935): 555–63.

56 David Smith, "The Authenticity of Alan Watts," in *American Buddhism as a Way of Life*, eds. Gary Storhoff and John Whalen-Bridge (Albany: SUNY Press, 2010), 13–39.

57 David Chidester, *Authentic Fakes: Religion and American Popular Culture* (Berkeley, CA: University of California Press, 2005).

58 Søren Kierkegaard, *Concluding Unscientific Postscript to the Philosophical Crumbs* (Cambridge: Cambridge University Press, 2009); Maurice Merleau-Ponty, *Phenomenology of Perception* (New York: Routledge and Kegan Paul, 1962).

59 Peter Berger and T. Luckmann, *The Social Construction of Reality: A Treatise in the Sociology of Knowledge* (Garden City, NY: Anchor Books, 1966).

60 Campbell, 49. Stewart Hoover, "The Cultural Construction of Religion and Media," in *Practicing Religion in the Age of the Media: Explorations in Media, Religion and Culture*, eds. Stewart Hoover and Lynn Schofield Clark (New York: Columbia University Press, 2002), 1–6.

61 Kierkegaard, 131.

62 Erich Fromm, *Escape from Freedom* (New York: Farrar and Rinehart, 1941), 256.

63 Fromm, 257.

64 Stewart Hoover and Knut Lundby, *Rethinking Media, Religion and Culture* (London: Sage, 1997).

65 Noah Levine, *Dharma Punx* (New York: Harper Collins, 2009), 4.

66 I define "human" as the totality of living, conscious beings who are involved with the immediate world in which they live, able to become aware of the contingent element of that involvement and the evolving nature of the self and capable of imagining alternative ways of being. My understanding is based on two trains of thought: first, the existential philosophy of Martin Heidegger, "This entity which each of us is himself . . . we shall denote by the term 'Dasein'" (Martin Heidegger, *Being and Time* [London: SCM Press, 1962], 27). "[Dasein is] that entity which in its Being has this very Being as an issue . . ." (Heidegger, 68); second, the Buddhist concept of sentient being. In Buddhism, sentient beings are composed of the five aggregates – matter, sensation, perception, mental formations, and consciousness – and are characteristically not enlightened and are thus confined to the death, rebirth, and suffering characteristic of saṃsāra. Kiyotaka Kimura, "The Self in Medieval Japanese Buddhism: Focusing on Dogen," *Philosophy East and West* 41, no. 3 (1991): 327–40.

67 In the pivotal article, "Popular Culture as the New Humanities," Ray B. Browne writes, "The so-called 'elite' or 'minority' culture may have some influence according to the

degree it is brought to the people and made applicable to their everyday lives. But the popular culture is already with the people, a part of their everyday lives, speaking their language. It is therefore irresistibly influential." Ray Browne, "Popular Culture as the New Humanities," *Journal of Popular Culture* 17, no. 4 (1984): 1.

68 Jacob Gruber, "Ethnographic Salvage and the Shaping of Anthropology," *American Anthropologist, New Series* 72, no. 6 (1970): 1289–99.

69 Laurence Moore, *Religious Outsiders and the Making of Americans* (Oxford: Oxford University Press, 1986); Sean McCloud, *Making the American Religious Fringe: Exotics, Subversives, and Journalists, 1955–1993* (Chapel Hill, NC: University of North Carolina Press, 2004).

Method

Empty your cup: Exploring
conventional ethnography
in a virtual world

> Nan-in, a Japanese master during the Meiji era received a university professor
> who came to inquire about Zen. Nan-in served tea. He poured his visitor's cup
> full, and then kept on pouring. The professor watched the overflow until he no
> longer could restrain himself. "It is overfull. No more will go in!" "Like this
> cup," Nan-in said, "you are full of your own opinions and speculations. How can
> I show you Zen unless you first empty your cup?"
>
> "Empty Your Cup" (Second Life note card)[1]

To collect the data for the investigation that follows, this chapter describes *Cyber Zen*'s team-based ethnographic method. As students of religion and media, my research team's onus was to create a method the purpose of which was to understand silent online meditation by making its implicit nature explicit.[2] In early January 2008, after a meditation session, Human Riddle, Rasa Vibration, and a few other community members invited me to tea.[3] Reflecting an informal Japanese tea gathering (*chakai*), "tea" was held in a teahouse just outside the main meditation hall and was an *event* that consisted of sitting around a brazier on which rested a small iron teapot.[4] Clicking the teapot gave me a tea bowl (*chawan*), which my avatar cuddled in its hands as if gaining warmth on a cold winter morning. The scene was cozy, intimate, with many threads of conversation simultaneously flying around in public and private chat – the opposite of the structured silence of online meditation. Human asked me about my research, and I began to explain my study, mostly copying from prewritten texts on my computer's desktop and pasting them into public chat. After I had gone on for quite a while, Rasa shared a note card on which was written, "You are full of your own opinions and speculations. How can I show you Zen unless you first empty your cup?"

Method describes how *Cyber Zen*'s data was collected by systematically dividing my research team's observations into categories that could be rationally explained and reliably applied. We could study virtual spirituality not only because it occurred in users' minds but also because it consisted of observable media practices that played across the screen. While an empirical study,

Cyber Zen is an interpretive rather than an experimental science. We did not go into the field looking for evidence to prove a preexisting hypothesis. Instead we were explorers who stayed close to the material by relying on thick descriptions to explain Second Life's Zen community by isolating and highlighting certain insider categories, specifying the relationship between the categories, and situating these in the group's underlying cultural matrix. As opposed to etic, or outsider theories, these emic categories are determined by local custom, meaning, and belief.[5] Ethnography exists in that liminal space betwixt and between cultures. I am not suggesting that ethnographers give the same meaning to, or even use the same, categories to investigate, as do insiders. Instead, ethnographers need to use categories that make insider experience intelligible to an outsider.

When we began the study, we assumed that the largest methodological issue would be the virtual nature of the material. Early on we decided that we would treat Second Life as a cultural field in its own right and not merely a supplement of real life. Because the virtual is obviously dependent on the actual, Second Life boundaries are porous and not hermetically sealed behind the computer screen. Often, as I describe in this volume's Introduction, the virtual is simply assumed to be unreal. As I discuss in *Cyber Zen*'s conclusion, however, the very interdependence between on- and offline social spaces generates the conventions of the virtual and actual. Accordingly, we shied away from asking real-life questions and only recorded them when they arose spontaneously. Our reluctance to ask about users' real lives was supported by Second Life's privacy regulations in the platform's terms of service and dictated ethically by our university's Internal Review Board, as well as being part of the virtual world's etiquette.

What slowly became apparent, however, was that silence proved to be a more difficult phenomenon than the virtual to document. This was particularly true because to understand Hoben Mountain Zen Retreat's spirituality, one needs to investigate silent media practices, which requires researchers to record not just the virtual world's content but also the procedures that comprise the cultural codes that make communication possible and interpretable by an outsider. One might assume the big data of quantitative research or historical analysis could capture such subtle practices. Maybe it would be enough to interview and survey members of groups such as Hoben or simply concentrate on written sources, which in the case of Second Life are available both inworld and on the World Wide Web. True. We actually use all these methods to support and contextualize our findings. What proved to be most effective for understanding silence, however, was the ethnographic method, which refers to the study of human behavior in the natural settings in which people live. Through fieldwork, ethnographic researchers describe cultural systems by immersing themselves in the ongoing everyday activities of a specific community for the purpose of describing the social context, relationships, and cultural processes relevant to the topic under consideration. Ethnographic analysis is inductive, building upon the perspectives of the residents studied, and emphasizes the analysis of people and communities through long-term relationships between the researcher and research participants.

To understand Second Life Zen's silent meditation, a method needs to attend to the group's media practices by recording its connotative context. Often this entails "emptying your cup" of preconceived biases. Between November 2007 and October 2011, our method emerged as a team-based conventional ethnography. "Team" refers to the fact that a principal investigator and five other researchers conducted the research. "Conventional" indicates that we approached Second Life as a unique social space and used a method grounded in participant observation and thick description. "Participant observation" indicates a qualitative method of data collection in which a researcher gains intimate familiarity with a group's ethos, or lived world, by living for an extended period of time with that group. "Thick description" is a method that describes both a practice and the social context that gives that practice meaning. We found that our three years of research followed a life cycle similar to that of an avatar – from *noobie*, to *middie*, to *elder* – and identified three chief ethical procedures: informed consent, anonymity, and transparency.

A conventional team ethnographic method

To record silent practices, our method extends the classic notions of the field from the observation of actual colocated, face-to-face physicality to digitally mediated real-time embodied interactions in a virtual world.[6] Using *avatars*, our research team engaged in a conventional ethnography using participant observation and thick description of Second Life's Zen Buddhist community between November 2007 and October 2011. The purpose of our study was to provide a coherent representation of Second Life spiritual media practices, that is, to draw a conclusion through interpretation based on certain descriptive facts. To collect these descriptions, Gregory Price Grieve (the author) gathered a research team that in its final form consisted of himself and five advanced undergraduates (Figure M.1). During our fieldwork we meditated, explored temples, prostrated before Buddha images, went to Dharma talks, and argued in open discussions about the nature of Buddhism. Our participant observation was recorded in shared field notes, *snapshots*, written documents, and material culture. In the final stages of the research, Grieve also conducted interviews, both inworld and using Skype, and conducted a series of surveys.

A "conventional theory" indicates two elements. First, as described in *Cyber Zen*'s conclusion, rather than an ultimate essential difference between Second Life and real life, we argue that virtual worlds constitute a distinct conventional social space, which offers new social fields with differing social positions, lifestyles, values, and dispositions. Any digital ethnography must choose where to draw the line that demarcates the limit of the field site. Although early studies of digital religion assumed a clear distinction between on- and offline practice, with the rise of smartphones and other tablets, the boundary has broken down

Figure M.1 Virtual research team. Principal investigator and five assistants: Rebecca Davis, Sabrina Epps, Kevin Heston, Michelle Lampley, and Jayme Mallindine.

(Second Life Snapshot by Gregory Price Grieve).

in both theory and practice.[7] Reacting against this, later studies argued that there is no difference between on- and offline knowledge formation.[8] Taking a middle position, we maintain that Second Life constitutes a conventional reality, which, while not a completely separate, isolated social world, dichotomized from real life, is socially differentiated by screening media practices as a distinct cultural field.

Second, to study Second Life Buddhist practices, we employed participant observation, a qualitative method in which, for an extended period of time, researchers live with participants in their own environment while documenting their everyday practices. Pioneered in the first half of the twentieth century by anthropologists such as Bronisław Malinowski, E. E. Evans-Pritchard, and Margaret Mead, participant observation is a qualitative method in which researchers take part in the daily activities of the group under study and record what they observe.[9] Following the work of Tom Boellstroff and Julian Dibbell, the social space we explored was a virtual world, and we conducted our study almost entirely from within Second Life using research avatars.[10] What makes participant observation a scientific research method is that one also needs to stand back and observe by watching and listening, while taking both physical and mental notes. Observation means logging concrete descriptions of social structures, examples of everyday life, and everyday utterances. We took "scratch notes" during our time inworld and then, after logging off, would spend almost as much time writing more detailed descriptions in our field notes, incorporating and describing snapshots, objects, and conversations.

We used our participant observations to produce thick descriptions framed in a first person perspective. Description concerns itself with the study of things as they appear, with bringing forth relationships of people and things rather than simply explaining or labeling them. Description goes beyond exposition and narration. Exposition supplies background information, while narration supplies the telling of events. Effective description emerges from carefully worded, sensory details that are enhanced by representing phenomena as a state of activity. Because of the subjective dimensions inherent in ethnography, we maintain that it is more transparent to write in the first person, framing our accounts with our own experiences and biases. As the principal investigator and ultimate author, Grieve did not want his voice to overly dominate the research and so decided to use the first person even when using field notes collected by other team members. In short, while Grieve takes ultimate responsibility, the "I" in these pages is a textual construct that utilizes the experiences, field notes, and research of all the team members.

If we have done our job effectively, readers will be able to imagine what it is like to be immersed in Second Life. For a moment, the world described will seem more real than the one at your elbow, and you will become immersed in our investigation. By describing both a phenomenon and also its cultural context in order for it to become meaningful to an outsider, thick description transforms mere description into a scientific method.[11] For instance, just describing the explicit meaning of Rasa's recitation of "A Cup of Tea" *kōan* does not explain its implicit meaning as a criticism. Only by contextualizing her statement in the social dynamics of the particular moment at the tea gathering that was produced by the culture, practices, and personal relationships of the Hoben community does the significance of Rasa's koan become intelligible to an outsider.

An embodied field

Determining what constitutes a "field site" is one of the main challenges that face ethnographers. Methodologically, a field site describes the locations where an ethnographer's work is conducted, the natural nonlaboratory location where the activities in which researchers are interested take place. Ethnographers are finding, however, that a bounded geographic locale is proving to be increasingly outdated and untenable as globalization blurs the boundary between "here" and "there."[12] Still, while the "tent-in-the-village" research model may be under pressure, many ethnographers are still surprised (if not appalled) at the thought of an online field site such as Second Life.[13] *Cyber Zen* contends that a field site can no longer be seen merely as a physical location but rather must be viewed as the intersection between people, practices, and shifting terrains, both physical and virtual. As such, as Christine Hine writes in *Virtual Ethnography*, "the internet and similar networks provide a naturally occurring field site for studying what people do when they are online."[14]

I maintain that Second Life avatar bodies are what demarcated our field. Much of the ideology surrounding virtual worlds has been sustained by a rhetoric of dematerialization, and it has often been argued that we leave our bodies behind upon entering virtual worlds. That is, that cyberspace makes the body obsolete. The inverse is also argued. Digital media are "body snatchers" that will destroy our bodies. Yet, as I illustrate in chapter four, residents have bodies. No doubt that when users log on to virtual worlds they never leave their seat, and being in a virtual world consists of digital media practices. *Cyber Zen* argues instead that the notion of body needs to be differentiated between "embodiment as performance" and "embodiment as (proprioceptive) sensation." A resident's virtual body, just like her actual body, is a stylized repetition of acts. It is precisely the repetition of acts, gestures, and discourses that produces bodies and enables ethnographers to comprehend a social practice, whether in real life or in a virtual world.

The life cycle of an ethnographic study

In hindsight at least, our research followed a life cycle similar to that of an avatar – from noobie, to middie, to elder (Table M.1).[15] Such a prolonged life cycle is crucial for any ethnographic project because it allows the researchers to become part of the group's everyday routines and to inhabit the insider's world, and it gives them the flexibility to "empty their cups" and to follow alternative hypotheses as they arise during the study. Initially, the research team consisted of Grieve, Kevin Heston, Jayme Mallidine, and Sabrina Epps, and we four engaged

Table M.1 Research timeline that followed a life cycle similar to that of an avatar – from noobie, to middie, to elder

	Dates: October 2007–October 2010	Investigators	Aims	Research Practices
Noobie	November 2007–May 2008	Grieve (PI), Epps, Heston, and Mallindine	Identification	Exploration, low-level participant observation, and collection of material culture. Aleph Technique survey (n=100)
Middie	June 2008–October 2009	Grieve (PI), Epps, Heston, Mallindine, Davis, and Lampley	Description	Participant observation (n=69) interviews, and collection of material culture
Elder	November 2009–Oct 2011	Grieve	Confirmation and control	Out of world interviews (n=13), surveys (n=1227, n=86, and n=108) and collection of material culture

Second Life as bumbling noobies. As we lumbered through the virtual world, our main aims were identification through exploration, engagement in low-level participant observation, and collection of material culture.

The second, or middie, stage lasted from June 2008 through October 2009 and was the most intense period of fieldwork. This period marked a change from exploration and discovery to reporting, and the research became more systematic and routinized. In the middie stage, we concentrated on description and engaged in participant observation and the collection of material culture. Two new researchers, Michelle Lampley and Rebecca Davis, joined the team, and we shared field notes using Google Documents and distributed material culture and screenshots using the web-based program Dropbox. Participant observation continued, with each researcher logging on for a minimum of two hours, three times a week. In June 2009, we ceased participant observation and engaged in a month of inworld open interviews, during which the research team spoke with sixty-nine residents.

The third, or elder, stage lasted from November 2009 to October 2011, and concentrated on confirmation, control, and fact checking. As the game researcher best known for being the cocreator of MUD1, Richard Bartle writes in *Designing Virtual Worlds*, "There comes a point when players have advanced so far that they feel they have achieved everything that they set out to achieve. They are no longer interested in activities that used to occupy their time: they feel they have 'made it.' The question then arises: What can they do instead?"[16] By the end of 2009, all of Grieve's student researchers had graduated, and he felt as if no new data were being generated by his own participant observation or inworld exploration. The research thus moved from concentrating on participant observation to structured interviews and surveys. With the key informants, Grieve conducted a series of long, out-of-world, open interviews using Skype or the telephone ($n=13$). Grieve also conducted three surveys in 2010. First, with the help of IDC Herzliya's Advanced Reality Lab, he used an animated avatar *bot* to conduct a broad survey of randomly selected residents that asked about religious affiliation ($n=1,227$). Second, with the assistance of Kevin Heston, who was now a graduate student, he used the web-based tool SurveyMonkey to administer a 100-question survey to Second Life religious practitioners ($n=86$); and third, he gave a similar survey to Buddhist Residents ($n=108$). Finally, between 2011 and 2013, Grieve used the qualitative data analysis program, Atlas.ti, to catalogue and code the team's field notes and 9,339 note cards and objects, as well as to data mine over 23,200 *groupchat* messages for key words.

Ethics

Ethnographic research must consider ethics from the very beginning. A virtual ethnographer's first and foremost responsibility is to those they study. Like the resident BodhiDharma Rosebud, people often bare themselves on virtual worlds and expose vulnerabilities that they might not in the actual world. For virtual ethnographers, this means that they must never forget that there are real users behind the on-screen avatars. We identified three chief elements of ethical research: informed consent, anonymity, and transparency. First, following the practices of the American Anthropological Association, we understood informed consent as being composed of the communication and comprehension of the study's goals and voluntary participation.[17] The second concern was anonymity, and we felt that each bit of data had to be carefully judged for an appropriate response. In addition to our own moral diligence, both our University's Institutional Review Board document, which monitored our research ethics and was based on a mix of institutional and national guidelines, and Second Life's terms of service required that informant identities and what they told us be kept confidential.[18]

Third, ethics was maintained through transparency, by rejecting such deceptive practices as being a "fly on the wall" and going "undercover" in the disguise of an alternative identity. That said, while investigators of virtual worlds need to be transparent, and need to clearly state their own actual world identity, playing an avatar that differs from your real-life self was part of the culture of Second Life and other virtual worlds. As long as they are transparent, researchers' avatars do not necessarily need to match their users. We found that "not playing" and maintaining too close a connection between user and avatar led one to being perceived as an expert. Not only did it not allow one to methodologically empty one's cup, but often, like colonizers' use of strict formal dress, it seemed like a way for researchers to distance and create a hierarchy over the "virtual natives." When doing actual world field work, ethnographers need to adapt to some of the customs of those they study; playing a character based too closely on one's actual identity often alienated residents and did not allow for complete understanding of a virtual culture's context.[19]

Conclusion

I stopped typing after I read Rasa's note card "Empty Your Cup." While I did not address it at the time, or even admit it myself, she had hurt my feelings. After a while, Human Riddle instant messaged me in private chat and laughed, "don't mind Rasa, she loves *drama,*" which the Second Life wiki defines as "A way of relating to the world in which a person consistently overreacts to or greatly exaggerates the importance of benign events in Second Life . . . as a way of gaining attention or making their own lives more exciting." Human went on to say that I sounded like an "explorer." He sent me a link to the Bartle Test of Gamer Psychology that categorizes players of MMORPGs into killers, achievers, socializers, and explorers.[20] I opened a web browser and completed the online test whose results did indicate what Human had surmised: I was an "explorer," a category that Richard Bartle's original paper describes as those who "delight in having the game expose its internal machinations to them.

They try progressively esoteric actions in wild, out-of-the-way places, looking for interesting features (i.e., bugs) and figuring out how things work."[21]

We maintain that ethnography is in the end a method of discovering new knowledge through exploration. Online ethnography can easily slide into a virtual tourism, in which investigators merely reinforce their prejudices. To conduct an effective ethnography, whether on- or offline, researchers first must empty their cups. Ethnographers do not have the option of cloaking themselves in the ceremonial objectivity of a white lab coat. Virtual or otherwise, an effective ethnography goes beyond a "deep hanging-out," however, because one cannot help going into a study with prejudices; even veteran researchers must be prepared for their biases and even to be challenged and transformed by the experience. The description of these transformations differentiates ethnography from other types of procedures and gives it methodological power.

Ethnography's effectiveness emerges from the everyday minute serendipitous details of exploration, which does not just discover what one doesn't know but uncovers what one doesn't yet know one doesn't know. Not just the content, but also the categories used to describe, explain, and analyze the data, need to emerge in a dialogue between researchers and the group being studied.[22] Ethnography moves forward not when you reconfirm your expertise but when you discover your ignorance. As described in this volume's Introduction, because of many preconceptions, researchers need to investigate the practice of religion in virtual worlds by "bracketing off" their own prejudices and suspending judgment so as to create a space for new knowledge to seep in. It is a methodological "emptying of one's cup," a type of methodological *shōshin*, or beginner's mind, a term often used by many at Hoben to refer to an attitude of openness, eagerness, and lack of biases. Emptying your methodological cup, however, means neither uncritically parroting back what people tell you nor searching for an objective reality. Instead, it is a middle-way method that means acknowledging that experts might not know everything and allows the categories of the data collected to be shaped and emerge in dialogue with one's exploration of the subject.

Notes

1 Versions of this koan can be found spread across the web, and in popular print. I traced back this version to the book by Paul Reps and Nyogen Senzaki, *Zen Flesh, Zen Bones: A Collection of Zen and Pre-Zen Writings* (New York: Tuttle Publishing, 1957), 19.

2 For the author's earlier work on virtual ethnography, see Gregory Price Grieve, "Virtually Embodying the Field: Silent Online Buddhist Meditation, Immersion, and the Cardean Ethnographic Method," *Online – Heidelberg Journal of Religions on the Internet* 4, no. 1 (2010), www.online.uni-hd.de/ (accessed November 4, 2015); "The Formation of a Virtual Ethnographic Method: The Theory, Practice and Ethics of Researching Second Life's Buddhist Community," *The Pixel in the Lotus: Buddhism, the Internet and Digital Media*, eds. Gregory Price Grieve and Daniel Veidlinger (New York: Routledge, 2014), 23–40; "Finding Liquid Salvation: Using the Cardean Ethnographic Method to Document Second Life Residents and Religious Cloud Communities," with Kevin Heston, in *Virtual*

Worlds, Second Life, and Metaverse Platforms: New Communication and Identity Paradigms, eds. Nelson Zagalo, Leonel Morgado, and Ana Boa-Ventura (Hershey, PA: IGI Global, 2011), 288–306.

3 See note 1 in the Introduction, page 24.

4 See note 2 in the Introduction, page 24.

5 See Alan Dundes, "From Etic to Emic Units in the Structural Study of Folktales," *Journal of American Folklore* 75, no. 1 (1962): 95–105.

6 Vered Amit, *Constructing the Field: Ethnographic Fieldwork in the Contemporary World* (London: Routledge, 2000).

7 We did not, as Lori Kendall warns in *Hanging Out in the Virtual Pub: Masculinities and Relationships Online*, attempt to treat Second Life as "a completely separate, isolated social world." Lori Kendall, *Hanging Out in the Virtual Pub: Masculinities and Relationships Online* (Berkeley: University of California Press, 2002), 9. Second, a conventional model necessitates collection of data almost entirely from within the virtual world, as Second Life *residents*. Tom Boellstorff, *Coming of Age in Second Life: An Anthropologist Explores the Virtually Human* (Princeton, NJ: Princeton University Press, 2008), 60–68. See Gregory Price Grieve, "Imagining a Virtual Religious Community: Neo-pagans on the Internet," *Chicago Anthropology Exchange* 7 (1995): 98–132; Christopher Helland, "Religion Online/Online Religion and Virtual Communitas," in *Religion on the Internet: Research Prospects and Promises*, eds. Jeffery K. Hadden and Douglas E. Cowan (London: JAI Press/Elsevier, 2000), 205–24.

8 See Alex Golub, "Being in the World (of Warcraft): Raiding, Realism, and Knowledge Production in a Massively Multiplayer Online Game," *Anthropological Quarterly* 83 (2010): 17–46.

9 *Nota Bene*: E. E. Evans-Pritchard, *The Nuer, a Description of the Modes Livelihood and Political Institutions of a Nilotic People* (Oxford: Clarendon Press, 1940); Margaret Mead, *Coming of Age in Samoa: A Psychological Study of Primitive Youth for Western Civilisation* (New York: William Morrow, 1928); Bronislaw Malinowski, *The Sexual Life of Savages in North-Western Melanesia: An Ethnographic Account of Courtship, Marriage and Family Life among the Natives of the Trobriand Islands, British New Guinea* (New York: Halcyon House, 1929); Bronislaw Malinowski, *Argonauts of the Western Pacific* (New York: E P. Dutton, 1961); Bronislaw Malinowski, *Magic, Science and Religion* (Prospect Heights, IL: Waveland Press, 1992).

10 Boellstorff; Julian Dibble, *My Tiny Life: Crime and Passion in a Virtual World* (New York: An Owl Book, 1998).

11 Clifford Geertz, "Thick Description: Toward an Interpretive Theory of Culture," in *The Interpretation of Cultures: Selected Essays* (New York: Basic Books, 1973), 3–30.

12 Richard Fox, "Introduction: Working in the Present," in *Recapturing Anthropology: Working in the Present*, ed. Richard Fox (Santa Fe, NM: School of American Research/University of Washington Press, 1991), 1–16; Akhil Gupta and James Ferguson, "Discipline and Practice: 'The Field' As Site, Method, and Location in Anthropology," in *Anthropological Locations: Boundaries and Grounds of a Field Science*, ed. A. Gupta and J. Ferguson (Berkeley: University of California Press, 1997), 1–46; Tamara Kohn, "She Came Out of the Field and into My Home," in *Questions of Consciousness*, eds. A. P. Cohen and N. Rappaport (London: Routledge, 1995), 41–59.

13 James Clifford, *Routes: Travel and Translation in the Late Twentieth Century* (Cambridge, MA: Harvard University Press, 1997); S. Delamont, P. A. Atkinson, and O. Parry, *The Doctoral Experience: Success and Failure in Graduate School* (London: Falmer, 2000).

14 Christine Hine, *Virtual Ethnography* (London: Sage Publications, 2000), 18.

15 Richard Bartle, *Designing Virtual Worlds* (Berkeley, CA: New Riders, 2004), 148–54.

16 Bartle, 451.

17 *American Anthropological Association Statement on Ethnography and Institutional Review Boards*, adopted by the AAA Executive Board June 4, 2004, www.aaanet.org/stmts/irb.htm (accessed August 22, 2013).

18 Tom Boellstroff, Bonni Nardi, Celia Pearce, and T.L. Taylor, *Ethnography and Virtual Worlds: A Handbook of Method* (Woodstock: Princeton University Press, 2012), 151–58.
19 See *The Office: Second Life Is the Same*, YouTube Video, 0:25, posted by yoyomaster, October 31, 2007, www.youtube.com/watch?v=U3d_fqDcN1s (accessed November 5, 2015); Robert R. Desjarlais, *Body and Emotion: The Aesthetics of Illness and Healing in the Nepal Himalayas* (Philadelphia, PA: University of Pennsylvania Press, 1992).
20 *Welcome to the Bartle Test*, http://4you2learn.com/bartle/ (accessed November 4, 2015).
21 Richard Bartle, "Hearts, Clubs, Diamonds, Spades: Players Who Suit Muds," http://mud.co.uk/richard/hcds.htmhttp://mud.co.uk/richard/hcds.htm (accessed November 5, 2015).
22 Gregory Price Grieve, *Retheorizing Religion in Nepal* (New York: Palgrave Macmillan, 2006), 19–21.

Part I

Chapter 1

Second Life

Your world, your imagination

I like to think, (it has to be!), of a cybernetic ecology, where we are free of our labors, and joined back to nature, returned to our mammal brothers and sisters, and all watched over, by machines of loving grace.

Richard Brautigan[1]

To contextualize *Cyber Zen*'s investigation, this chapter analyzes Second Life's media practices. I logged on to Second Life on December 12, 2009, after a Gmail "ping" pulled my attention out of the Microsoft Word document from which this very text would eventually evolve. Just a few minutes before, in an attempt to reboot my lagging fieldwork, I had contacted the *resident* Mystic Moon about a possible interview.[2] The ping marked the arrival of Mystic's positive answer and disentangled my awareness from my computer screen. I became conscious of my office's background noise: the jazz pianist Cedar Walton playing on my earbuds, the minor cord humming of the furnace, the large black cat in my lap, and a slight trembling from the train rattling by a half block away. In real life, Mystic was a twenty-six-year-old German who was finishing up his apprenticeship as a digital designer. In Second Life, Mystic was already a well-recognized *builder*, who had created the Buddhist garden of Gekkou, one of the most stunningly beautiful *sims* in Second Life.[3]

Second Life is a virtual world, a type of digital media practice that differs from other forms because it is a shared immersive cyber-social environment. In our interview, Mystic described Second Life as a "sim[ulation], or a multi-user platform such as World of Warcraft in which you take on an assumed persona and interact with other players." Second Life differs from flat digital media, such as the World Wide Web and email, because of a high rate of "immersion," which describes the feeling of "being in" a virtual world that occurs when a user's awareness no longer focuses on real life but has moved *inworld*. Many forms of media, from books to cinema, are immersive. Users often lose themselves in the narratives that media practices construct. Digital virtual worlds differ, however, because users share their immersion with others. As Mystic's partner, Fae Eden, who had come with him for the interview, added, "Second Life is a world because there are people."

The email message sent on December 12, 2009, contained a *SLurl*, a hyperlink, to Mystic Moon's location. By clicking the SLurl, I opened Second Life, a 3D graphic virtual world housed in cyberspace that users are able to access from any networked computer on the globe. Clicking the SLurl link opened a page in my web browser FireFox, which displayed on my computer's desktop a world map of Second Life centered on the region, or sim, of Gekkou.[4] While not actual, Gekkou was a "conventional reality," a term, which we detail in *Cyber Zen*'s conclusion, that describes mutually constituted and historically contextualized material discourses, practices, and objects by which people construct, interpret, and manage their everyday lives. As a conventional reality, virtual worlds indicate neither the natural world nor the solipsistic creation of an individual. Rather, they are a social reality conditioned through the repetition of public performative acts that create persistent lived worlds.

Once just the fantasy of science fiction writers and computer hackers, by the time of our study in 2008, popular culture had been seduced by the geeky siren call of virtual worlds. As Philip Rosedale, the founder and first CEO of Linden Lab, Second Life's corporate owner, prophesied in a May 16, 2007, interview in *The Guardian*, "Today Second Life, Tomorrow the World . . . This is only the beginning of the 3D web." While Rosedale's prediction has proven hubristic, virtual worlds and virtual realities continue to hold a clear presence in the popular imagination. Yet, what makes Second Life a social space perceived to be distinct from real life? If one leans back from the keyboard it is not immediately clear how the pixels and sounds that compose Second Life are any different from other types of digital media, such as websites, social media, and digital games. In all cases users never leave their chair. On the thin level of description, Second Life consists of merely moving pixels around on the screen through keystrokes and mouse clicks. As an interface, Second Life consists of programmable bits manipulated through the use of graphical user interfaces (GUI) as well as Windows, Icons, Menus, and Pointing devices (WIMP).

This chapter argues that residents' fantasies transform the pixels on the screen into a lived world. As the game researcher Richard Bartle writes, "virtual worlds are the places where the imaginary meets the real." Linden Lab's webpage, "What Is Second Life?," styles the platform as "a virtual world – a 3D online persistent space totally created and evolved by its users. Within this vast and rapidly expanding place, you can do, create or become just about anything you can imagine." When I asked the resident Algama GossipGirl why she used Second Life, she laughed and answered, "the world fascinates me." When I asked her why, she replied, "I can live out my fantasy." Often users' fascination with virtual worlds is assumed to stem from the digital media themselves or to boil up from the innate human desire to create ordered worlds of meaning. Rather than approaching virtual worlds as determined by digital media or by some innate human quality, this chapter describes the complexities of this early twenty-first-century everyday media practice in order to foreground human agency and historical context.[5]

To investigate how the virtual world's media practices transform the empty pixels on the screen into fantastic lived reality, we refract our analysis through Second Life's tagline, "Your World, Your Imagination." Taglines, like capitalistic catechisms, are statements made by a corporation that provide a concise explanation of what it offers. "World" refers to immersive screening practices, which are enabled by digital affordances and virtual world properties that are indebted to the history of the concept of cyberspace. "Imagination" describes the platform's creative software tools that enable resident fantasies, which are vital because they suture users into the virtual world. Second Life's use of the imagination emerges from a "digital utopianism" that arose in the 1970s from the unlikely marriage of computers and the 1960s counterculture. The "your" displays the tension between the promise of unlimited imagination and alienating Network Consumer Society, the cultural system that arose in the last quarter of the twentieth century, based on the desire to purchase goods and services, which do not merely fulfill biological needs but cater to consumer fantasy.

Since I ended our fieldwork in 2011, the appeal of digital media has not weakened and has if anything grown stronger. While Second Life will never become the cyber-frontier that early boosters predicted, because of how it engages the imagination, society will continue to be haunted by the specter of the virtual.[6] The chapter adds to our understanding of the culture and society of virtual worlds, particularly massively multiplayer online role-playing games (MMORPG), a genre of role-playing platforms in which a very large number of users interact with one another within a game setting. Also, by analyzing the part digital Zen plays in the construction of virtual worlds, this chapter lays the foundation that allows one to better diagnose the role religion plays more generally in emergent media. As the pioneer in the study of digital religion Lorne Dawson writes, "the lure of cyberspace remains strong and it is unlikely that the cultural, social, and psychological consequences of the Internet for religion can be avoided or reversed."[7]

World

The "world" in Second Life's tagline indicates the creation of an alternative conventional lived reality through immersive digital media practices, which are contextualized in the techno-fantasy of digital utopianism. The Second Life platform can be traced back to 1999 when the American entrepreneur Philip Rosedale founded Linden Lab, a privately held American Internet company.[8] In its alpha stage, called Linden World, the platform was not open to the public and was basically a primitive shooter game. The Second Life platform was publicly launched on June 23, 2003, and over the next few years there was a slow but steady growth in the number of users, and features such as teleporting and the inworld currency the Linden were added. Second Life caught the attention of popular culture when, on May 1, 2006, the resident Anshe Chung was featured on the cover of *BusinessWorld* and reported to be the first person to become a real-life millionaire due to a Second Life business. Chung's story brought a flood of media coverage and pitched the population growth further, and on October 18, 2006, the millionth resident joined.[9] In the mid-2000s, the platform was the darling of the press, with the American author Kurt Vonnegut's inworld interview, a congressional meeting on virtual worlds and terrorism, and of course the now infamous appearances on the NBC comedy *The Office* and Comedy Central's *The Daily Show*.[10] The honeymoon soon faded, and both critics and residents have been tolling the virtual world's death knells ever since. Second Life may have lost its luster. Still, outside the media hype, Second Life slouches along. As of April 2, 2014, there have been over thirty-seven million signups for Second Life, with a least one million users logging on every month and approximately 60,000 users logged on at any one time.[11]

Second Life's digital affordances and virtual world properties

When a virtual world is effective, however, users' awareness is organized in such a way that they communicate as if they are present in another place. As I typed on my computer, I was no longer just in my office but also aware of being in the region of Gekkou, if only virtually. Residents often talked about "falling" into Second Life, of being immersed and enveloped by the virtual world. Richard Bartle, in *Designing Virtual Worlds*, writes, "People want to be immersed. Designers want them to be immersed."[12] Yet how is this done? Second Life is not "virtual reality," which describes computer-modeled environments that simulate haptic physical presence using multimodal devices such as goggles, gloves, and treadmills. Rather Second Life is a "virtual world" in which users play a role and interact through their onscreen representations. Even while they danced or prayed, shopped or engaged in *edgeplay*, residents were never ignorant that Second Life was ultimately just pixels on a screen.

Second Life's digital practices immerse users through digital affordances that generate the properties of virtual worlds. "Affordance" refers to the properties that shape how an object can be used and can either block, increase, or decrease a particular action (Figure 1.1). For instance, a doorknob affords the opening of a door and the handle on a mug of coffee affords its consumption. One could force a door by kicking, but using the knob affords its smooth release, and one could drink the coffee without using the handle, but the grip affords its consumption without burning one's hands. Different media have differing affordances. Second Life is a "digital media practice," which, as opposed to "analog media" such as newspapers, film, and vinyl discs, consists of electronic technologies that are handled by computers as a series of numeric data. All digital media technologies are composed of programmable bits that can be used for semiotic manipulation and thus share common affordances. "Bit," a portmanteau of "binary" and "digit," is the basic unit of computer-assisted communication. Unlike analog media, which use a physical property of the medium

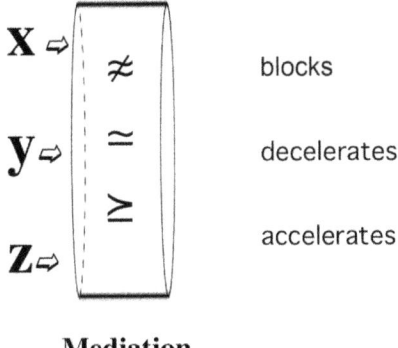

$$X \Rightarrow \quad \not\approx \quad \text{blocks}$$

$$y \Rightarrow \quad \approx \quad \text{decelerates}$$

$$z \Rightarrow \quad \geq \quad \text{accelerates}$$

Mediation

Figure 1.1 Affordances. The properties that shape how a medium either blocks, increases, or decreases a particular communication act.

to convey the signal's information (think of the needle on a vinyl record), digital media consist of digital bits, like a row of on/off switches, which can have only one of two values, most commonly represented as "0" and "1."[13]

Because users embody the world, they are not passive observers, like the readers of a novel or viewers of a film, but active participants who make choices based on their morals and desires. Digital media display four types of affordances: the spatial, participatory, encyclopedic, and procedural.[14] First, digital media's "spatial affordance" refers to how users perceive of logging on and imagine navigating through cyberspaces such as webpages as well as virtual worlds. Second, the "interactive affordance" indicates how digital media invites users to manipulate the represented space and can consist of hyperlinks and/or textual fields, or (as with my *avatar*) of maneuvering through a virtual environment. Third, the "encyclopedic affordance" points to digital media's high capacity for storing information and retrieving data, as displayed by Google's or Second Life's search engine. Consider, for instance, that one of the Hoben Mountain Zen Retreat's community's proudest features was a library that contained many hundreds of Buddhist texts. Finally, digital media's "procedural affordance" enables the ability to represent and execute conditioned behaviors. In a video game, when you shoot a zombie it dies, and when I clicked on one of the meditation cushions in Mystic Moon's Zen garden, my avatar would be animated by *LSL* (Linden Scripting Language) and sit in full lotus.

Yet, how do these digital bits become transformed into a world? Second Life becomes a world because, as a resident answered in our 2010 survey (*n*=108), the platform "allows creative development and also socializing." Creating and socializing in virtual worlds are shaped by four virtual world media practices, which break down into the locative properties of physics and persistence, as well as the social properties of avatars, and real time interaction. First, relying on digital media's procedural and spatial affordances, physics creates the world's "laws of nature," those underlying codes that dictate how automated rules simulate the laws of gravity, elasticity, and the conservation of momentum between colliding objects. Like the jump of video game hero Mario in the video game *Donkey Kong* (1981), virtual world physics need not, and in fact should not, map directly onto real world physics, but it must be fundamentally obvious and transparent and fulfill users' expectations. As Richard Bartle writes, "If I let go of an object, it will fall. That's gravity in action. When it hits the ground, will it bounce?"[15] Second, relying on digital media's encyclopedic affordance, virtual worlds need to be relatively persistent. While individual residents might come and go, unlike a conference call that ends when everyone hangs up, Second Life will continue to exist beyond one user logging off.

The virtual world's social space is also enhanced by avatars and real-time communication, and this is what really makes virtual places interesting to people – namely, other people. Contrary to early notions of virtual reality driven by technological fantasies of realism and total sensory immersion, it seems that the most compelling aspect of virtual worlds is other users. As Chip Morningstar and Randall Farmer, the developers of Habitat, an early and technologically influential online role-playing game, observed, a virtual world is "defined more by the interactions among actors within it than by the technology with which it is implemented."[16] Virtual worlds also differ from other types of digital practices, such as websites and social media, because users embody them through the use of avatars. As explored in chapter four, avatars represent the individual user inworld, and because users have a sense of control over them, avatars are more than just a "game token" but are strongly identified by a user as "self."

A genealogy of cyberspace

Second Life is indebted to both the technology and fantasy of "cyberspace," which by the mid-1990s had become the de facto synonym for online digital media. The March 1, 1995, cover of the special issue of *Time* magazine, *Welcome to Cyberspace*, displays rows of stacked computer circuit boards that disappear down a tunnel of infinite regress and beckon the consumer forward with the cursor-like words *Enter Here* >. Yet, what are users entering into? By the mid-2000s "cyber" had an almost an antique feel and had been superseded in the field of religion and media first by "new media," the term "digital," and finally "emergent." *Cyber Zen* consciously rehabilitates "cyber" in order to trace the genealogy of Second Life's digital virtual world's media practices.

As used by the mid-1990s, *cyberspace* denoted the mediated social space created by interconnected electronic communications.[17] It differs from telecommunications that have a sender and a receiver, because cyberspace occurs in an imagined virtual social environment, in that space between screens. As explored in *Cyber Zen's* conclusion, derived from cyberpunk novels as the opposite of "meat space," cyberspace is a fantastic place of the imagination. As can be seen, even in early discussions such as the American pioneer of digital technology Ted Nelson's 1974 *Computer Lib/Dream Machine*, often cyberspace is imagined as a fantastic place to transcend reality.[18] As technological fantasy, cyberspace emerged in the late twentieth century from the Cold War marriage of computers and the Internet. "Computers" are electronic devices that automatically carry out logical procedures and have their practical roots in World War II, particularly in figuring out artillery firing tables. In the 1940s the ENIAC (Electronic Numerical Integrator And Computer) was described in the January 14, 1946, issue of *Life* as "the Great Electro-Mechanical Brain" that "has been implacably working out the trajectories of shells for all the Navy Guns."[19] The second technological development was the Internet, the "network of networks" that has its roots in the military-university research complex and arose as part of the Cold War fear of nuclear mutually assured destruction. The Internet began in 1969 with the launch of the U.S. Advanced Research Projects Agency (ARPA) and was based on a concept first published in 1967.[20] At first the Net spread slowly, and was limited to a small community of researchers. New types of media practices were quickly developed, however, because rather than its original intent as a space of research, it quickly became a place for social interaction.[21]

Besides the hardware of the Internet, cyberspace is also dependent on an ontology, which, as touched upon in this volume's Introduction, can be traced to Norbert Wiener, who coined the term "cybernetics" in the late 1940s.[22] Wiener argued that cybernetics differed from hard empirical sciences because the focus was not material form but rather networks of organization, pattern, and communication made up of users and machines. As Wiener maintained, "Information is Information, not matter or energy. No materialism which does not admit this can survive at the present day."[23] Wiener envisioned cybernetics as offering a method for regulating the flow of information through such feedback loops between various interrelated components in order to predict and control the behavior of the whole system. Usually cybernetics pertained to messages occurring in standard communication systems or drew parallels between the ways that machines, such as computers, and the human brain process and communicate information.[24] Cybernetics, however, became more than just a way to describe systems but an ontological model of reality itself. By countering the disruptive forces of noise and entropy, Wiener saw communication as the organizing force that created the life of individuals and societies. As he writes near the end of his autobiography, *I Am a Mathematician*, "We are swimming upstream against a great torrent of disorganization."[25] As he writes in the *Human Use of Human Beings*, "We are but whirlpools in a river of ever-flowing water. We are not stuff that abides, but patterns that perpetuate themselves."[26]

Imagination

The virtual world's second tagline term is "Imagination," which describes media practices by which residents make their fantasies public. The website "What Is Second Life?" pulls users in with the claim, "Enter a world with infinite possibilities and live a life without boundaries, guided only by your imagination."[27] The imagination seems an obvious thing – when we take off the bells and whistles, it is simply the human capability to "make stuff up." On the philosophic level, imagination can be defined as the ability to form new images and sensations that are not perceived through the senses and allows for the synthesis and the creation of new knowledge. In Western thought, the concept of the imagination shoulders a wide range of meanings, from creating entirely new phenomena to producing a particular aesthetic experience, objects, and also, critically, the invention of the new ideas that fuel it all.

"Imagination" in Second Life's tagline, however, is more narrowly defined, as residents' creation of inworld content. These are media practices that constitute residents' fantasies afforded by digital media practices and the ideology of digital utopianism that emerged into popular culture in the early 1970s. Using software tools available to all users, residents can make *objects* with physical qualities and even give the objects scripted instructions and thus create buildings, environments, and even the bodies that residents inhabit. Central to Second Life's software are building tools by which residents can create objects using *prims* (primitives) – the most basic building blocks on Second Life.[28] There is also a procedural scripting language, LSL, which can be used to add interactivity to objects. Moreover, as investigated in chapter four, residents also create and *edit* their avatar's appearance by finding, purchasing, or designing clothing, as well as creating their own body's *shapes* and *skins*.

As analyzed in chapters three and five, imaginative media practices are also the means by which residents build their world by creating ways of living together and their methods of representing their collective life. Residents use *chat, instant message,* and *voice* to build together and even more to communicate about what they have built. With the rise of social media, the creative aspect of digital media seems to have been eclipsed. For Second Life, the creative aspect of digital media practices was crucial. Our survey found, however, that only 40.8 percent of those residents who practiced religion regularly indicated that building was important, while 71 percent indicated that socializing was important. Yet it was the builders, like Hoben's Cassius Lawndale and Gekkou's Mystic Moon, who not only imagined and built but also tended to own and run the different regions and spend the most time inworld. For instance, our survey data found that those who came to socialize spent on average zero to ten hours each week in Second Life, while those who found building important on average spent over forty hours a week inworld.

Sandbox

Second Life sells itself as a giant *sandbox*, which are inworld locations for residents to imagine and build their fantasies. Because virtual worlds offer no physical sustenance, Second Life's conventional reality was conditioned by imaginative fantasies, which are enabled by digital media's creative affordances. Throughout our fieldwork, residents generally agreed that whatever could be fantasized could be found, created, or mostly purchased in Second Life. As we explored the world, we found all sorts of things curious, weird, or, as the resident Fae Eden said, just plain "marvelous." Such statements reflect what the virtual world critic, Wagner James Au, in *Notes from the New World: The Making of Second Life*, refers to as "bepop reality": "a universe in which the fundamental laws of physics and identity are open to constant improvisation."[29]

One might assume that users become immersed in the virtual world because it is a game. However, when during interviews I asked if the platform was a game, almost all residents answered, as did resident Mystic Moon and his partner Fae in unison, "no." Others answered like the resident and self-described Zen gardener, Ashley Lee, who smiled and said that Second Life was "no more a game than real life." In the real world "some people play sports on fields, in Second Life there are *sims* for games like that." If not a game, what is it? When we asked residents to describe Second Life, most replied, as a survey respondent did in 2010, "I usually just tell people it's an online social/educational/roleplaying game. But that misses the point." In a typical answer to our question, a thirty-one-year-old, white female American, practicing Buddhist answered, "A social network, a place for art but constructed and musical, a place to imagine. Dreams made visible." Another resident answered on July 17, 2010, "it is a social network but it is more than that. Much much MORE than that!!!" (capitalization and punctuation in original).

Second Life is a place for play, but it is not a *gamist* play in which one collects points and levels up; rather, it is a type of serious pretend in which real life is bracketed off, allowing a space for public fantasies.[30] While Second Life uses a platform that looks similar to MMORPGs created by game designers, because the content is imagined by residents, the virtual world is more like early text-based social MUDs (Multi-User Dungeons), such as LambdaMOO, that de-emphasize competitive game play in favor of an environment designed by the users primarily for socializing.[31] During the time of our study, Second Life was unique among the large virtual world platforms because users created almost all the content, including objects, themselves, and communities, as well as reasons for play. Rather than being predesigned, a sandbox describes a digital environment that affords creativity and experimentation not only for builds and objects but also for imagining new forms of identity and community. As Linden Lab's community manager Brett Atwood writes, "A sandbox is a place for creativity and, on occasion, chaos. It's a place to play, a space in which to build. . . . a sandbox can also be an open place to roam and create freely without limits to your imagination."[32]

Figure 1.2 Second Life eye-in-hand logo.

As evidenced by Second Life's use of the eye-in-hand logo, imagination is the product that Linden Lab sells (Figure 1.2). In fact, while virtual worlds generate many tradable commodities that can be found on Second Life's Marketplace and eBay, Linden Lab's real product is the techno-fantasy of unlimited creative imagi-nation.[33] Au writes that imagination "was the uniqueness that [Linden Lab] stumbled upon, without quite planning it; that was the key feature that would distinguish Second Life from everything else on the market."[34]

Linden Lab advances Second Life's media practices as creative tools, which, by allowing individual creative manifestations of the imagination, are marketed as liberating, even god-like. An early 2002 blog entry describes the platform as "Playing God," because in Second Life, "you are the creator."[35] As the *Second Life Official Guide* reads, "From your point of view, Second Life works as if you were a god in real life. Not an almighty god, perhaps – more like one of those mytho-logical minor gods."[36] Yet, there is nothing inherently god-like about Second Life and other virtual world media practices. As we will see in the following section, the techno-fantasy that surrounds Second Life reflects the digital utopianism of early hacker culture, which emerged from a combination of California coun-terculture and computing.[37] For instance, the *Whole Earth Catalog*, an American counterculture periodical published by Stewart Brand between 1968 and 1972, contends, "we are gods and might as well get used to it."

Fantasy

Rather than making Second Life "unreal," fantasy transforms a screen of pixels into the reality of a conventional lived world. Fantasies are not opposed to real life but are those media practices that organize and give a face to users' desires.

The resident Algama GossipGirl described Second Life as a machine for creating desire, giggling, "people are running all-over with their id's hanging out." Emerging from computing, one might assume that screening media practices would be dry cool data, or at the very least that modeling enjoyment is supplemental to the medium's essential element of the transmission of information. Yet, as Theodor Nelson, writes, "America is the land where the machine is an intimate part of our fantasy life."[38] Second Life was never primarily about transmitting information. The Second Life viewer, particularly in its early forms, was never easy and required a steep learning curve that drove away many first-time users. Second Life's fantasies made the platform "sticky," which describes the amount of time people use particular media, and increased users' retention and duration.

Fantasy can be something seemingly trivial, such as purchasing a new pair of shoes, or profound, such as inhabiting a new type of body. Yet in all cases fantasy engaged with what people felt they were lacking in real life. On January 23, 2010, during a long interview with the resident Ashley Lee in her garden, I asked her why people came to Second Life. She answered, "they are looking for what is missing in their real life. I can't garden in real life." A few minutes later, she expanded on what she meant: "some come wanting the illusion of wealth, a different self, relationships, companionship or like me for spirituality." In Second Life, fantasy usually consisted not only of objects but more often of relationships to others. As the resident, Sophia Ebisu, said to me, on February 25, 2009, after I asked her what brought her to the virtual world, "★wink wink wink★ I'm working on building a man harem. Not sure what past behavior or thoughts drive that, but heck. Second Life provides!!!" (capitalization and punctuation in original).

Some of Second Life's fantasies, such as seeking financial success or education or living the dream of being a rock-and-roll star, were sanctioned by the mainstream. Other fantasies tended to be condemned, such as *edgeplay*, a term that refers to a broad spectrum of sexual encounters that challenge traditional "vanilla" conventions of heteronormativity.[39] The most powerful fantasies attached themselves to some kernel of *jouissance,* a French term that signifies a transgressive, excessive kind of pleasure that compelled certain residents to constantly attempt to transgress the normative social prohibitions.[40] The resident Rasa Vibration described Second Life as "ids gone wild," and, during our research, even in a cursory visit to Second Life, one could not help noticing the plethora of escort services and the cottage industry that provided for sex organs and fetish items.

Whether edgeplay or gardening, virtual worlds allow residents to engage in these imaginative acts publicly, and thus to externalize these fantasies. As Ashley described it, Second Life gave fantasy "a face." Moreover, because residents could never know exactly what others wanted, to many, fantasies seemed endless. Because digital fantasies are based on desires, and not biological needs that can be satisfied, they are never ending. Never quenched, fantasies crave what they lack and strive to hold onto pleasurable experiences and be separated from painful ones. Like a polarized magnet, fantasy does not seek out its self-image, however, but attracts what it feels it cannot have and thirsts to be filled or devour what it is denied. Residents' fantasies can be conscious or unconscious and can arise either from a feeling of "privation," wanting what others have but which you lack, or from "frustration," being refused attention by other people.

Digital utopianism

Why would users project their fantasies into cyberspace? After the triumph of digital media, the revolutionary force of screens seems obvious and inevitable. Yet, this was not always so, and early screens were crisp communication of data and little more. Second Life's fantastic media practices utilize "digital utopianism," a historic movement that started in the early 1970s when counterculturists and technologists joined together using cybernetic models to imagine cyberspace as a place of personal liberation and for the building of alternative communities. Digital utopianism advances the conception that cybernetic practices will create a postpolitical, nonhierarchical society by freeing individuals' imaginations from the system of traditional legal, governmental, and social conditions. For instance, the cyberspace pioneer Howard Rheingold, in *The Virtual Community: Homesteading on the Virtual Frontier*, describes cyberspace as an "electronic agora, an 'Athens without slaves' made possible by telecommunications and cheap computers and implemented through decentralized networks."[41]

In its more radical forms, digital utopianism promises a world of postscarcity, the transformations of human nature, and even the end of death. Take, for instance, the "cyberdelic" movement advanced by the advocate of psychedelic drugs, Timothy Leary. In *Chaos and Cyber Culture*, Leary proclaimed that the "PC is the LSD of the 1990s" and that "the one thing that no mass society can stand is individuals and small groups that go off to start learning how to program, reprogram, boot up, activate, and format their own brains."[42] In its more prosaic forms, digital utopianism assumes that all of a society's problems can be solved with digital technologies. As reported in the January 14, 2014, edition of the *Los Angeles Times*, digital utopianism drives such actions as the Los Angeles Board of Education's $1 billion goal "to provide a computer to every student, teacher and administrator."

From telegraphs and railroads, to radio and automobiles, digital utopianism is just the latest myth of technological advances through which America has imagined itself. Technology's role in America was heightened after World War II, however, because technological advance was popularly propagandized as the key to Allied victory, and then to winning the Cold War. Yet technology had a dark side. By 1959, President Dwight Eisenhower had cautioned Congress about the growing power of what he called the military-industrial complex. As seen in popular films, novels, and television, popular culture imagined that the computer threatened to destroy the human soul, overconsumption the environ-ment, and the atomic bomb the globe.

By the late 1960s, anxiety about the Cold War with Soviet Russia, and the growing hot war in Vietnam, as well as industrial pollution and social unrest at home, had led many intellectuals to see technology – particularly nuclear and computer – as the problem not the cure. In the 1960s, computers haunted the American imagination as bleak tools of the Cold War, and epitomized rigid organization and mechanical conformity. Consider the Californian social critic Theodore Roszak's 1968 book, *The Making of a Counter Culture: Reflections on the Technocratic Society and Its Youthful Opposition*. Roszak found common ground between 1960s student radicals and hippie dropouts in their mutual rejection of what he calls the "technocracy" – the system of corporate and technological expertise that dominates industrial society. For Roszak, the battle against tech-nology was the "paramount struggle of our day."[43] For Roszak, technology was more than just the physical machines – technology was the systematic tyranny of rationalism, bureaucratic regimentation, and ecological suicide. Roszak con-cludes that while technology had allowed humanity to achieve unattainable levels of efficiency, instead of liberating people, it had just enslaved them further in webs of control.

Starting in the early 1970s, however, a major shift occurred in how American popular culture imagined computers. Rather than agents of darkness, computers were rehabilitated as social saviors that allowed users to imagine existence from a god's-eye point of view. By the early 1970s, it was not drugs but computer technology that aided their imaginations, and digital media became a potential tool of liberation. Counterculturalists and technologists joined together using cybernetic models to imagine computers as tools for personal liberation and the building of alternative communities. Just three years after Roszak's 1968 work, Stewart Brand, who edited the *Whole Earth Catalog* from 1968 to 1971, wrote in an article for *Rolling Stone*, "Spacewar: Fanatic Life and Symbolic Death among the Computer Bums," "Ready or not, computers are coming to the people. That's good news, maybe the best since psychedelics."

The techno-fantasy of digital utopianism is laid bare in the information technology pioneer Theodor Nelson's manifesto *Computer Lib/Dream Machine*, where he writes, "computers are where it's at."[44] The 1974 first edition of *Computer Lib/Dream Machine* is an eleven-by-fourteen-inch paperback that ties together computer technology with a romantic notion of the imagination. Nelson's book has two covers – a front cover (*Computer Lib*) and, when rotated 180° and turned over, a flip side (*Dream Machines*) (Figure 1.3). The front cover, like a radical revolutionary graphic poster, shows a raised power fist and the title "Computer Lib," by which Nelson simply means, "making people freer through computers. That's all."[45] For Nelson, the "enemy" are "straight IBM (International Business Machines)" corporate "suits" and other computer pro-fessionals, whom he perceives as having centralized and sequestered computers away from the public. Nelson's "heroes" are the "hip" computer lovers, those

Figure 1.3 Theodor Nelson's *Computer Lib/Dream Machine* (1974) has two covers – a front cover (*Computer Lib*) and, when rotated 180° and turned over, a flip side (*Dream Machines*).

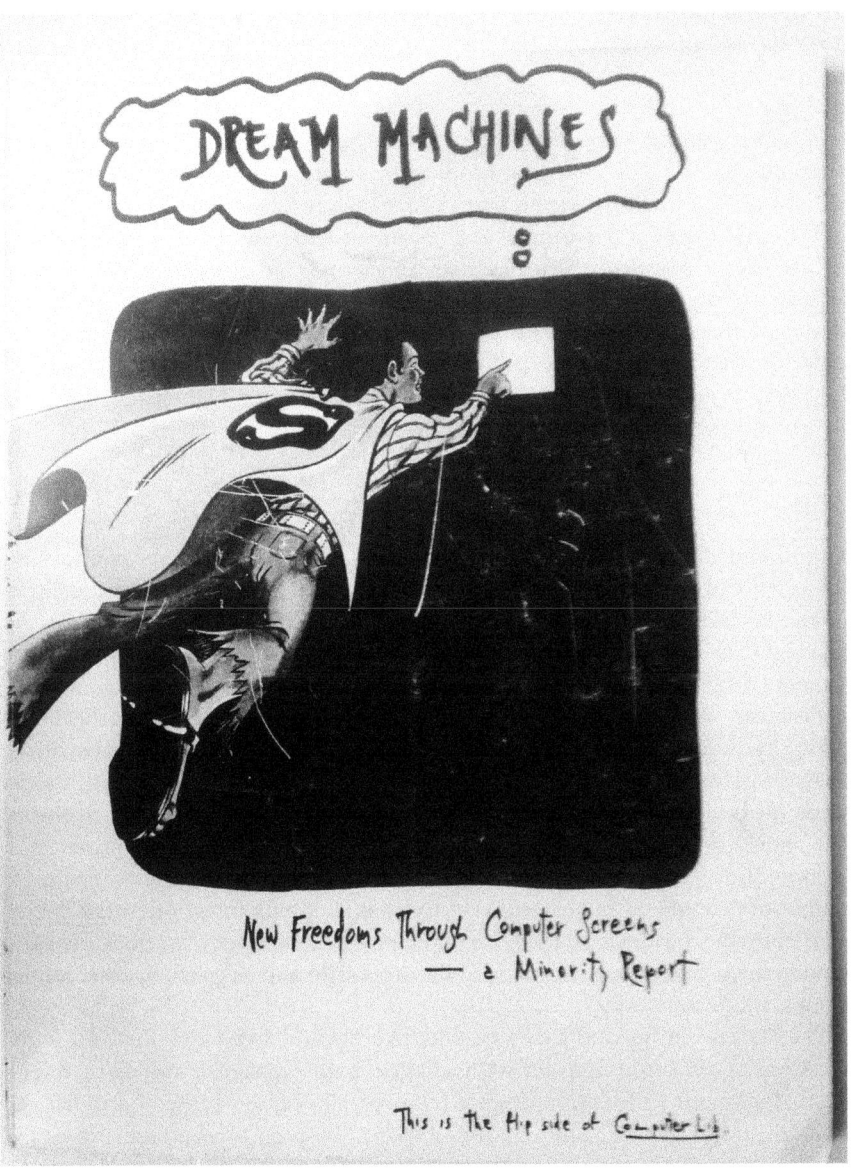

Figure 1.3 (Continued)

homebrewed "phreaks" and "heads," who would combine to create hacking culture and, ultimately, Silicon Valley.

Digital utopianism, however, is not just about computer technology. Something else is "a foot here," as the small cursive text playfully reads above a sandaled foot on the far left margin of the front cover. Following the foot leads to the back cover and accompanying pages, which depict digital media's relation to a counterculture spirituality, the idea that liberation lies in expanding one's consciousness. The 1970s digital utopic culture grew directly out of the countercultural use of hallucinogens, particularly lysergic acid diethylamide (LSD).[46] Like the B-side of a pop single, as Nelson writes, "the flip side of *Computer Lib*" is *Dream Machines: New Freedoms Through Computer Screens.*[47] The cover depicts a nerdy hippy dressed in tattered jeans, sandals, dress shirt, and Super Man cape that blissfully flies into a computer screen. Nelson's dream machine leads directly to Second Life's sandbox use of the imagination. As Nelson writes, the freedom that computer screens offer "is concerned principally with the theory and execution of systems useful to fantasy."[48]

Your

A third element, the "your" of Second Life's tagline, can easily be overlooked but is evident in much of the branding that surrounds Second Life, such as the eye-in-hand logo. Second Life residents engage in a participatory network consumerism where corporations such as Linden Lab only loosely control the content and in which "you" directly participate in the creation and circulation of meaning and values.[49] The "your" reveals the ideological tension between the digital utopian promise of unlimited authentic imagination and alienating network consumerism of its actual media practices. As described in this volume's Introduction, authenticity refers to a cultural model of media practices that allow users to innovatively explore and create alternative identities and communities. Yet, because Second Life is a privately held corporate company in which most residents' main creative activity is shopping, users often felt alienated from the product of their imagination. "Alienation" describes people's estrangement from their authentic ability to create and shape their own selves, groups, and lived worlds.

The "your" in Second Life's tagline, like Second Life's eye-in-hand logo, functions as a floating signifier with a vague, highly variable, unspecific referent that allows it to function despite (or maybe because of) the contradiction inherent in it.[50] Second Life's "your" denotes the unlimited imagination of a socially organic, egalitarian, and creative space that fosters unlimited individual creativity. Second Life's media practices alienate, however, because they sugarcoat corporate ownership with digital utopian fantasies.[51] Like fan fiction, Second Life's media practices lie in the play between these two extremes.[52] As detailed on the website, "The Second Life® Brand Center," the virtual world suffers a tension because, while it promises that it is "your" world, it is owned by Linden Lab. Second Life's building tools and even residents' avatars are always already subject to terms and conditions of use that "Linden Research, Inc. ('Linden Lab') grants." "If you don't agree to [the terms and conditions], do not use the Logo in any way."[53] After early confrontations, the Second Life terms of service provide that users retain copyright for any inworld content they create.[54] Residents do not, however, own the media practices by which these products are built and circulated and maintained. It is like owning your home's blueprints but not the land rights or even materials out of which it is constructed. Linden Lab may terminate residents' accounts at any time: "Upon Account termination, you will lose access to your Account and all licenses, Content, and data, and you understand this is a risk of participating in the Service."

The *SLogosphere* that surrounds the virtual world is filled with the tension between Linden Lab's corporate goals and the digital utopian fantasy displayed by many of Second Life's residents.[55] The post, "Your World, Your Imagination, Our Lawyers," from the Blog Magrathean, mocks Linden Lab's policies: "If you do something we don't like or try to compete with us we will just exercise our superspecial awesome *mod* rights and ban you into next Tuesday *n00b*."[56] Linden Lab's business mission seems to reflect a digital utopian ethic that has a deep faith in technology's liberating potential and a suspicion of vertical authority.[57] "The Tao of Linden" posted on the company's website reads: our "principles include working together, showing initiative, making day-by-day progress, being transparent and open, and having fun along the way." However, as a corporation, Linden Lab's bottom line is the bottom line. As founder and first CEO Philip Rosedale wrote on the Second Life blog, in a post titled "The Mission of Linden Lab," "It is certainly the goal of Linden Lab to operate profitably, and by doing so create returns for the shareholder-owners of the company."[58] Ultimately, Second Life's "your," to borrow a term from the French psychoanalyst Jacque Lacan, is a type of late capitalistic "symbolic castration" in which a person's fantasies are subject to the laws and conventions of authoritarian social reality in which they live and over which they do not have total control.[59]

Network Consumer Society

As revealed by the "your" and the eye-in-hand Logo, Second Life is a petri dish of Network Consumer Society, which defines the cultural, social, and economic system that arose in the last quarter of the twentieth century and is defined by the fluidity of financial capital, an intensification of the free market, radical individualism, and interconnected globalization. Network consumerism fosters a socioeconomic order based on the desire to purchase goods and services, which do not merely fulfill biological needs but cater to thirsts for pleasurable experiences and to be separated from unpleasant ones. Network Consumer Society is deeply entangled with digital media networks, which were originally built at the request of government agencies, military contractors, and educational institutions. Since the late- 1990s, however, digital networks have primarily served corporate interests.

Second Life's tagline's "your" displays the alienation inherent in Network Consumerism, in which the purchase of commoditized networks is how people express identities, form community, and engage desire. As a lived reality, consumerism is defined not just as the sale of goods but also by the fantasies that orbit around products. As Linda Grant writes, in *Laws of Desire*, "Because how you feel when you have your new coat or wrap dress is something so mysterious, complex and potentially transformative, that is almost metaphysical. It casts you in a new light to yourself." Commodities also make you desirable to others. Don DeLillo's novel *White Noise* captures perfectly consumer fantasies' projection of lack. The novel's protagonist, Jack Gladney, a middle-aged academic, is galvanized into going shopping because he worries about being unrecognizable, just a "big, harmless, aging, indistinct sort of guy."[60]

Virtual worlds are an extreme case that shows how Network Consumer fantasies magically transform ordinary objects into commodities and that it is through the consumption and circulation of commodities that selves, relationships, and communities are formed. Second Life offers the fantasy of unlimited imagination. What most residents actually do on Second Life, however, is shop. Our 2010 survey showed that 67 percent of respondents reported that shopping was very important or important to their second life. In fact, we found that 43 percent of residents reported that they spent over 50 percent of their time shopping. Using the Linden dollar, an inworld floating currency that is exchangeable for U.S. dollars or other currencies on market-based currency exchanges, residents spent a large amount of time consuming or talking about consuming.[61] Because there is no sensuous element, virtual commodities offer an ideal type. The perfect commodity is one that does not last, because desire emerges from attempting to fill a lack. If one actually satisfies a need, it is no longer a fantasy and is relinquished and no longer relevant.

Network consumerism is not false consciousness, however, but a media practice that structures residents' lived realities of the virtual world.[62] Residents know what they are doing and enjoy it, often saying that virtual goods are less expensive than real commodities. Residents on Second Life know what they buy is not actual, but the purchase of virtual goods structures social relations on- and offline and has real effect. Commonsensically, being a consumer seems to be all about knowing and satisfying one's own individual desires through choosing, buying, and enjoying. To be a consumer is to make choices, to decide what you want, to consider how to spend your money. Yet consumerism is not free choice. Consumer practices, and the marketplace ideology that support them, are conditioned by and frame consumers' horizons of conceivable actions by making some patterns of behavior more interpretable than others. As Eric Arnould and Craig Thompson write, in "Consumer Culture Theory (CCT):

Twenty Years of Research," "consumer culture denotes a social arrangement in which the relations between lived culture and social resources, and between meaningful ways of life and symbolic material resources on which they depend, are mediated through the markets."[63]

A genealogy of Network Consumer Society

The last quarter of the twentieth century saw the rise of Network Consumer Society. Take, for example, the Apple "1984" television commercial, which aired on January 22, 1984, during Super Bowl XVIII and marks the leading edge of Network Consumer Society. The advertisement introducing the Apple Macintosh Computer depicts a female athlete wearing an Olympic-like track uniform with an Apple logo smashing a hammer through a large blue-tinted television screen on which an Orwellian Big Brother–like image lectures. In the 1983 keynote address, which released the spot, cofounder of Apple Steve Jobs said, "it is now 1984. . . . IBM wants it all and is aiming its guns on its last obstacle to industry control: Apple. Will Big Blue dominate the entire computer industry? The entire information age? Was George Orwell right about 1984?"[64]

Like the hammer-wielding athlete, Network Consumer Society promises residents self-liberation through shopping. As the driving force of American society, consumerism arose in the second half of the twentieth century. While during World War II consumer goods were rationed and even cooking grease had been recycled, by the 1950s to shop was patriotic, and built-in obsolescence became an American virtue. Shopping was not merely materialism but allowed for the imagining of a shared American community outside of class, race, and ethnicity. During the war, Americans had (at least in the popular imagination) been able to put aside their differences. The postwar consumer-saturated technological society again allowed Americans of all kinds to imagine a shared community based on the myth of material success and technological improvement. As reflected in home appliances such as electric stoves, refrigerators, toasters, vacuum cleaners, and washing machines, the myth of technological advancement was key to imagining a harmonious American civil society led by scientists as well as a domestic realm ruled by homemakers.[65]

Until the 1970s, digital technological development mainly influenced labor. Starting in the last quarter of the twentieth century, Network Consumer Society began to emerge, as digital information technology, at a relatively inexpensive cost, afforded more sophisticated interactive capabilities. Network consumerism intensified "neoliberalism," a socioeconomic system that resurged in the late 1970s and that demands market deregulation as well as public sector reforms that force government agencies to operate similarly to private companies.[66] Under the euphemism of "flexibility" and "personal choice," neoliberalism has dissolved previously guaranteed permanent employment and sold consumers on the idea that as long as they have the money, they can buy any type of lifestyle, and if they are not satisfied, they at least have the freedom to choose another product.

The network consumerism that emerged in the early 1980s is built upon the digital utopianism that formed a decade earlier. As the article in the special issue of *Time*, "Welcome to Cyberspace," reads, "We Owe It All to the Hippies." The shift from the traditional models of corporate-controlled production and distribution to nonhierarchical, collaborative structures might seem more democratic than the traditional factories of solid modern production. Yet what at the time might have seemed liberating is now a web of network consumerism out of which there seems no exit. In hindsight we can see that Jobs was utilizing the techno-fantasy of digital utopianism for corporate profit. Apple and other Silicon Valley companies, such as Google, whose business was dependent on network consumerism would prevail, and the authority of modern production would be replaced by neoliberal authority. What at first seemed like a liberating technology that would disrupt the status quo has evolved into a media practice whose constant destabilizing pings control the very fabric of everyday life. The media practices that at first seemed so emancipatory have become a constant chore in which users have to constantly update their uncertain lives so that they do not become obsolete and out of date.

Conclusion

Ultimately, Second Life is just a screen of pixels that users manipulate through keystrokes and mouse clicks. Users never leave their chairs when they go inworld. Refracting our description through the tagline "Your World, Your Imagination," this chapter has illustrated that Second Life becomes a "world" neither because it mimics physical space nor because of an essential quality determined by digital media. Instead, residents turn the virtual world into a "second life" by using the platform's digital media practices to communicate public fantasies. As Robin Harper, the Linden Lab Vice President of Marketing and Community Development, wrote in 2003, "We had a lot of ideas for place names . . . Ultimately, though . . . We kept coming back to Life2, and then landed on Second Life as more interesting, more evocative and more what we hoped the world could become."[67] While residents create Second Life, however, they do not create it just as they please. While play exists in their choices, a resident's agency is always already shaped by the digital media's affordances, Network Consumer Society, and the techno-fantasies of digital utopianism that make the virtual world not only possible but desirable.

On December 12, 2009, just a few moments after the initial Gmail ping, my computer screened finally opened the Second Life Viewer (version 1.21.6), a software program needed to access the virtual world. Slowly the virtual world loaded. Once opened, the Second Life viewer displayed a blue-tinged rectangular computer window that filled my entire screen, blocking other windows. I logged on, and, after entering my password and hitting return, my avatar rezzed at Gekkou. I was no longer just typing on the keyboard but was also aware of standing in front of an immense stone image of Shakyamuni Buddha, framed by a forest of autumnal trees, over whose head was a twinkling rainbow.

In Network Consumer Society, people have many choices. Why at Hoben did residents pick convert Zen to counter the suffering created by Network Consumer Society? As evidenced by Mystic Moon's Zen Garden at Gekkou, while Second Life is the product of network consumer media practices, residents can still use it to imagine alternative social spaces. I often came to visit Mystic to get away from the shopping mall clutter and noise of many parts of the virtual world. As I show in the chapters that follow, while a popular form of spirituality, the groups, people, places, and events of Second Life's Zen community are authentic forms of religious practice. Scholars of religion and media need to be critical of the practices they investigate and see them not as timeless fonts of wisdom but as historically contextualized ordinary parts of everyday life. At the same time, however, scholars need to be alert to the particularly religious agency of the people being researched and not reduce their motives to other causes such as politics, psychology, sociology, ideology, and the economy.

There was no doubt that residents were logging onto Second Life for authentically religious reasons. As one adherent reported in our survey from 2010, "For my practice, I am unspeakably grateful to have this medium of access." Yet why Buddhism? As shown by my research team's and other scholars' surveys, the percentage of people reporting to be Buddhist online proved significantly higher than in the general public.[68] Convert Buddhist beliefs were also reported by many of the key figures who developed digital media. For instance, in 2010 Mark Zuckerberg, the founder of Facebook, listed "Eliminating Desire" (an obvious reference to Buddhism) as an interest on his Facebook page, and the Apple founder Steve Jobs's design for Macintosh was intricately intertwined with his idea of "Zen."[69] In the following chapter I illustrate that the strange fit between convert Buddhism and digital media occurs because cybernetic procedures were used in postwar America to translate many Buddhist practices into popular culture. Convert Zen has a genealogy leading from late 1940s cybernetic thought through Alan Watts, the Beats, California's sixties counterculture, the work of Robert Pirsig, and finally to the 1980s corporate mining of the concept of mindfulness. During World War II, Zen was the enemy. Yet with the defeat of the Japanese, Zen became a blank sign ready to be written upon. As America became the postwar consumer nation, cybernetics offered a frame on which Buddhist concepts and practices were hung in such a way to afford both spirituality and consumerism.

Notes

1 Richard Brautigan, *All Watched over by Machines of Loving Grace* (San Francisco: Communication Company, 1967).
2 See note 1 in the Introduction, page 24.
3 See note 2 in the Introduction, page 24.
4 "Meet Mozilla FireFox," Mozilla Foundation, www.mozilla.org/en-US/firefox/central/ (accessed February 6, 2012).
5 Stewart Hoover, "The Cultural Construction of Religion and Media," in *Practicing Religion in the Age of the Media: Explorations in Media, Religion and Culture*, eds. Stewart Hoover and Lynn Schofield Clark, 1–6 (New York: Columbia University Press, 2002), 3.
6 "A Second Life Holiday," *Gratuitous.com*, March 6, 2007, www.youtube.com/watch?v= EgtGcTHL2dI (accessed February 6, 2012); Philip Rosedale, "Life in Second Life," TED, www.ted.com/talks/the_inspiration_of_second_life?language=en (accessed February 6, 2012).
7 Lorne Dawson, "Doing Religion in Cyberspace: The Promise and the Perils," *Council of Societies for the Study of Religion Bulletin* 30, no. 1 (2001): 8. See Lorne Dawson and Douglas Cowan, eds., *Religion Online: Finding Faith on the Internet* (New York: Routledge, 2004).
8 James Wagner Au, *The Making of Second Life: Notes from the New World* (San Francisco: HarperCollins Publishers, 2008); Tom Boellstorff, *Coming of Age in Second Life: An Anthropologist Explores the Virtually Human* (Princeton, NJ: Princeton University Press, 2008).
9 "The Beginning of Second Life," Second Life Wiki, http://wiki.secondlife.com/wiki/ History_of_Second_Life (accessed April 1, 2014).
10 Sharon Weinberger, *Congress Freaks Out over Second Life Terrorism*, March 4, 2008, www. wired.com/2008/04/second-life/ (accessed November 6, 2015); Richard Koman, *Congress Goes Virtual in Online World Hearing by Mike Musgrove*, April 2, 2008, www.cio-today.com/article/index.php?story_id=0220020SF4V8, www.wired.com/2008/04/ second-life/ (accessed November 6, 2015); John Brownlee, "Kurt Vonnegut Interview in Second Life," www.wired.com/table_of_malcontents/2007/04/kurt_vonnegut_i/ (accessed November 6, 2015); Akela Talamasca, *Second Life Ranked 8th Most Effective Placement on TV in 2007*, December 30, 2007, http://massively.joystiq.com/2007/12/30/ second-life-ranked-8th-most-effective-placements-on-tv-in-2007 (accessed November 6, 2015).
11 "Second Life Grid Survey – Region Database," www.gridsurvey.com/ (accessed November 6, 2015).
12 Richard Bartle, *Designing Virtual Worlds* (Berkeley: New Riders, 2004), 239.
13 Consider the difference between Thomas Edison's tinfoil cylinder, which relies on the physicality of the medium to convey information, and a computer file of the same sound that is stored in an electronic device in a binary fashion as a series of ones and zeroes (see *ORIGINAL EDISON 1877 TIN FOIL RECORDING*, YouTube Video, 1:17, posted by THEVICTROLAGUY, December 2, 2012, www.youtube.com/watch?v=g3qPT30LejM (accessed November 6, 2015).
14 Gregory Price Grieve, "Religion," in *Digital Religion: Understanding Religious Practice in New Media Worlds*, ed. Heidi Campbell (New York: Routledge, 2012), 104–19; Janet Murray, *Inventing the Medium: Principles of Interaction Design as a Cultural Practice* (Cambridge MA: MIT Press, 2011); Ian Bogost, "Persuasive Games: Video Game Zen," *Gamasutra.com*, www.gamasutra.com/view/feature/2585/persuasive_games_video_game_zen. php (accessed January 2, 2014).
15 Bartle, 318.
16 Chip Morningstar and Randall Farmer, "The Lessons of Lucasfilm's Habitat," in *Cyberspace: First Steps*, ed. Michael Benedikt (Cambridge, MA: MIT Press, 1991), 274.

17 Benedikt; Edward Castronova, *Synthetic Worlds: The Business and Culture of Online Games* (Chicago: University of Chicago Press, 2005); Howard Rheingold, *The Virtual Community: Homesteading on the Electronic Frontier* (Reading, MA: Addison-Wesley Publications, 1993).

18 Theodor Nelson, *Computer Lib: You Can and Must Understand Computers Now/Dream Machines: New Freedoms through Computer Screens – A Minority Report* (Chicago: Hugo Book Service, 1974).

19 The ENIAC contained more than 17,000 vacuum tubes, weighed over thirty tons, and filled a room the size of a squash court. It could, however, complete calculations in under twenty seconds that had previously taken hours. By the end of 1947, nine such computers were being constructed in the United States and Britain, and soon the UNIVAC (universal automatic computer) would become the first commercially successful system. See Paul E. Ceruzzi, *A History of Modern Computing* (Boston: MIT Press, 2003).

20 Elmer B. Shapiro, "Computer Network Meeting of October 9–10, 1967," November 1967, http://web.stanford.edu/dept/SUL/library/extra4/sloan/mousesite/Archive/Post68/ARPANETMeeting1167.html (accessed November 6, 2015).

21 In 1970 the first electronic mail was sent, and by 1973 three quarters of all traffic on the Internet consisted of such messages. In 1975 discussion groups were added, and newsgroups in 1979. The arrival of relatively inexpensive personal computers in the early 1980s enabled many more users to log on. In 1990 the ARPANET was decommissioned, and by 1993 the administrative functions of the Internet were handed over to private corporations (Campbell, 4–5).

22 As a field, cybernetics falls into three stages. The first, from 1945 to 1960, was stimulated by a series of conferences sponsored by the Josiah Macy Foundation, which laid the foundation for the field by solidifying the concept that both humans and machines could be understood as information-processing systems (see Steve Heims, *The Cybernetics Group* [Cambridge, MA: MIT Press, 1991]). The second stage began in 1960 with the publication of Heinz von Foerster's *Observing Systems* (Seaside, CA: Intersystems Publications, 1981), which understood cybernetics systems not only as self-organizing, but as autopoitic, or reflexively self-making. The third stage began in 1972, when Myron Krueger coined the term "artificial reality" to describe the third Videoplace, which used projectors, video cameras, and other hardware to place users in an interactive computer environment (Myron Krueger, *Artificial Reality 2* (Reading, MA: Addison-Wesley Professional, 1991); *Myron Krueger – Videoplace, Responsive Environment, 1972–1990s,* YouTube video, 7:35, posted by "MediaArtTube," www.youtube.com/watch?v=dmmxVA5xhuo [accessed November 6, 2015]).

23 Norbert Wiener, *Cybernetics, or Control and Communication in the Animal and the Machine* (New York: Technology Press, 1948), 132.

24 W. Ross Ashby's *Design for a Brain* (London: Chapman & Hall, 1952) and F. H. George's *The Brain as Computer* (Oxford: Pergamon, 1961) were important works in this regard and suggest the early alliance among cybernetics, information theory, and artificial intelligence.

25 Norbert Wiener, *I Am a Mathematician: The Later Life of a Prodigy* (Cambridge, MA: MIT Press, 1964), 324.

26 Norbert Wiener, *Human Use of Human Beings* (New York: Houghton Mifflin, 1950), 96.

27 "What Is Second Life?," http://secondlife.com/whatis/ (accessed December 1, 2014).

28 Prims can be box, cylinder, and prism shaped, as well as sculpted (*sculpties*). Each prim's color, texture, bumpiness, shininess, and transparency can be adjusted; images (textures) can be applied to each surface to change its appearance; and mesh, textures for clothing or other objects, animations, and gestures can be created using external software and imported. In addition, a prim can have a mass that corresponds to seven materials: stone, metal, glass, wood, flesh, plastic, and rubber. http://community.secondlife.com/t5/English-Knowledge-Base/Build-Tools/ta-p/700039; for what was current during or field work see "Building Tools," http://wiki.secondlife.com/wiki/Edit_window#Edit_Tool

(accessed November 6, 2015). For a simple study of how mass is affected by prim shape/types see "Mass Lab," Second Life Wiki, http://wiki.secondlife.com/wiki/Mass_Lab (accessed November 6, 2015).

29 Au, xviii.

30 Compare Huizinga (Johan Huizinga, *Homo Ludens: A Study of the Play-Element in Culture* [Boston: Beacon Press, 1950]) to Donald Wood Winnicott, *Playing and Reality* (London: Tavistock, 1971).

31 "LambdaMOO," www.moo.mud.org/ (accessed November 6, 2015).

32 Brett Linden, "Introducing The Sandbox, the Official Second Life Newsletter," http://community.secondlife.com/t5/Community-General/Introducing-The-Sandbox-the-Official-Second-Life-Newsletter/ba-p/661318 (accessed November 6, 2015).

33 Thomas Malaby, "Beyond Play: A New Approach to Games," *Games and Culture* 2, no. 2 (2007): 95–113; *Making Virtual Worlds: Linden Lab and Second Life* (Ithaca, NY: Cornell University Press, 2009), 30. (See "Second Life Marketplace," https://marketplace.secondlife.com/?lang=en-US [accessed November 6, 2015], which used to be Xstreet. See http://wiki.secondlife.com/wiki/Category:Xstreet [accessed November 6, 2015]).

34 Au, 30.

35 "Second Life in 2002/News," http://wiki.secondlife.com/wiki/Second_Life_in_2002/News (accessed November 6, 2015).

36 Michael Rymaszewski, *Second Life: The Official Guide* (Hoboken, NJ: John Wiley & Sons, 2007), 7.

37 Fred Turner, *From Counterculture to Cyberculture* (Chicago: University of Chicago Press, 2006); Morris Dickstein, *Gates of Eden: American Culture in the Sixties* (New York: Basic Books, 1977).

38 Nelson, DM 13 (Nelson's book can be read in two directions. DM indicates Dream Machine, which is the "flip side" of the front cover).

39 As the inworld journalist Miller Copeland writes, "Although acted out through fantasy and roleplaying, the line between healthy and unhealthy behavior is deliberately blurred during such activities; hence the 'edge' in its name, and its continual controversy among even the BDSM community." (See Miller Copeland, "Edgeplay: The Dirty Little Secret of Second Life," *The Grid*, October 1, 2006, www.jasonpettus.com/inthegrid/itg01us.pdf [accessed November 6, 2015]).

40 Slavoj Žižek, *The Plague of Fantasies* (New York: Verso, 1997a), 50; Jacques Lacan, *The Ethics of Psychoanalysis: The Seminar of Jacques Lacan Book VII* (New York: Norton Company, 1986); Jacques Lacan, *The Seminar of Jaques Lacan: On Feminine Sexuality the Limits of Love and Knowledge. Book XX Encore 1972–1973* (New York: W.W. Norton & Company, 1988).

41 Howard Rheingold, *The Virtual Community: Homesteading on the Electronic Frontier* (Reading, MA: Addison-Wesley Publications, 1993), 240.

42 Timothy Leary, *Chaos and Cyber Culture* (San Francisco: Ronin Publishing, 1994), 37.

43 Theodore Roszak, *The Making of a Counter Culture: Reflections on the Technocratic Society and Its Youthful Opposition* (New York: Doubleday Books, 1968), 4.

44 Nelson, CL 4 (Nelsons' book can be read in two directions "CL" indicates Computer Lib, wich is the front cover of the "A side" of the book).

45 Nelson, DM 59, CL 1.

46 After almost half a century of "just say no" and antidrug morality, it is nearly impossible to understand the early 1970s attitude toward hallucinogens, particularly LSD (John Markoff, *What the Doormouse Said* [New York: Penguin, 2005], xvii). Consider the June 28, 1966, issue of *Look*, as the cover reads: "an entire issue on California/A new game with new rules." The magazine reports, "These people have tried LSD neither for kicks nor therapy, but to gain glimpses of new and rich worlds of consciousness (Nelson, DM 59). The use of hallucinogens was key for many Silicon Valley pioneers. For instance, Steve

Jobs believed that taking LSD was one of the two or three most important things that he had done (Markoff, xix). LSD and creativity were also important for Silicon Valley pioneers such as Doug Engelbart and Steve Brand (see Markoff, 61, 65–68; Turner, 60–61, 185).

47 Nelson, back cover.

48 Nelson, 5.

49 Louis Althusser, *Lenin and Philosophy and Other Essays* (London: Verso, 1970), 11.

50 Jeffrey Mehlman, *The "Floating Signifier": From Lévi-Strauss to Lacan* (New Haven, CT: Yale University Press, 1972), 10–37.

51 I would like to thank Jayme Mallindine for this insight.

52 Henry Jenkins, "Star Trek Return, Reread, Rewritten," *Critical Studies in Mass Communications* 5, no. 2 (1988): 85–107.

53 "License for Press Use of the Second Life Eye-in-Hand Logo," The Second Life® Brand Center, https://secondlife.com/corporate/brand/trademark/press.php (accessed November 6, 2015).

54 "Terms of service," Linden Lab, www.lindenlab.com/tos (accessed November 6, 2015).

55 Boellstorff, 220; Christopher Kelty, *Two Bits: The Cultural Significance of Free Software* (Durham, NC: Duke University Press, 2008); Lawrence Lessig, *Free Culture: How Big Media Uses Technology and the Law to Lock Down Culture and Control Creativity* (New York: Penguin Press, 2004); Geert Lovink, *Zero Comments: Blogging and Critical Internet Culture* (New York: Routledge, 2008); Peter Ludlow and Mark Wallace, *The Second Life Herald: The Virtual Tabloid that Witnessed the Dawn of the Metaverse* (Cambridge, MA: The MIT Press, 2007).

56 http://magrathean.ca/your-world-your-imagination-our-laywers/ (accessed February 1, 2012).

57 Malaby, *Making Virtual Worlds: Linden Lab and Second Life*.

58 http://community.secondlife.com/t5/Features/The-Mission-of-Linden-Lab/ba-p/533170.

59 "The Mission of Linden Lab," Philip Rosedale, https://community.secondlife.com/t5/Features/The-Mission-of-Linden-Lab/ba-p/533170 (accessed November 6, 2015).

60 Don DeLillo, *White Noise* (New York: Viking Press, 1985), 106–07.

61 One might question if "play currencies" like the Linden dollar, in "play worlds," like Second Life, have actual value. Yet, as Judge Eduardo Roberto writes in *Bragg v. Linden Research*, a 2006 Pennsylvania court case involving Second Life, "while the property and the world where it is found are virtual," the assets are real. www.paed.uscourts.gov/documents/opinions/07D0658P.pdf.

62 Slavoj Žižek, *The Sublime Object of Ideology* (London: Verso, 2008).

63 Erik Arnould and Craig Thompson, "Consumer Culture Theory (CCT) Twenty Years of Research," *Journal of Consumer Research* 3, no. 4 (2005): 869.

64 1983 Apple Keynote – The "1984" Ad Introduction, YouTube Video, 6:41, posted by The Apple History Channel, April 1, 2006. www.youtube.com/watch?v=lSiQA6KKyJo (accessed November 6, 2015).

65 TheBuddhaMachine – Computer.m4v, Gregory Grieve, 5:58, posted by Gregory Grieve, May 4, 2010, www.youtube.com/watch?v=qAbxGCuv6-Q (accessed November 6, 2015).

66 David Harvey, *A Brief History of Neoliberalism* (Oxford: Oxford University Press, 2005).

67 "The beginning of Second Life," Second Life Wiki, http://wiki.secondlife.com/wiki/History_of_Second_Life (accessed April 1, 2014).

68 The draw to Buddhism of online practice is evident in the numbers of practitioners. The Pew Forum on Religion and Public Life's "U.S. Religious Land Survey" showed that only 0.7 percent of Americans reported themselves as Buddhist (2008). Our large Second Life survey showed that 5.3 percent of residents reported being Buddhist. And when asked by our survey of residents who regularly practice religion in Second Life to "describe what

religion best describes you," 23.5 percent answered Buddhist. A 2009 survey, conducted by Daniel Veidlinger, of over one million Myspace profiles showed that 1.9 percent of users reported to be Buddhist. In August 2010, my own research team conducted a survey ($n=1,227$) of randomly sampled Second Life Residents and found that the percentage of Buddhists in the virtual world was 5.3 percent.

69 Jose Antonio Vargas, "The Face of Facebook," *The New Yorker*, September 2010, www.newyorker.com/magazine/2010/09/20/the-face-of-facebook (accessed November 7, 2015); Sam Littlefair Wallace, "Mark Zuckerberg says 'Buddhism Is an Amazing Religion'," *Lion's Road: Buddhist Wisdom for Our Time*, October 27, 2015, www.lionsroar.com/mark-zuckerberg-says-buddhism-is-an-amazing-religion/ (accessed November 7, 2015).

Chapter 2

Awake online

Understanding Second Life's Zen path of practice

I have found my lost spirituality here, I was distracted by many things in real life, Second Life has allowed me the freedom to find it again :)

Human Riddle (personal conversation, June 1, 2009)

This chapter analyzes the practice of convert Zen Buddhism on Second Life.[1] Many critics argue that digital religion technology "leaves no mystery," and authentic spirituality and virtual worlds are thus inherently antagonistic.[2] Numerous others assume that real religion and the market place are never compatible, and it seems obvious that digital media is opposed to mindfulness and that meditation is the means to counter society's high-tech thirst for networked consumerism. As the psychologist Philip Novak writes in "The Buddha and the Computer: Meditation in an Age of Information," meditation is a "tool for balance and sanity in an electronically over stimulated civilization, and perhaps the ultimate high-touch complement to our high-tech world."[3] Such blanket proclamations, however, do not adequately address the lived reality of everyday practice at the Hoben Mountain Zen Retreat. My research team found that for many adherents on Second Life, online Zen practice proved an authentic and meaningful part of their spiritual lives.

To study Zen on the digital screen, however, my research team first had to locate it. This quest proved difficult not for a lack of phenomena but rather because the word "Zen" operated in the virtual world as a shifting signifier whose meaning changed radically depending on the context. As one *resident* answered, on July 7, 2010, "What is Zen? What isn't?" During our research, "Zen" was a gun for hire, a shifting signifier utilized and transformed by different groups for different purposes. We quickly narrowed our search by asking, "What counts as authentic Zen practice?" As Gary Storhoff and John Whalen-Bridge ask in "American Buddhism as a Way of Life," "Where does a fashionable and trendy practice of Buddhism end, and where does a serious, committed, and devotional focus on Buddhism begin?"[4] As *Cyber Zen*'s introduction maintains, authentic religious media practices do not necessarily need to duplicate canonical sources, or even real-life practices, but are those that allow individuals and groups to engage innovatively with what they perceive as ultimately real.

Cyber Zen argues that for adherents the authentic Zen on Second Life is a practice-oriented spirituality. Studying Hoben's practice proved complicated, however, as I touched upon in the book's introduction, because it was often expressed as silence. The silence that surrounds Second Life practice is not that surprising. At Hoben, "Zen" was usually credited to the Indian monk Bodhidharma, who is recorded in the *Treatise on the Two Entrances and Four Practices* (sixth century C.E.) as coming to China from India during the time of the Southern and Northern Dynasties to carry a "special transmission outside of scriptures" which "did not stand upon words."[5] The founder of Hoben Zen Mountain Retreat Cassius Lawndale joked that the patriarch was mentioned so often "that we need a Bodhidharma emoticon."[6] Up until the mid-1980s, many scholars also invoked silence as the essence of Zen. As the German professor of the philosophy of religion and Jesuit theologian Heinrich Dumoulin writes in *Zen Enlightenment: Origins and Meaning*, "talking about Zen" is "basically useless. . . . the finger is not the moon and cannot pull the moon down."[7] The academic tide has turned, however, and Dumoulin and other scholars who searched for the essence of Zen have been heavily critiqued in recent scholarship as being custodians for the tradition who did not approach their subject critically.[8] Since the late 1980s, a wave of scholarship has seen through Zen, analyzing its practices as an all too human social construction.

Cyber Zen takes a middle path that argues that convert Zen is a social construction that is an authentic spirituality for its practitioners. Popular forms of meditation practice emerge in postwar America as both a product of and response to Network Consumer Society. We remain critical, however, of Zen's silence as being outside of language and approach silence as material media practices that do not have universal meaning but are dependent on a specific context for their significance.

How does one study silence, particularly if it is mediated by digital technologies? Luckily, in late 2010, Cassius placed a sign in Hoben's meditation hall (Figure 2.1). Titled across the top, in black letters and highlighted with lighter green, the sign read, "Understanding the Path of Practice" and displayed four possible interrelated states along a practitioner's journey: *Bodhisattva Vow, Karuṇā, Upāya, Śūnyatā*.[9] The sign was attributed to the popular Buddhist scholar, Mu Soeng, and a version of the diagram can be found on page thirty-three of his translation, the *Diamond Sutra: Transforming the Way We Perceive the World*. Soeng writes that the diagram provides "an in-depth discussion of the basic architecture of *Mahāyāna* [Buddhism]."[10] While Soeng's themes are taken from Buddhism, however, he arranges the four states of the path along a directed graph: a depiction of a feedback loop often used in computer science and related fields to describe the behavior of a system, which can be traced back to cybernetic thought. As we described in the last chapter, cybernetics emerged in postwar America and is an ontology modeled on computers that sees reality

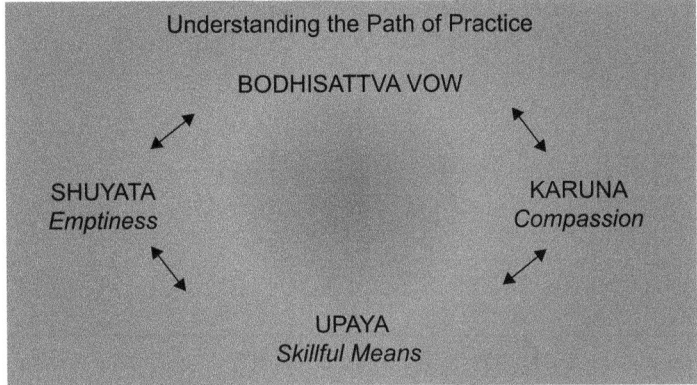

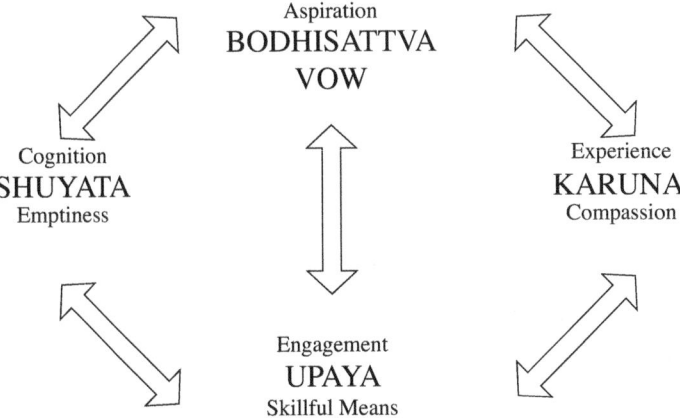

Understanding the Path of Practice

Aspiration
BODHISATTVA
VOW

Cognition
SHUYATA
Emptiness

Experience
KARUNA
Compassion

Engagement
UPAYA
Skillful Means

Figure 2.1 Resident Cassius Lawndale's sign, "Understanding the Path of Practice," a pictorial poaching of Mu Soeng's diagram of a "Thematic Understanding of the Prajnaparamita Tradition," from *The Diamond Sutra: Transforming the Way We Perceive the World.*

(Somerville, MA: Wisdom Publications, 2000), page 33.

as a system of feedback loops as navigated by a mindful steersman. In Soeng's case, the "system" is the spiritual path of a Buddhist practitioner. In fact, while the sign lists Buddhist concepts, the diagram most closely resembles the PDCA (plan-do-check-adjust) wheel popularized by the father of modern industrial quality control, Edwards Deming (Figure 2.2).[11] Such diagrams are a four-step management method for the control and continuous improvement of processes and products. As described below, the PDCA emerges from a strange feedback loop between Japanese and American culture.

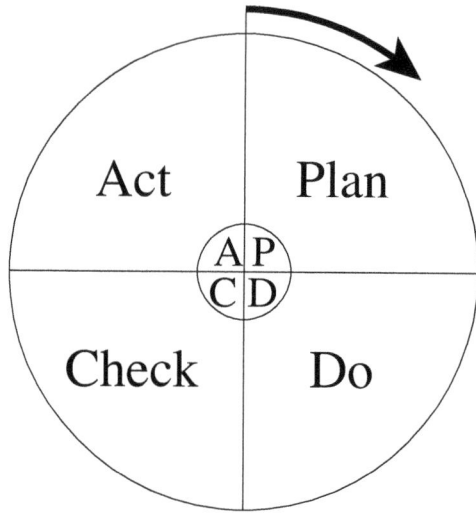

Figure 2.2 PDCA (a.k.a. the Deming Cycle, Shewhart cycle, or Deming Wheel) is an iterative four-step quality control strategy.

Using the sign "Understanding the Path of Practice" as a map, this chapter makes two arguments. First, it theorizes Second Life convert Zen as spiritual practices that enable residents to engage authentically with what they perceive as religious and thereby generate a moral economy that emerges from and engages with what they feel as ultimately significant in their lives. As Charles Prebish contends, in *American Buddhism,* just as the Chinese turned to Buddhism in the first century C.E., in the twentieth century Americans "turned to Buddhism to quench an intellectual thirst, an inquisitiveness fueled by this seemingly exotic religion."[12] Rather than being based on reading scripture, or belief, for the most part Second Life Zen Buddhism searches for the authentic practice of mindfulness, which practitioners describe as nonjudgmental focus on the emotions, thoughts, and sensations occurring in the present moment.

Second, the chapter maintains that convert Zen flourishes on Second Life because like virtual worlds, it has its historic roots in postwar American cybernetics. Accordingly, using the "Understanding the Path of Practice" sign as a touchstone, I trace Second Life's Zen's genealogy in order to comprehend what Buddhism is today and how its present form differs from the past. The goal is to see Zen more clearly. The chapter focuses on the historical conditions that have given rise to digital Dharma, specifically the mindfulness practice that one finds now on the web and in virtual worlds like Second Life. Specifically, the chapter uncovers the postwar American historical background that makes such phenomena as meditating in a virtual world not only possible but also desirable.

Cyber Zen argues that contemporary convert American Zen is not a timeless practice, nor simply an orientalist false consciousness, but a post–World War II creation, which was crafted in a tangled feedback loop between Asian practices and cybernetic procedures.

Convert Zen's history shows that while practice on Second Life has a family resemblance to classic Asian traditions, it has drifted in postwar America to a degree that its practices are only tangentially related to earlier forms. Cybernetics has had a significant influence on popular convert Buddhism: first, in the 1950s through the writings of Alan Watts and the Beats, and then in the 1960s through the hippie counterculture. The relation between convert Buddhism and cybernetics is clearest in Robert Pirsig's *Zen and the Art of Motorcycle Maintenance*, which in the 1980s and 1990s contributed to a Network Consumer business management style that has been reproduced in the many hundreds of "Zen and the Art of X" business titles and that flourishes in such tech companies as Google.[13] In this context, Zen and its nimbus of mindfulness is often assumed to be an ancient spirituality that has been updated with science. As the website Wisdom 2.0 Business reads, we explore "the next wave of innovation, mindfulness, and wisdom in business."[14] However, as we illustrate below, in a strange feedback loop the Zen that American corporate leaders brought back was a hybrid mix of a militant *bushido* wartime Buddhism and a cybernetic management style that had been introduced by occupation forces after World War II.

My aim is not to argue that the Zen of Second Life is inauthentic. While a social and historical human construction, Hoben's practices do not lack real and authentic spiritual meaning for their adherents. While people make religion, they do not choose the situations in which they make it and are thrown into given media environments. As Network Consumer Society tentacles its way into an increasingly large swath of contemporary life, residents in the developed world scramble to find authentic ways of being. One of the fascinating aspects of Second Life is that it lays bare the imagination of convert Buddhists, which displays wider tendencies in American spiritual life more generally. With less than 1 percent of the American population practicing it, Buddhism plays a part in the popular imagination far beyond the number of its adherents. Understanding such alternative religions is significant because, as Laurence Moore writes in *Religious Outsiders and the Making of Americans*, the study of American religion suffers from the providential myth of Protestant hegemony, while in fact it was "outsider" religions that shaped much contemporary practice.[15] Convert Buddhism is an "insider–outsider" religion that stands in a unique interstitial cultural space that defamiliarizes and makes conspicuous many contemporary spiritual practices.

Locating the Zen of Second Life

Before the chapter makes an argument, however, about what constitutes authentic Zen practice, the investigation needs to locate exactly what we are analyzing. Second Life's search engine proved an inadequate tool for limiting the study, and when filtered for "Zen" the searches returned tens of thousands of hits for a jumble of religions, alternative lifestyles, consumerism, creativity, and Eastern spirituality. The use of "Zen" ranged from a "cool" branding that was used to sell consumer goods to a classical handling that tied it to canonical scripture.[16] Next, my research team took a more boots-on-the-ground approach, and by the end of 2008, we had compiled over 163 Second Life regions that had Zen in their name. *Teleporting* through them alphabetically, we ran through a Buddhist hell, prostrated at a Thai *wat*, wandered through a Pure Land heaven, gathered information at a Jōdo Shinshū kiosk, climbed a mountain peak strewn with Tibetan prayer flags and a small *chörten*, as well as circumambulated a copy of the Nepali Swayambhunath *stūpa*.

There was no shortage of Zen on Second Life. Yet, what counted as authentic practice? From the perspective of Religious Studies, there is no one genuine form of Zen, and its practices have been adapted throughout history to the contours of the societies in which it has found itself. Just as Zen Buddhism has undergone significant changes in different geographical environments, it has undergone changes in different media environments.[17] Yet, without sliding down the slope to an essentialized version of a pure Zen, what definition can be used to find the authentic kernels while tossing away the chaff?

We maintain that Zen practice on Second Life should be studied "emically," an analysis that takes into account an insider's perspective rather than just importing an existing external theoretical framework. Defining Zen from an emic perspective proved complicated at Hoben, however, because, as explained in this volume's Introduction, the practitioners themselves took great pains not to describe it. How can one analyze an insider's silence? If asked for clarification on what Zen was, the community leaders would usually describe themselves as lay practitioners, saying that they did not have authority, and then would usually send a note card, or URL (Uniform Resource Identifier) link to other media. For instance, Cassius Lawndale indicated the YouTube video, "Orientation to Zen 01 – Zazen (Zen Meditation)," from the Victoria Zen Centre, that states, "Fundamentally Zen Practice is a very simple activity just sitting up straight and breathing and paying attention to where you are and what you are doing."[18]

As touched upon in *Cyber Zen's* Introduction, the ultimate goal of Hoben's silent meditation was to "wake up," which usually indicated mindful media practices. While spiritual, mindfulness was perceived as having nothing to do with a deity and to be empty of any doctrine, belief, or ideological system. When in an interview on May 4, 2009, I asked one of Hoben's leaders, Human Riddle, why he practiced Zen, he answered, "self examination, introspection, and most of all mindfulness." While perceived as devoid of content or even a goal, mindfulness was reported to be religious because it revealed the ultimate empty nature of reality. I asked Human to describe mindfulness. After a long pause he said, "We need to WAKE UP!!! from the waking 'dream' that we are living in during the course of our normal day. Mindfulness includes non-judging, non-interfering and non-striving. It is to be open to whatever arises. It is a mirror that does not add or subtract or improve or change" (capitalization in original). Mindfulness was pragmatically spiritual because it enabled compassion (*karuṇā*) that relieved suffering (*duḥkha*). As Human went on to add, "Being silent, in my humble opinion, is the most important thing we can do in this life for ourselves and the world in general, which is clearly, sorely in need of help. As Gandhi said, 'BE the change you want to see in the world.' Zen is a wonderful means of learning how to be that 'change'" (capitalization in original).

Spiritual but not religious

The first step to investigating Zen on Second Life is to analyze the emic use of the term "religion." On the night of February 25, 2009, after silent meditation, I went to visit the Zen practitioner Ashley Lee and her longtime friend Solojoe Magic who was helping her in the garden. Solojoe was dressed as a colorful hobo and described himself as a "homeless seeker." It was the first time I had met Solojoe, but Ashley, who had arranged the get-together, had spoken much about how he used Second Life to quest for spirituality. "He's everywhere, seeking the best of what Second Life has to offer." I asked Solojoe about his inworld practice, and he answered, "I think that whatever we do, whether 'here' or 'there,' acts to nurture something in our own garden." Ashley laughed, "and then once that seed ripens, whoot!" To which Solojoe added, "it can be a beautiful flower or a weed. Don't judge your spirituality. It is a personal path that few find revealed."

In Second Life's Buddhist community, an often heard phrase was "I'm spiritual but not religious."[19] Frequently this was expressed with passionate conviction. As the resident Imnotdana Zuul said at a Buddhist discussion on the night of July 23, 2009, "By the way, I loathe religion." The first few dozen times my research team encountered the phrase "I'm spiritual but not religious," we tried to filter it out as empty background noise. What became clear was that my research team and Second Life adherents were using the same word, "religion," but in different ways and that this difference was causing friction in our investigation. As referred to in the volume's introduction, my research team understood religion as those media practices by which people organize their lives by engaging with what they perceive as ultimately authentic. As can be seen in Imnotdana's statement, however, for many on Second Life, "religion" indicated oppressive forms of organized institutions that had lost the authentic search for the divine and instead used the authority of the divine to legitimize arbitrary and often exploitative dogma.

True, some Buddhist practitioners wondered if "spiritual" was the correct word to describe Zen, and a few, such as Cassius Lawndale, even questioned the use of the word "practice" itself. For the most part, however, the virtual world seemed to attract spiritual people – 21.4 percent of respondents in our large survey reported being spiritual but not religious ($n=1,227$). While we do not have statistical data, the perception from our fieldwork is that the percentage was even higher for residents reporting to be Buddhist. As a Buddhist practitioner wrote in our 2010 survey (n=108),

> It may have seemed a foolish thing to do, but one of the reasons I came to Second Life was to continue a spiritual journey that I was on. I had read that some Christian churches actually had services in [Second Life], and wondered what other religions might be represented. I needed a platform that allowed me to learn from multiple sources with a minimum of travel and expense, and found that in Second Life. The Buddhist *saṅgha* [communities] in Second Life have offered me that opportunity with such richness and variety that I am sometimes overwhelmed.

Three features of spirituality

The resident Ashley Lee defined Buddhism as "a spiritual set of guidelines for living well – for being a compassionate, kindly person." Describing convert Zen's spirituality proves difficult, however, because one of its defining features is its flexibility. Ashley Lee described Buddhism as "a many layered, many faceted practice, very ancient, that now takes a great many forms, some varying quite widely from what I understand to have been the original." Even more difficult, often residents pronounced spirituality as indescribable or even claimed that trying to define spirituality destroyed it. As the Buddhist resident Venomfangx Bardfield described in an interview on June 15, 2009, spirituality "can never be held, only sought after. Think of it as a catfish you pulled off your hook and grasped in your hand and with a wiggle maybe a poke from the spines . . . it slips from your fingers and back into the waters." We also quickly realized that residents were not concerned so much with defining spirituality as with its aesthetic and pragmatic value. As the resident RavensSong Merlin declared in an interview from May 29, 2009, "the 'meaning' of spirituality is like sunlight. You don't need to describe it, just enjoy its warmth."

While by definition, spirituality was perceived to be deeply personal, heterodoxic, and idiosyncratic, Second Life's spiritual practices consisted of three features: a focus on personal growth, anti-institutionalism, and spontaneity. First, residents focused on subjective experience and personal psychological growth that was perceived to be different for each individual and often depended on managing one's desires. This inward management was described by many Buddhist practitioners as taming one's "monkey mind," a term that can be found in classic Chinese texts and was usually used by convert Buddhists to describe the anxious unsettled state of living in Network Consumer Society.[20] The Buddhist resident Rasa Vibration described her practice as "sitting on a round black cushion on Monkey Mind Mountain, trying my best not to scream and run off."

Second, religious institutions, being tangential, were often seen by Buddhist residents as casual and transient at best and detrimental at worst to spiritual goals. What we observed was that "spirituality" as opposed to "religion" was perceived by many residents as an individual's personal pursuit of the divine that rejected traditional organized churches. As the practitioner Eliza Martinek said, "I don't consider my Buddhism a 'religion' *per se*. I try not to have too many compartments generally." In a similar fashion, Ashley said in our interview, "religion leaves you with an organized hierarchy where experts act as gatekeepers to the truth, Spiritual Truth is in a radically different context." She went on to add a few minutes later, "religion is the outward signs, and spirituality is what I believe and how I display it for ★me★."

Finally, spirituality was perceived to give people a personal authentic freedom, a spontaneity that countered the excess of the everyday existence of a Network Consumer life. A meditation note card, titled "Tap Dancing in Zen," attributed to Geri Larkin, the founder of the Still Point Zen Buddhist Temple, read, "We all have this freedom. The question is, how can we find the key, or keys, that will open our internal doors so we can all share in this knowing?" For many, Second Life afforded a flexible and inexpensive social reality to live out their spiritual fantasies. As Ashley said near the end of our interview, "Second Life is my place to lend freedom to my inner spiritual Zenpagan, who has taken a backseat to practical things for so long."

Three spiritual tactics

While residents felt that their practice was deeply personal, we found during our research three distinct spiritual tactics: fundamentalist dwellers, New Age seekers, and mindful practitioners. These tactics did not correspond to any particular religion but rather described how residents adhered to their traditions. In *The Practice of Everyday Life*, the French social theorist Michel de Certeau resorts to a distinction between "strategies" and "tactics." A strategy is an authoritative type of agency, such as the political, economic, scientific, and religious, that operates from a proper social location with standardized even routinized habitual forms of engagement.[21] On the other hand, while often poaching from traditional institutions, a tactic describes a type of agency that operates from outside bases of established authority, is used by more marginalized individuals, and by necessity is more flexible and innovative. As de Certeau writes, "A tactic insinuates itself into the other's place, fragmentarily, without taking it over in its entirety, without being able to keep it at a distance."[22] Spiritual tactics become necessary in contemporary culture because Network Consumer Society has dissolved traditional religious communities, identities, and institutions, leaving people anxious and unsure.

Dwellers and seekers

The first spiritual tactic found on Second Life is fundamentalism, which addresses networked consumerism by attempting to return to a traditional original essence. In *After Heaven: Spirituality in America Since the 1950s*, the sociologist of religion

Robert Wuthnow labels such individuals "dwellers" and writes, "for them, the congregation's mission will be to provide a safe haven amidst the growing uncertainties of the world in which people live."[23] Choosing to hold fast to an imagined tradition is a rational reaction to Network Consumer Society's dissolving of traditional social structures. Fundamentalisms hold on tight and center on a static essence as the spiritual force governing life. Fundamentalism tackles Network Consumer anxiety by setting sharp boundaries through personal discipline, steadfastness, and regular engagement with authoritative sources. For instance, the Second Life Christian group East Borough Church defined themselves in the following way: "we believe in all the fundamental doctrines of the evangelical Protestant church. For example, we believe in the inerrancy of Scripture, that the Bible, Old and New Testaments, is the inspired, infallible Word of God." Fundamentalists tended to pose a sharp dichotomy between Second Life and the actual world and saw the virtual platform primarily as a place of mission work, as a big *chatroom* for the transmission of information.

"New Age," the second spiritual tactic, sees in an increasingly pluralistic and moral and religious setting the need to negotiate one's own spiritual path in the midst of endless alternatives. Wuthnow calls these "seekers," a type of spirituality that "focuses on attention of the specifics of the moment but is likely to be insufficient to without an interpretive framework that provides coherence to individual biographies."[24] This is a tactic of letting go, of seeking wholeness by overcoming the barriers that separate people from one and another, and of emphasizing the feelings and experience in life more than a cognitive understanding. For the spiritual tactic of seeking reality is negotiable; whatever you believe is true – *at least for you.*

While New Agers stress the individualistic nature of their beliefs, a spirituality of seeking tends to have three main aspects. First is the understanding that union with the divine is possible. Second, it seeks a grain of truth in all religions. Finally, a spirituality of seeking has a monistic, or unified, worldview that seeks not membership in a particular faith but connections between different traditions. One can see this hybridity in Second Life's New Age group Energy Land, which perceived of the virtual world as more spiritual than real life. The New Age resident Thoth Sandy said to me during a guided meditation session,

> Concentrate on the divine light vehicle during the meditation here and feel the energy in *real life.* Second Life offers more energy models that can help you to increase your vibration, on physical and on mental levels. The great pyramid of Egypt, better known as the pyramid of Cheops, will generate energy.

As a place of fantasy, New Agers found Second Life to be a magical realm, often more real than the actual world, because the platform could allow their inner spiritual self to manifest.[25]

Practice-oriented spirituality

Clearly, the Second Life Buddhists were not fundamentalists. When we began our research on Second Life, we had assumed that the Hoben community would fit into the category of seekers, and at first blush the data might seem to confirm this view. For instance, in our 2010 survey ($n=108$) of Second Life Buddhists, not a single practitioner answered that they believed "my religion is the one and only true faith leading to salvation," while 61.4 percent answered "many religions can lead to salvation" and 75.3 percent maintained that "each person is free to interpret the teachings for themselves." As the community member RavensSong Merlin said, "there are all sorts of possibilities in all religions." As the resident Georgina Florida said, "while I practice Buddhism, I am fond of looking at the heart of other religions."

We slowly surmised, however, that Hoben fit neatly into neither the dweller nor seeker categories. Near the end of *After Heaven*, Robert Wuthnow introduces a third type of spirituality to "retrieve the neglected middle," a practice-oriented spirituality that offers an alternative to seeking and dwelling by combining elements from both.[26] The difference between the Buddhist spirituality and pure seekers is that the majority of community members perceived "belief" as secondary to "practice," which was reported to consist of experience and not the acceptance of a supernatural being. Take, for example, a conversation between regular practitioners and a new member of the community that occurred at Hoben in February 20, 2009. The *noobie* practitioner asked "what are we meditating to?" Cassius Lawndale replied, "Buddhism in general is a 'non-theistic' as opposed to a-theistic religion, which means that Buddhists don't discuss 'God' or a supreme deity because discussing it keeps it in the realm of ideas." The resident Human Riddle added, "you don't believe in the Buddha! Like a scientist you *do* Buddhism." RavensSong Merlin said at the same time, "Buddhists engage in practices which allow them to have a direct experience of the 'divine principle' that is the source of all creation. Zen practitioners take this admonition to put practice over belief to the highest degree of all Buddhists."

Like seeking, practice-oriented spirituality understands salvation as the outcome of one's personal effort. As Wuthnow writes, it "invokes the tradition of hard work, individual initiative, and responsible civic participation that has served the United States in the past and that is still widely shared at present."[27] Unlike pure seeking, however, because it entails actions, practice-oriented spirituality requires a space in which to dwell, which in the confusion of everyday life is only possible by carefully demarcating a place from its surroundings. For this reason, the New Age seeker Solojoe could be "homeless," without a community, yet, as we will see in chapter five, the practice-oriented adherents at Hoben required a communal place. Yet, unlike the spirituality of dwelling, these spaces are negotiable, and the point of engaging in spiritual practices is not to feel secure but to grow increasingly aware of their own ultimate authenticity through an understanding of oneself and one's place in the world. Such communities of worship define their mission as the strengthening of the spiritual practice of their members.

Mindfulness

Rather than being based on reading scripture, or personal belief, for the most part Second Life Zen Buddhism consisted of a practice-oriented spirituality that was expressed as mindfulness. Certainly, many thousands of pieces of Buddhist scripture and more popular accounts poached from magazines, books, and the web circulated among Hoben practitioners. And the community's Wisdom Center library, which contained hundreds of digitized texts and video links, was one of the group's proudest achievements. For the most part, however, rather than systematically studying these texts, such as was done in Christian groups with the Bible, Buddhist texts were poached to justify a practice-oriented path. Rather than a set of beliefs, practitioners saw Zen as a way of engaging with the world. One of Hoben's leaders, Tai Buckinghamshire, described Buddhism as "the path we walk through life." When I asked her to expand, she said, Zen is "a practice deriving from the Buddha which seeks to lay out enlightenment in a practical way which requires a different way of viewing the world, one that leads to clearer insight into oneself and others, which results in more effective dealings in the world."

In contemporary convert Zen practice, adherents report that when the clutter of everyday life is stripped away, what is left is "mindfulness," a nonjudgmental focus on the emotions, thoughts, and sensations occurring in the present moment. Derived from the Buddhist notion of *smṛti*, in contemporary convert practice the term is associated with "awakening" (*bodhi*), a clear and stable attention that affords a direct insight into the true nature of the world and self and the relationship between the two. When I asked Human Riddle to define mindfulness, he said, "keeping one's consciousness alive in the present reality." Human went on to add, "The practice of mindfulness/awareness meditation is common to all Buddhist traditions. Beyond that, it is common to, inherent in, all human beings." As I describe in chapter six, many practitioners felt that the simplest way to cultivate mindfulness was by being aware of your breath. As a note card titled, "Sitting With the Breath," written for the Hoben community by Human, who reported being a mindful awareness therapist in real life, stated, "we define sitting practice as simply sitting quietly . . . the goal is to see what there is to see, hear what there is to hear, breathe a breath and be there."

At Hoben, mindfulness was described as a spiritualized awareness of the interwoven relation of people and their environment, which leads to compassion. As the community leader Georgina Florida reported, "Compassionate awareness is who we really are." Mindfulness was understood as an absorption in the moment. As a meditative note card titled, "An Experimental Journey" reads, "'Just sitting,' 'just looking,' just doing anything. It's always about becoming completely absorbed in the experience in the moment. In fact 'absorption' is more than just an everyday word meaning getting lost in the activity. 'Absorption' is also a part of the meaning of the Pali 'jhana,' [*jhāna*] the Sanskrit 'dhyana' [*dhyāna*], the Chinese 'chan' and the Japanese 'Zen.'" When I asked Human why he practiced online silent meditation he said, "Self examination, introspection, and most of all mindfulness." I asked him to describe mindfulness, and there was a long pause. "Mindfulness is more capacity rather than a quality. As quality it includes non-judging, non-interfering and non-striving. It is to be open to whatever arises. It is a mirror that does not add or subtract or improve or change."

Bodhisattva vow

The aim of Buddhist practice-oriented spirituality is mindfulness, whose practice was diagrammed in the sign "Understanding the Path of Practice" (Figure 2.1). Cassius Lawndale attributed the sign to Mu Soeng's translation of the Diamond Sutra, a *Mahāyāna* sutra from the Perfection of Wisdom genre (*Prajñāpāramitā*) that emphasizes nonabiding and nonattachment. At the time Soeng was the scholar in residence at the Central Massachusetts Barre Center for Buddhist Studies, which is home of the Insight Meditation Society and whose website describes itself as "a non-profit educational organization dedicated to exploring Buddhist thought and practice as a living tradition, faithful to its origins, yet adaptable to the current world."[28]

Cassius's rendition of Soeng's sign displayed four possible interrelated states along the path to practice. First, centered at the top, just below the title "Understanding the Path of Practice," in large all capital letters Cassius had written "BODHISAT-TVA VOW," which was reported by many at Hoben to indicate an aspiration to wake up for the sake of all sentient beings. The meditation leader Dubhshlaine Gustafson's real-life profile tab read, "As long as Sentient beings remain in samsara [*saṃsāra*] may I too remain so that I may inspire them to recognize their own true nature, free from both attachment and aversion, hope and fear. The Prayer of the Bodhisattva (my favorite)." Above the large, all-capital letters, Cassius had written in small, almost invisible white font, "aspiration," which is slightly different from Soeng's diagram that reads "intention" yet fits more closely with how Hoben practitioners viewed *bodhichitta,* the desire to strive towards awakening. Soeng writes that "Mahayana [Buddhism] rests on the cosmological perspective in which the spiritual journey of the bodhisattva begins with. . . . being inspirited or awakened . . . to the point of an arousal of boddhicitta."[29] For many at Hoben, bodhichitta was tied into the regulation of desire, which was often described with the Buddhist term *tṛṣṇā*, which literally means "thirst" and defines an unquenchable craving that is the ultimate cause of suffering, anxiety, and dissatisfaction. In a late night conversation on August 1, 2009, the resident Mystic Moon declared that "Buddhism is the path of awakeness and awareness of our endless desires." As described in the last chapter, desire is not simply a want that can be filled but an attachment to an essential lacking that defines one's identity.

Compassion

Second, moving clockwise, a thin red double-headed arrow on the sign "Understanding the Path of Practice" pointed down and to the right, pointing to the words, "KARUNA" (capitalization in original), which Cassius translated as "compassion." Soeng writes, "as a result of [boddhicitta], the bodhisattva cultivates compassion for those beings still caught in the delusional world."[30] For many, compassion is their practice. As Ashley said, "Compassionate awareness is who we really are." A note card handed out on July 7, 2008, and excerpted from *Buddhadharma Magazine* read, "The roots of Buddhist practice are the attitudes of altruism and non-harm. In other words, the roots of Buddhist practice are loving-kindness and compassion." A note card titled "Eight Fold Path" and dispensed in Hoben's meditation hall described compassion as "Right Action [that] deals with refraining from killing, stealing and being unchaste. It helps one to develop a character that is self-controlled and mindful of the rights of others." Some like Human Riddle tied *karuna* into "engaged Buddhism," a term describing those who use mindfulness for political and social action. As Human said, engaged Buddhism "applies to a wide variety of human rights issues, such as antiviolence and environmental concerns, and to the lives of individual Buddhists living 'in the world'." More often, karuna was seen to arise from small everyday acts of kindness. Georgina Florida, when reporting about her infirm real-life husband, said, "Loving-kindness is beyond time and space. It has no set form. It's in the small moments and ordinary hopes of life every bit as much as in the grand gestures of saints. What's your prayer as you go about your life, caring for the people you love?"

Above the word KARUNA, Cassius had written in a small white font, "experience," which described the awareness of being interconnected. Through the concept of experience, Soeng ties together compassion with "tathata"(*tathatā*), which he translates as "suchness" and describes as "insight into the nature of the phenomenal world."[31] In a similar fashion, a note card titled "Kindness and Intimacy," dispensed on August 28, 2008 read, "This kind of intimacy means not being detached or separate from what is happening right now, in this moment, but rather being awake, open for the direct experience of life in the midst of it." At Hoben, such insight was seen as being generated by small mundane aspects of everyday life. In my conversation with Human Riddle, he described *tathata* as "seeing how the wind blows a leaf, or watching my daughter's face light up with a smile." Like Soeng, practitioners at Hoben saw the experience of tathata and karuna as intertwined. A meditation note card titled "The New Buddhism" and attributed to the American Buddhist writer Meredith Garmon read, "The skills of sustaining compassion and insight must be honed. Get down on that cushion. Put in the meditation time. . . . Know it in your bones not just on your lips. Retrain those neural pathways so that this awareness is a permanent habit rather than a fleeting glimpse."[32]

Upaya

Third, a second double-headed arrow on the sign "Understanding the Path of Practice" points down and to the left, where at six o'clock Cassius Lawndale had placed the word, "UPAYA" (capitalization in original), below which he had written "Skillful Means" and above in a small white font "Engagement." At Hoben, practitioners understood that compassion and insight were introduced to other sentient beings through *upāya*, a term that indicated that different sentient beings need different types of teaching. As the resident Buddha Hat described upaya, citing the Anglo-German scholar translator Edward Conze, it is "the ability to bring out the spiritual potentialities of different people by statements or actions which are adjusted to their needs and adapted to their capacity for comprehension."[33] As Mu Soeng writes, "Buddha's approach to teaching was primarily therapeutic – that he used a variety of strategies in assessment of the abilities of his audience to bring his listeners to a realization of nirvana."[34] A note card dispensed at Hoben tied upaya into "Right Speech that deals with refraining from falsehood, stealing, slandering, harsh words and frivolous talk."

For most at Hoben, upaya indicated not a system of ideas or rules, however, but a type of engagement. As Soeng writes, upaya indicates "the view that sees all of the Buddha's teachings as an antidote to suffering rather than an ideology." Often upaya was used to justify, or at least be mindful of, how Buddhism was being spread through new media. A note card handed out by BodhiDharma Rosebud before a meditation event, titled "Writer beware" and attributed to Allan Lokos, the founder of the New York Community Meditation center, read,

> When we consider skillful speech today, we must also consider a phenomenon that did not exist in the time of the Buddha: email. With the popularity of the telephone, we became a people that, for the most part, abandoned the practice of letter writing. What a perfect recipe for unskillful speech: a people long unpracticed at thoughtful letter-writing now equipped with the technological capability to churn out one quick email after another.[35]

Emptiness

Fourth, a double-headed arrow pointed straight up back to "BODHISATTVA VOW" (capitalization in original), while a final arrow pointed up and to the left, to nine o'clock, where Cassius had written, "SHUNYATA" (capitalization in original), under which was "Emptiness," and above in small white letters "Cognition." If there was one central concept that Hoben practitioners held in common it was emptiness, which practitioners indicated had a wide range of meanings: impermanence, not existing on its own, and as BodhiDharma Rosebud said, "to appear puffed up." The concept of impermanence was important, as a note card titled "Three Universal Characteristics" read: "The Buddha taught that all existence is impermanent because there is nothing internal or external whatsoever which is permanent. . . . Everything changes continuously. Existence is like the flowing water of a river or the burning flame of a candle, which is never the same in two consecutive moments."[36] When I asked the resident Algama GossipGirl to describe emptiness, she quoted *Alice's Adventures in Wonderland*, "Will you, wo'n't you, will you wo'n't you, will you join the dance?"[37]

Relying for the most part on writings by popular Buddhist teachers, however, practitioners usually related emptiness to the Buddhist concept of "dependent arising" (*pratītyasamutpāda*), particularly Thích Nhất Hạnh's concept of Interbeing, a term the Vietnamese monk coined to indicate the interconnectedness of human and nonhuman elements. As was written in Rasa Vibration's profile, "You are, therefore, I am . . . We inter-are." When I asked the self-reported classically trained resident Buddha Hat to define *shunyata*, he sent me the following citation from a commentary on the Heart Sutra: "Emptiness refers to the fact that no thing – including human existence – has ultimate substantiality, which in turn means that no thing is permanent and no thing is totally independent of everything else. In other words, everything in this world is interconnected and in constant flux."[38]

What was perceived to drive this system was karma, which literally translates from the Sanskrit as "action." For Zen practitioners on Second Life, however, karma was a spiritual concept reported to be deeply connected with the ethical implications of Buddhism because it denoted the moral consequences of one's engagement with the world. As an untitled meditation note card, handed out on January 21, 2009, and attributed to the Buddhist writer Barry Magid, which dealt with the Buddha's enlightenment, read, "To exclaim 'that's me' perfectly expresses the sudden delight of realizing nonseparation. That star is me, everything is me. And like the star, everything is in its own way clear, bright, and perfect."[39] When I asked BodhiDharma Rosebud, he answered, "Stuff and people only arise in dependence upon other people and stuff. No thing or person can exist as a singular isolated independent thing." Karma was believed not to be random, nor a system of rewards and punishment from a transcendent god. Rather karma was perceived almost like a part of nature that could be tested through scientific means and that had to do with intention. As a note card, handed out on April 4, 2008, titled "Karma," and attributed to the Buddhist writer Guy Claxton, read, "There is no belief at all which has to be accepted in developing insight into who we are. There is another, perhaps technically more correct, meaning of karma that refers to the intentions and the states of mind that lie behind and give rise to such actions, rather than to the results themselves."

The genealogy of cyber Zen

So far this chapter has aimed to emically describe the practice of Zen on Second Life. Emic refers to the ethnographical thick description of insider categories that are intelligible to an outsider. The second half of the chapter's goal is to ask, "What is the genealogy of the Zen of Second Life?" Often digital religion research, particularly studies of Buddhism, has tended to turn a blind eye to history and do little more than chronicle the platform. On one level this seems reasonable, because digital Dharma suffers a double dose of novelty: the digital is a new media, and Buddhism is often conceived as a newcomer to America's religious landscape. For instance, only in December 2003, with the creation of the Second Life *group* Zen Center, did Buddhism move onto digital virtual worlds. And only in August 1989, with the establishment of BUDDHIST@ jpntuvm0.bitnet, did Buddhism become digital.[40] By helping to spread the Dharma into the virtual world, Cassius Lawndale and other leaders of Hoben saw themselves as part of this historic move, as pioneers on the cyber frontier. Practitioners understood themselves as doing something new and in a note card response, described the Dharma leaders of the "first wave" of American Buddhism as playing a role similar to what "Bodhidharma did in ancient times when trekking to China."

Yet both "new media" and "new religions" are never fabricated out of whole cloth. Instead they emerge from bits and scraps of older media ecologies.[41] Digital Dharma recycles a field of entangled and confused media practices on sources that have been scratched over and recopied many times. The spreading of the Dharma to new geographic and new media technologies is not novel.[42] Since its inception, that cluster of discourses and practices, which has come to be called Buddhism, has, in the rhizomatic fashion of a banyan tree, undergone a continual process of displacement and relocation. Over the last 2,500 years, Buddhist practices have been shaped and reshaped as they spread throughout Asia. In the early 1900s, with the engagement of European powers, Buddhism changed again, reforming many of its institutions and beliefs. As it has moved west over the last century, Buddhism has taken new distinct forms in North America and other Western locations.

Once one takes a historical turn, one might assume that the place to look for digital Dharma's historical antecedents would be ancient Asian practices. Once one realizes, however, that the Zen practice found on Second Life bears only a family resemblance to canonical Asian traditions, one needs to look closer to home. Tracing its postwar American genealogy, one finds that the popularity of Buddhism, often in the form of Zen, came about because it entangled romantic antitechnological sentiment together with cybernetic thought. I argue that digital Dharma has a family resemblance, and genealogical relationship, to canonical Asian traditions but that these have been spread over a cybernetic ontology. This spiritual "mash-up" should come as no surprise. American popular religion often breeds such strange couplings of religion, media technology, and consumerism. From Henry Thoreau's *Walden Pond* to Henry Ford's conveyer belt, America seems to constantly be falling in and out of love with technology and its relation to a technologically driven consumerism.[43]

Cyber Zen illustrates that vital to understanding Second Life's practice-oriented spirituality is that mindfulness functions in a fashion similar to the cybernetic concept of the steersman. As detailed in chapter one, key to cybernetics are feedback loops composed of human and nonhuman elements that are governed by a steersman who is perceived to be vital to the system. Rather than being outside the system, the steersman is conceived as an essential part of it and as actually constituted by the system. However, the American mathematician and philosopher Norbert Wiener originally conceived of cybernetics not as a spiritual metaphysics but as a solution for antiaircraft guns. "At the beginning of the war, the German prestige in aviation and the defensive position of England turned the attention of many scientists to the improvement of anti-aircraft artillery."[44] The problem was that airplanes were much too fast and unproductively wiggly. Only by taking into account the voluntary activity of the pilot as a feedback loop could equations predict an airplane's flight. I am not equating silent online meditation with a German pilot. Rather, the formal similarity between a Zen practitioner sitting mindfully on his or her cushion and a aircraft pilot, as Wiener writes, is the Steersman. As he writes, "We cannot avoid the discussion of the performance of certain human factors."[45]

The counterculture Zen

In postwar America, Buddhism has functioned as a spiritual remedy to the excesses of consumer society. In the late 1950s, Zen came to be seen as a nature religion countering the overly technological square beige fog of American society. Consider the July 21, 1959, *Time* magazine article, "Zen: Beat & Square," which declares, "Zen Buddhism is growing more chic by the minute." Zen's value arose because it had an existential authenticity, which stemmed from the perception that it stood for everything Western consumerism was not. As the American poet and Buddhist teacher Gary Snyder writes in the manifesto "Buddhist Anarchism," "Modern America has become economically dependent on a fantastic system of stimulation of greed which cannot be fulfilled, sexual desire which cannot be satiated, and hatred which has no outlet."[46] As Stephen Mahoney, a self-proclaimed ex-Dharma Bum, writes in the November 1, 1958, issue of *Nation*, "For people who find the hothouse atmosphere of Western culture stifling . . . Zen is a cool, clean, early-morning breeze."[47] Mahoney goes on to write, "Zen is a nature religion. It is booming at a time when Western man's celebrated victory over nature is less convincing than ever – but when his alienation from nature, including his own nature, seems to be an accomplished fact."[48]

In the 1950s, Zen was rehabilitated. During the war years Zen had been a dangerous subject. As Robert Spencer wrote in 1948, in "The Social Structure of a Contemporary Japanese-American Buddhist Church," "The outbreak of the War with Japan was instrumental in disrupting Buddhist organizations."[49] Yet, once Japan was no longer seen as a threat, the notion that Eastern mysticism defied "the System" became a foundation stone for many in the 1960s counterculture, who perceived Zen as a politics of consciousness, as a means, like psychedelics, to expand one's mind and thereby reach one's authentic human potential. It is true that the 1960s saw some of the first serious academic study of religion in American universities, such as Wisconsin, Columbia, and Berkeley. Moreover, it was the first time that many American practitioners had had direct contact not just with the idea of Zen but also with actual Zen practice. However, in postwar America, Buddhism entered the mainstream not under the guidance of university scholars, Zen teachers, or ethnic churches but against the backdrop of a countercultural protest against social and religious unrest.

The rise of cyber Zen

I maintain that cybernetics had a deep effect on how Zen came to be translated into late twentieth-century American popular culture. The influence of cybernetics is clear on the Beat Generation, a postwar countercultural movement that rejected the status quo of consumerism and experimented with drugs, sexuality, and Eastern spirituality. The Beats were not against technology per se but were rather against the technocratic system that they saw as enslaving consciousness. In fact, the counterculture did not see technology as opposed to Zen and actually utilized technology as a means of poetic liberation. Consider Gary Snyder's "Look Out's Journal," from his ecological *Earth House Hold: Technical Notes & Queries to Fellow Dharma Revolutionaries*, which consists of the reports of radio transmissions between fellow Zen devotees Jack Kerouac and Philip Whalen during two summers.[50] In "Crater Shan," dated July 28, Snyder describes a moment that reflects Wiener's metaphor of the steersman, the digital Zen notion of mindful awareness, and the spiritual use of technology: "Down for a new radio, to Ross Lake, and back up. Three days walking. Strange how unmoved this place leaves one; neither articulate or worshipful; rather the pressing need to look within and adjust the mechanism of perception."[51]

Along with the Beats, the "square" popularizer Alan Watts often explains Zen through cybernetic metaphors. Take, for instance, *The Way of Zen*, where Watts sees delusion (*avidyā*) as "really a simple problem of what we now call cybernetics, the science of control."[52] Watts never actually cites Norbert Wiener directly, but there are a number of passages in *The Way of Zen* that are copied, sometimes word for word, from Wiener's *Cybernetics: Or the Control of and Communication of Animal and Machine*. Compare, for example, Watts's description of human self-consciousness as a "'feed-back' system" to Wiener's home thermostat (Figure I.2).[53] As Watts writes,

> Perhaps the most familiar example is the electrical thermostat which regulates the heating of a house. The temperature of the house is thus kept within the desired limit. The thermostat provides the furnace with a kind of sensitive organ – an extremely rudimentary analogy of the human consciousness.[54]

Presaging the Vietnamese Buddhist teacher Thích Nhất Hạnh's concept of Interbeing, Watt argues for a religious nondualism, a global skepticism against systems of thought that attempt to dichotomize the world between subject/ego and object/world.[55] Zen's cool liberation occurs when one becomes aware that we are composed of fields of thought. As Watts writes in *The Wisdom of Insecurity: A Message for an Age of Anxiety*, "In such feeling, seeing, and thinking life requires no future to complete itself nor explanation to justify itself."[56] Watts argues that the delusional split arises when one attempts to control the natural flow of the world. For Watts, suffering comes about from ignorance, those "vicious circles" when one forgets that one is part of a larger system.[57] As such, delusion arises when one forgets the relational nature of the self to the larger system.[58] As he writes in *The Tao of Philosophy*, "What you do is what the whole universe is doing at the place you call 'here and now,'" and you are something the whole universe is doing in the same way that a wave is something that the whole ocean is doing."[59] By the early 1970s, many American Buddhists saw their practice as a strategic way to counter the menace of technology.[60] As Thích Nhất Hạnh writes, in *Zen Keys*, "Western Civilization has brought us to the edge of the abyss. It has transformed us into machines. The 'awaking' of a few Westerners, their awareness of the real situation has . . . engaged them in the search for new values."[61]

Revisionist Zen

If Zen was antitechnological and countercultural, why and how does it flourish on Second Life, one of the most mediated communication practices and the epitome of Network Consumerism? The bridge is digital utopianism, which as I described in the last chapter defines the historic movement that started in the early 1970s when counterculturists and technologists joined together using cybernetic models to imagine cyberspace as a place of personal liberation. A sense of this ethos is evident in a lecture given by the countercultural critic Theodore Roszak at San Francisco State University in the mid-1980s. Unlike his 1969 *The Making of a Counter Culture: Reflections on the Technocratic Society and Its Youthful Opposition*, exhausted from the hippie "fragrance of barnyards and hunting camps," Roszak gave a lecture published as *From Satori to Silicon Valley*. In a chapter entitled "Machines of Loving Grace," Roszak, referring to Brautigan's poem, writes, "For the surviving remnants of the counterculture in the late seventies, it was digital data, rather than domes, archaeologies, or space colonies, that would bring us to the postindustrial promised land."[62] In this lecture, Roszak revised his argument about the relation between technology and the counterculture.[63] His countercultural heroes were no longer just hippies and beats but now also computer hackers, among whom Roszak perceived a new "postindustrial alternative."[64]

Instead of opposing all technology, he argued that along with the counterculture's "mystic tendencies and principled funkiness," there had always been a "deep ambiguity . . . a certain world-beating American fascination with making and doing."[65] Roszak ties these new innovative technologies to an "irrepressible Yankee ingenuity," which he sees in the "rebels and drop-outs [among whom] we can find the inventors and entrepreneurs who helped lay the foundations of the California computer industry."[66] For Roszak, these new technologies were revolutionary because they shared a spirituality with Eastern mysticism. In computers there "was an attractive hope that the high technology of our society might be wrested from the grip of benighted forces and used to restore us to an idyllic natural state."[67]

For Roszak, the "reversionary-technophiliac synthesis" of the small-scale computer industry offered a "short cut to satori."[68] In 1985, by using the term "satori," Roszak was looking back to California's countercultural roots. Roszak was also looking forward to the Silicon Valley ideology of the hacker's do-it-yourself, software-driven individualism. In late twentieth-century California, Roszak could tie together what would seem like dispersed fields of knowledge – Zen, computers, and nature – because they were all supported by an underlying cybernetic ontology.

Zen and the art of corporate management

Yet how did the mindful practitioner drift from the counterculture to corporate culture? To grasp how a popular cybernetic form of Zen became a bulwark of Network Consumerism, we need to address the 1974 publication of Robert Pirsig's *Zen and the Art of Motorcycle Maintenance*. Pirsig offered a post-countercultural perspective, which marked a turning point between the 1960s and 1970s. Pirsig reveals a new postsixties outlook, which argued for a systems analysis rather than dropping out of the system. Still, although his message was a watershed, Pirsig's Zen, like that of the Beats and Watts, was indebted to cybernetics. For instance, the opening paragraph of Pirsig's novel, a narrative retooling of Wiener's metaphor of a thermostatically controlled house, describes a cybernetic circuit composed of a system of feedback loops, weaving machine, animal, and environment. "I can see by my watch, without taking my hand from the left grip of the cycle, that it is eight-thirty in the morning. The wind, even at sixty miles an hour, is warm and humid."[69]

Reflecting Wiener's notion of the steersman, and Watts's nondeluded Zen adherent, the key for Pirsig is the concept of quality, which he sees as the communication that arises when subjects becomes mindful of the system in which they dwell. For Pirsig, technology and quality are not opposed, nor is technology essentially isolating. "A person who knows how to fix motorcycles . . . with Quality . . . is less likely to run short of friends than one who doesn't. And they aren't going to see him as some kind of object either. Quality destroys objectivity every time."[70] Yet, as Pirsig asks at the end of chapter fifteen, "what the hell is Quality? What is it?"[71] "By God," Pirsig discovers soon after, quality is neither "subjectivity nor objectivity, it was beyond both of those categories."[72]

Like Wiener's information, quality is neither mind nor matter, "it is a third entity which is independent of the two."[73] Pirsig's category of quality is nothing new and is similar to Wiener's questions "What is this Information, and how is it measured?"[74] Quality reflects a steersman's mindful awareness of the system in which it dwells. Like binary code itself, a quarter of a century earlier, Wiener perceived of information as an event that makes a difference: "one of the simplest, most unitary forms of information is the recording of a choice between two equally probable simple alternatives . . . a choice, for example, between heads and tails in the tossing of a coin."[75] In 1972, two years before the publication of Pirsig's novel, the English anthropologist Gregory Bateson defined information as "a difference which makes a difference" and saw it as a way out of the subject/object problem.[76] Similarly, for Pirsig, echoing Watts's mindful Zen, quality "is not a thing. . . . It is the event at which the subject becomes aware of the object."[77] Yet quality is not simply the flickering of a binary system; for quality to arise the system must become mindful of itself.

Closing the feedback loop

Pirsig's concept of Zen and the metaphysics of quality quickly found its way into corporate management. This trend started in 1978, when Richard Pascale, a consultant at McKinsey and Company and professor of management at Stanford University, published "Zen and the Art of Management: A Different Approach to Management for the 'Cards-on-the-Table' Executive, Which Works." In his study comparing Japanese and American companies, Pascale found only one significant difference, the quality of communication.[78] Pascale uses the term "Zen" "to denote these important nuances of interpersonal communication often enshrouded in a veil of mystique."[79] In fact, he goes on to argue that "the perspective imbedded in Eastern philosophy, culture and values helps make the implicit dimension more visible."[80] However, upon closer inspection, what Pascale is calling "Zen," is in fact a further telescoping of postwar cybernetic thought clothed in Eastern spirituality. Harkening back to Watts's wiggles and Wiener's German aircraft, Pascale suggests, "Let things flow. 'Success is going straight – around the circle,' says the Chinese adage."[81] Pascale's reference for this insight, however, is not an Asian source, but rather James D. Thompson's, *Organization in Action*, a text that distinguishes between the "rational closed system strategy" and the "flowing natural open-system strategy." Thompson in turn bases his distinction on Ross Ashby's *An Introduction to Cybernetics*, which employs Wiener's metaphors of thermostat and aircraft to describe the two types of systems.[82]

Pascale's use of Zen indicates two of cybernetics' key concepts as refracted through popular notions of Eastern spirituality: first, a new "Zen" management style that embraced more flexible models of team culture and innovation and reflected Wiener's steersman, as echoed off Watts's mindful subject and Pirsig's motorcycle rider; second, a Zen management style that leads to the adoption of just-in-time lean administrative methods that resemble cybernetic feedback loops and are key to the rise and management of neoliberalism and Network Consumerism. In the goal of increasing corporate America's efficiency, Pascale's article was the first of a myriad of management books that used the term "Zen" to make Network Consumer Society palatable.[83]

The Zen that American corporate leaders brought back as ancient Asian wisdom, however, was actually a new hybrid mix of a militant *bushido* wartime Buddhism and cybernetic management style that had been introduced by occupation forces after World War II.[84] While Buddhism is often depicted in American popular culture as a peace-loving religion, during World War II, by conflating Zen and the bushido warrior ethic, it contributed to some of the most egregious moments of Japanese militarism. Japan's defeat after World War II, however, as Brian Daizen Victoria argues in *Zen at War*, meant "not the demise of imperial-way Zen and Soldier Zen but only their metamorphosis and rebirth as corporate Zen."[85] While the ethos may have been bushido, however, the management system was a cybernetics that had been introduced by occupation forces after the war. Consider Edwards Deming, who had been invited to Japan at General Douglas MacArthur's request to rebuild war ruined industries and had within a few years completely transformed the Japanese economy.[86] Deming's theories relied upon cybernetic terms and philosophy, which he had learned during his time at Bell Laboratories.[87] Like Pirsig's motorcycle rider, and Watts's nondeluded practitioner, Deming's manager is a steersman checking a system for quality. Similar to Pirsig's question, however, Rafael Aguayo asks, in *Dr. Deming: The American Who Taught the Japanese about Quality*, "What is Quality?"[88] Quality is not preference, technological features, or overall design.[89] Like Pirsig's event, quality is an attitude toward the work that increases consumers' satisfaction.[90] Expensive new materials or design cannot improve Deming's quality – this would result in a new product. Instead, managers improve quality when mindful of how machines, humans, and environment run together smoothly.

The "Understanding the Path of Practice" sign emerged from this strange feedback loop in which the terms are Buddhist but the procedure is cybernetic and based on the Deming-Shewhart cycle of continuous improvement, which first plans a change (Boddhisatva vow), second does the change (compassion), next checks the results (emptiness), and finally decides what to do next (*upaya*) (compare figs. 8 and 9). In "Principles for Transformation of Western Management," Deming introduces what he labels the Shewhart cycle, tracing it back to Walter Shewhart's 1939 *Statistical Method from the Viewpoint of Quality Control*. During World War II, Deming worked for the U.S. Department of Agriculture and the Census Department. After the war, during the American occupation of Japan, General Douglas MacArthur employed him as a census consultant. During that time, Deming consulted with many of the leading Japanese industrialists, and many Japanese credit him with 1950s and 1960s "economic miracle."[91] In 1950, Deming presented the cycle at an eight-day seminar sponsored by the Japanese Union of Scientists and Engineers.[92] As Deming writes, "I called [the diagram] in Japan in 1950 and onward the Shewhart cycle. It went into immediate use in Japan under the name the Deming cycle, and so it has been called ever since."[93] During the 1950s many Japanese executives reworked Deming's diagram to produce the PDCA cycle, which is a four-step problem-solving tool in which managers ensure a product's quality by planning, doing, checking, and acting.

Conclusion

Employing the sign "Understanding the Path of Practice" as a map, this chapter traced the authorizing processes by which residents create and use Zen on Second Life, a pragmatic, individualist, system-oriented practice that is not hostile to technology and is actually preadapted for digital media, and Network Consumer Society more generally. The chapter illustrated two points. First, I have shown that Second Life convert Zen operates as a practice-oriented spirituality by which residents create authentic moral economies by using mindfulness media practices to engage with what they perceive as divine. Second, I illustrated that while having a family resemblance to canonical Asian traditions, the Zen found on Second Life is procedurally structured by post–World War II cybernetics. While it may be going too far to say that the Zen of Buddhism on Second Life has absolutely no relationship to Asian practices, its relationship is one of radical adaptation that resulted from the cutting and grafting of key Buddhist concepts onto cybernetics.

One could easily dismiss Cassius Lawndale's sign and the practices it indicates as reflecting a shallow consumerist understanding of Buddhism. Conversely, one could defend them as revealing a camouflaged deeply archaic essence, what the creator of the sign, Mu Soeng, calls "the basic architecture of Mahayana themes as they are understood within the Prajnaparamita tradition."[94] *Cyber Zen* has taken the neglected middle path and argued that all Buddhism, in fact all religion, is always already a hybrid construction that is shaped by its historical and cultural context. Buddhism has never been fixed or static but instead has continued to evolve and adapt to changing attitudes and circumstances, while its practitioners strive to retain a connection with the origins of the tradition. As Thomas Tweed writes in *The American Encounter with Buddhism*, when the Dharma spreads to new locales, it takes on "the shape and texture of the soil."[95] The point of historicizing digital Dharma in the present moment is not to show that it is the end of a necessary historical process, but rather to point out how a particular group of people in a particular historical moment used the flotsam and jetsam that has washed up on their cultural shore.

Understanding the attraction of cyber Zen for its practitioners, however, does not mean that we must bracket off and not judge the Zen of Second Life. As Theodore Roszak writes, much Zen was simply a "pretext for license."[96] It does mean that we need to begin from the perspective that convert Zen practices are authentic for their practitioners; then we can also begin to address the crisis in the contemporary study of American popular culture and Asian religions. Obviously cyber Zen is often a virtual orientalist practice, which can, as the blogger Justin Chin writes, generate "violence and bigotry directed toward Asian Americans."[97] Yet one cannot address these unless one understands the desire for its practitioners. The Zen of Second Life, and postwar American Buddhism more generally, fills a craving for those who use it. As Jack Kerouac writes at the end of *The Dharma Bums*, "Let there be blowing-out and Bliss forevermore."[98] Is this authentic? As Roszak writes, we "leave it up to the Zen Adepts to decide whether anything that deserves to be called authentic has actually taken root in our culture." He further writes, "it is indisputable, however, that the San Francisco Beats, and much of our younger generation since their time, thought they had found something in Zen they needed and promptly proceeded to use what they understood of this exotic tradition as a justification for fulfilling the need."[99]

Second Life Zen relieves the suffering of those who live a Network Consumer's life. Network Consumerism can be spiritually emancipatory because its residents are free to fashion new types of religious practice. What might at first seem liberating, even joyful, however, soon becomes a chore. "The newer understandings of spirituality are both liberating and frightening because," as Robert Wuthnow writes in *After Heaven: Spirituality in America Since the 1950s*, "they require people to do more work."[100] *Cyber Zen*'s following four chapters analyze the spiritual labor that Second Life Zen does. Rather than imposing outside structure onto the data, we organize our analysis of Second Life's convert Buddhist practices by filtering our findings through four categories poached from the Second Life search window: *group, people, place*, and *event*. Like with web search engines, residents can locate Second Life content by using a search window.[101] After residents search a term, they may filter the results through a number of tabs. Each of the following four chapters concentrates on one of the Second Life search window's filters to collect and analyze inworld Buddhist practice. We begin with "group," which the Second Life Wiki describes as simply "an organization which consists of at least two Residents."[102]

Notes

1 For sources on convert or Western practice, see Van Meter Ames, "Current Western Interest in Zen," *Philosophy East and West* 10 (1960): 23–33.
2 Setting the stage, an early account is the American media critic Jerry Mander's "Six Grave Doubts about Computers," where he presages the double threat as digital media's superabundant information and increasing pace of life. Mander maintains that "as the computer has sped up the information cycle for institutional activity, so it has done for human beings. As society increasingly emphasizes computers, we are receiving an ever increasing amount of data, most of it unusable in any practical sense" (Jerry Mander, "Six Grave Doubts about Computers," *Whole Earth Review* [1985]: 17–18). Cf. Jerry Mander, *Four Arguments for the Elimination of Television* (New York: Morrow Quill

Paperbacks, 1978); *In the Absence of the Sacred: The Failure of Technology and the Survival of the Indian Nations* (San Francisco: Sierra Club Books, 1991).

3 Philip Novak, "The Buddha and the Computer: Meditation in an Age of Information," *Journal of Religion and Health* 25, no. 2 (1986): 192.

4 Gary Storhoff and John Whalen-Bridge, "American Buddhism as a Way of Life," in *American Buddhism as a Way of Life*, eds. Gary Storhoff and John Whalen-Bridge (Albany, NY: State University of New York Press, 2010), 2.

5 Heinrich Dumoulin, *Zen Buddhism: India and China* (Bloomington, IN: World Wisdom, 2005), 9. Cf. Jeffrey L. Broughton, *The Bodhidharma Anthology: The Earliest Records of Zen* (Berkeley: University of California Press, 1999); John McRae, *Seeing through Zen: Encounter, Transformation, and Genealogy in Chinese Chan Buddhism* (Berkeley: University of California Press, 2003).

6 See note 1 in the Introduction, page 24.

7 Heinrich Dumoulin, *Zen Enlightenment: Origins and Meaning* (Boston: Weatherhill, 1993), 154.

8 As the Canadian Buddhologist Victor Hori writes in the introduction of the reissue of Dumoulin's *Zen Buddhism: A History, Volume 2: Japan* (New York: World Wisdom, 2005), this was "the last major scholarly work to put forward the vision of a 'pure' and 'authentic' Zen before Zen lost its Innocence" (p. xiv). And as the American scholar John McRae writes in the introduction to the reissue of *Zen Buddhism: A History, Volume 1: India and China* (New York: World Wisdom, 2005), Dumoulin "stood as a wonder-struck outsider to Buddhism, simultaneously baffled and awed by what he saw to be the deep spiritual truths its participants experienced" (xxx).

9 See note 2 in the Introduction, page 24.

10 Mu Soeng, *Diamond Sutra: Transforming the Way We Perceive the World* (Somerville, MA: Wisdom Publications, 2000), 33.

11 James Thompson and Jacek Koronacki, *Statistical Process Control: The Deming Paradigm and beyond* (London: Chapman & Hall, 2002).

12 Charles Prebish, *American Buddhism* (North Scituate, MA: Duxbury Press, 1979), 16–17.

13 Robert Pirsig, *Zen and the Art of Motorcycle Maintenance: An Inquiry into Values* (New York: Bantam Books, 1974).

14 "About Wisdom 2.0 Business," Wisdom 2.0: Living Mindfully in the Digital Age, www.wisdom2business.com/About (accessed November, 12 2010).

15 Laurence Moore, *Religious Outsiders and the Making of Americans* (Oxford: Oxford University Press, 1986); *Selling God: American Religion in the Marketplace of Culture* (Oxford: Oxford University Press, 1994).

16 Carl Bielefeldt, *Dōgen's Manuals of Meditation* (Berkeley: University of California Press, 1988) glosses Zen as "a common concern for the immediate, personal experience of enlightenment and liberation and, hence, by a common emphasis on the cultivation of spiritual techniques conductive to that experience " (p. 1). Bielefeldt writes that Dogen, the founder of the Sōtō school, "is concerned to ground his practice in history and identify it with the orthodox transmission of the Buddhas and Patriarchs" (p. 161). Prying it loose from its historic origins, R. H. Blyth, on the other hand, in *Zen in English Literature and Oriental Classics* (New York: Dutton, 1960), writes, "Zen, though far from indefinite, is by definition indefinable because it is the active principle of life itself" (p. 2). How does one separate popular Buddhism from what Hakamaya Noriaki, "Scholarship as Criticism," in *Pruning the Bodhi Tree: The Storm over Critical Buddhism* (eds. Jamie Hubbard and Paul Loren Swanson [Honolulu: University of Hawai'i Press, 1997], 113–37), defines as "true Buddhism" (p. 136)? One could start with a jingoistic or *nihonjinron* view that only Japanese culture can truly be Zen (Jamie Hubbard, "Introduction," in *Pruning the Bodhi Tree*; cf. Robert H. Sharf, "Modernism and the Rhetoric of Meditative Experience," *Numen* 42 [1995a]: 228–83;

"The Zen of Japanese Nationalism," in *Curators of the Buddha: The Study of Buddhism under Colonialism*, ed. Donald Lopez [Chicago: University of Chicago Press, 1995b], 107–61; Judith Snodgrass, *Presenting Japanese Buddhism to the West* [Chapel Hill, NC: University of North Carolina Press, 2003]; Daizen Victoria, *Zen at War* [New York: Routledge, 1997]). If this seems too narrow, one could enlarge the category and maintain, as Heinrich Dumoulin contends in *Zen Buddhism: A History, Volume 1: India and China*, that Zen "represents one of the purest manifestations of the religious essence of Buddhism" (p. xvii). One could move further out and argue, as Blyth writes, that "[w]herever there is a poetical action, a religious aspiration, a heroic thought, a union of nature within man and the Nature without: there is Zen" (vii). On the other hand, one could just give up on it all together and assume that "Zen" simply can mean whatever an individual wants it to mean, as Sharon Zukin implies in *Point of Purchase: How Shopping Changed American Culture* (New York: Routledge, 2004) 227–31. This "cool" understanding is often used in game design. See Big Fish, "Zen Games," www. bigfishgames.com/download-games/1707/zen-games/index.html (accessed January 21, 2014).

17 Daniel Veidlinger, *From Indra's Net to Internet: Communication, Technology and the Evolution of Buddhism*. Working paper. California State University, Chico (2015).
18 *Orientation to Zen 01 – Zazen (Zen Meditation)*, YouTube Video, 24:29, posted by Eshu Martin, April 30, 2012.
19 Cf. Robert Fuller, *Spiritual, but Not Religious* (Oxford: Oxford University Press, 2001); and Sven Erlandsson, *Spiritual but Not Religious: A Call to Religious Revolution in America* (Bloomington, IN: iUniverse, 2000).
20 Cf. Michael Carr, "'Mind-Monkey' Metaphors in Chinese and Japanese Dictionaries," *International Journal of Lexicography* 6, no. 3 (1993): 149–80; Kara Bussabarger, "Go Ahead, Lose Your Mind – 'Monkey Mind' That Is," *BizJournal*, www.bizjournals.com/louisville/stories/2008/03/17/story16.html (accessed November 7, 2015).
21 Michel de Certeau, *The Practice of Everyday Life* (Berkeley, CA: University of California Press, 1984).
22 de Certeau, xix.
23 Robert Wuthnow, *After Heaven: Spirituality in America Since the 1950's* (Berkeley, CA: University of California Press, 1998), 15.
24 Wuthnow, 188.
25 Cf. William Sims Bainbridge, *eGods: Faith Versus Fantasy in Computer Gaming* (Oxford: Oxford University Press, 2013).
26 Wuthnow, 16.
27 Wuthnow, 17–18.
28 "About Us," Barre Center for Buddhist Studies, www.bcbsdharma.org/about-us/ (accessed November 7, 2014).
29 Soeng, 34.
30 *ibid.*
31 *ibid.*
32 Meredith Garmon, "The New Buddhism," www.uufg.org/attachments/article/397/2006-August13-The-New-Buddhism-Garmon.pdf (accessed November 7, 2010).
33 Edward Conze, *Buddhism: A Short History* (London: Oneworld Publishing, 1980), 50.
34 Soeng, 35.
35 Allan Lokos, "By Working with the Lay Precept on Speech, We Can Learn to Say the Right Thing at the Right Time," *Tricycle*, www.tricycle.com/precepts/skillful-speech (accessed November 7, 2015).
36 "Disciplina Nomine Dharma," https://pieth.home.xs4all.nl/IPIR/philosophy/dharma/codex11-5.pdf (accessed November 7, 2014).
37 Lewis Carroll, *Alice's Adventures in Wonderland* (Toronto: Broadview, 2011), 137.

38 This version of the heart sutra is a meme that circulates on many websites; it was originally written by George Boeree, "An Introduction to Buddhism," http://webspace.ship.
edu/cgboer/heartsutra.html (accessed November 7, 2015). Cf. David Lopez, *The Heart
Sutra Explained* (Albany, NY: State University of New York Press, 1988); *Elaborations on
Emptiness: Uses of the Heart Sūtra* (Princeton, NJ: Princeton University Press, 1996).

39 Barry Magid, *Ending the Pursuit of Happiness: A Zen Guide* (Bloomington, MA: Wisdom
Publications, 2008), 66.

40 Matthew Ciolek, "Asian Studies Online – A Timeline of Major Developments," www.
ciolek.com/PAPERS/asian-studies-timeline.html (accessed November 7, 2015).

41 Michel Foucault, "Nietzsche, Genealogy, History," in *The Foucault Reader*, ed. Paul Rabinow (New York: Pantheon, 1984), 76–100.

42 Gregory Price Grieve and Daniel Veidlinger, *The Pixel in the Lotus: Buddhism, the Internet
and Digital Media* (New York: Routledge, 2014).

43 David Ney, *American Technological Sublime* (Boston: MIT Press, 1994).

44 Norbert Wiener, *Cybernetics, or Control and Communication in the Animal and the Machine*
(New York: Technology Press, 1948), 11.

45 Wiener, 11–13.

46 Gary Snyder, "Buddhist Anarchism," *Journal for the Protection of All Beings* #1 (San Francisco: City Lights, 1961).

47 Stephen Mahoney, "The Prevalence of Zen," *Nation*, November 1, 1958, 11. See Jack
Kerouac, *The Dharma Bums* (New York: Viking Press, 1958).

48 Mahoney, 12.

49 Robert F. Spencer, "Social Structure of a Contemporary Japanese-American Buddhist
Church," *Social Forces* 26, no. 3 (1948): 281–87.

50 Gary Snyder, *Earth House Hold: Technical Notes & Queries to Fellow Dharma Revolutionaries*
(San Francisco: New Directions, 1957). Cf. John Williams, "Techne-Zen and the Spiritual Quality of Global Capitalism," *Critical Inquiry* 37 (2011): 29; Thomas Malaby, *Making Virtual Worlds: Linden Lab and Second Life* (Ithaca: Cornell University Press, 2009).

51 Snyder, *Earth House Hold*, 4.

52 Alan Watts, *The Way of Zen* (New York: Pantheon, 1958), 57.

53 Watts, *Way of Zen*, 135. Cf. Wiener, 114–15.

54 Watts, *Way of Zen*, 135. Alan Watts was probably introduced to cybernetics through
Bateson, whom he knew from Esalen, a countercultural retreat center in Big Sur. In *Psychotherapy, East and West*, citing Bateson, Watts posed Zen as a type of "Psychotherapy,
as a Problem of Communication, 'The Social Matrix of Psychiatry'" (New York: New
American Library, 1961), 123.

55 Watts, *Way of Zen*.

56 Watts, *Way of Zen*, 152.

57 Alan Watts, *The Tao of Philosophy* (London: Tuttle Publishing, 2002).

58 Watts, *Way of Zen*, 56.

59 Watts, *Tao of Philosophy*, 18.

60 Prebish, 47.

61 Thích Nhất Hạnh, *Zen Keys: A Guide to Practice* (New York: Random House, 1974), 160.

62 Theodore Roszak, *From Satori to Silicon Valley* (San Francisco: Don't Call It Frisco Press,
1986), 39.

63 Roszak, 4.

64 Roszak, 5.

65 Roszak, 15.

66 *ibid.*

67 Roszak, 49–50.

68 Roszak, 48–49.

69 Pirsig, 3.

70 Pirsig, 351.
71 Pirsig, 178.
72 Pirsig, 231.
73 ibid.
74 Wiener, 61.
75 *Ibid.*
76 Gregory Bateson, *Steps to an Ecology of Mind: Collected Essays in Anthropology, Psychiatry, Evolution, and Epistemology* (Chicago: University of Chicago Press, 1972) 448.
77 Pirsig, 123.
78 Richard Pascale, "Zen and the Art of Management: A Different Approach to Management for the 'Cards-on-the-Table' Executive, Which Works," *Harvard Business Review*, March 1978, br.org/1978/03/zen-and-the-art-of-management/ar/1 (accessed January 26, 2014).
79 Pascale.
80 Pascale.
81 That Pascale's "Zen and the Art of Management" was *de facto* about cybernetic management is clear if we look at the trajectory of his later work. Consider *Surfing the Edge of Chaos: The Laws of Nature and the New Laws of Business* (New York: Crown Business, 2001), where he argues that managers should turn their companies into agile, adaptable "living systems." The book was a popularization of Pascale's article, "Intentional Breakdowns and Conflict by Design," *Planning Review* 22, no. 3 (1994): 12–19, which argued, "According to an obscure tenet of cybernetics, the Law of Requisite Variety: 'Any system must encourage and incorporate variety internally if it is to cope with variety externally.' In other words, it takes variety to manage variety" (p. 13).
82 Ross Ashby, *An Introduction to Cybernetics* (New York: Methuen, 1963), 4.
83 For instance, Williams (p. 29) lists thirty-three management books that use "Zen" in their name, and a total of eighty-seven "Zen and the Art of" titles (pp. 57–70). While Pascale's article was influential, however, the overdetermination of "Zen" can be traced to corporate America's anxiety with Japan in the early 1980s (Williams, 41–43). By the late 2010s, after the deflating of the Japanese economic bubble and American outsourcing of manufacturing to China starting in the 1990s, it is hard to imagine the overarching concern Western corporate managers had for Japan. Consider, for instance, the May 23, 1983, article in *Business Week*, "Chip Wars: The Japanese Threat," or documentaries such as NBC's *If Japan Can, Why Can't We* (Crawford-Mason, 1980) and PBS's *Japan: The Electronic Tribe* (1987). The consensus was, as John Micklethwait and Adrian Wooldridge write, in *The Witch Doctors: Making Sense of the Management Gurus* (New York: Random House, 1996) that "Japanese manufacturing trounced American ones in the 1980's because they embraced 'quality'" (p. 18). As reflected in the popular culture, this anxiety about quality and a Japanese spiritual discipline is evident in films such as Ron Howard's 1986 comedy *Gung Ho*, which tells the story of a Japanese corporate takeover of an American car factory. For instance, in a scene that appears after the auto factory has been reopened, a white-coated Japanese inspector tells a blue-collar line worker that his car is defective (31:40). The worker replies, "That's the dealer's problem. Every car can't be perfect." The inspector states, "In Japan, if there is defect, worker is ashamed. He stays [the] night to fix. In Japan, [the] goal is zero percent defect."
84 Williams, 42, 45.
85 Victoria, 186.
86 Williams, 42.
87 The influence of the Bell Telephone Laboratories on the development of cybernetics and other systems theories has been well documented. See Wiener, 4, 10, 60, 67; David Mindell, *Between Human and Machine* (Baltimore: John Hopkins University Press, 2002), 105–37; and Daniel Bell, *The Social Sciences since the Second World War* (New Brunswick,

NJ: Transaction Publishers, 1981), 31. Deming's theories were similarly influential in the development of Stafford Beer's "organizational cybernetics" (Stafford Beer, "Cybernetics and the Knowledge of God," *The Month* 34 [1965], 292).

88 Rafael Aguayo, *Dr. Deming: The American Who Taught the Japanese about Quality* (New York: Simon and Schuster, 1990), 35–50.

89 Aguayo, 37–38.

90 Aguayo, 50.

91 Masaaki Imai, *Kaizen: The Key to Japan's Competitive Success* (New York: McGraw-Hill Education, 1986); Kaoru Ishikawa, *What Is Total Quality Control? The Japanese Way* (New York, NY: Prentice-Hall, 1985).

92 Edward Deming, *Elementary Principles of the Statistical Control of Quality* (Tokyo: Union of Japanese Scientists and Engineers, 1950).

93 Deming, 88.

94 Deming, 33.

95 Thomas Tweed, *The American Encounter with Buddhism: 1844–1912* (Chapel Hill, NC: University of North Carolina Press, 1992), xxxiii.

96 Roszak, 136.

97 Justin Chin, *Mongrel: Essays, Diatribes, + Pranks* (New York: Macmillan, 1999), 177. See Jane Naomi Iwamura, *Virtual Orientalism: Asian Religions and American Popular Culture* (Oxford: Oxford University Press, 2011).

98 Kerouac, 155.

99 Roszak, 134.

100 Wuthnow, 13.

101 "Second Life Search," http://search.secondlife.com/ (accessed November 7, 2015).

102 "Group," http://wiki.secondlife.com/wiki/Group (accessed November 7, 2015).

Part II

Chapter 3

Groups

Relationships, cloud sanghas, and a cybernetic management style

> Zazen is the only true teacher.
>> Meditation note card (December 4, 2008, attributed to Kosho Uchiyama)

This chapter analyzes the Hoben Mountain Zen Retreat and the four other *groups* that make up Second Life's convert Zen Buddhist community. On July 23, 2009, I received an *Instant Message* (IM) from the *resident* Rasa Vibration requesting that I interview her. I hesitated, which may seem surprising.[1] One might assume that I would be pleased by such an offer. I and the other members of my research team had just spent the last two months *inworld* tracking down and cornering residents for just such interviews. Rasa, however, was known to create *drama,* which the Second Life wiki defines as "A way of relating to the world in which a person consistently overreacts to or greatly exaggerates the importance of benign events in Second Life . . . as a way of gaining attention or making their own lives more exciting."[2] After a second IM, I relented and clicked her *teleport invite* and found myself *rezzing* (materializing) in the jazz club Rick's Cafe. Unlike the *avatar* she used at Hoben, Rasa had taken on a highly sexualized form, with a dominating tall curvy figure and wearing a long flowing red ball gown. After refusing her offer of a dance, I sat down on a barstool. I asked Rasa why she logged onto Second Life. Because of her reputation as a *drama-queen,* I expected her to talk about herself. Instead, she brought up the importance of the Hoben community to her life and said, "We come together to sit online." She went on to add, "we are a *sangha,* a community, of like minded travelers on spiritual paths."

True, for many, especially for early adopters, the virtual world's primary attraction was building and/or exploring. The resident bUTTONpUSHER Jones writes, "in the early months the culture was definitely create-centric. At least I was. I love creating, and socializing is secondary to me."[3] By the end of the decade, however, socialization had eclipsed creativity. Our 2010 survey (n=108) showed that while building was very important to 14 percent of residents, socializing was very important to 87 percent. In fact, throughout our fieldwork we often heard remarks like those of the resident Charlanna Dmythrk, who said in an interview in July 5, 2010, "I came [to Second Life] out of curiosity, but stayed for the people. The creativity, culture and expression in Second Life are nothing short of amazing, but it is the connections that I've developed with people that keeps me here."

Cyber Zen theorizes community as media practices that enable "communitas," those intense feelings of social togetherness and belonging that are often afforded by religious practice.[4] As the community leader Georgina Florida said during a May 24, 2009, interview, "just like real life communities we are a close-knit group, our Second Life sangha is very strong and relationships develop." No one would doubt that Second Life allowed for the spread of information, and also for isolated practitioners to communicate with other Buddhist adherents. Global outreach was a key feature of how the leaders of Hoben attempted to legitimize their group. As the Hoben website reads, our virtual community "offers daily silent meditation with people from all over the planet." The resident BodhiDharma Rosebud, who, as touched upon in *Cyber Zen*'s introduction, reported living in a small town in Alaska, said that Second Life allowed him daily interaction with other Zen practitioners. As another Buddhist practitioner answered our 2010 survey on July 25, 2010, "I like the ability to practice my principles in Second Life and I love meeting other Buddhists – whom I see more regularly than real life."

As Rasa herself made evident during our research, people were logging onto Second Life and building what they perceived as a collective form of Buddhist sociability. Yet with neither physical presence nor face-to-face communication, can Hoben be a real community, let alone a Buddhist sangha? As *Cyber Zen*'s introduction describes, if one prejudices the need for physicality and face-to-face interaction, or if one defines authenticity as fidelity to traditional Buddhist communities, then Second Life Zen communities can never be considered real. Such an understanding, however, blindly replicates both a nineteenth-century romantic notion that theorized the only authentic community as face-to-face, village-like groups and also a romantic orientalist quest for an authentic Asia untouched by the modern West.[5] In such an understanding, any mediated form of Buddhism by definition will fall short and will at best create a pseudocommunity that is largely illusory. Networked communities based on mediated sentiment rather than physical proximity will automatically be reduced to insincere and simulated impersonal associations.

I argue that Second Life Buddhist groups offer authentic community but that these communities rely on new social structures for the virtual world, which do not necessarily mimic the actual world. A successful authentic online community does not merely upload real-life social systems. Instead, the formation of new types of online communities is necessitated.[6] *Cyber Zen* contends that Second Life Zen groups are best understood as "cloud communities" that are afforded by the virtual world, utilize network authority, and are based in a cybernetic management style that emerged out of the late twentieth-century telecommunications field. Created by Second Life's software, a "group" consists of an official association of at least two residents, who are joined together through the virtual world's media practices. "Cloud community" refers to online digital groups that take place primarily online. "Network authority" arises from consensual media interactions consisting of peer-to-peer egalitarian social ties. "Cybernetic management" describes a networked, entrepreneurial, noncentralized conception of personal interrelationships whose organizational style can be traced back to the 1920s and Bell Laboratories.

Digital cloud communities have become important because the passage into late modernity has dissolved traditional religious communities and institutions, so that individuals have to actively explore and create novel forms. The temporary, flexible, elastic and inexpensive nature of cloud communities make them perfect for Network Consumer Society, which is an uncertain life lived under constant shakiness. An investigation of the Hoben Buddhist sangha allows one to understand the distinctiveness of cloud communities, which in turn enables one to comprehend the role of popular spirituality in community formation more generally. Before we explore the media practices of *groups*, which tend to be larger, official, and public, however, we need to define the smaller private unofficial social unit of *relationships*, which describes the social interaction of two residents.

Relationships

On October 4, 2008, I was in a trolley slowly winding my way through Gibson Island, a 65,000 square meter region sponsored by the Gibson Guitar Corporation.[7] One of the more elaborate regions ever built, it was shaped like a guitar and had many theaters showing classic performances, stages for live music, shops giving away free guitars and other merchandise, and a path winding through a rain forest. Gibson Island was displayed at the time as a model of possible future corporate use of the virtual world. While incredibly well done, with hundreds of thousands of dollars and thousands of hours of labor, Gibson Island was unbelievably boring because I was alone. For all the time, hype, and expense spent on the region, it was completely empty of other residents and might as well have been a video or print advertisement.

For many network consumers, the largest lack in their life is personal relationships. When I asked Tai Buckinghamshire about her partner in Second Life, she answered, "I was not looking for a partner. It could also be said that intimacy has been missing in my life, both real life and Second Life, to have someone with whom you can share EVERYTHING" (capitalization in original). Many came to Second Life seeking relationships: frequently intense, often intimate interactions between two residents. When thrown into a virtual Second Life culture, residents intentionally look for friends or partners with whom to share the experience. They develop friendships, partnerships, or romantic companions, as well as even finding a Second Life family. The resident Algama GossipGirl said in an interview, "I love Second Life because you are never alone." The resident

Ashley Lee said that on Second Life "connection is everything." Second Life sociability transforms the screen's flat pixels into a world and keeps the "churn" rate down, the attrition rate by which subscribers leave Second Life. As Algama said, "playing any massively multiplayer online (MMO) game on your own is boring, but playing with a group, the social level makes you feel *obligated* to continue."

While not for everyone, relationships proved crucial for most residents and for many were the main reason for being on Second Life. Our 2010 survey (n=86) illustrates that 79 percent of residents reported that Second Life relationships "play an important part of who I am." A minority of residents, such as the "griefer" BlackFace Crow, found no emotional attachment. In a conversation in a public sandbox on January 5, 2010, she said, "folks are not very real here. This is a fantasy land." Some residents saw Second Life relationships as shallow. The self-proclaimed Second Life relationship expert Dr. Elov said of intimacy in the virtual world: "to some it is like real life. To others only pixels and nothing more. It's watching a cartoon version of porn." When asked how Second Life friendships were different from or similar to those in real life, one resident said, "friendships are shallow in Second Life . . . people let you see inside very little and only the bright part. So, you know . . . this is a fake world after all." Others worried that Second Life relationships were harmful, as Bunny Fierenza said, "because I don't think that they see this as hurting anyone else because you can just go on and never see the other person again."

Our fieldwork showed, however, that the vast majority of residents felt that Second Life relationships were virtually as strong as those of real life. Algama went on to say, "I think Second Life offers me the opportunity to explore a more deeper and OPEN relationship than real life does without all the ties and restrictions that are usually associated with real life relationships" (capitalization in original). The resident Rasa Vibration said in our interview, "I'm emotionally connected. I wish I was not. But I stopped fighting it." When I asked the resident Isabella Constantine, "Does Second Life offer something that real life doesn't?" she replied, "Yesss! Intimate relationships. I find that on Second Life you get to know someone on a deeper level . . . and the cuddling and chatting and dance and romance . . . is something that I enjoy." As the Buddhist resident Tai Buckinghamshire said, "I met my boyfriend in Second Life and we're together almost all the time." Sometimes "cybersex" was involved in relationships, a term describing the encounter between two or more residents in which they engage in mutual arousal in media practices that share sexual feelings and fantasies.[8] As Dr. Evol laughed, these are "one-handed" media practices that "get people off." From the start, cybersex has been part of virtual worlds. In 1996, the popular Internet author Harley Hahn wrote, in *The Internet Complete Reference*, "The goal of MUD sex is the same as the goal of regular sex (without the babies): to bond temporarily in a way that is physically and emotionally satisfying. To do so, two people will exchange messages so as to lead one another into a high level of sexual arousal, culminating in a well-defined resolution."[9]

In Second Life the relationships were usually platonic. As the resident Kenpo Soulsearch said about one of his friends, "we are both real life married so our agreement is to keep it on a brother-sister type basis and we do go dancing and so forth, nothing more than a family type hug."

Friends and partners

Relationships can be procedural or resident created. Procedural relationships, such as *friends* and *partners*, are afforded by the platform's code itself. As the Second Life wiki reads, "you can add other residents as 'friends' by right clicking on them and choosing 'Add Friend' from the pie menu, or accepting their friend offer."[10] Being a friend means that the other resident's name is listed in your conversation menu, that you can find each other on the *world map*, that you will be notified when the resident logs on, and that you can see whether the resident is online by going to the Second Life website. Residents hold varying opinions about friendships in Second Life, although virtually everyone has at least one friend. The resident RavensSong Merlin said, "friendship is an institution on Second Life. Closeness happens very quickly." When I asked the infrequent practitioner Skip Speech about friendship, he said, "not like I am here to swap phone numbers. But it is fun to have people to check out *sims* with." There are also some residents who believe the quality and depth of their friendships are the same in either world. I asked Skip whether there was a difference between Second Life and real life friendships. "Not too much. Just the same. Still real people behind the avatars." Others, such as Skip's friend Suzy Short, felt that Second Life friendships were deeper. "In real life you have the 'meat side,' here you haven't, but that makes friendships more genuine, I think. You don't make your judgments by how a person looks." I asked Ashley Lee the same question, and she replied more thoughtfully, "What I find with Second Life friendships is that often you are able to talk very deeply very quickly and connect very fast with someone. Yet, it is not the same as real life because they won't be coming to your dad's wedding. And they may disappear. And you know them only in certain contexts."

The second procedural relationship is partner. During our fieldwork, partnering on Second Life was a way for residents to indicate in their public *profiles* that they had a serious relationship. As Algama GossipGirl described it, "partnering means you are going steady." The resident Joselyn McLuhan described herself in an interview as *"partnered*, married with [avatar] kids, and *prim* babies." The website "Friends and Partnering" reads, "Second Life couples can make their relationships official. Whether you're married or just connected, you can designate your partner on your profile inworld and make your relationship visible to the rest of the community."[11] When I asked Ashley Lee about her partner, she replied, "I have eighteen friends in Second Life, all are female by choice. Of the eighteen friends, four have made a lasting impression on me. One of the four asked to me to partner in Second Life which I was happy to agree to."

Partnership neither affects how residents interact nor has any legal bond, but it does make the relationship visible to others, and for most was the equivalent of marriage. When I asked Suzy, "What does it mean to be partnered in Second Life?" She answered, "to be married." Dr. Evol said, "I have partnered two times so far in Second Life. The first time meant more to me than it did to her. The second time was wonderful. We wrote our vows and had a ceremony and invited all our friends to attend it, even had a reception. It was for all intensive [*sic*] purposes a wedding in its truest sense."

Dominant/submissive and adoption

Beyond those offered by the Second Life platform are resident-created relationships, social arrangements that residents fantasized and over which Linden Lab did not exercise control and made no specific efforts to review. Two main relationships include dominant/submissive and adoption. "Dominant/submissive" describes a relationship involving the giving over of obedience and control of one person to another, usually in erotic *roleplaying*. In December 2007, I struck up a conversation with a resident at the Buddhist Shrine of Varosha in the region of Crazy Devil. She had come to buy a Tai Chi mat, and, as I photographed the many Buddha images, I spoke with her about her spirituality. She told me how in a few short months, Second Life had enabled her to more deeply know her true self. Suddenly, a fierce-looking resident with a tiger tattoo across his bare chest, a large bow across his back, and a whip on his belt appeared. The female resident dropped to the ground kneeling and the man attached a leash. She IM'd me – "My Master needs me. I have to go. He is collaring me next Saturday" – and she sent me an invitation. At the ceremony, I found out that they were Goreans, a lifestyle based on the pulp novels of John Norman that combines philosophy, erotica, romance, and science fiction.[12]

Our research showed that the *collar* was the ultimate symbol of the dominant/submissive relationship. The Second Life wiki states that collars "can be a 'simple' piece of jewelry, often worn by *neko* or *furry* avatars, though many collars are scripted in order to allow the wearer certain features. Quite common features let the wearer grant certain permissions to a third person, like animating their own avatar, limiting its mobility, tracking if the collar is worn or not, etc."[13] Second Life media practices were regularly used to empower residents through abilities like flying and what in real life would be supernatural powers such as clairvoyance and out-of-body experiences. Interestingly, even more common was residents' use of the virtual world's media practices to voluntarily disempower themselves, by restricting and confining possible ways of being and acting. Residents could give control over to others, who governed their avatars to change clothing, force them to sit, block chat, or teleport them elsewhere. These disempowering media practices were usually used by *submissives*, often called "subs," to give control over to others. For instance, the Restrained Love viewer was an alternative to the Second Life viewer, "mostly aimed at enhancing BDSM play [erotic practices involving dominance and submission]. It is aimed at making restraints more secure and more restrictive, by giving the 'top' more tools to keep the 'bottom' under control."[14]

Adoption consists of adult users playing children avatars, by which they then form families. Early in the study, I came across a playground swarming with child avatars. I quickly found out that it was an adoption agency. For many residents this was one of the stranger parts of Second Life, and a long thread on the topic of adoption ran on Second Life's General Discussion Forum.[15] Most of the comments were negative, complaining that the practice should be stopped, or that it was just a means for the "children" to scam for Linden. One resident wrote in the practice's defense, "It can be a great joy. Remember they are adults playing on child avatars. Most will pay their own way with clothes and such." There was obvious attachment generated by the relationships. As the post went on to say, "but here is the kicker. It's like having a Second Life partner, you never know when they are going to up and leave. I had three adopted kids and they were great and slowly but surely they all left, probably off to play an adult avatar. Just like having a partner you miss them when they leave. But I'd do it again if the timing was right." Adoptive families tended to stay in character, and it was difficult to know when they were speaking of real life and when they were speaking of Second Life. As one adopter said about her family, "luckily I got a great husband he hands me money so I can spoil these kids. And they deserve spoiling. All my girls play their characters well." I asked another adopter if she enjoyed her Second Life family. She answered, "We have a very good girl, but most didn't work out they were just users who got what they could and flew the coop."

To be clear, residents at Hoben Mountain Zen Retreat tended to utilize only friendships and partnerships, and the more edgy types of relationships such as dominance/submission and adoption were at odds with the goals of the leaders of the Buddhist groups. I never once saw an adoption relationship at Hoben, and while it sometimes surfaced, dominance/submission was marginal at best. As the community leader Yidam Roads said, "we are seeing an influx of *BDSM* types in the Buddhist groups. I talked to some and they seem to be genuine Buddhists. Some tried to explain the submission issues but I just don't get it." At a Second Life wedding that I attended, I noticed that many of the avatars were kneeling. I asked a bridesmaid about it, and she replied, "I don't understand why these type of people are coming to Hoben. It goes against Buddhism and attachment. They tried to explain bondage to me, but it didn't make any sense." When I asked Cassius Lawndale if it was having any effect on the region, he paused and said, "I don't think it does anything one way or the other." Still, these types of relationships did go on. Algama sheepishly confessed to being a submissive. "When I heard the collar click for the first time it transformed me. It is hard to describe, my heart trembled, I shivered in real life, and I felt dominated and loved. Protected, but terrified. I wanted to please."

Group

I define "relationships" as private media practices that afford sociability between two residents and use "group" to indicate the function of the platform's software that ties together a public association of residents. Groups are joined together through networked communication practices such as *groupchat*, and these are by far the most popular and effective way of reaching and organizing social units of like-minded residents. During the time of our study, Second Life groups enabled up to ten different governing *roles* that gave varying amounts of authority. Also, like individual residents, groups could own land. Any resident could create a group for L$100 (about US$0.60) and groups could have members of up to twenty-five. Groups could be open (any resident could join) or closed (joinable by invitation only). Groups were important for our research, because while residents and *places* came and went, the groups, like ripples in a virtual stream, remained more or less stable.

Groups were at the center of Second Life's Buddhist community. Being inexpensive and hard to disband, they tended to be quite stable and were the backbone of different social clouds. While many residents initially logged on for the recreation, those who continued to come back were almost always integrated into some type of group. The Second Life webpage "Community: Groups" states that groups "congregate around any topic you can possibly imagine." When I mentioned to the resident Algama GossipGirl some of the more edgy groups in her profile, she replied, "There is a group for just about everything, silly." For instance, sampling Algama's groups, they could hinge on role-playing, such as the Noxious City – Main Group, with 8,136 members. They could be pedagogical, such as the Second Life Educators with 39 members. They could be for entertainment, such as the group Kinky Sex Stuff, with 544 members. Interestingly, many groups centered on religious interests. On July 18, 2013, when I searched for religious groups, a representative sample included "Second Life Christians," with 1,383 members, described as "for all those who follow Jesus. Purpose: to strengthen, encourage, and build up one another; to learn and grow; to have life in great abundance"; "Bayt al-Hikmah," with 115 members, who describe themselves as "spiritual-minded people who are seeking better understanding of Islam in general and Sufism in particular"; "Jewish Torah Learning," with seventy members who state that "this group is for Jewish studies in Second Life. We hope to have classes in Jewish philosophy, ethics and law, for interested members of the Jewish faith here in Second Life"; and "pagan," with 598 members, which is "for the Second Life Pagan and Pagan friendly community. We are the oldest Pagan community in Second Life. Founded in 2003."

The five core Zen Buddhist groups

On September 1, 2009, Second Life's Zen Buddhist cloud consisted of five core groups: Bodhi Center, Gekkou Buddhist Group, Hoben Mountain Zen Retreat, Zen Center Retreat, and the Zen Sitting Group (Table 3.1).[16] Four of the groups

Table 3.1 Second Life's Zen Buddhist cloud community (compiled on September 1, 2009)

	Bodhi Center	Gekkou Buddhist Group	Hoben Mountain Zen Retreat	Zen Center Retreat	Zen Sitting Group
Membership	674	157	1358	430	257
Philosophy	Buddhism must be unequivocally and purely taught by experienced monastics and laypeople	Free Form for Buddhists and spiritual Beings from all over the world	Not teachers, but lay helpers creating a space where people can come together for community	A gathering place for those on the path to awareness.... Mostly, it's about Sitting quietly, doing nothing."	You are welcome to join our practice to nurture inner and outer peace in SL and RL.
Meditation Style	Western/Silent	Traditional, Golden Sentences	Western/note card	No regular events/ Sitting quietly	Western/ note card
Founder	Zeus Ides (2007)	Mystic Moon (2007)	Cassius Lawndale (2008)	Wayne Wanderer (2003)	Yidam Roads (2007)
Creation Date	2008	2008	2008	2003	2007
Managers (no. of roles/ no. of people)	5/13	2/6	3/33	1/2	2/21
Traffic	1742	2753	4841	42	630
Notices (weekly)	31.5	30	33	0	23.5
Meditations/ Talks/Concert	15/2/0	3/0/0	21/0/1	0	7/1

Overlap of Buddhist Cloud at officer level. 1 = Agnostic Buddhist Sangha; 2 = Hoben Mountain Zen Retreat; 3 = Zen Sitting Group; 4 = Bodhi Center; 5 = Gekkou Buddhist Group

were formed nearly at the same time in late 2007 or early 2008. The remaining group, the Zen Sitting Group, was formed very early in Second Life's history in 2003, and during 2008–2009 had no regular events and was mostly used for *cross-posting* for groupchat by the other Zen groups. All the groups claimed to be Buddhist, and all were led by teams of experienced lay practitioners. They all came into existence in reaction against what the founders saw as inauthentic, even harmful, forms of practice that other Second Life residents were calling Buddhism.

In September 2009, the largest of the Zen groups, with 1,358 members, was Hoben, which was described as "an owned and operated Buddhist practice center in the virtual universe of Second Life." At the start of our research, Hoben was the largest, most popular, and also the fastest growing group, and with weekly traffic of 4,841, it was the most popular location for Zen meditation in Second Life. By the end of our research, however, it had been eclipsed by the

Bodhi Center. Hoben was founded by Cassius Lawndale, but unlike some of the other groups, was very much a community endeavor, with a large group of over thirty people taking some part in management. Hoben's traffic was generated both by meditation sessions and also by the purchase of Buddhist-inspired commodities available at the shopping mall.

In September 2009, besides Hoben there were two other important groups. First was the Bodhi Center, created by Zeus Ides, which was the second largest group. The Bodhi Center was, as a note card described, "open to everyone," and its mission was to "introduce more disciplined practice into Second Life." Its basic tenet was that Buddhism "must be unequivocally and purely taught by experienced monastics and laypeople of Second Life." The Bodhi Center supported itself by selling many of Zeus Ides's Buddhist-inspired objects, such as *maṇḍala* paintings and Buddha statues. The second group, Gekkou, differed from Bodhi Center in at least two ways. It was more elitist in its approach, was spread mostly by word of mouth, and was composed of residents who spent more time *inworld*. First, it only had 155 members. Second, its founder, Mystic Moon, described its philosophy as a "traditional free flow improvisation," which centered on his self-authored Golden Sentences, which he used during meditation sessions as "seeds for insight." Unlike the larger groups, Gekkou was supported by donations, and the members had near the end of my team's ethnography closed the last of their retail stores. It was also more exclusionary than the other groups, in that you had to be invited to join.

The last two groups were the originals for the Zen cloud but had by the time of our research been eclipsed in activity and number of members. First, the Zen Center Retreat was described as "a gathering place for those on the path to awareness." Wayne Wanderer, who was an early Second Life adopter with an avatar created in 2003, founded the group. The Zen Center Retreat's build was a very well-crafted monastery building that was created on December 10, 2003, making it one of the oldest religious sites that we encountered. During our research, however, the Zen Center Retreat had more or less been abandoned. It had only two active managers, with no events or notices. The final group was the Zen Sitting Group founded by Yidam Roads, which sought "to nurture inner and outer peace in Second Life and real life." Its chief function was to "sponsor twenty minute Zen meditation daily at 6PM Second Life Time." It was located on Second Life's Mainland, and the region was a very beautiful Zen-inspired garden. When we began fieldwork, the Zen Sitting Group was the most active, and it was the first to specifically design practices for Second Life, such as the "note card" version of meditation detailed in chapter six.

Demarcating Second Life's Zen cloud

We identified these five groups as part of Second Life's convert Zen cloud, because they shared a coherent ontology and ethos, as well as the practice of silent meditation. By "ontology" we refer to denoted pragmatic models of reality, and by "ethos" to the often-connoted tone and character of residents' lived worlds. As detailed in the last chapter, the groups in the Zen cloud were also demarcated by the spiritual practice of mindfulness, which practitioners describe as nonjudgmental focus on the emotions, thoughts, and sensations occurring in the present moment. Most vital, as we explore in chapter six, however, was the practice of online meditation, which differentiated these groups from other religious and even agnostic Buddhist communities.

The five groups of the Zen Buddhist cloud formed a coherent community that differentiated itself from similar social units. Our research team belonged to many groups that engaged with Buddhism, from the "Agnostic Buddhist Sangha" to "Zen Temple at Mystical Mastery." At first sight there was no clear division between the convert Zen groups and the other communities that blended into the Zen Buddhist cloud, such as the Tibetan, Theravada Buddhist, New Age, and to some degree pagan and Liberal Christian Community groups. Yet our research uncovered a clear distinction between these and the Zen cloud that could be observed. Our 2010 survey often revealed the existence of the Zen cloud. A typical answer from July 25, 2010, was "Hoben Zen Retreat is what I consider to be my Sangha, but I also belong to the Bodhi Center, Gekkou, and the Zen Sitting Group." In an interview, when I asked the group leader Dubhshlaine Gustafson if there was "A Buddhist community in Second Life, a Sangha?" she answered, "definitely. Many. The Bodhi Center, Gekkou, Hoben, and the Zen Sitting Group all sanghas. They are as much my sangha as my real life one."

Besides explicit description by residents, the convert Zen cloud community coherence can be seen clearly in four ways. First, there was a consistent overlap of members in each group, especially at the officer level (Figure 3.1). Second, members attended each other's groups and actually led events. Third, group members cross-posted events on each other's groups. Fourth, as we explore in chapter six, near the end of our fieldwork there was an attempt between these groups to form the Second Life Buddhist Council in order to coordinate online sitting schedules.

In addition to these four pieces of evidence, the Zen cloud also held a coherent convert Buddhist ontology and ethos centered on the practice of silent online meditation. As illustrated in chapter six, the main way that the groups in the convert Zen cloud differentiated them from other communities were events centered on the practice of silent online meditation, which not only afforded community in the virtual world, but was key for convert Zen on Second Life more generally. The practice of online meditation differentiated them not only from the few ethnic Buddhist communities, but also from Buddhist philosophy groups such as the Agnostic Buddhist Sangha, which at first glance might seem part of the community, but whose media practices mainly focused on the rational discussion about religion, not its online practice. As one of the leaders, Skeptical Starshine, said during an interview on June 12, 2009, "the core Teachings of the Buddha indicate that an agnostic approach is called for − agnostics

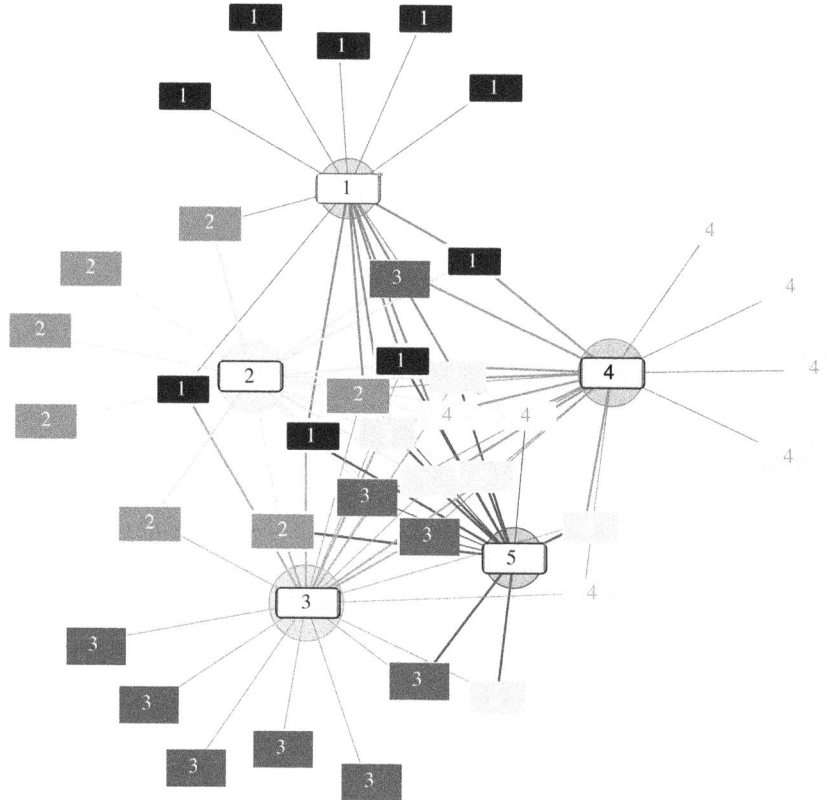

Figure 3.1 Network of Buddhist cloud at officer level. 1 = Agnostic Buddhist Sangha; 2 = Hoben Mountain Zen Retreat; 3 = Zen Sitting Group; 4 = Bodhi Center; 5 = Gekkou Buddhist Group.

refrain from clinging to views – and that the agnostic approach enables us to be more creative and less dogmatic in our lives and in sharing the Dharma."

Sangha

While residents first logged on for many motives, community was the main reason that they stayed and was an important part of Buddhist practice on Second Life. During an interview on May 21, 2009, I asked the resident Dawn Arietta, "Do you belong to a real life Buddhist community?" She took offense at my use of the word "real" and answered, "Second Life is my main Buddhist sangha, and it is very ★real★ in my humble opinion." For most Buddhist practitioners on Second Life, "sangha" indicated, as a 2010 survey taker responded, "Any group of people working to support each other in a Buddhist spiritual effort – local, regional, global, virtual, etc." Some residents worried about the effects of the virtual platform. As the builder and Buddhist practitioner Bob Tinker said, "It's not ideal, but community can exist here." For the most part, the fact that community existed was taken for granted. I asked the resident Starlight Qunhua whether she thought Buddhist sanghas existed in Second Life and whether she belonged to one. She replied, "It ★does★, and I ★do.★" Similar to Dawn's annoyance, in an interview on June 6, 2009, I asked the Buddhist practitioner Lana Rossini whether she thought "Second Life Buddhist communities are possible?" Lana replied playfully, "but . . . of course ★rolls her eyes★."

The Zen cloud shared a coherent ontology based on mindfulness and the practice of online silent meditation. A Second Life Buddhist practitioner wrote in our survey on July 3, 2010, "Firstly, sangha are the ones who practice Buddhism with the intention of eventually attaining either liberation (the state of an Arhat) or complete enlightenment (Buddhahood). Secondly, those who have attained it, or some degree of it and guide us on our journey." One Hoben resident responded to our 2010 survey to the question "what is the sangha," by writing, "All of us on the path. We are the sangha, the sangha is us." Bob defined sangha as "a community of fellow practitioners and students to the Dharma." When I asked Starlight to describe "sangha," she replied, "A supportive community of practitioners following the teachings of the Buddha to get to that clearer insight of being awake." The Buddhist notion of community differed from other groups, such as Christian believers. As one Christian resident reported in our 2010 survey, "I see our community as a group of people growing in the Lord together, rejoicing together, and seeking God together."

Community was an important part of most adherents' practice. In an interview, the Hoben group leader, Tai Buckinghamshire said that "sangha is one of the Three Refuges, the group that upholds you and who holds you accountable and supports your practice." A meditation note card, titled "The Fertile Soil of Sangha" and attributed to the Vietnamese Buddhist monk Thích Nhất Hạnh, read,

> If you have a supportive sangha, it's easy to nourish your *"bodhichitta"* [awakened consciousness], the seeds of enlightenment. If you don't have anyone who understands you, who encourages you in the practice of the living Dharma, your desire to practice may wither. Your sangha – family, friends, and co-practitioners – is the soil, and you are the seed.[17]

Hoben practitioners often mentioned the search for community, or sangha, as their main reason for logging on to Second Life. As the resident Ashley Lee offered, "I appreciate the great effort others put into supporting the community by creating places of practice and leading practice and hope to support the practice of myself and others by partaking in group sittings."

A cloud sangha

Because of the wide variety of types of media practices that go under the rubric of "digital religion," there is a need to differentiate between differing patterns of emergent media configurations. Second Life's Zen groups form a "cloud sangha," a more or less stable, online network of personal relationships. In ancient India, the term "sangha" originally connoted any group of people living together to pursue a unified purpose that ranged from trade guilds to political groups to religious orders. The term "sangha" in Buddhism initially referred to the community of monks but came to denote the larger community that also includes lay practitioners and in the most general sense denotes the assembly of all beings on the path to awakening.[18] Over the last century, Buddhism has taken new forms in America and other Western locations; this includes spreading online through digital media. In 1991, the term "cybersangha" was coined by Gary Ray in the "BodhiNet Bylaws" to indicate any online Buddhist group, which he defined as "a community of persons who actively scout their way to truth; who have, as an additional gift, the ability to communicate instantly without regard for their geographical proximities."[19] In 2003, the resident Wayne Wanderer founded the first Second Life sangha called the Zen Center Retreat, which was "a gathering place for those on the path to awareness. There are occasional meetings; Some instruction, of a sort, but, mostly, it's about 'sitting quietly, doing nothing'."

The term "cloud" is similar to the concept of a networked community, a term that describes groups that are bound by particular interests rather than notions of shared geography and familial ties.[20] Cloud communities differ, however, from networked communities because while networked communities often have a significant actual world presence as part of their makeup, cloud communities consist primarily, even consciously, of online digital media practices.[21] We borrow the notion of the "cloud" from computing, where it signifies an architecture in which users access resources online from a host of different servers – during our research, Google Docs, Blist, and Sliderocket would have been examples. In cloud computing, users do not invest in infrastructure. Instead, they rent what they need when they need it.

Buddhist residents joined the cloud community for many reasons. Yet it was the spiritual practices, particularly online silent meditation, which glommed them together as a group. The Zen cloud allowed users from different isolated geographic regions, those engaged in identity play, busy, or just shy, to come together as a community. Hoben group members reported that they engaged with community because some found it easier than real life, and others were seeking emotional bonds that they saw lacking in their real life. Some found it easier to interact with other practitioners online. An infrequent but long attending Hoben Group member, Skip Speech, said in conversation, "I feel more comfortable walking into the Second Life *zendo* than a real life one." I asked if he felt part of the community. Skip answered, "Yes _/!!!_ [emoticon for *gasshō* with extra exclamation points for emphasis]." As one practitioner responded in our 2010 survey, "As an almost pathologically shy homebody, who is more comfortable in solitude than in crowds, I'm surprised at how important the sangha has become to me. I am part of a group of people who are supportive of my growth and with whom I can engage in the kind of debate and discussion that I cherish."

Authority

Authorized media practices enjoy positions of privilege, in which they can do what they will, without having to explain themselves. One might assume that a Zen cloud community would be free of authority. Because digital media tend to disrupt traditional social arrangements, they are often assumed to be inherently free of authority, or even dissolving of authority. For instance, Howard Rheingold, in *The Virtual Community: Homesteading on the Virtual Frontier*, describes community as an "electronic agora, an 'Athens without slaves' made possible by telecommunications and cheap computers and implemented through decentralized networks."[22] On Second Life, the practice of Zen was also often seen as free of authority, as a note card handed out July 19, 2008, titled "Zen Anarchy" and attributed to the author of "The Surre(gion)alist Manifesto," Max Cafard, read, "to the extent that [Zen] follows its own path of the awakened mind; it is radically and uncompromisingly anti-authoritarian and anarchistic." No doubt Zen displays a myth of antiauthoritarian religious practices. Yet the notion that Zen was free of authority can be seen to emerge, as described in chapter two, from the 1950s and 1960s countercultural Zen and also, as explored in chapter one, from the 1970s digital utopianism.

While Second Life and convert Zen might seem all about innovation, play, and peer-to-peer interactions, the Zen groups did not lack governance, control, and even power. Some residents ultimately held more authority than others. As seen in the experience of *noobies*, at Hoben there was a visible pecking order in which different group members communicated with more authoritative media practices. Inworld was often a tangle of competing whirling strands of discourse, displayed on the screen in a web of overlapping public and private media practices that included text, voice, the exchange of images, and the avatar appearance and gesture. As a noobie, it was sometimes disconcerting, if not impossible, to make oneself heard and not always clear why one felt ignored in the swirl of conversation. It was not that one could not communicate, but that the more established members of the group would not build on your communication. Some of my first field notes from December 23, 2007, describe one of my first meetings: "There was no leader, and it reminded me of a Quaker meeting with people talking when they felt moved. There were about twenty people there. But really only about four or five people participated in the conversation. It will be interesting to learn what are the unstated rules."

Even if community members acted as if they were part of a well-defined and harmonious group, disruptions and disputes often arose. Authority was necessary to mediate disputes, which in the Zen cloud were either intergroup or intragroup. Intergroup disputes occurred between different groups and were usually clashes over *event* scheduling and the legitimacy of real-life credentials. For instance, as the Hoben founder Cassius Lawndale said to me in conversation on March 4, 2010,

> The Bodhi Center present themselves as the watchdog of other Buddhist groups. Since they are one of the largest groups they do as they please, when they please. Taking all the prime times of the day without checking with other groups. Also they claim to be concerned over other groups' teachings yet never speak to others or give the real life credentials of their teachers. If you're going to try to be the Buddhist Vatican in Second Life ALL [capitalization in original] teachers must supply their credentials or just admit they're really no different than any other group.

When I asked Dawn Arietta, one of the leaders of Bodhi Center, about this she said, "I didn't realize that notices for Buddhist sittings were spam. I work closely with the other Zen groups to make sure that our sitting schedule does not overlap."

Intragroup dispute refers to conflicts internal to Hoben, which usually involved a tangle of leadership and practice. A major dispute began in July 2010 between Human Riddle and Cassius, over the style of practice. Up until this point, as founder, Cassius had been the de facto leader. The July 2010 dispute led to an election, with Georgina Florida and Jashar Silence winning as cogroup leaders, but also created a crisis and the need for new meditation leaders. Once elected, Georgina argued that all meditation leaders must follow the five Buddhist Precepts (*pañca-śīlāni*). She refused to use *voice chat,* however, to verify her real-life identity, which led many to believe she was *gender bending* and was male in real life. Rasa Vibration denounced her for "precept abuse" and suggested a trial, which led to Georgina resigning and leaving the group. Rasa was also banned but came back as an *alt*[ernative avatar] and was banned again. The need for voice chat was dropped by Hoben, and Georgina returned but no longer held much power and was no longer in a leadership role. By the end of the summer, there were no new elections, and by consensus, the partnered couple Tai Buckinghamshire and Venomfangx Bardfield became the group's de facto leaders.

A multilayered hierarchy of authority

Rather than being absent, authority in Second Life takes a multilayered pattern of media practices, which, while similar, are distinct from the real world. Obviously, real-life communication patterns are often replicated online. Female avatars were often silenced, for instance, and avatars of color were also prejudiced.

Also, Hoben's media practices were authorized by Linden Lab, region own-ership, and reference to real life. Still, a unique type of online power I call "networked authority" played a major role of communication in the Hoben community. On May 24, 2009, when I asked Georgina Florida if the group had leaders, she answered, "there are people who have earned the respect of the Second Life community through their actions and understanding." For anyone who has spent time in online Buddhist communities, or in convert Zen real-life centers, this assumption proves utopic and politically naïve. True, if one is looking for legal, traditional, or charismatic authority, Second Life groups might appear to have no governance. In a media practice that is pictured as play, and divorced from work and often experienced as commoditized leisure, the role of authority might not seem obvious. On the other hand, there is always the need for day-to-day governance and dispute resolution.

The ultimate authority was Linden Lab, the corporate owners of the plat-form. Like a *Deus Absconditus* (Hidden God), the *Lindens*, however, rarely inter-fered in the affairs of the residents and usually only entered the world when the functioning of the platform itself was threatened. During my many years inworld, I only met one Linden, because a butterfly dispenser on a plot of land I owned was causing *lag* to one of their servers. While more or less absent from residents' everyday lives, Linden Lab did possess two forms of governance. The foundational layer was the procedural logic of the platform's code, which ultimately conditioned the world but played little conscious part in residents' day-to-day lives. As the game theorist Richard Bartle writes in *Designing Virtual Worlds*, "If the physics don't allow it, you can't have it."[23] During the time of our research, Second Life used a Havok engine to simulate actual world physics that managed collisions and interactions between objects.[24] As described in chapter one, Linden Lab also enforced a bureaucratic authority legitimized by legally enacted rules and regulations as spelled out in their Terms of Service (ToS), which gave residents almost no rights.[25]

Second, as an extreme case of neoliberalism, in the virtual world, property rights reign supreme, and after the Lindens, authority rested with each owner of a region; these owners often acted like small feudal lords. An owner can have as little as 512 square meters of land, or they can be one of Second Life's land barons who control huge swaths of the virtual world. The resident Ram Chi-wanga compared regions to "burbclaves," from Neal Stephenson's cyberpunk novel *Snow Crash*, which are small suburban nation-states that are a metaphori-cal extension of gated communities.[26] Each owner rules like a small princeling, holding almost ultimate authority, making the rules, which they can enforce by *freezing, ejecting,* or *banning* any resident they wish to, with or without cause. An avatar that is frozen cannot move, interact with objects, or chat but can still send and receive instant messages. Ejecting an avatar teleports them to an adja-cent parcel. A banned resident cannot move onto or over an owner's land and perceives a barrier of red lines that read "access denied." Owners can also limit sound and gestures, use of scripts, building rights, and *maturity rating.*

As seen in the case of Rasa Vibration, at Hoben, the ejecting and banning features were used, but infrequently and for personal drama rather than to enforce orthodoxy. Other Second Life religious regions, however, did use the ownership privileges to police doctrine and practice. During one heated debate at a region focused on the teachings of Martin Luther, I witnessed four residents ejected and banned within the space of a few minutes – two for their beliefs and two because they refused to take off their angel wings. At Hoben, and most religious groups in Second Life, these land-governing features were used not to enforce orthodoxy but were almost exclusively for *griefers*. As an Islamic group posted in a note card, "griefers and those here to argue and stir up strife will be banned and may be reported. We do this to protect everyone else. Doing things like that only makes the one doing it look silly anyway." The term *griefer* indicated those residents who deliberately irritate and harass others through abusive language, *pushes and hits, cages, orbiters, deformers, spoofing*, as well as *texture spamming*. For instance, at a meditation event, a resident, Dr Oooodles, began to create and materialize an attack of *grey goo* penises that was accompanied by the sound of heavy breathing. Grey goo describes a viral attack of self-replicating objects, which not only annoy other users but place a strain on the platform servers, causing extreme lag and even *crashing* the *grid*.

Beyond the Lindens' authority, and owner's privilege, media practices at Hoben were authorized by reference to real-life community. As a way to legitimize his new Second Life community, early on Cassius Lawndale had built a lineage room that displayed images and texts from his own Dharma transmission. The lineage model was most apparent during Dharma talks by prominent actual world authorities. For instance, in October 2009 an abbot from an American Midwest Zen center gave an hour-long Dharma talk in Second Life. He talked about the nature of Second Life and used it as a *kōan* to discuss the nature of reality and to remind everyone that "the real event here is the question and being present in the moment." Over the next year, spearheaded by Cassius, Hoben hosted a series of talks by different Dharma teachers. Interestingly, while these talks were meant to give legitimacy to the Second Life community, what occurred was a "swirling controversy" over the abbot's own claimed real life lineage. In a 2012 comment on a Facebook page in response to the abbot's claims, a commenter wrote, "I hope you can see how maybe these questions have some bearing on all of these people's self-professed claims and standards for their legitimacy."

Network authority

While all these layers of authority played a part in Hoben's governance, on an everyday level the most important type were consensual networks of peer-to-peer, egalitarian social ties of network authority. Network authority was entangled with the concept of "being spiritual but not religious," which, as was explained in the last chapter, focused on personal growth, anti–institutionalism, and spontaneity. At Hoben, the spiritualized use of network authority was legitimized by silent online meditation, which for many practitioners was "the only real teacher." On May 24, 2009, I asked Georgina Florida if she had a teacher. She answered, "Being aware of life just as it is. Everything is Dharma. Honestly, my accountability is between me and my cushion. Just me and Buddha _/!_."

This network of soft religious authority was not an overt system of power and hierarchy but rather authorized spiritual discourse by celebrating the voluntary nature of practice, and the right to cross class, gender, culture, and ethnic divides in search of personal spiritual liberation. The egalitarian nature of the Zen cloud was evident in the prominence of women in leadership roles and in a practice-oriented spiritual support of nontraditional lifestyles, particularly with regard to sexual preferences, which were not only tolerated but celebrated. At Hoben, the network authority was nonsectarian. As the practitioner TypesZen Sideways said about the community, "we embrace Dharma without dogma." Many saw the nondogmatic vision of the group as an umbrella under which different ethnicities, practices, and beliefs could be addressed in a constructive and productive fashion. There were still leaders and followers. As Cassius said, "I think we're one of the more popular spots for meditation in Second Life for a number of reasons, not the least of which is the fact that we have about ten devoted *meditation leaders* available to lead our sits at any given time." The leaders, however, came from various backgrounds in Buddhism, and some identified as Christians or pagan.

Yet these differences were secondary to the authority of silent meditation that was experienced as transcending any faith tradition. As Cassius said, "Religious affiliation is not a concern of ours, and while we present ourselves as a Buddhist community, we believe that fundamentally meditation is for everyone." Early in our research, I asked Cassius Lawndale which sect of Buddhism the community practiced. He replied, "we aren't at all sectarian, even intentionally nonsectarian, and we're not even religious, really. Absolutely anyone is welcome here, provided they are respectful." He illustrated his point by describing how the actual world *rōshi*, Hakuun Yasutani, founder of Sanbo Kyodan Zen Buddhist organization, "once told one of his Christian practitioners that there is Zen Buddhism, and there is simply Zen. I guess I agree with that sentiment." When I asked BodhiDharma Rosebud about the nonsectarian nature of the group, he said that Second Life afforded for the first occasion in history for every type of Buddhism, and every Buddhist on the globe, to come together in one place to meditate at the same time.

Cybernetic management

What is the genealogy of Hoben's networked authority? It is neither the more typical Buddhist structure of the laity supporting monks through *dāna* (gift giving) nor even of the Zen monastic structure based on the transmission of Dharma through the hierarchical teacher student relation. In the Second Life groups, the

vast majority of both teachers and students were not monastics but household-
ers who meditated. As a note card handed out on March 29, 2008, and titled
"Butterfly Kiss for the Buddha," read, "One of the unique features of Buddhism
in the West is how many serious meditators are fully engaged in daily life and
also committed family people." Without doubt, the community's democratizing
process is more consistent with American conceptions of democracy and also
reflects real-life American Zendo and lay sitting groups. Second Life's Zen cloud,
however, more closely resembles the global, entrepreneurial, noncentralized conception of community as envisioned by Linden Lab. As the website "Welcome
to the Second Life World" stated in 2008, "We are a global community working
together to build a new online space for creativity, collaboration, commerce, and
entertainment. . . . We believe in free expression, compassion and tolerance as
the foundation for community in this new world."[27]

I am not arguing against actual freedom but rather that discourses of choice,
freedom, and innovation hide the ideology and genealogy of network authority. *Cyber Zen* argues that the creative, nonhierarchical, networked authority
reflects a "cybernetic management" style, whose organizational approach was
assumed by technology companies, and can be traced back to 1920 and Bell
Laboratories, and whose management structure was modeled on telecommunications relay systems. Hoben's spiritualized network authority reflects cybernetic management – a networked, entrepreneurial, noncentralized conception
of personal interrelationships. Such spiritual entrepreneurism meshes into a
general notion of convert Buddhism as nonhierarchical and flexible, with only
meditation as a leader.[28] In a response to a question about group governance,
on March 7, 2010, Cassius Lawndale wrote in an email,

> Let the community run itself. This point took me some time to embrace,
> because for a long time I had little trust that others could carry on the
> original vision of the place. I thought that I had to do everything or the
> place would fail. But really the place runs so much better now that this idea
> has become a reality.

Near the end of our research, just before he logged off on a permanent basis, Cassius wrote in an email, "we are totally group owned now – one of the best things
to happen with us." He went on to say, "Today Second Life feels like much less
of a burden. I am free to build for the sake of building now, and I know that if
I'm not here the sim is ok without me. Tai Buckinghamshire and Venomfangx
Bardfield, and many others, do wonders for the group that help it stay afloat."

Networked authority's genealogy

Rather than traditional Buddhist notions of governance, the conception of Second Life's Zen cloud reflects a more general notion of virtual communities as
entrepreneurial, global, and noncentralized liberating spaces and was assumed

by many pioneers in the study of computer-mediated-communication (CMC). Howard Rheingold, in *The Virtual Community: Homesteading on the Electronic Frontier*, writes, "I conclude that whenever CMC becomes available to people anywhere, they inevitably build virtual communities with it, just as microorganisms inevitably create colonies."[29] Rheingold argues that digital media automatically create community and creativity. For Rheingold, digital media cannot help but "bring conviviality and understanding into our lives."[30] He celebrates the entrepreneurial nature of cyberspace and argues that it is inherently nonhierarchical and egalitarian and that digital media are a great equalizer by which ordinary citizens can counter the forces of central control. "The political significance of CMC lies in its capacity to challenge the existing political hierarchy's monopoly on powerful communications media, and perhaps thus revitalize citizen-based democracy."[31]

Cyber Zen contends that "freedom," "flexibility," and "choice" are often just network authority under a different name. Networked authority governs through a cybernetic management that employs the "law of requisite variety": rather than attempting to limit the flow of communication, a cybernetic manager, like the steersman of a ship, regulates the system through a large variety of data that must be equal to or larger than the variety of the disruptions. In theory, this creates an adaptive system that not only runs smoothly but also creatively transforms itself to meet changes in the environment.[32] Starting in the late 1950s, the economist Stafford Beer retooled the law of requisite variety for the management of corporations and called it the Viable Systems Model.[33] By the 1970s Beer had put this model into action for a variety of corporate clients, and even national economies, the largest of these was the entire economy of Chile. From 1971 to 1973, Beer created a real-time communications network, called Cybernet, which linked Chile's industrial base to computers in its capital.

Building on the work of Norbert Wiener, and also the British cyberneticist Ross Ashby, Beer applied cybernetic laws to human organizations and institutions. Beer argued that the uncertainty of postwar markets called for a new type of organization that was flexible, entrepreneurial, and open to rapid change. For Beer, these "exceeding complex systems" were best managed through a cybernetics informatics that would transform systems by governing their flows of information.[34] Cybernetic management regulates through real-time feedback, understands information as structures in which actors operate, and perceives managers as an integral part of the system, not detached from it. For Beer, as in Norbert Wiener's model of a furnace, Robert Pirsig's motorcycle rider, Alan Watts' nondeluded subject, and the convert Zen practitioner meditating on a black cushion, key for such management is homeostasis, the ability of a system to creatively respond to changes in its environment.

For Beer, cybernetics had both political and spiritual outcomes, which hinged on the conception that traditional systems of governance were not structured to take into account the huge variety and overwhelming amount of information that was made possible by changes in media technologies. In October 2001,

Beer wrote, "Last month [September 2001], the tragic events in New York, as cybernetically interpreted, look quite different from the interpretation supplied by world leaders – and therefore the strategies now pursued are quite mistaken in cybernetic eyes."[35] Beer's spirituality was also entangled with his cybernetic ontology. He began life as an Anglican, converted to Catholicism, and ended a self-proclaimed Tantric Yogi. In his 1965 article, "Cybernetics and the Knowledge of God," Beer treats the divine in a similar way as he does a corporation. Beer argues that while God is ultimately too complex to be known, one can articulate useful models as long as one realizes that they are revisable practices and not fixed and definitive representations. Just as managers can gather data, although never adequate, and still learn about their corporations, spiritual seekers can pursue to understand the divine, even if it is ontologically unknowable through information. "In fact," Beer suggests, "we – that is men – have a whole reference frame, called religion, which distinguishes between orders of creation precisely in terms of their communication capacity."[36]

Don't be evil

As seen in Google's motto, "Don't be evil" (which was dropped in October 2015), digital media's entrepreneurial, global, and noncentralized liberating potential was soon commodified, corporatized, and branded. Google reports that its organization style runs like the Internet itself: fast moving, bottom up, and decentralized. "We were born in the Internet time," writes Megan Smith, vice president of business development at Google, "so our company's like our products in some weird way."[37] As evidenced by the annual Wisdom 2.0 Conference, there is no doubt that Buddhism has influenced Silicon Valley corporate culture. As a July 23, 2012, *New York Times* article reads, "Founders from Facebook, Twitter, eBay, Zynga and PayPal, and executives and managers from companies like Google, Microsoft, Cisco and others listened to or participated in conversations with experts in yoga and mindfulness." The entanglement, however, leads both ways, and Hoben's authority can be seen to reflect the same underlying cybernetic ontology as Google's. As the section from Google's "2004 Founders' IPO Letter," titled "Don't Be Evil," included as part of their S-1 Registration Statement with the Securities and Exchange Commission, reads, "We aspire to make Google an institution that makes the world a better place. . . . With our products, Google connects people and information all around the world for free."

For Google, cybernetic management and networked authority are key to their success in creating networks of spontaneous entanglement of dense, vibrant, webs of playful interactions. For instance, Google's campus is intentionally packed full of people. As the directory of facilities George Salah said, "We want to pack those buildings not just because it minimizes our [environmental] footprint, but because of the interactions you get, just accidental stuff you overhear."[38] Play was also important. As the "2004 Founders' IPO Letter," reads, "This empowers [employees] to be more creative and innovative.[39] For this reason Google works hard at maintaining a sense of play. One of the most important days in Google culture is April 1, when employees are encouraged to pull elaborate pranks. For instance, on April 1, 2001, Google released "MentalPlex," a search engine that could read your mind.[40] Play is also evident in the key performance principle for the work environment, a "Googley atmosphere."[41]

Google's management style reflects the cybernetic organization approach pioneered by Bell Laboratories, which was founded in the 1920s and whose organizational style was modeled on telecommunications switching relays. Bell Lab's buildings, both at the original Manhattan site and the later Holmdel Complex in New Jersey, were constructed to be spaces of dense spontaneous human interactions. For instance, the Bell Lab employee Claude Shannon, often called the father of information theory and credited with the creation of digital computer and digital circuit design theory, imagined the laboratory as a highly complex set of relays made of people and machines: "a really beautiful example of a highly complex machine. This is in many ways the most complex machine that man has ever attempted, and in many ways also a most reliable one."[42] Like Second Life and Google, Bell Lab's management style was structured to produce innovation and flexibility. Management had to be technically competent and were all former researchers. Researchers were allowed a sense of play, because they were freed from the pressure of raising funds and not damned for failure.

Conclusion

This chapter has described Second Life's relationships and groups. Relationships are usually intense private interactions between two residents, while groups define a more cool and mediated interaction among a larger public. While relationships are often short-lived and intimate, groups tend to be more steady and are the most basic and stable Second Life social unit. Hoben illustrates that rather than simply connoting living in the same physical vicinity, the term "community" ought to define a group whose media practices form relations over time by interacting on a regular basis around a shared set of experiences. We have illustrated that Second Life's convert Zen groups are cloud communities that utilize network authority and are based in a cybernetic management style that emerged out of the twentieth-century telecommunications field. Frequently, Second Life community was fueled by a desire for authentic close personal interactions, as opposed to the indirect, formalized impersonal roles that were seen to compose much of real life Network Consumer Society. When I asked the resident Eliza Martinek to describe Hoben, she said in an interview, "Warm and generous, Ferociously smart, true." The musician Venomfangx Bardfield described Hoben as "a spiritual, fun-loving. close-knit group." One resident on our 2010 survey simply responded "joy."

As I argue in chapters five and six, the practice of silent online meditation is what affords authentic community in Second Life. Online meditation enabled community because it gave residents a reason to regularly log on and come together as a group. Residents felt a responsibility toward others, and a duty towards themselves. As the Hoben leader Tai Buckinghamshire said in conversation on March 5, 2010, "Being a 'lone practitioner' it's sometimes difficult to keep constant practice going. I need that extra ★nudge★ from others. By logging into Second Life and attending a meditation session or a Dharma talk, I get that virtual nudge that I can transfer to my real life." More intensely, it was the communitas generated through the practice of online meditation that afforded residents feelings of togetherness. In a similar fashion, during our fieldwork many religious groups in Second Life used music to create a collective effervescence that fused the individual residents into a community. On a daily basis, Christian, Jewish, and pagan groups all used music and dancing to create a communal experience. While Hoben did have regular Friday night music at its *campfire*, this did not involve dancing and was secondary to the feeling of community created by online silent meditation. Interestingly, the group Agnostic Buddhists Sangha, which had talks about Buddhism but did not have a regular sitting practice, actually dissolved over the issue of whether it could create a virtual community.

Still, we are left with a lingering question: Why are there so many Buddhists online? It might simply be that Buddhists, like human beings more generally, are social animals and they will form relationships however they can, whenever they can, whether on- or offline. This chapter speculated, however, that convert Zen cloud communities flourish because they are entangled with the same cybernetic ethos that also fuels digital media and contemporary telecommunications management styles. As we saw in the last chapter, up until the early 1970s computers were seen by the vast majority of spiritual practitioners and counterculturists as the most odious technology for the corporate and military occupation of everyday life. Beginning in the mid-1970s, however, the notion that digital media could supply alternative social spaces emerged in California's Bay Area in a long-running collaboration between the counterculture and the emerging technological hacker culture of the Silicon Valley. Enabled by digital media and the belief that there ought to be online community, by the mid-1980s these strong, weak social ties, allowed a variety of imagined communities to thrive online.

Is Second Life's Zen cloud authentic? All communities – even Buddhist ones – are socially constructed and dependent on and maintained by media practices. As the political scientist Benedict Anderson argues, in *Imagined Community*, media are necessary for "all communities larger than primordial villages of face-to-face contact (and perhaps even these)."[43] Since at least the early 1990s, digital media have allowed people to imagine online spiritual communities. Second Life is no different. Hoben's sangha illustrates the need to redefine the politics of authentic religious community and view popular forms of online spirituality as possible alternatives, which are not only a viable option, but are also desirable. While the virtual does not displace strong real-life social ties, for many residents

Second Life sociability was an important part of their everyday community that offered authentic human interaction. For many, the Zen groups began merely as an augment to real-life Buddhist sanghas; often, however, the weak social ties of the virtual world became the center of their practice. The other residents became community members and close friends. As Rasa Vibration said near the end of our interview,

> Being isolated from Buddhists in general, I was extremely glad to have found Buddhists in Second Life. I had no idea they would even have a presence there. I originally looked at it as a sangha because I had no real life sangha, and for that it was wonderful. It has become my sangha, and allowed for a safe and supportive environment to explore and share Buddhist thought, Dharma and friendships.

Notes

1 See note 1 in the Introduction, page 24.
2 See note 2 in the Introduction, page 24.
3 Michael Rymaszewski, Wagner James Au, Mark Wallace, Catherine Winters, Cory Ondrejka, Benjamin Batstone-Cunningham, Philip Rosedale, *Second Life: The Official Guide* (Indianapolis, IN: Wiley Publishing, 2007), 277.
4 Edith Turner, *Communitas: The Anthropology of Collective Joy* (New York: Palgrave Macmillan, 2012).
5 Cf. Ferdinand Tönnies, *Gemeinschaft und Gesellschaft – Abhandlung des Communismus und des Sozialismus als empirischer Kulturforment* (Leipzig: Fues's Verlag, 1887); David Lopez, *Prisoners of Shangri-La* (Princeton, NJ: Princeton University Press, 1997).
6 Gregory Price Grieve, "Imagining a Virtual Religious Community: Neo-pagans on the Internet," *Chicago Anthropology Exchange* 7 (1995): 98–132.
7 *Gibson Island Second Life! – Home of Gibson Guitar Corp,* YouTube video, 4:35, posted by Earth Primbee, www.youtube.com/watch?v=8hnOd2ZsIxA (accessed February 21, 2012).
8 N. R. Deuel, "Our Passionate Response to Virtual Reality," in *Computer-Mediated Communication: Linguistic, Social and Cross-Cultural Perspectives,* ed. S. Herring (Amsterdam: John Benjamins Publishing Company, 1996), 129–46.
9 Harley Hahn, *The Internet Complete Reference* (New York: Osborne McGraw-Hill, 1996), 570.
10 "Friends in Second Life," http://wiki.secondlife.com/wiki/Friends_in_Second_Life (accessed November 8, 2015).
11 "Friends and Partnering," https://community.secondlife.com/t5/English-Knowledge-Base/Friends-and-partnering/ta-p/700067 (accessed November 8, 2015).
12 "Gorean Roleplay in Second Life," Second Life Adventures, www.second-life-adventures. com/gorean-roleplay-in-second-life/ (accessed November 8, 2015).
13 "Collar," http://wiki.secondlife.com/wiki/Collar (accessed November 8, 2015).
14 "LSL Protocol/Restrained Love Relay/Introduction," http://wiki.secondlife.com/wiki/ LSL_Protocol/Restrained_Love_Relay/Introduction (accessed November 8, 2015).
15 "Does Anyone Have Experience with the Adoption of a Child or Teenager?," http:// community.secondlife.com/t5/General-Discussion-Forum/Does-anyone-have-experience-with-the-adoption-of-a-child-or/td-p/1451217 (accessed November 8, 2015).
16 See note 1 in the Introduction, page 24.
17 Thích Nhất Hạnh, *Cultivating the Mind of Love* (Berkeley, CA: Parallax Press, 1996).

18 Charles Prebish, *Luminous Passage: The Practice of and Study of Buddhism in America* (Berkley, CA: University of California Press, 1999), 203–32.

19 J. H. Steingrubner, "Cybersangha: Building Buddhist Community Online," *Cybersangha: The Buddhist Alternative Journal*, www.newciv.org/CyberSangha/stein95.htm (accessed June 1, 2008).

20 Heidi Campbell, *Exploring Religious Community Online: We Are One in the Network* (Oxford: Peter Lang, 2005).

21 Christopher Helland, "Religion Online/Online Religion and Virtual Communitas," in *Religion on the Internet: Research Prospects and Promises*, eds. Jeffery K. Hadden and Douglas E. Cowan (London: JAI Press/Elsevier, 2000), 205–24; "Online Religion as Lived Religion. Methodological Issues in the Study of Religious Participation on the Internet," in *Online – Heidelberg Journal of Religions on the Internet* 1, no. 1 (2005), www.ub.uni-heidelberg.de/archiv/5823 (accessed November 3, 2015).

22 Howard Rheingold, *The Virtual Community: Homesteading on the Electronic Frontier* (Reading, MA: Addison-Wesley Publications, 1993), 240.

23 Richard Bartle, *Designing Virtual Worlds* (Berkeley, CA: New Riders, 2004), 317.

24 "Second Life Havok 4 – No Lag with 2000–3400 Physical Prims," www.youtube.com/watch?v=t5_Lzxvuizg (accessed November 8, 2015).

25 Linden Lab, "Terms of Service," www.lindenlab.com/tos (accessed November 6, 2015).

26 Linden Lab.

27 "Second Life Community, "http://secondlife.com/community/ (accessed January 26, 2008).

28 Stafford Beer, *Cybernetics and Management* (London: English Universities Press, 1959).

29 Howard Rheingold, *The Virtual Community: Homesteading on the Electronic Frontier* (Reading MA: Addison-Wesly Publications, 1993), 6.

30 Rheingold, 14.

31 *ibid.*

32 Ross Ashby, *An Introduction to Cybernetics* (New York: Methuen, 1963).

33 Stafford Beer, *Brain of the Firm* (London: Penguin, 1972).

34 Stafford Beer, *Cybernetics and Management* (London: English Universities Press, 1959), 17.

35 Stafford Beer, "The Impact of Cybernetics on the Concept of Industrial Organization," in *Proceedings of the First International Congress on Cybernetics* (Paris: Gauthier-Villars, June 1956), 26–29; reprinted in Beer, *How Many Grapes Went into the Wine? Stafford Beer on the Art and Science of Holistic Management* (New York: Wiley, 1994), 75–95. Stafford Beer, "What Is Cybernetics?" acceptance speech for an honorary degree at the University of Valladolid, Mexico, October 2001, *Kybernetes* 33 (2004): 853.

36 Stafford Beer, "Cybernetics and the Knowledge of God," *The Month* 34 (1965): 292, 297.

37 Cited in Steven Levy, *In the Plex: How Google Thinks, Works, and Shapes Our Lives* (New York: Simon and Schuster, 2011), 158.

38 Cited in Levy, 132.

39 "'An Owner's Manual' for Google's Shareholders," 2004 Founders' IPO Letter, https://investor.google.com/corporate/2004/ipo-founders-letter.html (accessed November 8, 2015); "S-1/A 1 ds1a.htm AMENDMENT NO. 9 TO FORM S-1," www.sec.gov/Archives/edgar/data/1288776/000119312504142742/ds1a.htm (accessed November 8, 2015).

40 "MentalPlex," https://archive.google.com/mentalplex/ (accessed November 8, 2015).

41 Levy, 130.

42 Cited in Jon Gertner, *The Idea Factory: Bell Labs and the Great Age of American Innovation* (New York: Penguin Press, 2012), 136.

43 Benedict Anderson, *Imagined Communities: Reflections on the Origin and Spread of Nationalism* (New York: Verso, 1983), 6.

Chapter 4

People

Buddhist robes, cyborgs, and the gendered self-fashioning of a mindful resident

Algama GossipGirl:	"Namaste _/!_, Clint ;)"
Human Riddle:	"You are getting really close"
Algama:	"Does this look okay?"
Human:	"That is really good I think ★smiles★"
TypeZen Sideways:	"Looks good. You just need to make your breasts smaller . :-)"
Human:	LOL
Algama:	"Such a production •★´″'★•.„.•★´″'★•., giggles,.•★´″'★•.„.•★´″'★•"

Transcript of conversation at
Hoben Mountain Zen Retreat
(February 23, 2010)

Concentrating on the role of gender in identity formation, and refracting our analysis through free virtual Buddhist monk robes (*kāṣāya*) handed out at Hoben Mountain Zen Retreat on February 23, 2010, this chapter explores how *residents* used Second Life's media practices to fashion mindful selves. When I logged on the day the free version became available at Hoben, I came across an almost carnivalesque group helping a female human *avatar*, Algama GossipGirl, *edit* the robes so that they would fit (Figure 4.1). As a default, the robes had been made for men. We found, however, that they tended to mostly be modified and worn by female avatars. I maintain that for female avatars the Buddhist robes played a part in fashioning selves that were both politically and spiritually liberating.

Yet, what type of selves did the robes fashion? And why did mostly female avatars tend to wear them? Frequently studies of online subjectivity either frame their analysis in a dystopic lament over the loss of an essential coherent modern self or, conversely, a utopic hagiography praising the liberating potential of constructed postmodern fluid identities.[1] Compare for instance, the scholar of science and technology Sherry Turkle's later work, *Alone Together*, to her earlier work *Life on the Screen*.[2] Neither of these two choices, however, adequately described the everyday reality that we came across on Second Life. To give a more accurate account, this chapter first uses the Second Life search engine filter of "people" to locate "residents." The term "resident" describes cyber-social beings that are activated in the virtual world by the feedback between

Figure 4.1 Free Buddhist monk robes from Hoben Mountain Zen Retreat.

Figure 4.1 (Continued)

"user" and "avatar." Users are the flesh and blood individuals behind the screens, and avatars are the virtual appearance that descends into the virtual world. Rather than emphasizing the real world or virtual world, I theorize residents as "cyborgs," hybrid systems of machine and biologic organisms, and trace the roots of the contemporary concept of the term in postwar popular American culture.

Second, this chapter employs the cyborg model of self to explore how Second Life media practices are used to fashion alternative residents through a careful cultivation of *shapes*, *skins*, and virtual dress. To analyze such alternative self-fashioning, I employ the category of gender, which I theorize on Second Life not as a natural phenomenon but as emerging from the play in media practices between a user's desire, agency, and social norms.[3] My goal is not simply to add to the ample literature on gender and online identity, but to use the category of gender to explore how residents fashion selves that are both products of and alternatives to the norms of Network Consumer Society. Early in the study, on May 23, 2008, for instance, the resident RavenSong Merlin described Second Life as "an alternate reality where you can recreate yourself" and went on to describe the platform as a "sandbox for the self." As described in chapter one, a sandbox consists of digital media practices that afford creativity and experimentation not only for builds and objects but also for imagining new forms of identity and community.

Third, this chapter illustrates how for many residents self-fashioning was part of their spirituality and explores how women's dress was woven into their media practices. As I explained in *Cyber Zen*'s introduction, spiritual media practices are those that address the deeper existential anguishes that arise from the very condition of being human. Touching back upon chapter two, I first explore three tactics for spiritual self-fashioning: fundamentalist, New Age, and mindful. Fundamentalism policed authenticity by maintaining a networked cisgendered rigidity between users and avatars and regulating modest dress for female avatars. As the opposite of transgender, "cisgendered" describes a person whose identity matches with their biologically given body.[4] "Networked cisgendered" refers to the majority of nongender swapping users whose real-life gendered identity matches with that of their avatar. The New Age celebrated the free play of the imagination, and because fantasy revealed a user's inner self, saw creative avatars as revealing residents' authentic selves. New Agers did not seem overly concerned with networked cisgenderness. Still, their media practices systematically reinscribed "heteronormativity," the assumption that human beings divide naturally into the complementary genders of male and female and that heterosexuality is the only normal sexual orientation.

As the final section of the chapter narrates, our analysis became more complicated, however, because it turned out that Algama was "gender swapping." The scholar of online community and identity Amy Bruckman refers to "gender swapping" as the ability "to pretend to be the opposite gender" and notes that "in these virtual worlds, the way gender structures basic human interaction is often noticed and reflected upon."[5] Gender swapping is an ethical issue, which often falls into a dichotomy between those who see it as immoral and those who praise it as an emancipating media practice. I sidestep the dilemma and instead maintain that religious studies cannot theorize universal moral judgments about gender swapping but should instead analyze the fine-grained tactics of its everyday use. Using the gender swapping Algama's donning of Buddhist robes as a touchstone, I argue that Second Life convert Zen residents follow a third spiritual tactic of self-fashioning, mindful media practices that are codependent on users and avatars. In a mindful approach, authenticity lies neither solely with the avatar nor with the user, but rather in the awareness of the play between Second Life and real life. As the Buddhist resident Yidam Roads said on May 22, 2009, "If you change avatars especially, I think it can help you explore different facets of personal identity and perhaps hold your identification with 'self' more lightly."

The chapter argues that the mindful donning of robes at Hoben liberated female avatars both politically and spiritually. On a political level, the robes allowed female avatars to fashion online identities that traversed Second Life's intense heteronormativity. On a spiritual level, by affording an experience of the empty nature of gender, the robes enabled a glimpse of the empty nature of the world more generally. As described in chapter two, the Buddhist concept of emptiness (śūnyatā) does not contend that the phenomena of conventional reality are unreal, but only that they have no essential core and only arise through a codependence on other human and nonhuman elements. Second Life's fantasy-driven self-fashioning does not allow users to actually know what it is like to be someone different, but its media practices do allow residents to become something virtually different that allows them to experience that while we need social roles, these roles can do violence to those who don them. As I flesh out in *Cyber Zen*'s conclusion, being mindful of the constructed nature of lived reality enabled residents to imagine alternative ways of being. As Algama said near the end of our conversation, "I don't think playing a girl, ever allowed me to really know what it is like to be really be a girl, mostly, but I did see how being a guy was like, ya know, different."

Virtual monk robes

Often clothing is reduced to need, and no doubt, as naked apes, human beings must cover against the elements.[6] Fashion emerges, however, not just from what clothes do but also from what they mean and, especially in contemporary society, has more do with engaging desire and marking distinction than with physical necessity. One might think that fashion is just added adornment and thus not in need of serious analysis. However, because in Network Consumer Society desire outstrips need, contemporary fashion is not superfluous but for many consumers a necessity for being considered a full-fledged citizen. As defined in chapter one, Network Consumer Society indicates the cultural, social, and economic system that arose in the second half of the twentieth century and is defined by the fluidity of financial capital, an intensification of the free market, radical individualism, and interconnected globalization.

As an extreme version of Network Consumer Society, while just pixels on the screen, fashion on Second Life was a crucial aspect of everyday life in the virtual world. During our research, Second Life lacked the fixity of ranks and status of traditional societies, and thus fashion emerged as the central focus of many residents. Second Life identity was not usually regulated through public institutions but fashioned through consumer choices. Consumerism was vital to fashioning. As Algama GossipGirl answered ironically to my question of whether she shopped in Second Life, "I buy therefore my avatar is." From Jesus baseball caps and *yamakas* to yoga pants and angel wings, the centrality of self-fashioning was also true for many Second Life religious groups. Interestingly, however, even more than other traditions in Second Life, dress played a key role in convert Zen Buddhism. This may come as no surprise, for monk robes have always played a crucial role in Buddhist practice. In his classic article, "Quand l'habit fait le moine," the Buddhologist Bernard Faure writes, "the monastic garment became the symbol *par excellence* of the Dharma, outperforming other symbols and relics, and occupying a prominent place in the Buddhist imaginary."[7]

The free robes handed out in February 2010 were created by the talented builder Ryusho Ort and were based on his popular Soto So-Fuku robes that he described as "Japanese Soto monk kesa (robes). Also applicable for Chinese and Korean Traditions." Following some twenty-five centuries of custom, which had traveled from India and been adapted as Buddhism spread through Asia, Ryusho's robes consisted of the "triple robe" style: a lower covering (*antarvāsa*) made of a *skirt* and *pants*, an upper covering *(uttarāsaṅga)* made of a *shirt*, and an outer robe (*saṃghāti*) made of a *jacket* and *flexi attachments*. In Second Life, skirts, pants, shirts, and jackets describe different layer-based textured clothing that can be applied directly to a user's avatar. Flexi attachments are *prims* (primitives) that are set to "flex" so that they mimic the physical movement of cloth, such as being blown in the wind.

Resident

Early in the study, after I had completed one of my first meditation sessions, I sat impatiently waiting for the customary follow-up discussion. I watched as the other practitioners began to rouse themselves from their digital slumber; their avatars suddenly began to move as their users returned fingers to keyboards. Much to my surprise, one of the first questions directed towards the group from the leader was the rather ambiguous, "Who are you?" In real life this seems a simple enough question to answer. In Second Life it proved much more difficult. Was I the user, the avatar, or some *mashup* between the two? I also started to wonder: Out of what material are selves fashioned? Am I my thoughts? My words and actions? What about possessions and relationships? Do virtual objects and fashion count? As the American philosopher and psychologist William James writes in *The Principles of Psychology*, "between what a man calls *me* and what he simply calls *mine* the line is difficult to draw."[8]

Selves are fashioned. As Lila Abu-Lughod, the professor of anthropology and women's and gender studies writes, "the self is always a construction, never a natural or found entity."[9] Virtual worlds make self-fashioning more conspicuous, because there is no actual world referent and ultimately selves are just media practices. On Second Life selves are roles that stem not from an already given body but are instead constituted by repeated media practices that are renewed, revised, and consolidated through time. Yet selves are never made out of whole cloth or completely under conscious rational control. Like a half-improvised script, the virtual world reveals that selves are templates that are structured through repeated communication that socially sanctions possible types of behavior. Social roles regularly function to define the situation for those with whom one communicates and are standardized systems that define the physical, temporal, emotional, and cognitive limits by which users communicate their identity. These include such identity markers as age, race, and rank, which are displayed through clothing, size, posture, speech patterns, and bodily gestures.

How ought one to theorize selves fashioned on Second Life? Much of contemporary theory on subjective formation, whether on- or offline, falls between a modern essentialist position that posits a static bounded self and a postmodern position that suggests a fluid, socially constructed identity. The modernist position usually privileges the actual, while the postmodern celebrates the virtual. To sidestep this dilemma, I turn to Second Life's own category of "people," which filters the platform's search engine for "residents," those cybersocial entities created from digital media practices that entangle virtual avatars with their organic users. In my analysis, I employ the term "user" to refer to the actual person behind the screen and "avatar" to refer to a user's virtual representative, and I poach the Second Life term "resident" to indicate the cybersocial entity afforded by the virtual world media practices that consist of the avatar, operated by the user, and socialized by interaction with *groups* of other residents, and occasionally the users themselves (Figure 4.2).

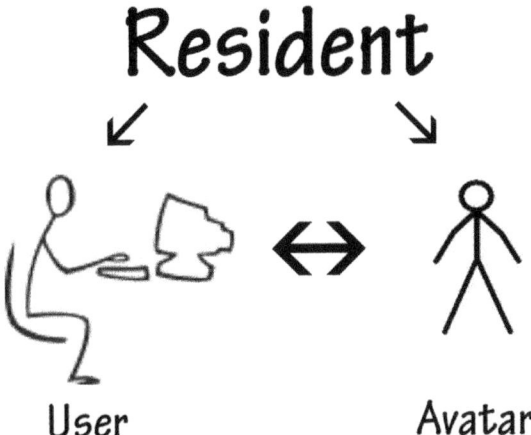

Figure 4.2 Resident as cyborg, hybrid feedback loops of machine and biologic organisms, composed of user and avatar.

Residents do not exist before users log on but rather emerge from Second Life media practices. Employed throughout the platform and the surrounding *SLogosphere* instead of the term "player," the term "resident" is "meant to give users a feeling of 'belonging' and ownership of the virtual world."[10] "Resident" was used almost from the beginning of Second Life and can be seen as far back as 2003 in the beta testing website, which states, "residents of Second Life will face a host of choices daily . . . [in this] multi-layered boundless universe that is constantly changed by – and constantly changes – its inhabitants."[11] "Resident" is meant to capture how the Second Life experience differs from the "flat" technology like email and describes someone who dwells in a three-dimensional virtual environment. As Robin Linden, the avatar for Robin Harper, Vice President of Marketing and Community Development, who coined the term, wrote in a Second Life Forum from July 2006, " . . . the word 'users' doesn't do a very good job of describing the two-way nature of Second Life . . . We also thought about 'members' (boring!), 'citizens' (too political!), and 'players' (too game-y). 'residents', however, seems most descriptive of people who have a stake in the world and how it grows."[12]

Residents emerge from the feedback between users and avatar. Linden Lab defines a "resident" as "a uniquely named avatar with the right to log into Second Life, trade Linden Dollars and visit the Community pages."[13] Second Life residents are governed by terms of service, which specifically allow users to retain all intellectual property rights in the digital content they create or own on the virtual world, and are held to Community Standards, which operate as best practices.[14] It is important to remember that a "resident" is not always a one-to-one relationship between a real-life user and a virtual representation. As with most website user accounts, several alternative avatars (*alts*) might belong to one user, and conversely one avatar might be operated by more than one user sequentially, or in some cases by more than one user at the same time, as in the situation of one avatar controlled by nine disabled persons.[15]

Users and avatars

A "user" is the real-life person in front of the screen with fingers on keyboard. As the Hoben group leader Tai Buckinghamshire said on January 10, 2009, "I never forget that the people I interact with are very much real flesh and blood on the other side of the screen." Tai was the avatar of the user Jessie Harrison, one of the study's main informants. Jessie was a psychologist from the mountains of Virginia, who described herself as "a long time meditator, informed by Buddhism." Reflecting the community, Jessie was female, middle-class, North American, highly educated, liberal, white, and in her late thirties.[16] While in a slight minority (46.7 percent), women tended to hold many positions of authority and often played key roles in maintaining the community. For instance, Tai often found herself mediating between different members of the group and making sure that events were staffed. Jessie, like almost all users (86.6 percent), was white. This percentage reflects convert Buddhism more generally. Like Jessie, while Hoben users were from twenty-six countries, the majority (56.6 percent) were from America, and 17.7 percent were from other Anglophone countries such as Canada, England, Australia, and New Zealand. Like Jessie, who held a Ph.D., a small majority (34.2 percent) of Buddhist residents had postgraduate degrees, followed by a college degree (34.3 percent) and by some college (24.4 percent). Politically, users were progressive, with 62.5 percent describing themselves as liberal and only 3.8 percent as conservative. Jessie's career as a psychologist also reflected the community. A very small majority of Hoben's users (18.2 percent) worked in information technology, followed by art and design (16.9 percent) and education (13 percent). Jessie's age was also typical. Ages at Hoben ranged between seventeen and seventy-four, with a mean of forty-five, a median of forty-four, and an average age of forty-three years and three months.

Avatars are the inworld resident's presence. On June 11, 2015, the Second Life sign-in webpage, titled "Create your Avatar," stated, "Be anyone or anything you want," and then asked "Who do you want to be?"[17] In computing, avatars are on-screen representations, which can be a three-dimensional model such as in Second Life, a two-dimensional icon as used in many chat forums, or a written description as used in text-based Multi User Dungeons (MUDs). In Second Life, avatars were fashioned from media practices that included voice, open and private chat, and note cards and textures for sending textual and graphical data. Avatars can have possessions such as clothes, furniture, weapons, and currency, which are frequently stored in an inventory. Second Life avatars also have profiles that contain identifying information such as name, group affiliations, and interest.

Avatars are not simply game tokens but embody highly personal manifestations of fantasy that often emerge from Network Consumer Society. Second Life's "Create your Avatar" webpage offered to get you started "with a free avatar, customize your appearance, [and] shop the marketplace." In Second Life, the default avatar shape is humanoid, and one can choose to be ether male or female, but it can be customized through a graphical user interface to modify gender, body shape, skin, hairstyle, and clothes. Moreover, residents can purchase or create bodies and clothes as well as *attachments, animation,* and sonic (voice) overrides. Such customization results in male, female, and androgynous human avatars, as well as animal, robot, *neko, furries,* and other fantasy creatures such as dragons.

Body

By the end of our research, every member of our research team employed a human avatar; early on, however, each of us had experimented with a variety of types. Interestingly, the only type that consistently caused trouble was an invisible avatar. We found that the lack of an avatar body was the quickest way for a resident to be *ejected* and *banned* from a region. This is to say, that much of the ideology surrounding virtual worlds has been sustained by a rhetoric of dematerialization and disembodiment. Yet, virtual worlds do not lack bodies. What they lack is the face-to-face physical interaction of oral communication that is often considered necessary for authentic interpersonal relationships. Because of resident embodiment, however, Second Life was more than just a chat room and differed in fundamental ways from text-only digital media such as email and chat. Residents' bodies mediated communication because they both structure and were structured by virtual world media practices. During our research we found that some residents treated Second Life as little more than textual chat. Our experience was that these users tended not to spend much time in the virtual world and were often marginalized to *noobie* status and even seen as potential *griefers* because their avatars seemed underdeveloped.

Avatars differ from other digital media practices because of bodies. Unlike film that shows bodies, as well as print and radio that tell about bodies, virtual worlds afford embodiment. This does not mean that like the film *Tron* (1982), one takes one's biological body with oneself when one logs on. Instead, logging on extends users' bodies and their body meshes through media practices with the screen. As the American postmodern literary critic Katherine Halyes writes in *How We Became Post Human*, in digital media, "it is not a question of leaving the body behind but rather extending embodied awareness in highly specific, local, and material ways that would be impossible without electronic prosthesis."[18] In the simplest sense, a virtual body is one that inhabits a virtual world. In the most general sense, embodiment signifies the experience of being in one's body and challenges the assumptions that subjectivity can be reduced to mind and that media practices are merely about the conveyance of disembodied information.[19]

Bodies are not natural. To assume that actual world embodiment is the only authentic embodiment imputes a naturalist and romantic notion of an unmediated encounter with the world. Human beings may have no choice in the biological body they are given, but bodies never exist outside of media practices. Embodiment, paradoxically, is not about material manifestation of the body, but rather about how the body is enacted. People communicate bodies in fluid and shifting media practices that emerge out of the continuing stylized repetition. People with actual world disabilities illuminate the social constructed nature of bodies both on- and offline. Since the earliest days of text-driven MUDs, scholars have noted the potential for allowing disabled persons to be embodied virtually in nondisabled forms. The resident Twinkle MoonLight, who often took the form of a *tiny* avatar, told me that in "real life I'm pretty much confined to my home and this room. . . . I don't know many people." And she pointed out that Second Life allowed her "to perform, and sing. I love to sing. I *love* to dance."

Cyborg

The constructed nature of the embodied self is all the more obvious in virtual worlds. Algama and other residents did not exist before they logged on but rather emerged from Second Life's media practices that aggregate users' actual world "meat" and the avatars' virtual "pixels." Second Life residents are "cyborgs," a portmanteau of cybernetic organisms, which emerge from online media practices that create a system of feedback loops between user and avatar. I employ the term "cyborg" here to trace the movement of residents as they shuttle back and forth across the screen, entangling lived worlds of the virtual and the actual, of reality and fantasy, of self and other. As the feminist theorist Donna Haraway writes, in "A Cyborg Manifesto: Science, Technology, and Socialist-Feminism in the Late Twentieth Century," Second Life residents are a "cybernetic organism, a hybrid of machine and organism, a creature of social reality as well as a creature of fiction."[20]

As only part of the cyborg, avatars neither simply represent nor erase a user's real-life self. Second Life residents are nondual, existing simultaneously in both lived worlds, virtual and actual, real and imagined. A minority of residents attempted to maintain a strict separation between Second Life and real life, and researchers often came across the phrase "Second Life is Second Life and real life is real life, please don't ask." For most, however, the enjoyment of the virtual world came from the feedback loop between the two fields of lived reality. As the resident Superman Lemon's profile read, "Second Life and Real Life are all mixed up, it makes it so much more fun!" While the boundary between the actual world and the virtual world was porous and never dichotomized, each, however, was treated as a distinct social space. Superman's first life profile read, "I share real life with good friends and have nothing to hide, but not looking to expand real life through Second Life. We can't help mix them some or there would be nothing to talk about."

During our research, residents tended to describe the relationship between users and avatars in one of three main ways. First, users frequently treated their avatars as dolls, to dress up and play with in the serious play of a role-playing situation. As the resident Avi Long said, "this is just pixels. I had hard time to find a human avatar, I was a *fur* for a long time, but then Halloween came and I bought an outfit that had this shape and a skin." Second, often avatars were treated as tools, to be used for building, communication, and for making money. The resident Yidam Roads said, "I started out identifying fairly strongly with my avatar, tried to make her look like my real life self, but when I build, the avatar is a tool – in fact, I don't even know where I've left it." Third, residents might be "merged," which indicated that user and avatar were so closely meshed that it seemed as if Second Life was unmediated and users were there inworld. As Algama said about her avatar, "She is me. I am here right now." When I asked Algama how she would define this, she said after a long pause, "I guess I would have to dub it lifestyle-play? Play might offend some, and lifestyle others, but,

I don't want to draw this into a real-life relationship. I respect others' feelings, and can even understand that at some times the lines blur in this virtual world." While users tended toward one style, often, in quick succession, they cycled through a number of relations between user and avatar as merged, roleplay, and tool.

Cyborgs in popular culture

Cyborg is not a naturally given universal category, and its contemporary meaning emerges from a particular social and historic context. I contend that the cybernetic media practice of resident and the subject position that it creates have roots in postwar popular culture. In the late twentieth century, with the increasing intrusion of technology into everyday life, the distinctions between human and nonhuman dissolved in a flurry of pixels. The concept of cyborg emerged from the breakdown of three boundaries in postwar culture: the boundary between human and animal, organism and machine, and the physical and nonphysical. These blurrings are reflected in popular culture, from the original Doctor Who's 1966 introduction of the Cybermen, *Star Trek: The Next Generation*'s introduction of the Borg in 1989, to the 2000 *Deus Ex* cyberpunk-themed first-person action role-playing video game. What drives these blurrings are networks of desires. Cyborgs are most distinct from other twentieth-century technological beings, such as the classic all-metal robot, because they have desires. Compare the powerful, but emotionless, eight-foot tall robot Gort, from *The Day the Earth Stood Still* (1951) with the sexy, dangerous, and mysterious queen of the Borg Collective from *Star Trek: First Contact* (1996).

Cyborgs are entangled with cybernetics and can be traced to Norbert Wiener's *Cybernetics: Or the Control and Communication in the Animal and the Machine.*[21] It was not until 1960, however, when the astrophysicists Manfred Clynes and Nathan Kline coined the actual term "cyborg" to define a "self-regulating man-machine system . . . for the exogenously extended organizational complex functioning as an integrated homeostatic system."[22] In 1965, Daniel Stephen Halacy, in *Cyborg: Evolution of the Superman,* promised a "new frontier" that was "not merely space, but more profoundly the relationship between 'inner space' to 'outer space' – a bridge . . . between mind and matter."[23] The early 1960s also found the creator of the field of cybernetic management, Stafford Beer, attempting to use feedback loops to make "biological computers" using children, mice, and also microscopic organisms.[24]

If robots epitomized the cold world of modern factory production, cyborgs presented the anxious desires emerging from postmodern Network Consumer Society. Often cyborgs display the monstrous – an unease with contemporary society's overdependence on technology, a loss of free will, and the use of advanced technology by the military. An image from Clynes and Kline's article illustrating "one of the first Cyborgs, . . . a 220-gm rat has under its skin the osmotic pump designed to permit continuous injections of chemicals" displays this disturbing monstrous quality.[25] In the late 1980s, however, the image of the cyborgs transmorphed from a symbol of dominance into one of possible transgressive identities that promised a utopic potential for a posthuman existence. New alternative identities could be fantasized into being, and new possibilities for refiguring subjectivity in the face of rapid cultural change emerged. Donna Haraway used the image of the cyborg "to build an ironic political myth faithful to feminism, socialism, and materialism."[26] Haraway calls for moving away from essentialist notions of self and uses the cyborg as a more fluid model of sexual desire and gendered embodiment. As Haraway writes, "Gender might not be global identity after all, even if it has profound historical breadth and depth."[27]

Fashioning a resident

As the website "Create Your Avatar" shows when residents initially log onto Second Life, the first thing they do is use the virtual world's media practices to fashion themselves. All new residents, when they sign up for Second Life, choose a default avatar but may modify the avatar depending on their imagination, editing skills, and *Linden dollars*. Residents could, with the click of a few buttons, choose to be either male or female and also change their appearance by wearing different shapes and skins. During the time of our research, one could purchase or find many shapes, or one could customize one's avatar through the appearance menu. Skins wrap around the avatar's wire mesh, and like shapes could be purchased, found, or created. An avatar's hair and eyes could also be customized. In later versions of the Second Life viewer, users could also change their avatar's *physics*, customizing the way their avatar's breasts, belly, and butt bounced and swayed. Residents could also change their appearance by finding, purchasing, or designing clothing. Seemingly infinite styles of clothing could be obtained in Second Life and worn with just a few mouse clicks.

Avatars revealed users' desires and fantasies. For many, as the resident Human Riddle said, "*tongue in cheek* Second Life is all about playing with yourself." During the time of our research, customizing one's avatar became a necessity. If one did not want to appear a noobie, or be banned as a griefer, residents quickly learned how to make or acquire customized clothing, hair, and even bodies. For residents, shopping was not extra but a central part of the virtual world's media practices. There was a necessary style, knowledge, and hard work to employing the media practices to make oneself the same but different. A few residents could not keep up with the strain of fashioning. After an important early informant stopped logging on, I emailed her. She replied by email, "I just can't keep up with Second Life. It was fun to shop at first. Now it is just a chore, and I have enough work in my real life." While plunging many residents into uncertainty, Second Life's self-fashioning also opened up new fantastic possibilities. For most, however, fashion allowed them the freedom to create alternative selves. As Ashley Lee's friend, Megan Megadon, said, "that's what Second Life is about isn't it? . . . being what you are not able to in real life." Ashley nodded and agreed, "Second Life is my place to lend freedom to my inner freak, who has taken a backseat to practical things for so long . . . to have the balls to make my hair very freaky colors that I could have dyed it when I was young."

Some types of avatars went beyond Second Life's libertine community standards. For instance, "Linden Lab Official: Clarification of policy disallowing *ageplay*" reads, "Under our Community Standards policy, real-life images, avatar portrayals, and other depictions of sexual or lewd acts involving or appearing to involve children or minors are not allowed within Second Life."[28] Besides ageplay, there was a strict policy on the use of *bots*, avatars controlled by a software program rather than by a human user. As the webpage "Linden Lab Official: Bot policy" reads: "bots *per se*, are allowed and have legitimate uses, but inappropriate uses are violations of this policy."[29] Using bots to "game" traffic, send an excessive number of messages, and purchase mainland parcels was not allowed. We used a bot in our large survey (*n*=1,227). Residents' responses to it were often vitriolic. As the resident Mild Winter replied after being contacted by our bot, "Piss off. fuck off. damn you. You are reported to Linden Lab."

Virtual gender

The role of fantasy and desire in fashioning residents is clear in gender. Naïvely, when we first logged on, we assumed that, freed from physical bodies, there would be no gender trouble. When one is able to fashion any body, Second Life might seem to conform to a voluntarist, even rational, theory of gender invention. It might seem that the "I" that is being bodied somehow precedes the avatar. Yet avatars are always constrained and constituted by cultural norms, conventions, and laws. One does not have a gender on Second Life but rather enacts gender through media practices that create fantasies that bridge what is desired with what is possible.[30] For instance, during our research, when sitting, residents were usually given a choice of clicking on blue *poseballs* for male or pink for female characters. Poseballs are common scripted objects that usually appear as round colored spheres that play an animation on the avatar that clicks on them. If one clicked on a blue poseball, one's avatar would sit like "a male." If one clicked on the pink ball, one's avatar would sit like "a female." The poseball reproduces the normative contemporary Western convention that women regularly cross their legs when sitting, while men sit with open legs.[31] Often gender items could be purchased. The website Xcite Sexual Equipment offers, for L$1500, the Xcite X4 female starter pack, which includes "the complete sexual survival kit with the X4 Vagina," which includes the Xcite!® X4 Core, X4 'Jasmine' vagina shape, X4 Ass with 'Caboose' Shape, and X4 Nipples with 'Hot Button' Shape."[32]

Cyberspace has often been regarded as a place where gender and sexual identities can be performed in liberating ways. Unfortunately, on Second Life there is a good deal of online sexual and gender play that objectifies women and marginalizes queer identities, and a heteronormative gender matrix is actually more pronounced in Second Life than in real life. Often Second Life's heteronormativity reflected the actual world. Frequently, female avatars were silenced in communication. This occurred not because they were told to be quiet (female avatars' conversation actually takes up more public chat) but rather because others did not follow up on their utterances. As in the actual world, often, dress was gendered. Especially at many religious locations, if a female avatar came scantily dressed, she would be asked to leave, and if she did not, she would be banned from the region.

While entangled with the actual world, Second Life's fashioning of gender does not merely recreate or simulate real practices but is a unique and significant example on its own terms which forms gender along three axes: how an avatar appears, how an avatar communicates, and how an avatar performs. Appearance is everything in Second Life. At a basic level of the platform's programming, residents have to choose between being male or female inworld by clicking a gender button. Gender was also constituted by how an avatar communicates. The most obvious is voice, which is often assumed to assure a match between avatar and user but can be modified through voice morphing. Gender was also communicated through chat. Female chat tended to be more affectionate and used more emoting functions, such as nodding, smiling, giggling, and blushing. Gender was also communicated by gestures. Embedded in avatars are animations and gestures that enable practices of the body such as sitting, dancing, or fighting. In Second Life, one can change posture and gestures. Vista Animation's Perfect Lady AO (animation override), was created "For All of You: Beautiful, Pretty, Elegant, Sexy, Sensual, Business Women." The Vista AO included "9 walks: hips movement from less to more, hands on hips, pockets hair . . . and a standard sexy walk; and 23 animated stands: Perfect transitions. Versatile stands for all occasions."

Most residents engaged in a cisgendered relationship where the user identity and that of the avatar match. Second Life residents could, however, "jam" these enforced heteronormative identities, and during the time of our research we ran across some very transgressive examples. "Culture jamming" defines a communications tactic that disrupts dominate messages through alternatives, which often parody the mainstream. For example, Algama GossipGirl described herself as "a sissy girl. It fits me better than any other term. A 'girl' is feminine, soft, beautiful, young, like, wow, and free. A 'sissy' isn't male or masculine, mostly, but it implies that I am not biologically female."

A sandbox for the self

For the most part, a resident's virtual identity matched the actual world. Still, for many residents, Second Life afforded a space to play with selves, which, while without flesh, were not entirely without bodies. For some this was obvious. Residents edited their avatars' appearance, adapting their real-life identity or discarding it altogether. Many played with multiple selves by morphing between different avatars in a single interaction and explored, experimented, and played with invented, variable, flexible, and fluid selves. Often this was seen as a type of self-therapy. As the resident Mystic Moon said in an interview, "Second Life is a great way to open yourself and find doors to yourself without costs, except of course the time." Such self-experimentation was not always seen as "safe and sane," as the resident Dr. Evol described it. "Many people here are playing games with people's hearts and souls. Many people here in Second Life are using Second Life as a form of Self Therapy instead of getting real life help and taking their medication."

One of the main ways residents played with identity was gender swapping. While only 7 percent of Buddhist residents reported gender swapping regularly, the practice illuminates how Second Life can operate as a spiritual sandbox for the self. The anonymity offered by digital virtual worlds gives people the chance to express multiple and often unexplored aspects of the self and opens windows to unexplored identity and to the trying out of new ones.[33] Obviously avatar bodies emerge from the platform's media practices and do not exist before users log on. Yet while users choose their avatars, and can buy or make just about anything, residents could not become anything they desire. Residents are objects of the virtual world's media practices, shaped by community standards and the procedural logic of the platform's code. Still, because Second Life detaches individual subjects' gender performances from the perceived sex of their bodies, it makes these roles more visible and more available for analysis. Even for those residents strongly identified with their real-life genders, playing with gender in virtual worlds makes the communication of gender more apparent. The resident Yidam Roads said in conversation, "I've tried a male avatar but didn't do much with it, but I did notice one thing. I went to a discussion group and people thought I was a 'genius.'" People are always trying to 'enlighten' me. No one listens to my female avatar. I did enjoy being listened to [and] having my ideas well regarded ★LOL★."

Such self-play was an important part of many Buddhist practitioners' spiritual path. Sixty-six percent of the Buddhist residents surveyed in 2010 ($n=108$) stated that learning about oneself through Second Life was important or very important. A few moments later in my interview with Algama GossipGirl, she added, the virtual world allowed her to "be who I really am when not just spending my life working at a job." Mystic Moon described his time inworld like putting a puzzle together: "you are a puzzle piece you can figure it out and figure out how you fit in." At the end of a long interview, the *builder* and *scripter* Ashley Lee called the virtual world "a great sandbox for personal development!" She stressed that for most "Second Life is a place where you can experiment with your self-image and learn about yourself and your boundaries." I asked her to expand on what she meant, and she replied, "Let me give you a *snapshot* by telling you a dream I had recently about Second Life. I was at a class I run at the Red Parrot sandbox, with friends I enjoy, and we were switching faces and identities. We were the same person, but playing by changing."

Three tactics for spiritual self-fashioning

Fashion is at once the most visible and overlooked of signs in popular culture and also reflects and affects larger historical trends. The dynamic that emerged in the different Second Life religious groups was a tension between the myth of liberating self-play and a fairly rigid adherence to norms. This might not be surprising in more conservative Christian and Islamic regions. As seen through fashion, however, even in convert Buddhist groups, who prided themselves on being egalitarian and were usually run by female avatars, there was a prevalent heteronormativity – male avatars were usually offered monk robes, while women were offered such things as Tibetan tribal costumes.

As described in chapter two, in Second Life we found three distinct forms of spiritual media practices: dwelling fundamentalists, seeking New Agers, and mindful practice–oriented Buddhists. I maintain that how different spiritual groups address clothing, particularly women's dress, illustrates how they address the spiritual self in relation to Network Consumer Society. While clearly different, we found that that the three groups tended to regulate the bodies of female avatars through a similar procedure. First, the women's clothing had to be distinct from that of typical Second Life dress, and second, the clothing had to be aligned with the group's ultimate reality. As Catherine Bell writes in *Ritual Theory Ritual Practice*, for a practice to be sacred, it must be different than the norm but also must "align [a practitioner] within a series of relationships linked to the ultimate source of power."[34]

To be clear, female avatar bodies were highly regulated in many groups, not just in spiritual groups. There are large communities of Goreans, a role-playing cloud based on the hyperpatriarchal novels by the author John Norman, who are infamous for their strict gender rules and themed clothing. During our research, upscale dance clubs like Rick's Place, based on a 1940 nightspot, also enforced formal attire in the form of ball gowns. And some regions, like Huntington Bay Nude Beach, required a lack of clothes for female avatars. In other words, for the spiritualization of dress to be effective, it was not enough for a practice to simply differentiate itself from the norm; it also needed to be associated with a group's ultimate reality. For instance, while a lack of clothes plays one function at Huntington Bay Nude Beach, at the Skyclad Wicca Coven, lack of clothing ties practitioners into, as an information note card read, "your natural self" – what this group of witches articulates as their ultimate source of power.

Fundamentalist

The first of the three strategies we uncovered was a dwelling fundamentalism, which addresses networked consumerism by attempting to occupy a traditional ultimate reality. Choosing to hold fast to an imagined tradition is a natural reaction to consumerism's enforced individualization, which tackles

Network Consumer uncertainty by setting sharp boundaries through personal discipline, steadfastness, and regular readings and prayers. Most fundamentalists expressed the notion that the avatar was little more than a mask for the authentic real-life self. There was a strict policing between the identity of the user and the avatar he or she played. The group Real Ladies was run by the resident Judy Judge, who oversaw some of the most important Christian regions. After Judy suspected that many users were gender swapping, she created the group. After speaking with Judy (which was her name in both the virtual and actual world) on the phone, residents could join the group and use the title "I'm a Real Lady."

Even some religious groups who described the platform as nothing more than a chat room, and thought of avatars as "a little silly," often treated female avatars' bodies as important. The region of Scripture Island required that female avatars dress appropriately. Scripture Island described itself as a "neat place where there is all kinds of Bible studies," but warns "PLEASE DRESS MOD-ESTLY" (capitalization in original). The reason given was that Scripture Island was a "Family Area" where many children watch their parents as they come there to study the Bible. When one teleports in, the first thing one encounters is a sign that reads, "Dear Ladies, Please cover yourself up so you do not show any cleavage or stomach and please have your dress long enough so that when you sit down it laps over your knee (1 Timothy 2:9–10)."[35] At the landing point is a *teleporter* offered for women that sends them to a dressing room that offers "plain dresses, modest undergarments, and flat shoes." No such appropriate dress was available for men. In a similar fashion, a note card titled "Clothing" from a Muslim region reads, "In Islam, dressing modestly is an obligation placed on us by Allah (God)." For women the "whole body is required to be fully covered except face, hands and feet. . . . especially if you are inside any mosque on the *sim*, or near the Holy Kaaba."

New Age

During our research, the second of the three strategies was a seeking New Age spirituality, which saw in the increasingly pluralistic, immoral, and religious setting of consumer society the need to negotiate one's own spiritual path in the midst of endless alternatives. This is a strategy of letting go, of seeking wholeness by overcoming the barriers that separate people from one another, and of emphasizing intuitive feelings more than a cognitive understanding. For the spirituality of seeking, the divine is negotiable; whatever you believe is true, as the pagan practitioner, Megan Megadon said, "at least for you." As described in chapter two, a spirituality of seeking tends to have three main aspects. First, it puts forth the understanding that union with the divine is possible. Second, it seeks a grain of truth in all religions. Finally, a spirituality of seeking has a monistic, or unified, worldview that seeks not membership in a particular faith but connections between different traditions.

For New Agers, spiritual authenticity tends to lie with the avatar, because it allows users to reveal their true inner nature. As the New Age resident Thoth Sandy said, "People lose themselves all the time or even identify more with their avatar here than their self in real life." For the New Age, Second Life is a magical space that allows them to use their will to create reality, and an authentic resident was one who used his or her avatar to reveal his or her inner spirituality. A note card described the Pagan Learning Grove as "a place for people to freely find their path of spiritual growth." As Thoth went on to say, "because real life does not always show one's true self." Ironically, in this world of individuals, how one marks one's distinction was often through shopping. Such growth was seen to stem from one's inner self, which was often made visible to others through dress. In New Age regions, there is no uniform or habit, like at Scripture Island. Instead, vast regions on Second Life were devoted to New Age shopping. The owner of one store, Megan said, "spirituality should not tell you what to wear, but what to wear to be yourself. If you are going to follow a religion that favors diversity. Wear whatever you desire!"

For New Agers authentic gender was not based on your real-life body but on your core inner self. Still there was not much room for in-betweens. You could be whatever you wanted as long as you were clearly defined as a male or female. As can be seen in the many fashion outlets, in Second Life these norms are easily purchasable. Interestingly, while an authentic gender did not rely on a networked cisgendered resident, those whose avatar matched the gender the user was assigned at birth, New Ager groups often ended up with binary gender roles similar to those of fundamentalists.[36] While my research team was unable to follows up, we hypothesized that the systematic heteronormativity may have to do with a neopagan belief in male and female deities. As the blogger and GreenPatch Witch Chi writes, in "Disenchantment and a Sense of True Polarity," "It's somewhat troubling to walk into the local New Age shop and see a sculpture of Pan who looks like he's on steroids, or a poster with Rhiannon who looks like she's impersonating a prostitute from a bad sci-fi film – complete with a 21 inch waist and boobs roughly the size of her head."[37]

Mindful

As described in chapter two, convert Zen Buddhists engage Network Consumer Society through mindfulness, a practice that cultivates a calm awareness of one's body functions, feelings, content of consciousness, and consciousness itself. The mindful tactic sees ultimate reality as empty, an important aspect of which is the impermanent nature of the self (*anātman*). The mindful approach obviously differs from a fundamentalist logic that argues that there is only one truth and one way of being human based on that truth. Convert Buddhism also differs from New Age practices because of how it engages the self. New Agers maintain that because all ideologies lie, all you have is yourself – that inner stable core. Convert Buddhism, on the other hand, maintains that there are neither permanent ideologies nor permanent selves. As the Buddhist practitioner BodhiDharma Rosebud stated, "people say 'me me me' as if it belongs to us. But it was given to us by our parents, and also by plants and animals. We have taken it from others."

Hoben's virtual robes illustrate a mindful resident religious identity that is neither fundamentalist nor New Age. As can be seen through the lens of fashion, the fundamentalist mode, in response to the uncertainty of the Network Consumer Society, sees the need to police an authentic identity based on a correspondence between user and avatar. Contrary to this, the New Age tactic sees spiritual authenticity in the avatar's ability to create an online self freed from the constraints of the real world. The convert Buddhist sees authentic personal growth stemming from being mindful of the relationship between user and avatar, between the actual and virtual worlds. In the convert Buddhist context, mindfulness leads to a realization of emptiness (śūnyatā), a term that describes that nothing possesses essential, enduring identity. For convert Buddhists it is the realization of emptiness, which, in Bell's words, "aligns one with the ultimate source of power."[38]

The mindfulness of the self as empty was often described as "being the Buddha." For practitioners of Second Life's Zen cluster, as the "awakened one," the Buddha was not someone to be worshiped as divine but a model of practice to be emulated. A meditation note card titled "Entering the Heart of the Buddha" read, "Buddha was not a god. He was a human being like you and me, and he suffered just as we do." Because he was pictured as a model of awakening, many practitioners held, as Yidam Roads said in an interview from May 22, 2009, that they were "virtually walking in the Buddha's footprints." When I asked Human Riddle to describe the Buddha he answered, "you practice what you are." Twinkle MoonLight said, "the Buddha was a mortal man, not a god. The whole point of our practice is for everyone to become a Buddha (you probably already know that). But of course he was a supreme example!"

To become the Buddha was not, however, to transcend everyday life, but rather to cease suffering. When on May 25, 2009, I asked the resident Buddha Hat to describe the Buddha, he said, "an individual who realized Buddhahood – the end of suffering." For many at Hoben, what was ultimately authentic was the emptiness of the phenomenal world, as it appeared both in the actual and virtual forms. A typical answer to my question "are avatars real" was that they are no less real than the actual world, and residents often used the fashioning of avatars to indicate how the real-world personas are also ultimately empty. BodhiDharma Rosebud replied to my question about the reality of the virtual world: "A patriarch said, 'At the moment of profound insight, you transcend both appearance and emptiness. Don't search for the truth; just let go of your opinions.' Second Life and real life are no different. What you see is what you get."

The mindful spiritual path lay neither in the real-life user nor in the virtual avatar but in being mindful of the play between the two. After a Dharma talk, I asked Skeptical Starshine, "would you say you see your avatar as a mask, a reflection of a Real Life self, or as a projection of an inner self?" She answered, "At different times it is any of those things. Just like the self I project into the world via flesh." The gender-swapping resident Algama said, "I am both in real life, and Second Life, meat and pixels its all me, it's all me." One evening I was talking to Ashley Lee about her robes and asked, "I've got an abstract question, Do you see your Avatar as a mask, reflection of your real self, or as a projection of an inner self?" She laughed and replied, "mostly I just take classes, make things, garden, and make friends." There was a long pause, and she added, "Not a mask, for sure. Both my real life and Second Life me's are me." Pondering, I added, "I guess the question is 'what is that *real* self'?" Ashley smiled, "a moving point of balance. Water crashing against rocks. That's what makes trying to be real so tricky – need to be awfully mindful! Authentic. Integrity . . . that kind of thing."

The liberating fashion of virtual robes

Still a final question remains: Why did female avatars tend to wear the robes? And why in particular did a gender-swapping resident find the robes spiritually significant? I contend that for female avatars wearing the robes operated similarly to the American philosopher and gender theorist Judith Butler's theory of "drag," which refers to the clothing associated with one gender role when worn by a person of another gender. Butler argues that drag is subversive because, as she writes in *Bodies That Matter*, it "disputes heterosexuality's claim on naturalness and originality."[39] Butler contends that because drag exposes gender binaries, it makes the constructed aspect of gender obvious.[40]

Cyber Zen's claim is not that the female use of robes is a type of drag but that the virtual robes operated in a similar formal way and that by making avatars mindful of how gender functioned inworld offered a creative alternative to conventional heteronormative roles on both a political and spiritual level. Being mindful of gender does not deny that it is a real-world concern. Algama GossipGirl did not stop being a "guy" in real life because his avatar was female. Rather as a cyborg, s/he was nondual and revealed that ultimately gender is a socially constructed category, which nevertheless has inescapable implications in the conventional everyday lived world. Residents need gender norms in order to live. Yet they are constrained by these roles.

As with the practice of drag, the robes made the socially constructed nature of femininity more apparent. As Algama said, "when you are a male, man, you are just you for yourself. But when you are a girl, oh boy, you seem to be everyone's concern." In our conversation, Algama explained how she had always fantasized about being a girl, but that once she actually played one it had not been what she expected. "It was a lot of work!" Speaking about her avatar in the third person she admitted, "I still can not believe how concerned everyone seems about her looks. Or more realistically, I am concerned about how others think she looks. I'm not sure if this is just my problem, or if maybe people feel freer to comment on a woman's looks." She wondered if the appearance of a female avatar was always a public concern. "I just want to have fun, or do my job, and everyone is sticking their nose into my business." Algama admitted that she got better at playing herself and also that much of being a female avatar was dependent on Second Life's media practices. After a suggestion she had bought her avatar an *animation override (AO)*, a scripted attachment that replaces standard animations with animations created by residents.[41] "Now she looks natural, instead of like a brick wall. I also think that it makes her look more 'believable' in a way, because she looks more realistic and natural."

On a political level, the robe's austere and simple form allowed the fashioning of female avatars that were distinct from the hyperheteronormativity that dominated Second Life, and by extension Network Consumer Society more generally. Algama "*giggled*" that the robes gave "me an outfit that wasn't pink." On a political level, the robes expose Second Life's ideology of heteronormativity. The robes illuminated that inworld gender is constructed through residents' performance of a stylized repetition of acts, an imitation or miming of the dominant conventions of gender. Because gender is a performative act, the robes illuminated that in Second Life, there is no gender that precedes logging on. Also, because virtual gender subsumes real-life biological gender, the robes exposed that a user's real-life biological sex is also a social construction.

On a spiritual level, the robes afforded mindfulness of the constructed but necessary role of conventional reality. Like a form of mindfulness practice, the virtual robes enabled Algama to be mindful of her desires, which indicate that she did not escape gender but rather traversed through the fantasy that gave it power. For Algama, wearing of the virtual robes operated as a spiritual media practice because by affording an experience of the constructed empty nature of gender, it afforded a perception of the empty nature of the world more generally. "Being a girl in Second Life, kinda made me see how being a guy, was like you know, different, like role play." For convert Buddhists the authentic spiritual resident was nondualistic, which indicates that things appear distinct while not being separate and affirms the understanding that while distinctions exist, dichotomies are illusory phenomena. This does not mean that the gender roles are masks in a game of public presentation – because for the convert Buddhists there is no self behind the mask. Instead, the self is the practice. The robes allowed those who used a female avatar a media practice to explore the fluid and empty nature of identity. As Algama said, "I am a combination of my experiences, perceptions and understandings, both in Second Life and real life."

The Buddhologist Bernard Faure writes, in "Quand l'habit fait le moine," that above all monastic robes embody the "Buddhist Two Truths," a Mahāyāna

Buddhist doctrine that maintains that while there is a distinction between conventional reality and ultimate reality, in the end they are nondual and part of
the same lived world. As the Buddhist philosopher Nāgārjuna, writes in the
Fundamental Verses on the Middle Way (Mūlamadhyamakakārikā),

> The Buddha's teaching of the Dharma is based on two truths: a truth of
> worldly convention and an ultimate truth. Those who do not understand
> the distinction drawn between these two truths do not understand the
> Buddha's profound truth. Without a foundation in the conventional truth
> the significance of the ultimate cannot be taught. Without understanding the
> significance of the ultimate, liberation is not achieved.[42]

Conventional reality (*saṃvṛti-satya*) refers to the experience of everyday existence. Ultimate reality (*paramārtha-satya*) indicates emptiness (*śunyatā*), the perception that phenomena are impermanent collections of causes and conditions
that are designated by mere conceptual labels. In a similar formal fashion, just
as drag shows the constructed but necessary nature of gender, monastic robes,
whether virtual or actual, bring together an experience of these two truths and
show the necessary but conventional nature of lived worlds. As Faure writes,
through "the ideological manipulation of the symbols adhering to [monk
robes], the Zen adept gradually learned how to read through the superposed
symbolic systems, using the logic of the Two Truths, and to move from one
symbolic system to another."[43]

Conclusion

This chapter concentrated on the virtual robe-wearing gender-swapping resident Algama GossipGirl. Second Life gender swapping makes the media practices out of which gender emerges more conspicuous and allows researchers an
understanding of why female avatars tended to wear the robes. The wearing of
robes illustrates the interplay between gender, fashion, and spirituality on one
hand and the back and forth between user and avatar on the other. Hoben's
robes indicate how, while there is some room for play and agency, community standards and the platform's code shape residents' spiritual identity. In the
virtual world, there is no natural sexual difference and all gender is created
through media practices. One is not born a resident but rather becomes one.
There are genders on Second Life, however, if only virtual. The fact that they
are detached from the perceived biological sex of an individual's body makes
one more mindful of the fashioning of gender – it becomes more visible and
available for analysis.

To be clear, *Cyber Zen*'s point in this chapter is not simply to add to this
already abundant literature but rather to use the phenomenon of online gender
swapping to explore the role of Second Life spirituality in addressing an authentic self. In Second Life, each resident is a unique cybernetic being self-created

through media practices linking user and avatar. Cyborg captures the back-and-forth experience of the relationship between user and avatar and illustrates how selves are shaped online by the play of social forces compiled from the physical, biological, psychological, social, cultural, and spiritual aspects of its residents. Just as in the actual world, a virtual body employs the historical and cultural norms that define the gender: how it should look, walk, talk, and sit, for example. Fashion is significant in this investigation, because Network Consumer Society has dissolved traditional social roles, and in contemporary society people often wear clothing not just to protect themselves against the elements but also to shape identities.

An investigation of the robes is significant because they display how convert Zen's spiritual media practices fashion alternative subjectivities that operate as a product of and resistance against Network Consumer Society. Residents on Second Life are obviously formed through media practices that make the act of constituting one's identity and its roles more transparent. Hoben's virtual robes illustrate that convert Buddhist identity is neither a postmodern fragmented or modernist essentialist self but rather a mindful approach. Algama's modification of Hoben's virtual monk robes focuses the chapter's investigation on gender and allows us to observe different spiritual responses to the dissolving of traditional social roles. The virtual robes are significant because they have the capacity to denaturalize and thus articulate how bodies are constituted by norms. The virtual robes afford a mindfulness of how gender often reinscribes heteronormativity, and at other times playfully, even outrageously, disrupts it.

The wearing of virtual robes amounts to inhabiting a space between genders. Even if it does not immediately translate into political action and subversive identity politics, mindfulness engages in a profound social critique of heteronormativity. Wearing virtual robes probably does not confront conventional conceptions of agency as resistance to the social and political structures of control. Yet it does afford the possibility of different modalities of agency that transcend the conceptual binary of resistance versus submission. Being mindful of gender challenges and moves beyond this external-internal dynamics by illustrating that social norms are necessary for the articulation of not only subjectivity and the enactment of agency but of spirituality. Spiritual subjectivization secures a subject's subordination and is also the means by which she becomes a mindful agent.

The following chapter moves from the fashioning of individuals to the building of locations. As described in chapter two, convert Zen proves to be a practice-oriented spirituality that requires locations for its performance. Third places are community spaces that are neither home nor work, such as taverns, coffee shops, and beauty salons, and that host regular, voluntary gatherings that are marked by a playful mood.[44] Third spaces need not necessarily be physical locations but can also emerge through media practices.[45] While Second Life may be a third space allowing for experiments in new types of religious practices, residents are ultimately poachers who not only live in a corporate-owned reality but borrow liberally from a wide spectrum of popular spirituality. Poaching, as described by the American media scholar Henry Jenkins, is media practice that raids authoritative sources. As Jenkins writes, poaching is "a type of cultural bricolage through which readers fragment texts and reassemble the broken shards according to their own blueprint, salvaging bits and pieces of found material in making sense of their own social experience."[46]

Notes

1 For a menagerie of sources see: Charles Taylor, *Sources of the Self: The Making of the Modern Identity* (Cambridge, MA: Harvard University Press, 1989). Cf. Valentine Daniel, *Fluid Signs: Being a Person the Tamil Way* (Berkeley: University of California Press, 1984); Bruce Fink, *The Lacanian Subject: Between Language and Jouissance* (Princeton, NJ: Princeton University Press, 1995); Gregory Price Grieve, "There Is No Spoon? *The Matrix*, Ideology, and the Spiritual Logic of Late Capital," in *Teaching Religion and Film*, ed. Greg Watkins. American Academy of Religion's Religious Studies Series Teaching (Oxford: Oxford University Press, 2009, 189–207); Nicholas Negroponte, *Being Digital* (New York: Alfred Knopf, 1995).

2 Sherry Turkle, *The Second Self: Computers and the Human Spirit* (New York: Simon and Schuster, 1984); *Life on the Screen: Identity in the Age of Internet* (New York: Simon and Schuster, 1995); *Alone Together: Why We Expect More from Technology and Less from Each Other* (New York: Basic Books, 2011).

3 Anne Balsamo, *Technologies of the Gendered Body* (Durham, NC: Duke University Press, 1996).

4 Mark Hansen, *Bodies in Code: Interfaces with Digital Media* (New York: Routedge, 2006).

5 Amy Bruckman, "Gender Swapping on the Internet," Presented at the Internet Society, San Francisco, CA, August 1993, www.cc.gatech.edu/~asb/papers/gender-swapping.txt (accessed November 9, 2015).

6 See Ruth Barnes and Joanne B. Eicher, *Dress and Gender: Making and Meaning* (New York: Bloomsbury Academic, 1997); Barbara Burman, *Material Strategies: Dress and Gender in a Historical Perspective* (Malden, MA: Blackwell, 2003); Fred Davis, *Fashion Culture, and Identity* (Chicago: University of Chicago Press, 1992).

7 Bernard Faure, "Quand l'habit fait le moine: The Symbolism of the Kāsāya in Sōtō Zen," *Cahiers d'Extrême-Asie* 8, no. 3 (1995): 335.

8 William James, *The Principles of Psychology* (New York: Henry Holt and Company, 1890), 291.

9 Lila Abu-Lughod, "Writing against Culture," in *Feminist Anthropology: A Reader*, ed. Ellen Lewin (Malden, MA: Blackwell Publishing), 155.

10 "Resident," http://wiki.secondlife.com/wiki/Resident (accessed August 23, 2013).

11 "Press Room," *Linden Lab*, http://lindenlab.com/press_2.php (accessed February 3, 2010).

12 "Who Coined the Term 'Resident'?," Second Life Forums Archive," http://forums-archive.secondlife.com/139/e9/125712/1.html (accessed March 22, 2012).

13 Linden Lab, "Company Fact Sheet," 2007, www.lindenlab.com/.

14 "Linden Lab Official: Terms of Service Archive," http://wiki.secondlife.com/wiki/Linden_Lab_Official:Terms_of_Service_Archive (accessed November 9, 2015); "Community Standards," https://secondlife.com/corporate/cs.php (accessed November 9, 2015). Cf. "Terms of Service," Linden Lab, www.lindenlab.com/tos (accessed November 6, 2015).

15 James Wagner Au, *The Making of Second Life: Notes from the New World* (San Francisco: HarperCollins Publishers, 2008), 202.

16 Valerie Babb, *Whiteness Visible: The Meaning of Whiteness* (New York: New York University Press, 1998).

17 "Create Your Avatar," http://go.secondlife.com/landing/avatar/ (accessed August 28, 2016).

18 Katherine Hayles, *How We Became Posthuman: Virtual Bodies in Cybernetics, Literature, and Informatics* (Chicago: University of Chicago Press, 199), 291.

19 Kaja Silverman, *Male Subjectivity at the Margins* (New York: Routledge, 1992); *The Subject of Semiotics* (New York: Oxford University Press, 1983).

20 Donna Haraway, "A Cyborg Manifesto: Science, Technology, and Socialist-Feminism in the Late Twentieth Century," in *Simians, Cyborgs and Women: The Reinvention of Nature* (New York: Routledge, 1994), 149.

21 Norbert Wiener, *Cybernetics, or Control and Communication in the Animal and the Machine* (New York: Technology Press, 1948).

22 Manfred Clynes and Nathan Kline, "Cyborgs and Space," *Astronautics* (September 1960), 27.

23 Daniel Stephen Halacy, *Cyborg: Evolution of the Superman* (New York: Harper and Row, 1965), 7.

24 Andrew Pickering, "The Science of the Unknowable: Stafford Beer's Cybernetic Informatics," in *The History and Heritage of Scientific and Technological Information Systems*, eds. W. Boyd Rayward and Mary Ellen Bowden (New Jersey: Information Today, 2004), 29–38.

25 Clynes and Kline, 27.

26 Haraway, 149.

27 Haraway, 180.

28 "Linden Lab Official: Clarification of Policy Disallowing Ageplay," Linden_Lab_Official:Clarification_of_policy_disallowing_ageplay (accessed November 9, 2015).

29 "Linden Lab Official: Bot Policy," http://wiki.secondlife.com/wiki/Linden_Lab_Official:Bot_policy (accessed November 9, 2015).

30 Judith Butler, *Gender Trouble: Feminism and the Subversion of Identity* (New York: Routledge, 1990); *Bodies that Matter: On the Discursive Limits of "Sex"* (New York: Routledge, 1993); *The Psychic Life of Power* (Stanford, CA: Stanford University Press, 1997); *Undoing Gender* (New York: Routledge, 2004b); *Precarious Life: The Powers of Mourning and Violence* (New York: Verso, 2004a); *Giving an Account of Oneself* (New York: Fordham University Press, 2005).

31 Iris Marion Young, *On Female Body Experience: "Throwing Like a Girl" and Other Essays* (Oxford: Oxford University Press, 2005).

32 "X4 Female Starter Pack," www.getxcite.com/item_v2.php?product=2288 (accessed November 9, 2015).

33 Turkle, *Life on the Screen*, 192.

34 Catherine Bell, *Ritual Theory, Ritual Practice* (Oxford: Oxford University, 1992), 141.

35 "In like manner also, that women adorn themselves in modest apparel, with shamefacedness and sobriety; not with braided hair, or gold, or pearls, or costly array; but (which becometh women professing godliness) with good works." 1 Timothy 2:9–10 (KJV).

36 Kristen Schilt, "Doing Gender, Doing Heteronormativity: 'Gender Normals,' Transgender People, and the Social Maintenance of Heterosexuality," *Gender & Society* 23, no. 4 (2009): 440–64.

37 "Disenchantment and a Sense of True Polarity," www.witchvox.com/va/dt_va.html?a=uswa&c=gay&id=13741 (accessed November 10, 2015).

38 Bell, 141.

39 Butler, 1993, 125.

40 Butler, 1990, 179.

41 "Don't Know What an Animation Override Is You Need to See This – Second Life Viewer 2.3 Beta Tutorial," www.youtube.com/watch?v=0ZmSmO2dhV8 (accessed November 9, 2015).

42 Jay L. Garfield, *The Fundamental Wisdom of the Middle Way: Nagarjuna's Mūlamadhyamakakārikā* (New York: Oxford University Press, 1995), 296, 298.

43 Faure, 365.

44 Ray Oldenburg, *The Great Good Place: Cafes, Coffee Shops, Community Centers, Beauty Parlors, General Stores, Bars, Hangouts, and How They Get You through the Day* (New York: Paragon House, 1989).

45 Stewart Hoover and Nabil Echchaibi, "Media Theory and the 'Third Spaces of Digital Religion'," Center for Media, Religion, and Culture, University of Boulder, 2014.

46 Henry Jenkins, "*Star Trek* Rerun, Reread, Rewritten: Fan Writing as Textual Poaching," *Critical Studies in Mass Communication* 5, no. 2 (1988): 86.

Chapter 5

Place

Cosmologicalization, spiritual role play, and a third place zendo

> Only if we are capable of dwelling, only then can we build.
> Martin Heidegger, "Building Dwelling Thinking."[1]

To understand what enables convert Zen adherents to dwell online, this chapter investigates how to *build* an authentic spiritual *place* on Second Life. "Dwelling" indicates more than mere immersion, the perception that you are in a place, but that the space has a deep lasting meaning that emerges from social interaction and embodied practices that make a world livable. On Wednesday evening, January 21, 2009, I sat in Hoben Mountain Zen Retreat's empty *zendo*, or meditation hall. Because it provided a location for *events*, functioned as a meeting point for casual conversations and *Dharma talks*, and also operated as a symbol of the community, the zendo was the hub for most Second Life convert Buddhist practice. In the meditation hall, *zafus* (meditation cushions) were laid out in semicircular lines, so that when people sat on them they faced the central altar on which sat flowers, burning incense, and a statue of Siddhārtha Gautama Shakyamuni Buddha (Figure 5.1). There were two cushions facing away from the altar, and between them a meditation gong (*kesu*), which was referred to as the *bell*. I sat on a cushion facing away from the altar so that I could act as the meditation leader or *timekeeper*, who — and I quote from information given to me when I trained for this job — "is the person who holds the meditative space for the sitting practice of others. It is a practice of great generosity and deepening of mindfulness."

Can Hoben's virtual zendo be considered an authentic spiritual place? One might argue that the meditation hall has at best only a family resemblance to an actual zendo. As described in *Cyber Zen*'s introduction, however, authentic spiritual media practices do not necessarily mimic real life but are those that allow users to innovatively explore and create alternative identities and communities in relation to what they perceive as ultimately real. One might also argue that the digital media by their very nature are spiritual because they enable fantastic places.[2] Yet no place, either actual or virtual, is inherently religious, and much of Second Life was no better than a haphazard strip mall. In *Map Is Not Territory*,

Figure 5.1 Hoben Mountain Zen Retreat's zendo (meditation hall).

the historian of religion J. Z. Smith writes, "Religion is the quest, within the bounds of the human, historical condition, for the power to manipulate and negotiate ones 'situation' so as to have 'space' in which to meaningfully dwell."[3] Hoben's historical condition was digital media, and its situation was Network Consumer Society, which by disrupting many traditional real-life places of worship left a need for "third places." As we use the term, "third place" refers to social locations that are liminal alternatives between work and home, which in contemporary society are composed of a hybrid mix of everyday media practices and real-life locations.

Hoben's zendo, is a clear example of using digital media practices to create an authentic spiritual third place, and illustrates that such social environments transform the flat pixels of the screen into a sacred space. While in common usage the terms "place" and "space" are more or less interchangeable, I theorize space to indicate the abstract raw potential of unoccupied territory and use place to describe particular builds that people have made habitable by using cosmologies to turn space into organized lived places that have meaning and value for those who dwell there.

Hoben residents transformed the raw abstract potential of cyberspace into a place through virtual bodies interacting with virtual objects that afforded immersion and social interaction. During my research team's fieldwork, what changed

Hoben's virtual places into spiritual locations in which to dwell were *saṃsaric* cosmologies. Cosmologies are neither preexisting states of being nor cognitive maps of the world. Cosmologies are world-building media practices that residents employ to create and maintain lived realities by turning first order space into second order place. For most at Hoben, this was done through the cosmology of *saṃsāra*, which was tied into the Buddhist notion of dependent origination (*pratītyasamutpāda*), that all things arise only in relationship to other things. As I illustrate below, for many convert Buddhists, these cosmological media practices were entangled with a cybernetic model of feedback and networked systems. This cybernetic relation to contemporary Zen can be found in scholars such as the American deep ecologist Joanna Macy but at Hoben was best revealed by the Vietnamese Buddhist monk Thích Nhất Hạnh's concept of "Interbeing," which describes how people exist only in relation to other human and nonhuman elements.

Understanding how Zen practitioners built an authentic spiritual place is significant because Second Life allowed convert Buddhist innovative cosmologies of ideal places. Many Second Life Buddhist practitioners wanted a virtual place that did not merely copy the actual world, but as the resident Mystic Moon declared, was "better than real life." By this, Mystic meant a place that by manifesting a fantasized Buddhist "pure" cosmology afforded authentic spiritual practice that might be lacking in the actual world. In real life, convert Buddhists usually lived in cities, often had to meet in less than ideal spaces, used the implements at hand, dressed to meet climate conditions with available materials, and were forced by their circumstances to associate with a particular local group and its lineage.[4] In Second Life, they could build places that were constrained only by their imagination and the limits of the Second Life platform. I maintain that Hoben's zendo is not just an isolated case but rather offers a glimpse of how popular forms of spirituality are both a product of and response to Network Consumer Society. Laurence Moore writes, in *Religious Outsiders and the Making of Americans*, the study of American religion suffers from the providential myth of Protestant hegemony, while in fact "'mainline' has all too often been misleadingly used to label what is 'normal' in American life and 'outsider' to characterize what is aberrational or not-yet-American."[5] Moore goes on to suggest that the "American religious system is 'working' only when it is . . . producing novelty."[6]

A virtual zendo

The Hoben community built their virtual zendo. On Second Life, "builds" refer to virtual environments created or modified by residents using the platform's built-in *building tools* to create and manipulate *primitives* as well as employing *textures* and *scripts*. As the website "Building Tools" reads, "The Second Life viewer has built-in tools to create and modify objects, a process known as 'building.' Once created, objects can be stored in your personal inventory, shared with other users, or placed somewhere within the 3D world."[7] Primitives (or just prims) refer to three-dimensional shapes such as cubes, spheres, and cylinders that residents can edit and cut to a variety of shapes, color, add different textures, add parameters and properties, and make flexible as well as cause to emit light. "Textures" are images that are used to cover the faces of a virtual object. "Scripts" refer to the Linden Scripting Language (LSL), which can be inserted into builds so that they give behaviors to Second Life objects and avatars.

Using the platform's building tools, the Second Life Zen community built spiritual places that focused on zendos. In Japanese, *zen-dō* translates as the "place of Zen" and is where *zazen* (sitting meditation) is practiced. Hoben's zendo was at the center of the region and also at the center of practice. It sat in the middle of a forested island that was surrounded by rough seas and modeled on an Asian mountain retreat. During our research, the region's other buildings included three meditation halls, two temples, a monks' retreat, rental cabins, a gift shop, a lounge, spaces for Tai Chi and concerts, as well as a wisdom publication library, HIV (human immunodeficiency virus) Awareness Center, and an Addiction Recovery Center (Figure 5.2).

In hindsight, it was really not surprising that we found a virtual zendo on Second Life. During our research it seemed as if residents had built just about

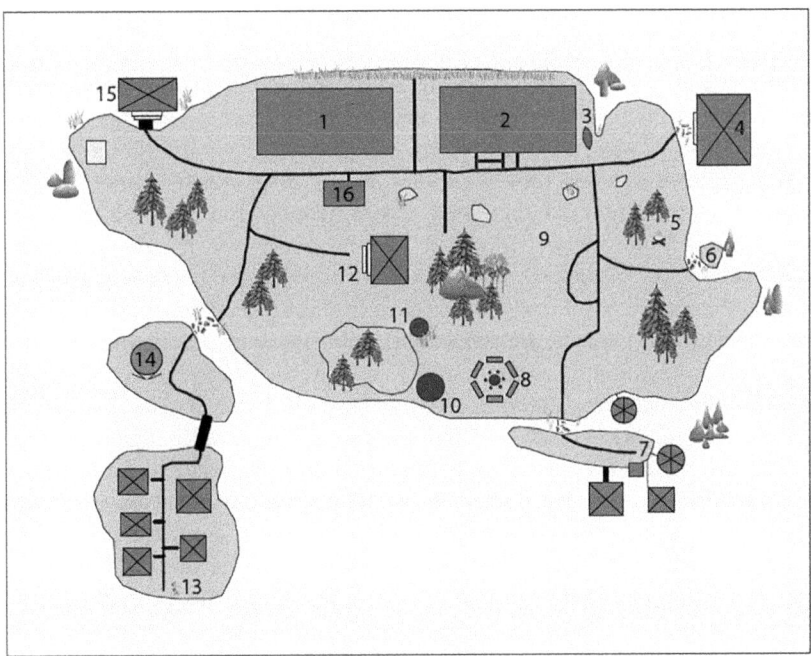

Figure 5.2 Map of Hoben Mountain Zen Retreat, July 2010. (Map key: 1, Entrance/Imports; 2, Zendo/Game Room; 3, Canoe Tour; 4, Five Peak Sangha; 5, Live Music Events; 6, Tai Chi; 7, Residences; 8, Drumming Circle; 9, Majestic Forest; 10, Sweat Lodge; 11, Tree Stump; 12, Temple; 13, Human's Garden; 14, Hot Air Balloon Tour; 15, Myohoji Temple; 16, HIV Information.)

(Map created by Kristin B. Johnston.)

everything one could imagine, from the Vietnam War Memorial and the Great Wall of China, to the Hollywood Airport, where I kept my zeppelin, to a surreal version of Pfaffenthal in Luxembourg City, where I went to buy a bowler hat. Because sacred locations proved to be some of the most potent cosmological locations, Second Life builds included many religious places. Inworld, my research team found Hindu temples, Christian churches, synagogues, Pagan fire circles, virtual Hajjs, and even a Buddhist hell. Religious builds either mimicked real life, such as a copy of the Saint Michael shrine from Tarpon Springs, Florida, or they could be fantastic places straight out of the imagination, such as the Grove of the Greenman. One might assume that because the Saint Michael shrine mimicked a real-life structure that it would be the most religiously authentic. We argue that while the Saint Michael shrine was an almost perfect copy of an actual world structure, it did not function as an authentic spiritual place because it was not the focus of religious practice. On the other hand, the Grove of the Greenman, which was pure fantasy, operated authentically because it was almost always filled with practitioners.[8]

Hoben's zendo, reflecting their practice of mindfulness, lay somewhere betwixt and between the two extremes of mimicry and pure fantasy. I found that New Age groups often privileged the imaginary space of Second Life, giving the platform's fantasy more authenticity than the real world itself. Fundamentalist groups, on the other hand, tended to shy away from Second Life and privileged the authenticity of the real world, often using the platform as little more than a *chat room*. Hoben residents took a mindful middle path, which did not copy any one particular building but rather was a compilation of ideal convert Zen practice spaces translated into the virtual world. Hoben's zendo was pragmatic in that it incorporated many of the practical elements of convert Zen practice spaces. Yet it was also fantastic, in that it displayed an ideal Buddhist environment. In more traditional Asian Zen practice, the meditation hall is set apart, and communal social spaces tend to revolve around food, such as the kitchen. As the scholar of Korean Buddhism and Chinese Buddhism Robert Buswell writes in *The Zen Monastic Experience*, the meditation hall is a "training ground" and "a laboratory in which the ideal atmosphere for practice is maintained."[9] In American convert Buddhism the zendo is key for both social interaction and spiritual practice. Convert American Buddhists simply do not have as much space and often make do with the architecture that they find at hand. As the scholar of American Buddhism Jeff Wilson writes, in *Dixie Dharma*, "the pattern of Buddha-cizing preexisting spaces by simply bringing in Buddhist images and ritual implements is repeated across the country, in houses as well as apartments, storefronts, garages, and even barns."[10]

Places

On Second Life, "places" are the virtual environments built by residents in which avatars dwell and consist of an almost unimaginable variety of venues. As a *builder* said to me as I was *scripting* in a *sandbox*, "If you *rez* it, they will come." Filtering the Second Life search engine for "places" reveals parcels of virtual land larger than 144 meters^2.[11] The Second Life wiki, "Land," describes a parcel as "an area of land owned by a single user or group, which is at least 16m^2 and at maximum 65,536m^2, all within one region."[12] Land emerges out of Second Life's abstract *grid*, whose code is stored on computers and made available through the Internet. The grid is the underlying structure of Second Life and consists of a collection of network computer servers that implement the presentation of land and inworld physics.

Building on Second Life allowed residents to express their lived reality and themselves. Their cosmologies coincided with their building, both what they build and how they built it. If the land is abstract space, then Second Life cosmological media practices turn the raw potential of the grid into locations in which residents dwell. Places are not found but must be painstakingly built up from raw pixels through many hours of labor. By labor, we do not simply mean the hours spent clicking a mouse and typing on a keyboard. Labor defines the creative ability of people to make manifest their fantasies in the world through building and socializing.[13] As the resident Khandroma Cypress, a builder and creator, said on May 22, 2009, "The whole concept of [Second Life] and what you could do fascinated me. Once I got here, I got hooked on the possibilities for creativity and networking."

In Second Life places are not inherently meaningful but must be built by residents to create a place to dwell. In Second Life, building allowed for dwelling and is what makes virtual worlds distinct from other online flat digital media practices such as email, websites, and social media. We theorized dwelling as a phenomenological experience of abiding in an authentic place. In "Building Dwelling Thinking," the German phenomenological philosopher Martin Heidegger describes dwelling as the ability "to cherish and protect, to preserve and care for."[14] As I described in the last chapter, such care depends upon a sense of embodied perception, in which the body plays a central role in how people engage with the world. Residents not only experience the virtual world around them but also see themselves in Second Life. As the French phenomenologist Maurice Merleau-Ponty writes in "Eye and Mind," "The world is made of the very stuff of the body."[15] The dwelling resident and the virtual world are entangled, and media practices and body are intimately interwined. As Merleau-Ponty envisions, they are of the same "fabric," the same "flesh."[16]

Objects

Virtual objects afford dwelling. One might assume that, being made out of just pixels and code, virtual objects are unreal. Scripted objects make Second Life different from nonvirtual world digital media practices such as the World Wide Web and email. Obviously in the end there really is no difference between a virtual world and the web. Both are merely pixels on the screen that are controlled by users through keystrokes and mouse clicks. On the conventional level of lived media practice, however, virtual objects have a "materiality," a term that refers not only to the concrete physical world but also to the fact that objects are pragmatic as well as semantic. As a *New York Times* article from September 9, 2007, reminds us, "Even in a Virtual World, 'Stuff' Matters."

Inworld, as the Second Life wiki "Object" reads, "an object is either a single prim or a link set (a collection several linked prims). An object can be attached to an avatar and there are various scripting functions that can affect an object."[17] In Second Life objects can be such things as cars, houses, jewelry, and even less obvious things like hair and clothing. Residents usually make objects inworld using the built-in editing tools that set shape, color, and texture. Second Life objects can be set to seven materials that determine physical occurrences like friction and collision sound. Such virtual objects are linked to a set of primitives that often contain *scripts*. Script refers to the LSL, which has a syntax similar to C and allows for the control of inworld objects. For instance, if one puts the default script, "Hello, Avatar," into an object, that object will say in public chat "Hello, Avatar!" when the object is touched.[18]

All religious practice requires material culture, and it is through interaction with it that practitioners become entangled with a tradition. Virtual Buddhism does not differ. While often perceived as purely philosophical, in real life, Buddhists use objects in their practice that are often not only material but sensual and convey not only an ontology but an ethos. Almost every actual world Buddhist monastery has a temple with at least one statue of the Buddha, and often the laity have in their houses a small shrine or at least a picture of Buddha with a tiny altar before it.[19] Because of how religion becomes translated into the virtual world, this materiality is even more apparent on Second Life. During our research there was no lack of Second Life religious objects that were significant not only because of their aesthetic qualities but more often because they engaged with a group's ultimate reality, those ontological models that include both the content of what is ultimately real and what is not but also the larger cultural matrix that shapes the abstract idea of reality itself. Sometimes the connection for religious objects was for actual world resemblance. Take, for example, the Christian object, the Cross Necklace, whose accompanying note card reads, "The cross is the symbol of our faith. We wear it as a testimony of the price that Jesus Christ paid that dark day of his crucifixion." For New Agers, objects often stood in for an ultimate concern perceived to be lacking in the actual world. To give a few examples, pagan objects included such things as a Goblet of Mead, Black Marble Altar, and an Impoloc Candle. As described below, convert Zen objects, such as the virtual meditation cushion, were significant neither for transmitting the meaning of a symbol, nor because they filled what was missing in real life, but because by communicating silence they structured bodily practices.

Social interaction

Objects enhance cosmological media practices through social interaction. During our research, built places afforded a sense of "immersion," the feeling of being there, which our 2010 survey (n=108) showed 86.7 percent of residents felt always or often when using Second Life. Immersion describes the feeling of being in a place that emerged from interactivity with Second Life's builds and shifts users from merely seeking information to navigating through places. In Second Life, residents are able to walk, run, fly, swim, or *teleport* throughout immensely variable, virtual physical environments; they are able to dance, hug, and even sit in full lotus. The media practices of an "immersed" user are different from those of one seeking to extract information or a passive viewer. Instead of text-based experience aimed at finding and connecting pieces of data, or giving in to a cinematic gaze, the goals of an immersed user include bodily sensory awareness. As Wagner James Au writes in *The Making of Second Life: Notes from the New World*, "[t]o be immersed in an online world is to be helped into a similar illusion, but also to feel enveloped within it, as a bodily sensation. And if you run through that waterfall, your stomach will lurch in the moment that you leap and see the sharp rocks rushing up at you."[20]

While mediated by digital media, however, ultimately what people on Second Life are interested in is other people. To actualize a place's immersive qualities interaction with other residents was key. While virtual environments enable social interaction, the desire to interact with other residents makes Hoben a community and Second Life a place. Our survey in 2010 showed that 98.8 percent of Buddhist residents had felt a connection with other residents at some time when using Second Life. Such social interaction is what draws residents in and keeps them coming back. As the pioneer of digital virtual worlds Richard Bartle writes in *Designing Virtual Worlds*, social interaction "makes virtual worlds incredibly sticky – much stickier than related leisure-time pursuits such as books, computer games, movies and television."[21] "Sticky" describes the amount of time people use a particular media and the increased users' retention and duration.

A virtual cushion

Convert Buddhists took a middle path between mimicry and pure fantasy, and the object central to their practices was the zafu, or meditation cushion, that affords mindfulness by communicating silence (Figure 5.3). Although it was acknowledged, as Cassius Lawndale said, "that true Buddhist practice does not start or stop on the cushion," the meditation cushion was at the heart of Second Life Buddhist practice because it communicated silence. Scripted objects were especially important to Zen groups because meditation cushions ritualized residents' bodies by affording animations that signify silence. As explored in the following chapter, while embodiment plays a part in many of Second Life's

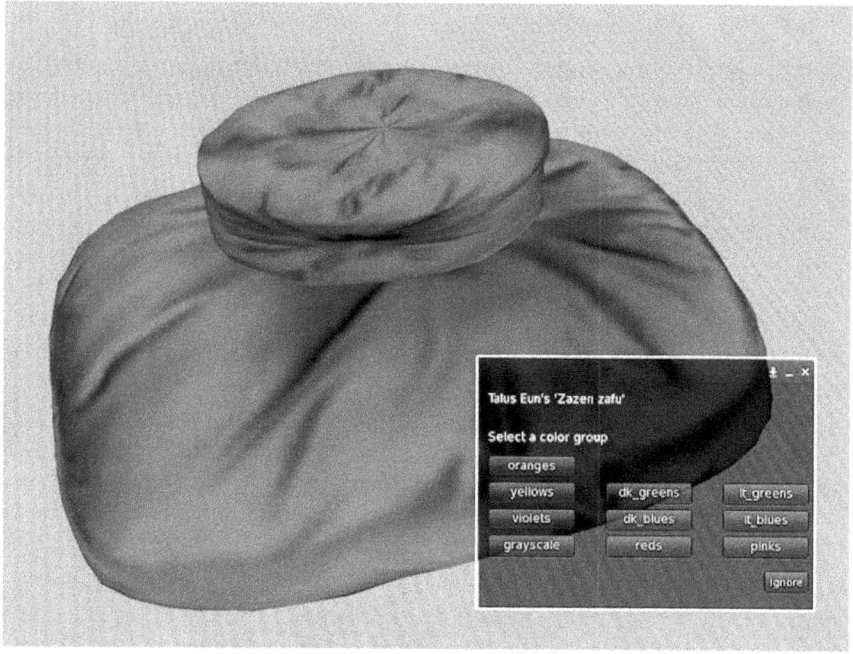

Figure 5.3 The Peaceful Warrior zafu and zabuton created by the resident Talus Eun.

(Second Life Snapshot by Gregory Price Grieve).

groups, such spiritual bodily practice is particularly important to the religious imagination of convert practitioners because they tend to imagine authentic spirituality as transmitted outside of language.

Cushions make evident that to some extent online silent meditation events exchange information about Buddhist teachings; what is key, however, is an online ritual component that spiritualizes silence. Virtual meditation cushions pragmatically determine how practitioners ritualize silence. Because Buddhism is a material practice as well as a matter of beliefs, it is dependent on objects and spaces as much as, or more so, than on ideas and doctrine. The cushion, whether virtual or actual, is important because it illustrates that convert Buddhism is more than images of the Buddha, particular scriptures, and even statements of belief such as the Four Noble Truths. At its heart convert Buddhism understands itself as a practice. At Hoben, as for most convert Buddhists, because meditation cushions both signify and enable the enactment of the practice of silent seated meditation, they indicate the "marrow" of the tradition. As BodhiDharma Rosebud said when I first asked him what to do in the meditation hall, "just remain on your cushion without expecting anything."

All religious groups that we encountered during our research used objects. Consider, for instance, "Holy Spirit Righteousness, Peace, And Joy Version 1.0" that residents could wear. Every ten minutes when wearing the Holy Spirit it would read a line of the New Testament in public chat. Meditation cushions, however, were different because they engaged with the community's core spiritual ontologies not through content but by creating ritualized media practices centered on the resident's body. Unlike a film or book, one does not simply read a virtual world but is immersed and embodied by it. Online silent meditation is a diachronic procedure of movements executed by residents, which instead of being read as a text, are enacted using the unique affordances of the virtual world.

In real life, a zafu, often translated in English as "sewn seat," is a meditation cushion used for zazen, or Zen meditation. Typically a zafu is a round shape about 15 inches across and packed tight with kapok, a silky fiber obtained from the fruit of the silk cotton tree. Meditation cushions are often placed on a *zabuton*, a mat used in Japan for sitting on the floor. In convert Buddhism, "the cushion" is not just a prop but is often used as a synecdoche for spiritual practice. The website "Buddhism in the West," on buddhanet.net, describing a ten-day retreat at the Blue Mountains Insight Meditation Center in Australia, states, "The basis of Buddhist practice in the West, as in the East, is meditation, and people may sit on cushions with their legs folded and hands in laps."[22] Yet, more important than their symbolic content is that cushions channel bodily practice. James William Coleman's study, *The New Buddhism: The Western Transformations of an Ancient Tradition*, pivots on a description of convert Buddhist practice, which concludes by saying, "Each person goes to the front of one of the black cushions and bows. Turning to their right they bow again, and finally they mount the platform and take their place on the cushion."[23]

Online silent meditation was often signified through reference to "the cushion." For example, at the start of a meditation session on May 5, 2010, the resident Artemis Huckleberry introduced himself by saying, "I've come for an empty cushion, to sit in emptiness." While modeled on real life, during our research, Second Life meditation cushions varied from simple and scripted for a single position to intricately sculpted and multiply scripted ones. For instance, the "Simple Zafu" was ubiquitous throughout Second Life's Buddhist community and can be traced back to the originally named "Japanese Sit Pillow," which was created by CrystalShard, a well-known builder, who had created them as a *freebie* to be included along with one of the first items she had ever designed, a sushi table created in 2004. Because the cushion was *full perm* (free to *copy, modify,* and *transfer*), over the years the Japanese Sit Pillow had become a meme; residents have customized and changed the original, and versions of it can be found all over Second Life. The Peaceful Warrior zafu and zabuton was a more complicated cushion created by resident Talus Eun that can be purchased for L$100 ($0.73 USD) and was "created as an aid to your Second Life Meditation Practice." Eun's cushion offered the sound of "restful breathing" and a *menu* with 512 separate colors choices and hundreds of poses. The resident BrokenBridge commented on the "Senshi: Art and Arms'" webpage, "by far the best looking zafu/zabuton I have found and I find the subtle breathing very centering."

Spiritual places

Hoben was not just any place, however, but was a spiritual location for the community's practitioners that addressed what was seen to be ultimately lacking in a Network Consumer's life. Besides Buddhism, spiritual places were a major feature of many Second Life regions and included Christian, Islamic, Jewish, and neopagan regions. When we first started fieldwork, my team attempted to catalogue all the religious regions by *landmarking* them, but after mapping over five hundred, we stopped. The problem was not just with the sheer number but that, like ice in a quickly flowing stream, the places were forming and dissolving at such a rate that it was difficult to give an accurate count. Unlike the actual world where abandoned buildings leave ruins, in Second Life all that remains is an error code.

Because they were built by residents, Second Life's religious places both afford and display a group's spirituality, which as I described in chapter two refers to media practices that create moral economies of what groups perceive to be ultimately real but lacking in the actual world. A Christian group laid out their cosmology in a note card titled "Code of Conduct," "Love, Respect and Honor God Above all Else. No Nudity at any time! No Abusive or Vile Language. Treat All Others with Dignity and Respect." Beyond just written rules, residents could literally embody their cosmology by crafting spiritual places constrained only by the limits of the platform's media practices. Practitioners could conjure up any type of image or item they wished to virtually interact with; they could dress their avatars however they chose; they could cobble together as many elements of as many religions as they fantasized, as well as introduce other traditions' elements or invent new things. Beyond the owners of a region, during our research on Second Life, there was no specific local authority policing anyone's identity or its representations, and it could thus be as orthodox or innovative as a resident desired.

While the rationales and strategies for spiritualization differ, a cosmological space is, ultimately, a place that has been set apart and tied to an ultimate reality. American convert Buddhists at Hoben strove for a landscape of silence and visual simplicity embedded in an aesthetics strongly influenced by a romanticized notion of a premodern Asian landscape. The Hoben landscape afforded mindfulness and was built to draw a resident's attention toward spiritual practice. Community members moved among the landscapes and buildings, acquiring a sense of direction and a spiritual frame of reference that created place by structuring events, relationships, and avatars' bodies. Visual elements dominated: buildings, mountains, and forests. Also, just as in real life, sound helped guide community members – the splash of running water, the ringing of a bell, and scripted chanting gave a sense of dwelling. Of crucial importance was silence. As the opposite of the usual noisy and visually cluttered strip mall–like quality of the virtual world, silence signified Hoben as a place that differed from typical Network Consumer Society and residents' hurried and uncertain lives. Places were crucial to such practices. As one resident responded to our 2010 survey, Hoben is a "way to exit reality and just concentrate on images in front of you. It's hard in this day and age to Meditate in a calm setting in the hustle and bustle of the city. In Second Life I choose the surroundings I feel at home in." As the resident Ashley Lee said in a conversation, Hoben's virtual calm "is a breath of fresh air."

Cosmologicalization

Cosmology is neither a preexisting phenomenon out there in the world nor merely a cognitive map existing in people's minds. Cosmologies are the spiritual media practices that turn space into place. As I described in chapter two, spiritual Second Life locations are not unreal but are media practices that generate a moral economy that engages with what is perceived to be ultimately lacking in particular social situations. Often cosmologies are understood simply as how a particular group views the universe. We theorize cosmologies as world-building media practices that transform abstract space into lived places. As such, cosmologies are not inherent but define a group's ultimate fantasies about existence that transform first order space into second order place.[24] Cosmology's ability to transform abstract territory into place is true both for physical space and cyberspace, which as I described in chapter one, indicates the social space created through computer networks.

Cosmologicalization defines the media practices by which people build spiritual places and these spiritual places fold back and constitute the users and their lived world. Cosmologies are not an expression of an already existing reality; rather, a place is made habitable through world-building media practices. Cosmological media practices are dialectic in that they are the products of residents, and nothing but the product of residents, yet these cosmological media practices continuously act back on their producers, shaping them.[25] Second Life's media practices create cosmologies through a three-step process: externalization, objectification, and internalization. First, users externalize a cosmos by communicating with other residents. "Externalization" denotes residents acting upon and creating the virtual world. One sees this clearly in Second Life where residents build not only objects, practices, and even themselves but also relationships and communities. Second, these externalized phenomena become an objective social reality. "Objectification" signals when humanly constructed phenomena have taken on a social life of their own that shapes residents and channels their actions. "Objectification" occurs when a lived world created by a group of people – as material objects, concepts, and human relationships – confronts them as a facticity external to and other than themselves. Even in a virtual world, because it consists not just of pixels but also of networks also of people, once produced cannot simply be wished away. It is something "out there," which resists the desires of its producers. Third, residents internalize the objectified media practices. "Internalization" signifies when the facticity of the world becomes subjectified and is apparent in Second Life during immersion, when users become so caught up in a world that it obliterates attention to the actual world.

Role play

Cosmologicalization was enhanced through spiritual media practices that borrowed from role play. Many residents, and the corporate owners of Second Life, Linden Lab, vehemently denied that Second Life was a game and instead wanted to characterize it as a three-dimensional chat room. This has a ring of truth. If one limits the definition of play to sport – what residents in Second Life often called "gamist" – then Second Life is not. The virtual world did not have points that players could gather by vanquishing opponents as in a first person shooter game. Residents could not level up by completing quests or other challenges as in classic video games. In fact there was no way to "beat" Second Life. Play on the platform was like the "elder game" of more traditional video games. "Elder game" describes when a player in a traditional digital game has beaten it but does not want to leave and spends time socializing and creating.[26]

Yet if one extends play to include "pretending," like in playing house, or theater, then Second Life is a "game" in which residents' media practices manifest and become immersed in fantastic worlds. *Cyber Zen* contends that the jump from play to spirituality, from fantastic to cosmological, is more than merely a leap of faith but involves authentic media practices that are enabled by the serious pretend of role play. Lying between the inner and outer worlds, the British psychologist D. W. Winnicott argues that play serves as the basis for creativity and the discovery of authentic forms of being in the world. As he writes in *Playing and Reality*, "In this play area the child gathers objects or phenomena from external reality and uses these in the service of some sample derived from inner reality."[27] For Winnicott, play refers not just to what children do, but to adult creative arts and sports. It is only in these moments of creativity that an authentic self can be achieved. As Winnicott writes, "Only the true self can be creative and only the true self can feel real."

During our research, such play was labeled *role-playing*, which the Second Life wiki describes as "simply pretending to be someone or something to simulate an experience, usually interacting with others doing the same. The simplest 'game' is just a gathering of friends, indulging in a common tale."[28] The different role-play spaces were described as *realms*: "The setting of the 'game'. It contains other things than just the visual surroundings, it includes some story elements and background data of the world the game is placed in."[29] The different role-play avatars were often described as *characters*, a "tailored avatar for the part, like a movie actor one should pre-meditate the outlook & characteristics of a character."[30]

Spiritual role play

We argue that Hoben's cosmology was enacted through serious spiritual role-playing. Often a dichotomy is assumed between serious spirituality and frivolous play. We want to stake a claim for an intermediate media practice of imagining alternative fantasy worlds, which is actually at the center of religion and art, and may be what ultimately makes us human. In the second appendix to *Man and the Sacred*, the French scholar Roger Caillois makes "the most daring thesis," that is, "the identification of play and the sacred."[31] Relying on game theorist Johan Huizinga's concept of the "magic circle," Caillois contends that games and religious practices are intimately entangled. For instance, the popular game Chutes and Ladders is based on a Tibetan game describing the stages of liberation to enlightenment, and the Game of Life is based on the Checkered Game of Life that instructed players in morality.

Even more daring, Caillois goes on to describe a formal similarity between play and sacred spaces. From an emic perspective, both practices seem to make stuff up. Because both create worlds of meaning set apart from everyday life, play spaces and sacred spaces have both physical and temporal limiting boundaries, as well as rules and narratives. The Dutch historian and one of the founders of game theory, Huizinga argues that both ritual and play occur within magic circles, which are socially imagined places that are differentiated by a social membrane constituted by location, duration, and order. Huizinga writes, "Just as there is no formal difference between play and ritual, so the 'consecrated spot' cannot be formally distinguished from the play-ground." They are "all temporary worlds within the ordinary world, dedicated to the performance of an act apart."[32] Magic circles are differentiated by location. Consider, for instance, the soccer field, which is marked off from everyday life. As Huizinga writes in *Homo Ludens*, play "transports the participants to another world."[33] And just like in sacred space "inside the playground an absolute and peculiar order reigns."[34]

On Second Life it was not always easy to separate spiritual media practices from role-playing. It has been argued that while playgrounds and sacred spaces have formal similarities, their orientation to the world differs radically. As the theorist of the religion of virtual worlds Rachel Wagner argues, in play the fate of the world is suspended, while in religious practice, the very fate of reality is at stake.[35] People play to fantasize outside of the actual world's limitations. In play, they engage with roles that may enhance learning, as well as self-healing and exploration, but in the end are mostly just fun. Religious practice, on the other hand, is ultimately about engaging ultimate reality in order to enhance transformation and salvation. A difficulty with Second Life is that it is difficult if not impossible to know when the media practices change from play to religious practice. There are some clues, such as the separation of *OOC* (Out of Character) and *IC* (In Character) communications and avatar clothing. Yet, at Hoben, there was a tendency to even use role-play conventions in every-day communication, such as the employment of asterisks to indicate actions (e.g., *bows and gasshos*) and also, as explored in the last chapter, to wear "in realm" attire such as Buddhist robes.[36]

Samsara

The cosmology, or realm setting, for Hoben's cosmology was *saṃsāra*, a Sanskrit word meaning to pass through a series of states or conditions that is also uti-lized by Hinduism, Buddhism, and Jainism. Many Hoben residents spoke about Second Life in terms of samsara. Late in our research, on the night of Friday, October 23, 2009, I asked the resident BodhiDharma Rosebud if Second Life was real. He answered, "Second Life and Real Life are both samsara, wheels turning wheels turning wheels turning wheels turning wheels." Interestingly, Linden Lab, Second Life's corporate creators, also often used the term "samsara" to refer to the platform. For instance, Robin Harper, Linden Lab's Senior Vice President of Community, writes, "We had a lot of ideas for place names – one of my favorites was Samsara, which was not only euphonic, but had an interest-ing meaning in the original Sanskrit, meaning roughly 'ever changing world'."[37] Also, Second Life's main grid is called Agni, named after the Hindu god of fire. The platform's preview grids are also named after Hindu gods, Shiva, Durga, Aditi, and Soma.

  Hoben's practitioners often understood the virtual world and its relation-ship to real life through the Buddhist concept of samsara, which indicates the constructed nature of existence and refers to both transmigration and the lived reality of the phenomenal world.[38] For convert Buddhists, samsara indicated not that Second Life was unreal, an illusion, but just impermanent and created from the interconnected desires of sentient beings. In one of my first conversations with the resident Rasa Vibration she said, "Second Life is just another layer of samsara, just one more layer of illusion created from your desires." For most Hoben members, phenomena, virtual and actual, were empty (*śūnyatā),* which means that they are impermanent and void of any inherent essential qualities. For many at Hoben, there were obvious differences between real life and Second Life. Yet they were similar because they both were characterized by suffering (*duḥkha*) and created by the process of dependent origination (*pratītyasamutpāda*) that was fueled by *karma*. Dependent origination describes how all phenomena only exist because of their relationship to other things. For Hoben practitio-ners, the lived conventional reality of samsara was created by karma, which was fueled by desires (*tṛṣṇā*). Karma refers to the spiritual belief that one's actions will influence the future condition of one's existence. As described in chapter two, desire for many at Hoben was pictured as a "thirst," which was based on ignorance and led to being stuck (*duḥkha)* in samsara. As Rasa said, "I suffer because I keep having the same relationship over and over again."

Interbeing

While residents' cosmological understanding of samsara has a family resemblance to Asian canonic texts, we maintain that it was entangled with cybernetic understanding of systems. This is part of a late twentieth-century tendency of conceiving of "world" as a system that is evidenced, for instance, in the writings of the American scholar Joanna Macy, who compiles Buddhist thought with systems theory and deep ecology. Systems theory studies self-regulating systems, and while some maintain that it predated cybernetics, there is no doubt a close correspondence between the two movements.[39] In *Mutual Causality in Buddhism and General Systems Theory: The Dharma of Natural Systems,* Macy writes that the general systems theory's "view of reality as a process, its perception of self-organizing patterns of physical and mental events, and the principles that it discerned in the dynamics of these natural systems struck me as remarkably consonant with the Buddha's teaching."[40] Macy finds a similarity between cybernetics and Buddhist thought in the idea of dependent arising. As she writes on her blog, "I have been deeply inspired by the Buddha's teaching of dependent co-arising. Helping me understand the non-hierarchical and self-organizing nature of life, it is the philosophic grounding of all my work."[41] Much like the resident Rasa Vibration, Macy understands that the codependence of the system is fueled by desire. "Neither factor is reducible to the other because they are mutually generative: As ignorance propels our craving, so does craving mire us in ignorance."[42]

At Hoben the entanglement of the cosmology of samsara with cybernetics was clear in the community's use of the Vietnamese Buddhist monk Thích Nhất Hạnh's concept of "Interbeing," which he defines as the cosmology that all "phenomena are interdependent . . . endlessly interwoven."[43] As the resident BodhiDharma Rosebud said, "we all breathe the same air, and piss the same water." Thích Nhất Hạnh maintains that we are all made up of interwoven human and nonhuman elements. As a Hoben note card titled "Going Home Part 3" and attributed to Thích Nhất Hạnh reads, "if you continue to look deeply, you will see that in the present moment, you continue to be a rose, a rabbit, a tree, and a rock. This is the truth of interbeing. You are made of non-you elements." A meditation note card handed out on April 4, 2008, titled "Zen Keys" and attributed to Thích Nhất Hạnh gives a sense of what Buddha was expressing. "Defiled or immaculate, increasing or decreasing – these concepts exist only in our minds. The reality of interbeing is unsurpassed." Many at Hoben perceived that interbeing was not just a cognitive thought but was experienced in the body. Interbeing has a spiritual element. As the resident Buddha Hat said, when we were talking about interbeing, "You need to do the spiritual work, put your time in on the cushion, to make and maintain interbeing as a lived truth, to understand that the natural world is our very own body and not merely as cognitive knowledge but as mindfulness."

Conclusion

This chapter explored Second Life's spiritual places, those virtual religious environments built by residents in which avatars dwell. Hoben residents transformed the raw abstract potential of cyberspace into a place through virtual bodies interacting with virtual objects that afforded immersion and social interaction. The chapter argued that residents' interaction with virtual objects afforded immersion and that immersion differentiated Second Life from non-virtual world digital media practices such as the World Wide Web and email. In other words, cosmologies consist of spiritual media practices that turn raw space into a spiritual place. Hoben's practitioners tended to understand the virtual world and its relationship to real life through samsara, a Sanskrit word meaning to pass through a series or states of conditions. While residents' cosmological understanding of samsara has a family resemblance to Asian canonic texts, the chapter maintains that it was entangled with a cybernetic understanding of systems, particularly the Vietnamese Buddhist monk Thích Nhất Hạnh's concept of interbeing.

Understanding how Zen practitioners built an authentic spiritual place is significant because Second Life allowed convert Buddhist innovative cosmologies of ideal places. The virtual spiritual place created was perceived as a calm and mindful alternative to the often chaotic and overstimulated reality of Network Consumer Society. While virtual, and based at least in part on fantasy, the zendo provided comfort and order to the practitioners who were often faced with uncertainty. The zendo might be a virtual place, but it was built in response to authentic needs and desires. Because Network Consumer Society has dissolved many of the traditional social spaces, one of the main reasons for the rise of digital media practices, particularly virtual worlds, is their third place sociability.[44] Virtual third places are cyberspace environments that lie between work and home and allow for relatively unstructured community.[45] While they might not substitute for real life, scholars have indicated that because contemporary Network Consumer Society has disrupted traditional third places, both digital media and multiplayer online games often come to act as third places.[46] These "virtual third places" afford a "home away from home," which enables users to interact in a neutral place, in which status is not tied closely to the outside world. Sociability is key, and media practices are marked by play, frivolity, and verbal word play.[47]

As described in the following chapter, convert Zen Buddhist "third places" are enabled by and a response to a Network Consumer life. On that Wednesday evening in January 21, 2009, as I sat on my cushion in Hoben Mountain Zen Retreat's empty zendo, I was a little nervous. I was about to lead my first *online silent meditation event*. I waited, my finger hovering above my mouse button, getting ready to click the bell and lead the practitioners in an online meditation event. The following chapter details Second Life's online silent meditation events, which communicated silence through ritualized media practices that disrupted typical practices and engaged practitioners with the group's often unstated ultimate reality.

Notes

1 Martin Heidegger, *Poetry, Language, Thought* (New York: Harper and Row, 1971), 160. Cf. Martin Heidegger, "A Dialogue on Language between a Japanese and an Inquirer," in *On the Way to Language* (New York: Harper & Row, 1971), 1–57.
2 Brenda Brasher, *Give Me that Online Religion* (San Francisco: Jossey-Bass, 2001).
3 J. Z. Smith, *Map Is Not Territory: Studies in the History of Religions* (Chicago: University of Chicago Press, 1978), 291.
4 I would like to thank Jeff Wilson, Associate Professor, Religious Studies and East Asian Studies, from the University of Waterloo for this insight.
5 Laurence Moore, *Religious Outsiders and the Making of Americans* (Oxford: Oxford University Press, 1986), 208.
6 Moore, 208.
7 "Building Tools," http://wiki.secondlife.com/wiki/Edit_window#Edit_Tool (accessed November 6, 2015).
8 Christopher Helland, "Religion Online/Online Religion and Virtual Communitas," in *Religion on the Internet: Research Prospects and Promises*, eds. Jeffery K. Hadden and Douglas E. Cowan (London: JAI Press/Elsevier, 2000), 205–24; Anastasia Karaflogka, *E-Religion: A Critical Appraisal of Religious Discourse on the World Wide Web* (London: Equinox, 2006).
9 Robert E. Buswell, *The Zen Monastic Experience* (Princeton, NJ: Princeton University Press, 1992), 161.
10 Jeff Wilson, *Dixie Dharma* (Chapel Hill, NC: University of North Carolina Press, 2012), 61.
11 "Second Life Search," http://search.secondlife.com/ (accessed November 7, 2015).
12 "Land," http://wiki.secondlife.com/wiki/Land (accessed November 10, 2015).
13 Karl Marx, *The German Ideology* (London: Lawrence & Wishart, 1965), 32.
14 Heidegger, *Poetry, Language, Thought* , 147.
15 Maurice Merleau-Ponty, "Eye and Mind," in *The Primacy of Perception*, ed. James E. Edie (Evanston, IL: Northwestern University Press, 1964), 163.
16 Maurice Merleau-Ponty, 168.
17 "Object," http://wiki.secondlife.com/wiki/Object (accessed August 28, 2016).
18 "Hello Avatar – Second Life Wiki," Wiki.secondlife.com (accessed November 10, 2015).
19 Richard Gombrich, "The Consecration of a Buddhist Image," *Journal of Asian Studies* 26, no. 1 (1966): 23–36.
20 James Wagner Au, *The Making of Second Life: Notes from the New World* (San Francisco: HarperCollins Publishers, 2008), xi.
21 Richard Bartle, *Designing Virtual Worlds* (Berkeley: New Riders, 2004), 55.
22 "Buddhism in the West," www.buddhanet.net/e-learning/buddhistworld/to-west.htm (accessed November 10, 2015).
23 William James Coleman, *The New Buddhism: The Western Transformation of an Ancient Tradition* (London: Oxford University Press, 2002), 12.
24 Gregory Price Grieve, *Retheorizing Religion in Nepal* (New York: Palgrave Macmillan, 2006), 50–51.
25 Peter Berger, *The Sacred Canopy: Elements of a Sociological Theory of Religion* (New York: Doubleday, 1967).
26 Bartle, 451–58.
27 Donald Wood Winnicott, *Playing and Reality* (London: Tavistock, 1971), 49.
28 "Role Play," http://wiki.secondlife.com/wiki/Role_play (accessed November 10, 2015).
29 *ibid.*

30 *ibid.*

31 Roger Caillois, *Man and the Sacred* (Urbana and Chicago: University of Illinois Press, 2001); 154. Cf. Roger Caillois, *Man, Play, Games* (New York: Glencoe, 1961).

32 Johan Huizinga, *Homo ludens: A Study of the Play-element in Culture* (Boston: Beacon Press, 1950), 10.

33 Huizinga, 18.

34 Huizinga, 10.

35 Rachel Wagner, "The Importance of Playing in Earnest," in *Playing with Religion in Digital Games*, eds. Heidi Campbell and Gregory Price Grieve (Bloomington, IN: Indiana University Press, 2014), 192–213.

36 Spiritual role-playing is not limited to virtual worlds. In "Constructing a Small Place," in *Sacred Space: Shrine, City, Land*, eds. Joshua Prawer, B. Z. Kedar, R. J. Zwi Werblowsky, Benjamin Kedar-Kopfstein (New York: New York University Press, 1998), 19–31, the scholar of religion Jonathan Z. Smith argues that one of the strategies by which practitioners make place is through "miniaturization." This process describes how people create a smaller model of a larger object as a way of transporting its cosmologicalization. Miniaturization cannot help but have an element of play. As Smith writes, "the 'little' temples and shrines . . . are treated as if they were major edifices housing a divine image and cult table" (p. 19).

37 "Linden World," http://secondlife.wikia.com/wiki/Linden_World (accessed November 10, 2015).

38 Gregory Price Grieve, *Retheorizing Religion in Nepal* (New York: Palgrave Macmillan, 2006), 87–103.

39 Ludwig von Bertalanffy, *General System Theory: Foundations, Development, Applications* (New York: George Braziller, 1968), 12–16.

40 Joanna Macy, *Mutual Causality in Buddhism and General Systems Theory* (Albany, NY: State University of New York Press, 1991), xii.

41 "Dependent Co-Arising," *Joanna Macy and Her Work* www.joannamacy.net/dependent-co-arising.html (accessed November 10, 2015).

42 Macy, 57.

43 Thích Nhất Hạnh, *Love in Action: Writings on Nonviolent Social Change* (Berkeley: Parallax Press, 1993), 129.

44 Nicolas Ducheneaut, Nicholas Yee, Eric Nickell, and Robert J. Moore, "Virtual 'Third Places': A Case Study of Sociability in Massively Multiplayer Games," *Computer Supported Cooperative Work* 16, no. 2–7 (2007): 129–66.

45 In *The Great Good Place*, the American urban sociologist Oldenburg argues for the importance of third places such as cafes, clubs, or parks for anchoring community and maintains that a third place should be welcoming, inexpensive, accessible, and involve both regulars and the possibility of new friends (Ray Oldenburg, *The Great Good Place: Cafes, Coffee Shops, Community Centers, Beauty Parlors, General Stores, Bars, Hangouts, and How They Get You through the Day* [New York: Paragon House, 1989]).

46 Stewart Hoover and Nabil Echchaibi, *Media Theory and the 'Third Spaces of Digital Religion'*, Center for Media, Religion, and Culture, University of Boulder, 2014.

47 Edward Soja, *Thirdspace: Journeys to Los Angeles and Other Real-and-Imagined Places* (Oxford: Basil Blackwell, 1996).

Chapter 6

Event

Online silent meditation, virtual cushions, and the cybernetic steersman

There are no enlightened beings, only enlightened actions.
Coming to the End of Your Quest for Enlightenment [in One Minute]
Meditation note card attributed to Franz Metcalf[1]

On Sunday, January 23, 2010, I logged on early to Hoben Mountain Zen Retreat's *zendo,* or meditation hall. I had arrived before the *event* because I wanted to *rez,* or materialize, my new Peaceful Warrior *zafu,* or meditation cushion, mentioned in the last chapter (Figure 5.3).[2] I thought the meditation hall would be empty, but sitting on one of the *timekeeper's* cushions was Georgina Florida, who was about to lead the upcoming event.[3] Before I *unboxed* my zafu, I hesitated for a moment, because there was only Georgina and myself and I was unsure of the community's rules and felt intimidated by her. She radiated authority and had a stunningly beautiful avatar. Sensing my indecision, Georgina *Instant Messaged* (IMed) me on *private chat* and said, "take a cushion," and then assuming I was a *noobie,* sent a *note card* titled "How to Meditate," which stated, "We sit on the cushion, follow our breath and watch our thoughts. We simplify our whole situation." Not wanting to disturb, I decided that I would unbox the meditation cushion later at a *sandbox.*

Consisting of 87.1 percent of all convert Buddhist events, Second Life's Zen's chief activity was such silent online meditation, frequently called *zazen* or more often just *sitting* (Figure 6.1). As I explain in this chapter, during such events residents rested their avatars on virtual meditation cushions for twenty to thirty minutes and usually remained inactive in front of their computer screens just counting their breath. Often, as the technologist David Levy argues, in "No Time To Think: Reflections on Information Technology and Contemplative Scholarship," there is an assumed negative correlation between digital media and authentic spiritual practice.[4] While digital media may afford distraction, however, others argue that there are mindful methods to using digital media. The American monk Bikkhu Suwattano writes in "Mindfulness and Insight on the Internet," "When we begin to cultivate mindfulness it is enough to just pay attention to our movements . . . When we click on a link or a function

Figure 6.1 Online silent meditation.

(Second Life snapshot by Gregory Price Grieve).

on our monitor screen, we know we are clicking – we can say to ourselves 'clicking.'"[5]

In this chapter, rather than assuming that digital media practices determine authentic spirituality, I look at the practice from an insider's emic perspective and ask: How does online silent meditation work, what spiritual labor does it do, and what is its historical genealogy? The key to unlocking these questions is to make sense of silence. If, as many convert Buddhists hold, the core of Zen is a transmission outside of words and scripture, how can it be communicated, let alone communicated over the Internet? Often to answer this question scholars either pose "Zen" as the essential religious experience or reduce popular forms to a false consciousness. I take a middle path, however, and maintain that Second Life online meditation is a spiritual media practice that ritualizes silence, and while socially constructed and culturally contextualized, is an authentic response to contemporary Network Consumer Society. As I stated in *Cyber Zen*'s introduction, authenticity indicates media practices that allow users to innovatively explore and create alternative identities and communities in relation to what they perceive as divine. Networked Consumer Society, as explained in chapter one, refers to the cultural system that arose in the last quarter of the twentieth century based on the desire to purchase goods and services, which do not merely fulfill biological needs but cater to consumer desire.

As we touched upon in *Cyber Zen*'s introduction, we contend that silence does not hold a preexisting universal meaning. Instead of preexisting, silence emerges from media practices, which may not denote meaning but do connote particular situational significance. "Situation" refers to locations that gather together people's bodies, social roles, and cultural discourses.[6] Situational significances do not necessarily symbolize something beyond themselves. As the historian of religion Catherine Bell writes in "Performance," such emergent practices "bring about social and ontological change by virtue of the doing itself."[7] If one tries to give a semantic interpretation to such wordless practices as

Hoben's zazen, one risks reducing them to something else. To be clear, as argued in chapter two, *Cyber Zen* is not perpetuating the ideology that "Zen spoken is not the real Zen." Instead, I maintain that to make sense of online silent meditation one must situationalize the media practices from which it emerges by analyzing together its bodily practices, social roles, and the discourses that frame it.

We argue that online silent meditation communicates silence by denoting "nothing" but by connoting mindfulness, which is experienced by practitioners as an authentic spirituality that counters the anxiety of living in Network Consumer Society. Spiritualized silence on Second Life is communicated by ritualized procedural media practices that disrupt typical habits and engages these with the group's perception of their ultimate reality. A procedure indicates an established method for executing a series of actions in a certain order. As in any ritual practice, the procedure during silent meditation is that residents perform something different from the norm. As I investigate below, in online silent meditation, rather than the hurried day most adherents experienced both on- and offline, for twenty to thirty minutes residents' avatars sat silently on virtual cushions, while users meditated in front of their computer screens. For such (in)activity to become spiritualized, however, it needs to be contextualized in the group's ultimate reality. During our research, key for understanding this process was the convert Buddhist concept of "mindfulness." As described in chapter two, derived from the Buddhist notion of *smṛti*, in contemporary convert practice mindfulness refers to a nonjudgmental focus on the emotions, thoughts, and sensations occurring in the present moment. At Hoben, mindfulness was described neither as a god nor as a sacred phenomenon but rather as a spiritual method of perceiving the world that revealed reality's interconnected (*pratītyasamutpāda*) empty nature (*śūnyata*).

To make sense of the silence of online meditation events, this chapter makes three intertwined investigations. First, the chapter describes online silent meditation as a media practice dependent upon both on- and offline bodies that are hinged together by virtual meditation cushions. Second, the chapter argues that online silent meditation is a ritualized procedural process, which by doing "nothing" connotes mindfulness. Finally, the chapter suggests that Hoben's contemporary practice of online silent meditation, while it has a family resemblance to the Buddhist concept of *ānāpānasmṛti* (mindfulness of breathing) and is informed by Protestant rejection of ritual and celebration of inner experience, has since the 1950s been entangled with the cybernetic conception of the "steersman" (*kybernḗtēs*).[8] As I described in chapter one, cybernetics was coined in the second half of the twentieth century to describe systems composed of machines and animals but can be traced back to Plato's *The Alcibiades*, where it signifies "the study of self-governance."[9]

Making sense of silent meditation is significant for three reasons. First, by giving a thick description of a particular spiritual digital media practice, it illuminates digital religion more generally and highlights a middle path between media determinism and the myth of complete rational agency. The dynamics of online silent meditation make researchers aware that Second Life residents are active builders of virtual religion, both as they invent new forms and adopt and modify actual world practices. Yet Second Life residents cannot do whatever they imagine; they are restricted by the software code, and the platform's social conventions are limited by the virtual world's media practices. Second, by offering a slightly askew reflection of convert Buddhist practices, this chapter allows one to see more clearly the function and labor that Buddhism does in contemporary American popular culture. Convert Buddhism is authentic not because it is a perfect copy of Asian practices but rather because it engages with, and is a product of, Network Consumer Society. Third, online meditation causes one to critically examine the role of silence both in contemplative practices and in society more generally. Users know silence when they do not hear it but are not accustomed to thinking about it in its own right; rather, they think of it as the lack of something else. Once silence is critically examined, however, one finds that its significance is not static but changes according to the social situation.

Silent online meditation events

After Georgina Florida had given me the note card, I walked slowly to one of the zendo's meditation cushions that were spread in a semicircle around the altar. I clicked. The script inside the cushion sat my avatar down in a perfect lotus position. I waited with Georgina a few minutes more as twenty-three other practitioners slowly wandered in and sat down. As they entered, most of the practitioners said, "namaste," a customary greeting used in South Asia when meeting or departing, or they typed the gassho (*gasshō*) emoticon "_/!_," the Japanese term for the *añjali mudrā*, a gesture in which the palms are placed together pointing upwards in prayer position, that can be used for prayer or as a sign of greeting.

Hoben's community members came for many reasons, but they tended to stay to meditate, and zazen is what sustained the community and practitioner's individual spirituality. No doubt that for many online silent meditation was just an excuse to be with other "Zennies." As one practitioner said, on October 3, 2008, "Second Life *sitting* is a little goofy, but some actually *sit* along, at home. I just come for the people." Yet, as Ashley Lee, a self-proclaimed Zen gardener, said in an interview, "at first I logged into [Second Life] out of curiosity and then to build and go to discussions and explore about anything that comes my way. Now I usually just sit." A small number of community members spoke of koans (paradoxical spiritual anecdotes or riddles), and others the use of *mantras* (a sacred utterance); for most practitioners, however, "just sitting" on the cushion was enough. As Georgina Florida summarized in a conversation, "sitting is my guru." To be fair, silent online meditation was not for everyone. As one resident answered in our 2010 survey (*n*=108), "Well . . . I tried to meditate once in Second Life, but I find it very strange. It's like a very artificial situation. I do prefer to meditate when I'm not playing at all."

Second Life revolves around such "events," which include activities related to arts, culture, charity, support groups, commerce, discussion, education, games, contests, nightlife, entertainment, pageants, and sports. As the Second Life web-page reads, "Looking for something to do in Second Life? Featured Events includes fun and interesting virtual world activities, such as fashion hunts, live music performances, conferences and more."[10] Throughout my research team's fieldwork, we encountered a vast number and variety of Second Life spiritual events, and at first, besides Zen, we observed and participated in Islamic, Chris-tian, Jewish, Native American, neopagan, and secular Buddhist events. Islamic events included information sessions and virtual pilgrimages. Christian events included such practices as prayer meetings, weekly services, and bible study. Jewish events included candle lighting, dances, and services. Native American events included sweat lodges and dances. Pagan groups held events such as Imbolc, a Celtic festival celebrated on the second day of February.

As our research entered its second year, however, we began to concentrate on convert Zen Buddhist events (Figure 6.2). During 2008 and 2009, Hoben held approximately fifty events a week of a vast variety, such as *campfire concerts*, *Dharma* and book discussions, *Dharma talks* and interviews, and more rarely weddings and memorials. Campfire concerts were a common Second Life social activity and were musical events that occurred around a virtual fire pit. Dharma discussions were a Zen event in which practitioners would have informal conversations, usually led by one of Hoben's owners, about spiritual practice. Dharma talks were events in which real-life experts would be invited to give a lecture that was usually followed by a question and answer session.

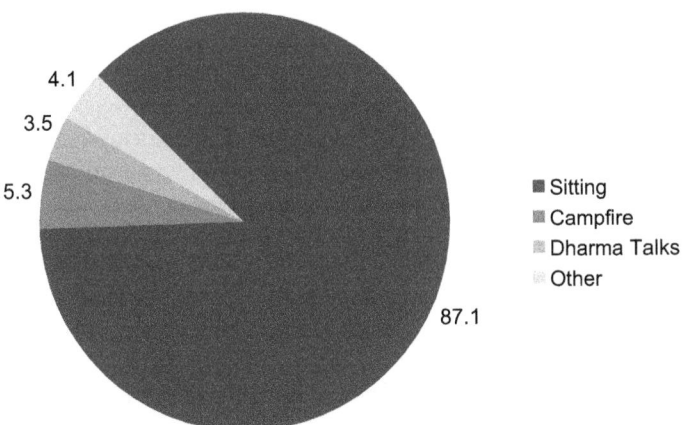

Figure 6.2 Percentage of types of events at Hoben Mountain Zen Retreat: 87.1% online silent meditation, 5.3% campfire and other musical events, 3.5% Dharma talks, 4.1% other, including events such as memorials, weddings, interviews, and one-time events such as Tsunami relief.

Interviews were more rare and were a chance for practitioners to have *doku-san*, a conversation with a real-life teacher about practice. By far the most prevalent and significant practice, however, was silent online meditation, which describes a media practice in which users rest their avatars on virtual meditation cushions.

For most residents at Hoben, zazen referred to sitting forms of silent meditation, usually practiced in the lotus position, which was perceived as both affording a direct experience of mindfulness and also as a form of mental therapy. As a Hoben note card, Short Instructions reads, "Zazen is a particular kind of meditation, unique to Zen, that functions centrally as the very heart of the practice. In fact, Zen Buddhists are generally known as the 'meditation Buddhists.' Basically, zazen is the study of the self." When I asked the resident BodhiDharma Rosebud to describe Zen, he answered, "the heart of Zen is Zazen / which means sitting Zen / Without Zazen there is no Zen." After laughing at how many times he used the word Zen in one sentence, and repeating the first lines from the children's author Dr. Seuss's *Green Eggs and Ham*, BodhiDharma became serious and went on to explain that silent meditation was not a doctrine but an experiment. "The Buddha was already experimenting, and it was refined by countless training centers ever since." As touched upon in chapter two, because it focused on bodily procedures and not belief, most residents did not perceive Zen as a religion but rather as a spiritual practice. As Boon Thinker said in a public discussion at the Agnostic Buddhist Group, because Buddhism "is a direct entrance to the spiritual without addressing the supernatural. It does not need ceremony but is clinical like psychology. It does not ask you to believe, but only to do what works for you."

Silence

When asked to define "Zen," most at Hoben would simply remain silent. As touched upon in *Cyber Zen*'s introduction, silence is not simply an absence of sound that somehow exists outside of language, nor does silence have a universal meaning that conveys the same significance across all social situations. Silence is a media practice dependent on context, or more precisely the absence of communication within a particular procedural situation. At Hoben's meditation events, silence referred to the fact that during the twenty to thirty minute sessions residents did not communicate in public *chat*. Hoben's silence was considered spiritual neither because it semantically symbolized a deity nor because it represented a doctrine, belief, or ideological system. Practitioners repeatedly indicated that silence was empty of belief. As the resident Human Riddle said in conversation,

> To me, belief is sadly lacking in meaning and the ability to significantly raise one's level of consciousness. In my humble opinion, Zen gave me the opportunity and the techniques to experience that for myself instead of just

'thinking' about it and knowing it through 'ideas.' Belief is like going to a restaurant and eating the menu, Zen is eating the real FOOD!!!!!

[capitalization in the original]

Not only was sitting silent, but adherents were hesitant to speak of their practices. The Hoben community's silence was usually justified in one of two ways. The first reason was a humble ignorance. Often when my research team asked Hoben's visitors to define Zen, they would say that they were just beginners and did not really know what it was. They would tell me to "google" it or that I should ask one of the community leaders. The community leaders were also hesitant to define Zen. They described themselves as lay practitioners, saying that they did not have authority to define Zen, and would often send a note card, or URL (Uniform Resource Locator) link to other media. For instance, the founder of Hoben, Cassius Lawndale, indicated the YouTube video, "Orientation to Zen 01 – Zazen (Zen Meditation)," from the Victoria Zen Centre, that states, "Fundamentally Zen Practice is a very simple activity just sitting up straight and breathing and paying attention to where you are and what you are doing."[11]

Investigating silence

Silence might seem hard to study. While a personal and silent form of spiritual practice, zazen could be researched, however, because my research team could speak with members of the community about it, and there was a consistent publicly observable procedure for silent practice. While Zen meditation on Second Life was described as silent, the practice was neither empty of significance, nor were people silent about talking about it. Of the 2,716 convert Buddhist primary documents collected during our research, over 77 percent contained the words "silent meditation," "sit," or zazen. Moreover, if one compiles these with the 6,623 *group instant messages* collected, the number rises to over 93 percent.[12] Even more significantly, timekeepers would often hand out a note card before a meditation event. As Cassius Lawndale wrote in a long email message when describing the procedure of online silent meditation, "We'll begin each meditation with a quote one of us likes." The meditation note cards were described by practitioners as seeds for the silent meditation and ranged from a piece of Buddhist scripture to an excerpt from a popular meditation guide, but most often the note cards engaged the concept of mindfulness.

Silence was not just an absence of communicating but was key to understanding Second Life Buddhism's authentic situation. When we asked about silence, two basic meanings surfaced. First was the understanding that from silence emerged the ultimate reality of the Buddha-nature (*tathāgatagarbha*). As the resident Mystic Moon wrote, "it is through silence that the Buddha speaks." Mystic then chatted on for several paragraphs that "the Zen that is typed is not the true Zen" and that in the "now of namelessness" lay the "mother of all reality." Or more concisely, as he wrote in a note card titled, "Golden Sentence of Awareness," Zen was "awareness= ' ' <- – there." The second meaning, a more common one at Hoben, was that silence is a form of skillful speech (*upāya*). As the resident BodhiDharma Rosebud, said, "Silence is double edged, it helps keep order and keep concentration. In Real Life I facilitated a weekly sangha. We didn't even say, 'I agree with him,' or 'My sister went through the same thing.' All we did was listen." BodhiDharma went on to say that "Zen is seeing clearly. It can not be labeled in words." He laughed and typed, "_/! ," which he explained a few minutes later as the emoticon for "one hand clapping," a koan.[13]

If asked about silence, residents could formulate answers. These answers, however, seemed to have little to nothing to do with the actual day-to-day practice of the community and often seemed composed to satisfy researchers.[14] For most at Hoben there was no instruction on what silent meditation meant. When I asked resident BodhiDharma about what goal I should be aiming for while sitting, he laughed, "just sit. Everyone is already the Buddha there is nothing to gain. Just sit. Just sit. Just sit." When I pushed him for an explanation, he sent me a white lotus flower, and typed in public chat, "_/!_" (the emoticon for *gasshō*). BodhiDharma was pointing to Mahākāśyapa, one of the principal disciples of Shakyamuni Buddha. In the Flower Sermon, the Buddha held up a white flower. All the other disciples just looked on without knowing how to react, but Mahākāśyapa smiled faintly, and Shakyamuni Buddha picked him as the one who truly understood him and the one worthy to be his successor.[15]

Procedure for ritualizing silence

There are many ways to do nothing. At Hoben, during our research, silent online meditation began with the timekeeper ringing the bell three times in audio. For practitioners who may not have heard the bell, the timekeeper usually keyed a brief reminder, such as, "Let us prepare for 30 minutes of silent meditation. May our minds be one with the Dharma." At Hoben, zazen was considered silent, because for the duration of the sitting residents' avatars would remain still and they would not type in public chat. For the most part, users were usually assumed to be sitting quietly in front of their computer screens minding their breath.

Mediated forms of meditation are not new to contemporary American society, and as early as 1967 practitioners in California were practicing together via telephone.[16] At least since 1998 and the opening of the website "Daily Zen Meditation," online practice has been offered on the World Wide Web, and starting in 2004 regular silent meditation started in Second Life at the resident Wayne Wanderer's Zen Center, "a gathering place for those on the path to awareness." Such engagement with digital religion continues to change and evolve to the digital mediascape with Buddhist-inspired smartphone applications. For instance, the application Mindfulness Meditation offers "simply the best way to learn and enjoy mindfulness meditation."[17] As the user MetaHipster comments in the application's webpage, "I've tried zen sitting and walking group meditation. I've tried silent zazen sitting and kneeling meditation on my own with a timer app. I've tried several other meditation apps, some with sound effects, some with music." This is "the first app that's helped me achieve a meditative state."[18]

At Hoben, beyond the ringing of the bell, almost no instruction was given on how to do silent meditation, and if asked, most community leaders would instruct noobies to just sit there, or to simply count their breath. As the founder of the group, Cassius Lawndale said, after I asked him about instruction in a formal interview, "I do not think it is a good idea to 'teach' that here. There are many much more reliable places one can find that information already on the web, along with visual aids to boot. When I asked Human Riddle to describe practice at Hoben, he sent me a note card titled "What We Practice," attributed to Cheri Huber, an American independent Soto Zen teacher, which read, "Our practice does not require much from us; we do not have to figure out anything. I would encourage everyone to just show up, with no ideas about how the practice should be. The practice itself provides all the standards that we need: One, sit down. Two, be still. Three, pay attention."

While there was minimal content, and almost no direct instruction, residents were still being trained in spiritual practice. During our research, silent online meditation events were a type of ritualized procedural performance. A procedure, like the code of a computer program, is a step-by-step practice that emerges from a set of rules for performing a particular operation. Similar to how the gamer theorist Alexander Galloway describes play, the Zen of Second Life "is an activity defined by rules in which players try to reach some sort of goal." It "can be played alone or in complex social scenarios."[19] Like BodhiDharma's white lotus, important in online silent meditation is not what actions mean but what they do in a particular situation.[20] Because silent online meditation is primarily procedural and not narrative or symbolic like a game, it is often cumbersome to describe. As Markku Eskelinen writes, in "The Gaming Situation," "If I throw a ball at you I don't expect you to drop it and wait until it starts telling stories."[21] In a similar fashion, "Zen" was usually explained as a type of performance. For instance, in a note card handed out on April 23, 2008, titled "Can I Be Honest With You?," the author describes "Zen" not through a narrative of belief but through action: ". . . thought turns into speech, which turns into action, which ultimately affects our whole world . . ."[22]

The procedure-like nature of zazen was similar to how residents reported practicing their actual world meditation. For instance, in July 2008 when I asked BodhiDharma how to sit in real life, he replied, "I use the full lotus when sitting [in the actual world]. Reputed to be the best for seated meditation." I responded, "you must be quite flexible." To which he said, "I use a little *seiza* [kneeling bench]. I'm old. Hahaha, bad knees, no hair, no teeth." I asked him for how long did he meditate. "Forty minutes is usual at traditional zendos, with a ten minute break for *kinhin* [slow walking meditation]." I asked him what posture to take. He said, "only important to be upright and comfortable, not rigid like a Marine at attention, but not slouched either. Somewhere in between, needs to be comfortable and relaxed, but in good posture – not forced." He then went on to add "that some things are kinda important, gotta sit upright. I tried it while prone flat on my back just went to sleep." I asked him, "should you have your eyes closed?" To which he answered, "Better to have eyes open, otherwise – easy to sleep or daydream. They say to cast gaze about three feet in front." We talked awhile about the difference between staring down and straight ahead and then he went on to add "We – Soto Zennies – face the wall as we sit very close to the wall two–three feet." Finally I asked him about *mudras*, hand positions. He said, "Hands should be comfortable on lap. A special 'mudra' not necessary. I think mudras are really just Buddhist 'gang signs' hahahaha."

Ritual

As described in the last chapter, the virtual cushion was Hoben's ultimate message, not because it represented semantic content or transmitted information but rather because it ritualized silence through bodily performances that involve both a resident's user and avatar. Ritualization, the production of ritualized acts, can be described, in part, as that way of acting that sets itself off from other ways of acting by virtue of the way in which it does what it does.[23] Network consumerism is typified by constant and often frenzied media practices. In contrast, silent online meditation creates a media practice in which resident bodies remain motionless and silent. Consider, for instance, a note card written by the Hoben community leader Human Riddle: "we define sitting practice as simply sitting, quietly."

Rituals are dynamic actions that emerge in space and time. In her seminal article "The Ritual Body and the Dynamics of Ritual Power," Catherine Bell analyzes religious performance through the lens of "ritualization," a way of doing certain activities that differentiates those activities from more conventional ones. Bell gives the example of the Christian Eucharistic meal that differs from a normal meal, in what one eats, when one eats, where one eats, with whom one eats, and whom one eats. In Second Life, ritual also depended on such practices. For instance, mirroring the actual world, Second Life's Hindu Shri Ganesh Temple required that avatars take off their shoes, and many Islamic sites required that female avatars veil before entering a mosque. An obvious ritualized convert Zen Second Life media practice is the gassho emoticon, "_/!_." Typed into public chat, or instant messaged, Second Life Buddhist residents use the _/!_ as a way of greeting each other, showing thankfulness, and also marking communications as having particular reverence, such as at the beginning and end of a group meditation.

As Bell goes on to argue, however, it is not enough for ritualization to simply do something different: these differing actions must be tied to a group's ultimate reality. As Bell explains, "ritualization always aligns one within a series of relationships linked to the ultimate sources of power."[24] While mindfulness is certainly the ultimate concern neither of all Buddhists nor even of all Buddhists practicing on Second Life, because it was a concern of a majority of Hoben's practitioners it played a major part in shaping the practice of online silent meditation. For Zen practitioners the nonactivity of just sitting was tied to mindfulness that was seen to transcend not only specific cultures and historical locations but also language itself. For instance, when I asked the resident Buddha Hat what Zen meant, he replied, "it comes from *chán*, which is a Chinese translation of *dhyāna* . . . meditation . . . It's all about mindful sitting in direct experience, as opposed to conscious thinking. It is silence." Mindfulness was perceived by many practitioners to be the ultimate source of power, which lay beyond each person. As a meditative note card, titled "One Way to Stop Yourself from Running Late," reads,

> To cultivate the healing power of mindfulness in your life requires more than just sitting in a meditative posture, or following a set of meditation instructions or listening to a tape. . . . . The focus is on you and your life as it unfolds moment by moment. And this way of learning happens from the inside out.[25]

Through the procedure of online meditation's media practices, silence's difference was tied to mindfulness. As the note card "Can I Be Honest With You?" reads, "the first step is to cultivate awareness through mindfulness meditation. Using your breath as a home base for your wandering mind, notice when you get caught up in thought and your attention strays from the breath."[26] Rather than semantic content, it was the procedure of online meditation that had ultimate authority. As the note card handed out by Georgina Florida on January 13, 2008, and attributed to the Sōtō Priest Kosho Uchiyama read, "From the beginning, I have said that the *zazen* each of us practices is the only true teacher."[27]

Bridging worlds

Meditation cushions linked Second Life and real life. On Sunday, January 13, 2008, a random resident wandered into Hoben's zendo and interrupted to ask in public chat, "what are you doing?" Georgina Florida answered, "We are about to meditate." The resident asked, "Do you meditate in Second Life and Real Life at the same time?" To which Georgina Florida answered, "yes. I always do. This is a practice that bridges both worlds." Georgina's answer was similar to other residents, of which 81.2 percent reported always or usually meditating in real life when their avatar meditated in Second Life. When I asked residents what they did when their avatar meditated, a few answered to our 2010 Survey ($n=108$) with responses such as "Tidy, drink coffee, get my messages." Most reported as one person responded in our survey, "I sit in front of my monitor in my chair." Others were more detailed. "I meditate. Sit in Burmese style, hands in Universal Mudra, breathing and counting, or holding attention in a 'still point' as much as possible."

Such bodily performances, whether on- or offline, can be reduced neither to scriptural texts that can be analyzed nor to the mere execution of a pre-existing ideology. Instead, bodily performances such as silent online meditations are effective because they use the body in ways different from the norm. Second Life's virtual cushions are unique, because they tie together into one ritual system the inactivity of avatars with the conscious breathing of users. If we take into consideration, as described in chapter four, that residents' bodies are compiled from real word and Second Life aggregates, then we can see that online silent meditation tends to consist of conscious breathing in the actual world and scripted meditation cushions in the virtual world. As the resident Tai Buckinghamshire said in an interview, "Obviously, in Second Life our avatars sit silently on the cushions provided. . . . In real life, you also sit in front of your computer screen, until you hear the bell. The leader of the group rings the gong at the start."

The typical procedure for Hoben's zazen consisted of users counting their breaths, while their avatars remained sitting in a lotus position on a meditation cushion. After the meditation event on January 23, 2010, I asked Georgina Florida how to meditate. She sent me a note card that read, "In the little pause at the end of the out breath, count, first breath out 'one', second breath out 'two' and so on up to ten, and then start over with 'one'." A note card titled, "Sitting With the Breath," written for Hoben by Human Riddle, one of the community's core members and a mindfulness awareness therapist in real life, stated, "we define sitting practice as simply sitting quietly . . . the goal is to see what there is to see, hear what there is to hear, breathe a breath and be there." Beginners and more seasoned practitioners both employed conscious breathing. Also, when newcomers to the community asked what they should do, conscious breathing was the chief suggestion. Early on in my research, when I instant messaged one of the meditation leaders, Buddha Hat, for clarification on what I should be doing while we sat, he replied with a note card that read, "Just sit in Second Life. Follow your breath, in and out. It's helpful to find a location in your body to focus on. Perhaps the rising and falling of your chest or stomach, perhaps your nostrils where the air enters and leaves, perhaps imagining the path of the breath in."

As described in the last chapter, in Second Life virtual zafus (meditation cushions) were *objects* that lay at the heart of online silent practice. The cushions afforded ritualizing by animating avatars in a lotus position. *Scripts* created with the Linden Scripting Language give behavior to objects, including *animations* that afford avatars the ability to perform a variety of acts such as walking, sitting, and flying as well as dancing, and shaking hands. The importance of meditation animations was evidenced by the amount of time residents placed in the procurement of and discussion about them. For instance, BodhiDharma Rose-bud always refused to sit on meditation cushions that made his avatar do nonlo-tus animations, such as the Yoga Surya Namaskar. Meditation cushions bridged these two sets of practices into one system. Consider, for instance, as described in the last chapter, the Peaceful Warrior zafu and zabuton set that I had placed on the deck of my home in Second Life. Sitting on the cushion automatically placed one's avatar in a full lotus position, and the sound of restful breathing was played. Its documentation read, "This Zafu and Zabuton Set is created as an aid to your Second Life meditation practice. The zafu enhances meditation by helping you get in touch with your breath, and correctly angles your back and legs."

My Peaceful Warrior meditation cushion did not stand in for real-life medita-tion cushions, nor did real-life meditation cushions represent Buddhism the way a cross does for Christianity, or even, as mentioned in *Cyber Zen*'s introduction, as a *dharmacakra* represents the Buddha's teaching. Rather virtual meditation cushions pragmatically inferred how practitioners ought to interpret silence.[28] Virtual meditation cushions do determine the practice of online meditation yet are not symbols that represent spiritual content; rather they are signs that train bodies how to practice. That is, virtual cushions play a crucial part in the ritual-ization and are neither just ornament nor mere symbol but rather are a form of self-reflexive "metapragmatic" media practices that channel virtual and actual bodily practice. Metapragmatic describes the effects and conditions of a media practice that uses itself as the object of discourse.[29] Because of the metapragmat-ics, Second Life practice was treated as complete in itself. As the community leader Cassius Lawndale said during an interview, "What others do while they sit here is their own business. Some might be smoking a cigarette in IM, or read-ing a blog elsewhere, and maybe, just maybe . . . some are actually taking that time to sit in their real life at the same time. But, no matter what they are doing, I don't consider that any business of mine. It is the Dharma."

Remedy to anxiety

Silent online meditation events contrasted themselves to other events by doing nothing and bridged both virtual and actual worlds, as well as spiritual practice and everyday life. Because online meditation also enabled a second bridging between the meditation event and users' everyday life, "doing nothing" was perceived as an antidote to the suffering generated by living in Network Con-sumer Society. Bill Kwong, founder and abbot of the real-life Sonoma Moun-tain Zen Center, maintains that the key to Zen is "to have a good seat – sitting on the zafu [cushion] and getting a glimpse of your original nature, your Bud-dha nature. It's a bridge . . . from the Zendo [meditation hall] to your practical life."[30] The logic of ritualization specifies that such bodily practices as online silent meditation must satisfy in order to be meaningful and as such are recipes or methods for accomplishing specific results, solving problems, or performing tasks. This was true for online meditation as well. The mindfulness produced by silence was perceived to cure the suffering of living in Network Consumer Society. A meditation note card handed out April 28, 2008, titled "Why Do People Do Zazen?" and attributed to the American Soto Zen priest Jiho Sargent read that most people practice zazen for "the most common reason for undertaking any sort of religious practice: a sense that life is not satisfactory in one way or another, to one degree or another."

At Hoben, practitioners experienced silence as an antidote to the uncertain anxiety of living in Network Consumer Society because it produced "mindfulness," which as Georgina Florida described in a note card, is "a gift given to you every moment." She went on to add,

> As I once told a friend recently, Buddha gives us Eskimo kisses 24/7. His teachings are being played out in front of us all the time. We just have to be aware of them. . . . These timeless, perfect expressions, of life just as it is, are everywhere around us. Gifts waiting for us. Look and see for yourselves. :).

While some practitioners wished for a calmer life, and others mystical experiences, for most silent online meditation's mindfulness was perceived as a way to relieve suffering through compassion. Compassion was seen to relieve suffering because of Interbeing, which as I described in the last chapter refers to how people exist only in relation to other human and nonhuman elements. As the note card titled "You don't just sit there," from an April 23, 2008, meditation session, states, "the ideal of Buddhist practice is to bring wisdom and compassion into the world and our relationships and to relieve suffering in all walks of life." As the community leader Tai Buckinghamshire said in an interview on May 20, 2009, "I practice mindfulness to hone my skills, to lessen my reactivity, to reduces stress and to help the sangha."

Cybernetic steersman

To sit on the cushion was to be mindful of the one's place in the world. Yet what model of self does such self-awareness entail? The Buddhist concept of no-self (*anātman*) emphasizes that there is no stable quality of self and that one's self exists only in a conditioned existence, which is transient and in a constant state of flux. For those at Hoben, the mindful self was, as the resident Ashley Lee described it, "a moving point of balance." When I asked BodhiDharma Rosebud whether he saw his "Avatar as a mask, reflection of your real-life self, or as a projection of an inner self?" He replied, "No simple origin, real life and Second Life are reflecting pools. Our self is the blind spot." After a pause he added, "The Sharpest sword can not cut itself; the finger-tips cannot touch finger-tips; self cannot know self." As described in chapter four, in convert Zen discourse the self is conceived simultaneously as ultimately empty but shaped by conventional reality. When I asked the residents Bob Tinker and Starlight Excellence about the relation between avatars and self, Bob said, "your ideas of you don't exist." And in the same instance, Starlight told me that I existed, "even if virtually."

On the surface, the content of convert Buddhist practice has a family resemblance to canonical Asian traditions. *Cyber Zen* maintains, however, that the procedures of convert Zen practices are historically entangled with postwar American cybernetics. As I described in chapter one, cybernetics refers to the scientific study of systems, particularly feedback loops, which emerged in the second half of the twentieth century from systems theory, information theory, and related sciences. Because it pictures the world as a series of systems that contains individuals, societies, and ecosystems and because it is concerned with describing the patterns that form from their emergence, one can see that while Convert Buddhism was influenced by them, it differs from canonical Asian sources. As described above, the word "cybernetics" was forged from the Greek *kybernetes,* or "steersman," and is defined as "the entire field of control and communication theory, whether in the machine or animal."[31] As described in chapter two, convert American Zen's entanglement with cybernetics begins in the late 1940s and is entangled with Alan Watts, the Beats, California's sixties counterculture, the work of Robert Pirsig, and finally 1980s corporate poaching of the concept of mindfulness.

The mindful notion of self that Hoben practitioners described was an entanglement of the cybernetic concept of self as a governor and the Buddhist concept of "no-self." As detailed in chapter two, key to cybernetics are feedback loops composed of human and nonhuman elements that are governed by a "steersman" who is perceived to be vital to the system, aware of the system, and emerging from the system. Rather than being outside the system, the steersman is conceived of as an essential part of it and as actually constituted by the system. The twentieth-century popularizer of Buddhism Alan Watts expanded the concept of the "nondual self" to describe the self not as an isolated unit but as a cybernetic system of mutually conditioned transactions in which "the line between myself and what happens to me is dissolved."[32] As Watts argues in *The Book: The Taboo against Knowing Who You Are,* while we habitually confront reality as a self that is acted upon by the world, in fact "the world outside your skin is just as much you as the world inside."[33] Particularly important for Watts was the concept of nondelusion (*avidyā*) that the individual ego was not separate, but was really part of a larger system. In *The Way of Zen,* Watts writes, "This is really a simple problem of what we now call cybernetics, the science of control."[34]

Silence as spiritual media practice

By mindfully focusing the bodily performance of both user and avatar, silent online meditation media practices act as a bridge that ties real life and Second Life together as well as spiritual practice and everyday life. What affords online silent meditation are the media practices that constitute virtual meditation cushions, or zafus. While meditation cushions are the message, the cushions did not symbolize content but rather ritualized silent bodily practices. Because mindfulness is pragmatic rather than semantic, it does not require faith in anything. Because it does not require a belief in content, it operates well as a spiritual practice in a society where all solid traditional forms of religious authority are melting into pixels. As the meditation note card titled "Zen Wrapped in Karma Dipped in Chocolate, Part 1," reads, "The practice of zazen is unassailable. It doesn't matter what you think. It doesn't matter what you feel. It doesn't matter if you hate it or love it. The practice itself transcends all attempts to box it in."

Cyber Zen argues for the middle ground when analyzing silent meditation events. There is no essential spiritual element, nor is the practice false consciousness. Online silent meditations are authentic media practices that force scholars to confront silence because there is nothing more than the performance of silence itself. As the resident Algama GossipGirl said in an interview on June 16, 2009, "zazen just is. You just are . . . you just are you . . . when you sit on your cushion." However, nothing is inherently silent, and no practice is inherently empty. Rather than mere absence, silence is a material media practice – like the Mahakasyapa's white lotus – that is culturally specific, plays out in space and time, and is transmitted through material systems of communication. At Hoben silent online meditation was significant pragmatically rather than semantically. Semantics refers to the content of a message, while pragmatics refers to how messages create meaning from context. To understand the semantic meaning of a media practice, one needs to synchronically "decode" its message. To understand the pragmatic meaning of a media practice, one needs to diachronically investigate the message's cultural situation. It is important to return to the cushion here, because what the cushion shows is that "just sitting" is a mix of bodily practices (*dhyāna*), discourses (*sūtra*), and a Buddhist religious matrix (*tathāgatagarbha*). As scholars of religion, we must remember that we need to be aware of how both operate; one can neither reduce the body to text, nor the text to body, and both text and body cannot exist independently of a cultural frame that shapes media practices.

Conclusion

The sitting period ends with one ring of the bell, followed by a brief prayer, the simplest and most frequent being "By this merit may all sentient beings attain complete awakening." The timekeeper then types the emoticon "_/!_" (for *gasshō*). Most of the other people present also type this emoticon into their computers, which causes a cascade of _/!_s to flow down the screen. On Sunday, January 23, 2010, after the sitting period had ended, I stood, "gassho-ed" to the altar, and walked slowly out of the zendo. I then said good-bye to my companions, teleported back to my house, and logged off. I shut down the computer and stood up from my chair. Once again my attention was brought back into the actual world.

Understanding Hoben's silent online meditation events resolves *Cyber Zen*'s original question of why did BodhiDharma Rosebud go online, as well as gives us the tools to answer in the following chapter the larger query about the ontology of two intertwined realities, the virtual/actual and conventional/ultimate. For the majority at Hoben, online silent meditation events did not merely symbolize ultimate reality but molded media practices such that they engaged with its perceived lack. On May 24, 2009, I asked one of Hoben's leaders, Georgina Florida, "How would you define Buddhism?" She answered, "Awakism." Georgina went on to describe Zen as a therapeutic practice that deeply penetrates the nature of reality, showing that reality and the self are empty of any inherent meaning. Georgina described this process as a mindful attentiveness to everyday life, particularly one's own identity, and gave as an example washing her ill husband. "I gave him a mindful bath and realized in a real way that self overlays no self."

Was Georgina's answer authentic? As we described in *Cyber Zen*'s Introduction, this question boiled down to a critical inquiry of the authenticity of online spiritual practice. As the Introduction contended, if one understands authenticity as fidelity to real life, then the answer can only be negative. As became clear during a conflict over community authority, Georgina's husband probably was a fantasy, and she was probably male in real life. If on the other hand, one understands authentic practice as that which enables individuals and groups to engage innovatively with what they perceive as ultimately real, then Second Life Buddhism is an authentic spirituality. In *Cyber Zen*'s conclusion, I use the ruptures in Second Life's media practices to map Second Life Zen community's understanding of ultimate reality itself. To be clear, my goal is not theological. I am not making any ontological claims about the ultimate nature of being. Instead, I am analyzing how practitioners at Hoben described their experience of ultimate reality. Such a map was not difficult to draw. My research team was not sure if the virtual world attracted users with a philosophical bent or if its media practices afforded ontological pondering. Either way, we often found ourselves talking with residents about "what was real." I do not claim that Second Life holds the final answers. Rather it enabled an attitude of openness, eagerness, and a lack of preconceptions that emerged out of the gaps, kinks, and stutters in our research.

Notes

1 The note card was attributed to Franz Metcalf, a popular Buddhist author. This quote circulates on the Web normally as, "There are, strictly speaking, no enlightened people, there is only enlightened activity" and is frequently attributed to the Sōtō Zen monk and teacher Shunryu Suzuki. See Igor Kononenko, *Teachers of Wisdom* (Pittsburgh, PA: RoseDog Books, 2010), 311. I could not locate the original citation.
2 See note 2 in the Introduction, page 24.
3 See note 1 in the Introduction, page 24.
4 David M. Levy, "No Time to Think: Reflections on Information Technology and Contemplative Scholarship," *Ethics and Information Technology* 9, no. 4 (2007): 237–49.

5 Bikkhu Suwattano, "Mindfulness and Insight on the Internet," www.budsas.org/ebud/ebmed008.htm (accessed November 11, 2015).

6 Keith H. Basso, "'To Give Up on Words': Silence in Western Apache Culture," *Southwestern Journal of Anthropology* 23 no. 3 (1970): 213–30.

7 Catherine Bell, "Performance," in *Critical Terms for Religious Studies*, ed. Mark C. Taylor (Chicago: University of Chicago Press, 1998), 209.

8 On classical sources for mindful breathing see Steven Hein and Dale Wright, eds., *The Zen Canon: Understanding the Classic Texts* (Oxford: Oxford University Press, 2004). On cybernetics see Ross Ashby, *An Introduction to Cybernetics* (New York: Methuen, 1963). On Protestantism see Richard Bauman, "Let Your Words Be Few: Speaking and Silence in Quaker Ideology," in *Let Your Words Be Few: Symbolism of Speaking and Silence among Seventeenth-Century Quakers* (Cambridge: Cambridge University Press, 1983), 20–31.

9 Nicholas Denyer, "Introduction," in Plato, *Alcibiades*, ed. Nicholas Denyer (Cambridge: Cambridge University Press, 2001), 1–26. Cf. Charles M. Young, "Plato and Computer Dating," *Oxford Studies in Ancient Philosophy* 12 (1994): 227–50; Michel Foucault, *The Hermeneutics of the Subject: Lectures at the Collège de France*, 1981–1982 (New York: Picador, 2005).

10 "Featured Events," http://secondlife.com/destinations/events (accessed November 11, 2015).

11 *Orientation to Zen 01 – Zazen (Zen Meditation)*, YouTube Video, 24:29, posted by Eshu Martin, April 30, 2012.

12 While we did not analyze the entirety of the non-Buddhist group's documents, a random sampling of 100 documents showed that only 3.3 percent contained the term "meditation" and that meditation was understood differently. For Christian groups, meditation was a subset of prayer. For example, as the resident Shaker Beatle said during a *Bible study*, Matthew 13:1–9 "is a really good meditation text . . . you can read it and then quietly contemplate the Lord's presence." And for New Age groups such as the Energy Island, meditation was about Energy work models that "can help you to increase your vibration, on physical and on mental level."

13 Victor Hori, *Zen Sand: The Book of Capping Phrases for Kōan Practice* (Honolulu: University of Hawaii Press, 2003).

14 Charles L. Briggs, *Learning How to Ask: A Sociolinguistic Appraisal of the Role of the Interview in Social Science Research* (Cambridge: Cambridge University Press, 1986).

15 Albert Welter, "Mahākāśyapa's Smile: Silent Transmission and the Kung-an (Kōan) Tradition," in *The Kōan: Texts and Contexts in Zen Buddhism*, eds. Steven Heine and Dale S. Wright (Oxford and New York: Oxford University Press, 2000), 75–109. Cf. Heinrich Dumoulin, *Zen Buddhism: A History, Volume 1: India and China* (New York: World Wisdom, 2005), 9.

16 Vincent Horn, "Two-Player Meditation," Buddhistgeeks Lab, www.buddhistgeeks.com/2011/03/two-player-meditation/ (accessed November 11, 2015).

17 "Mindfulness Meditation," Mental Workout, www.mentalworkout.com/store/programs/mindfulness-meditation/ (accessed November 11, 2015).

18 "Meditation/Mindfulness Apps for Smart Phones." WE MEDITATE [caps in original], http://wemeditate.weebly.com/apps.html (accessed November 11, 2015).

19 Alexander Galloway, *Gaming: Essays on Algorithmic Culture* (Minneapolis: University of Minnesota Press, 2006), 19.

20 Catherine Bell, "Performance," in *Critical Terms for Religious Studies*, ed. Mark C. Taylor (Chicago: University of Chicago Press, 1998), 215–16. Cf. Catherine Bell, "The Ritual Body and the Dynamics of Ritual Power," *Journal of Ritual Studies* 4 (1990): 299–313; *Ritual Theory/Ritual Practice* (Oxford: Oxford University Press, 1992).

21 Markku Eskelinen, "The Gaming Situation," *Game Studies* 1, no. 1 (2001). www.gamestudies.org/0101/eskelinen/ (accessed November 11, 2015).

22 The note card gives citation to a September 2007 issue of *Shambhala Sun* and the author Cyndi Lee.

23 Bell, *Ritual Theory/Ritual Practice*, 140.

24 Bell, *Ritual Theory/Ritual Practice*, 141.

25 Jeffrey Brantley, *Calming Your Anxious Mind: How Mindfulness and Compassion Can Free You from Anxiety, Fear and Panic* (Oakland, CA: New Harbinger Publications, 2007), 72.

26 Mindful Staff, "Can I Be Honest with You?" *Mindful*, August 25, 2010, www.mindful.org/can-i-be-honest-with-you/ (accessed November 11, 2015).

27 Kosho Uchiyama, *Opening the Hand of thought: Foundations of Zen Buddhist Practice* (Delhi: Wisdom Publications, 1993).

28 Michel Silverstein, "Metapragmatic Discourse and Metapragmatic Function," in *Reflexive Language*, ed. J. Lucy (New York: Cambridge University Press, 1993), 32–58.

29 Michael Silverstein, "Shifters, Linguistic Categories, and Cultural Description," in *Meaning in Anthropology*, eds. Keith Basso and Henry A. Selby (Albuquerque, NM: University of New Mexico Press, 1976), 11–55.

30 Cited in Michael Downing, *Shoes Outside the Door: Desire, Devotion, and Excess at the San Francisco Zen Center* (Washington, DC: Counterpoint, 2001), 81.

31 Norbert Wiener, *Cybernetics, or Control and Communication in the Animal and the Machine* (New York: Technology Press, 1948), 11.

32 Alan Watts, *The Book: The Taboo against Knowing Who You Are* (London: Jonathan Cape, 1969), 124.

33 Watts, 20.

34 Alan Watts, *The Way of Zen* (New York: Pantheon, 1958), 57.

Conclusion

Mind the gap: Screens, ontologies, and the far shore

> If it (the world) were not empty,
> How could there be another world?
> If the world were unlimited,
> How could there be another world?
> *The Fundamental Wisdom of*
> *the Middle Way,* XXVII.21[1]

Cyber Zen has shown that for convert Zen Second Life practitioners, to be awake online was to mind the gap between the real and the actual, so that one was mindful of the gap between lived conventional reality and the ultimate empty nature of existence. The Conclusion utilizes Second Life's gaps to investigate the convert Zen Buddhist ontologies that not only make silent online meditation possible but desirable. Ontology describes pragmatic models of reality, not only how reality is discussed, but also the social procedures that generate everyday lived worlds.[2] On Wednesday, February 23, 2011, near the end of the research period, I logged on to what would prove to be one of my last times in Second Life. I no longer felt like a *noobie*. I felt immersed in the virtual world, having *friended* many residents, and I was a central member of numerous *groups*. After over three years of fieldwork, it all seemed easy, transparent, and smooth. I had come to identify with my avatar and felt competent, even arrogant. Yet, as I logged on to Second Life there was an incredible amount of *lag*, the colloquial name for the platform's slow reaction time that can be caused by anything from inadequate Internet connection to residents' usage of too many *scripts*. Phenomenologically, I was no longer immersed. Rather I was in two locations at once, in that gap between Second Life and real life. In the actual world I was typing and clicking – struggling with my computer screen, a cold cup of tea in my hand. In the background I could hear the laughter of a neighbor's child and my kettle starting to whistle. In the virtual world, I was fighting lag, which as Jeff Zaleski comments, in *The Soul of Cyber Space*, "This seemingly small thing is, actually, no small thing. It breaks up the flow of the online experience, and tests one's patience time and time again."[3]

My second life was deconstructing.[4] I couldn't move. My *inventory* wasn't loading. I tried to *edit* my *appearance* by changing into my Zen robes but found myself wearing nothing but a *box* that I had attached to myself when trying to unpack its contents. As other residents stuttered past me in lag-produced jerky motions, a few let me know in *instant message* that I had on no clothes. The resident Algama GossipGirl stopped in front of me and handed me a t-shirt and a pair of pants. I put them on and noticed that the shirt, like the one she was wearing in her profile picture, had a logo from the London underground, "Mind the Gap." When I asked her why the "Mind the Gap" shirt, she replied, "*★giggles★* If you don't understand that by now hun . . . like, you don't know anything about Second Life" (Figure C.1). Using the "gap" as a theoretical lens, *Cyber Zen*'s conclusion employs the evidence gleaned from the preceding chapters to investigate Hoben's modes of reality. By focusing on the gap, the chapter can illuminate how Hoben's reality was produced by Second Life's media practices and thus answer *Cyber Zen*'s original question: "Why did the resident

Figure C.1 "Mind the Gap" shirt.

(Second Life snapshot by Gregory Price Grieve).

BodhiDharma Rosebud and the other members of Second Life's convert Zen Buddhist community log on to the virtual world?"

The usual suspects

My research team uncovered the radical fact that people do not stop being human when they log on and that, for many users of digital media, religion plays a central part in how they imagine their humanity. Throughout *Cyber Zen* we have illustrated that residents log on to Second Life's Zen cloud for many reasons: they may seek community because they are geographically isolated; they may desire a convenient way to practice because they are overscheduled; they may be disabled and housebound and quest for relationships; and they may be engaged in some type of identity play. Practitioners logged on to the Hoben Mountain Zen Retreat for all these motives. Yet, what glommed these residents into a Buddhist community was the quest for spiritual liberation. As the resident BodhiDharma Rosebud said in a June 23, 2009, interview, when I asked him why he practiced on Second Life, "To be awake, just that, In My Humble Opinion, the most important thing we can do in this life for ourselves and the world in general (which is clearly, sorely in need of help) is to 'WAKE UP!!!'" (capitalization and punctuation in original).

Often virtual worlds are accused of leaching away users' humanity and their connection to reality. If a culprit exists in our study, however, it is not popular forms of digital media but rather the frequently simplistic and thin descriptions that rob Second Life residents of their agency and imagination. Yet as *Cyber Zen*'s introduction asked, are popular online forms of spiritual practice authentic? Scholars of religion regularly seem scandalized by popular online Buddhism because it is often perceived to have at best a tenuous connection to canonical Asian forms. Yet an original pure Buddhism has only ever existed in adherents' fantasies, and actual everyday practices are always hybrids of hybrids that have taken on the shape of the cultures into which they were introduced. I have illustrated that cybernetics occupies a central place shaping Second Life's Zen. *Cyber Zen* contends that there is a direct genealogical link between the convert Zen practitioners meditating on their cushions and the cybernetic steersmen, who are theorized as a part of, emerging from, and aware of the system in which they dwell. Throughout *Cyber Zen* I have illustrated that understanding the everyday media practices of Second Life's Zen causes one to rethink the notion of authenticity, which for practitioners does not merely entail fidelity to original sources but rather indicates effective spiritual practice in the present moment. As explored throughout the book, the difficulty with studying religion at Hoben was that it was ultimately a silent practice. As argued in the Introduction, and fleshed out in chapter six, silence is neither simply an absence of information that exists outside of language nor does silence have a universal meaning. Rather, silence exists in the gaps produced within specific media practices.

Gap

As illustrated in the preceding chapters, often for Hoben's residents Buddhist Dharma's most consequential aspects were signified by what was not there. When I asked the resident Yidam Roads to define Buddhism, she answered, "to follow the Buddha is to follow in the gaps that he left behind." For many at Hoben, such gaps were significant because they were perceived as outside of representation, as bits of ultimate reality that bubbled to the surface of everyday life. When I asked Human Riddle what it meant to be Buddhist, he sent me the following note card, attributed to Layman P'ang, a legendary seventh-century Chinese sage often considered the exemplar of the nonmonastic practitioner: "Well versed in the Buddha way, I go the non-Way, without abandoning my ordinary person's affairs. The conditioned and name-and-form, all are flowers in the sky. Nameless and formless, I leave birth-and-death."[5]

Gaps were not a thing that existed outside of the virtual world's media practices and were represented by it. Like my experience of lag, on Second Life gaps occurred when media practices broke down, stuttered. And stopped. On the platform, gaps emerged at both the pragmatic material level of the signifier and also on the semantic conceptual level of the signified. For instance, it was not uncommon on Second Life during our research to see pigs fly (Figure C.2).

Figure C.2 Second Life flying pig.

Such conceptual impossibilities are like lag, in that they cause stutters in the seamlessness of the virtual world. They make it seem unreal. While all too common in digital media, such gaps are excluded from representation but at the same time are communicated by what they exclude. On a pragmatic level, my lag was not represented by the platform but communicated by the interruption in the smooth flow of using the media practices. On a semantic level, the flying pig does not only signify an airborne pig but also communicates a lack (that pigs can't fly in the real world).

The lag I was experiencing as I tried to move highlighted that the gap between Second Life and real life was also a breach between residents' actual world existence and their uploaded fantasies. Because users experience this gap as a lack, they desire to close it, to fill it in, to replace it with their fantasies. Yet the gap can never be completely closed and thus disrupts Second Life's media practices and exposes them as conventional and constructed. At the same time, however, the screen communicates and holds a fascinating power over users, because residents' fantasies are virtual, almost real.

Screening desire

It is only when screening media practices break down that we take notice.[6] As I spoke with the resident Algama GossipGirl, I was no longer *inworld*, immersed in the act of communication, but became aware of the screen in front of me. I was frustrated, lost in the gap between the virtual world's promises and its practice. Screens are treated as almost real not because they mimic actual reality, but because they circulate desire. As described in *Cyber Zen's* introduction, screening describes how users engage with their digital devices through a flat digital visual interface. What sticks users to the screen and makes virtual worlds real are the users' desires. Unlike need, desire cannot be satisfied even when needs are met but is an endless shifting from goal to goal, a thirst (*tṛṣṇā*) that cannot be quenched, an itch whose scratching only makes it worse.[7] Desire is the continuous force of the craving to seek and hold onto pleasurable experiences and avoid unpleasant ones. David Webster writes, in "The Philosophy of Desire in the Buddhist Canon," that desire is a "'lack,' or absence, or deficiency."[8] Consider, for instance, a person who is dehydrated and desires a drink of water. If the water is easily available, no thirst occurs. Only when water is lacking are people thirsty. This understanding of desire was clear in the Hoben community. For instance, a meditation note card, titled "Turning to Love," reads, "The refrain, of course, underscores the Buddha's second noble truth, that suffering is the product of attachment. How painful it is to want – until that wanting is fulfilled and there is momentary peace and happiness. That is, until the next wanting comes forth."

As a spiritual media practice, virtual worlds are attractive not because they simulate real life but rather because they give a space for "rezzing" what the actual world lacks. Yet screens do not quench desire, but rather give it a face. Residents' fantasies are hardly fulfilled. Rather, by chasing after their fantasies, the platform's media practices cover over the virtual world's stuttering lack, which keeps residents glued to their screens. The pixels take on a reality because the screen fills the lack of communities, identities, locations, and practices that users imagine but are ultimately unable to obtain in real life. The lost object causes desire, and this desire structures the virtual world and momentarily screens off anxiety and insecurity. Like fabric laid over a hole, Second Life's media practices contour the typography of desire. What gaps mask is not some other alternative but rather a void in the real world that pulls users into the virtual world.

Screens constitute reality by modeling desire in three ways: as a surface for projecting what is missing in real life, as a porous shield protecting against lack, and as a window revealing fantasies. First, screens afford Second Life by acting as a surface on which to project users' desires. Second Life users' fascination with screens frequently occurs because they project upon it what they feel they lack.[9] Residents reflectively know that Second Life images on the computer screen are not actual but nevertheless give the screen a reality because they desire to become enmeshed with what it depicts. Second, screens act as a porous shield that veils desire. Although users attempt to eliminate what they lack by trying to screen it off completely, the lack pierces the screen. This occurs because users only have partial control over media practices, and they feel the tug of desire through the screen of something other than themselves. As such, screens are more than merely a medium that leads us away from reality but shields users from what is desired and what is possible. Like a veil, screens are porous shields that simultaneously divide but also frame reality by allowing glimpses of a fantasized other. Third, screens afford reality by opening a window onto virtually impossible desires. As the cultural critic Slavoj Žižek writes in *The Abyss of Freedom*, "what defines the properly 'human dimension' is the presence of a screen, a frame, through which we communicate with the 'suprasensible' virtual universe to be found nowhere in reality."[10]

Ontologies

"What is really real, luv?" was one of the first questions that the resident Algama asked me when we first met. Such ontological questions were endemic to my research team's time inworld, and the reality screened by a group determined the type of spiritual practices that they found possible in the virtual world. Buddhists, it seemed more than other groups, wrestled with these issues. As the resident Yidam Roads's profile read, "Second Life mirrors the first, or is it the other way around?" When I asked BodhiDharma Rosebud whether the virtual world was real, he said, "Second Life is like a shining mirror, never let the dust accumulate." I asked him to expand and he replied, "Second Life does not exist, where can the dust itself accumulate?" I laughed and told him that he was just butchering Huineng, the sixth and last Patriarch of Zen Buddhism. There was a long pause and BodhiDharma wrote. "It is, it isn't, it isn't isn't, and it isn't isn't isn't."

I was taken back by Algama's question. I was not sure what the Hoben community conceived as real. Ultimately virtual worlds are utopic, because users actually go nowhere. I'd been rushing and had to slow down to decipher what she had said by going back and picking her text out of the chaos of many overlapping lines of chat. I'd been trying hard to politely brush her off, because on the surface she appeared interested in little more than shopping and having a good time (and involving me in both activities). Algama, however, was neither the first nor would she be the last resident to ask this question, and such ontological inquiry emerged often during our research. To a certain extent, the questions about the nature of reality arose because of the presence of my research team. The type of questions we were asking likely triggered residents' curiosity.[11] Also, no doubt, just being sentient presupposes inquiry into the nature of reality and existence.[12] We maintain, however, that Second Life's media practices accelerate examination into the nature of reality and that the virtual world often seemed to transform normal individuals into metaphysicians who were forced to face the meaning of reality.

Residents' ontologies transform the programmable bits displayed across a screen into lived reality. "Reality," as the way the world actually is, may seem like too big a concept to fail. It is often assumed that reality holds the commonsensical ground on which culture is spread like ideological icing. To what extent, however, does reality as a phenomenon exist unmediated and to what extent do media practices determine our experience of it? One strains to imagine a world without reality. Yet the modern use of the term emerged only a few hundred years ago from early Enlightenment thought and was tied to elite male European encounters with other groups of people both internal and foreign.[13] Over the last 100 years, however, twentieth-century psychology, physics, and philosophy have all in their own ways challenged the concept of an unmediated reality at the most basic level.[14] Reality has also bent under the weight of postwar American spirituality. As the American sociologist Robert Bellah writes in *Beyond Belief: Essays on Religion in a Post-Traditional World*, "reality is never as real as we think it is."[15]

Extrapolating from Second Life's residents' perceptions, we make two claims about Second Life ontologies. First, reality on the platform does not exist objectively but rather emerges from media practices. As James Carey writes, in *A Cultural Approach to Communication*, "reality is brought into existence, is produced by communication."[16] Media practices do not necessarily have to invent reality out of whole cloth but recycle what has come before. Rather than an essential category, these "realities," as the sociologists Peter L. Berger and

Thomas Luckmann originally argue, are a "social construction" that proves a "human product, or more precisely, an ongoing human production."[17] To call something socially constructed is to emphasize its dependence on contingent aspects of our social selves, which are dependent on both human and non-human elements. Social reality is conditioned through the repeated repetition of public performative acts that create persistent lived worlds, which in the American philosopher of language John Searle's words, "persist through time independently of the urges and inclinations of the participants."[18] Second, we contend that how different religious groups perceived the relationship between the sacred and profane shaped how they perceived the relationship between the virtual and actual. By breaking the platform, the lag made the constructed nature of the virtual world obvious, which made the modes of reality on which it is based more conspicuous and available for analysis.

Virtual/actual

Reality at Hoben was screened through two interwoven pairs of Möbius strip–like bands of media practices: virtual/actual and ultimate/conventional (Figure C.3). Residents were conscious of the boundaries between these different

Figure C.3 Interwoven pairs of Möbius strip–like bands of media practices: virtual/actual and ultimate/conventional.

realities but passed through the borders often unaware. The Möbius effect indicates that media practices are in flux and that the virtual/actual, as well as the conventional/ultimate, never exist on their own but only emerge in relationship to each other. Each member of each pair as well as both pairs were, to borrow a Buddhist term, interdependent (*pratītyasamutpāda*), and while distinct, the different realities interpenetrated each other and in the end were just empty pixels on the screen. As touched upon in chapter two, at Hoben, dependent origination was often tied to Thích Nhất Hạnh's idea of "Interbeing," a state of the connectedness and interdependence of all phenomena, and ultimately had entangled with cybernetic procedures.

For convert Buddhists Second Life and real life were different but the same, and Second Life's empty nature illuminated the illusory quality of real life. Conditioned reality is produced through desires, which in the case of Second Life turn the flat pixels of the computer screen into a virtual world, which could not exist on its own but is always dependent on human beings and their material systems of communication. Second Life and real life were obviously different because one was actual and the other virtual. They were similar, however, because both Second Life and real life were conditioned conventional realities, those mutually constituted and historically contextualized material discourses, practices, and objects by which people construct, interpret, and manage their everyday lives. Because of emptiness, for many Hoben practitioners, while just a media-created fantasy, Second Life was an authentic conventional reality, not just a fake copy of the actual world. As the resident Mystic Moon wrote, on December 2, 2008, in a note card titled, "Golden Sentence of Reality (version 1)," "Reality, based on the concept of the social teaching of what your senses tells you, is an illusion linked with terms and forms in your mind. But that doesn't mean that it doesn't exist." A few days later he wrote, "Golden Sentence of Reality (version 2): "When reality is an illusion, and let's all agree that Second Life is an illusion. We are also aware we can call illusions reality – therefore, Second Life is also reality!"

Like a Möbius strip, while the boundary between Second Life and real life is ultimately unreal, just a human-made fiction emerging from digital media practices, from the perspective of immersed users, Second Life operates as a conventional social reality whose structure is created through media practices. While Second Life may be nothing more than a screened fantasy, the virtual world's media practices do create a unique social space that has very real consequences for its users. Media practices are not solipsistic. While individual residents play a part in the construction of these other realities, because it is such an intersubjective complex system, it conditions them in ways over which they have no control. Because of the interaction with the platform's code, as well as other residents, their media practices become an object that confronts them as a facticity external to and other than themselves. Once produced, the social worlds created on the platform cannot simply be wished away. As I learned during my many months of "*noobhood*," even if it is a social construct, one can be incorrect about Second Life's conventional truths. They become something "out there," which resists the actions of its producers. Like any "lived reality," a location where residents and their roles are set, there is a difference in Second Life between getting it right and getting it wrong.

Being pixels on the screen, ultimately there was no difference between the virtual and actual. Like a Möbius strip, if you were to engage Second Life's media practices you would always return to the starting point of actual keystrokes and mouse clicks, having traversed both the virtual and the actual world, but without ever having crossed an edge. Yet, while in the end there is no difference between the two, there was a distinction on the social level of lived reality. In an interview with the resident WinterSong Camelot, I asked her whether she had any real life friends whom she had met in Second Life. She answered, "I haven't actually crossed the thin line that separates the two." Similarly, during an interview in May 21, 2009, the resident Ashley Lee said, "I am still finding boundaries between Second Life and real life, that is what makes it fun."

The actual and virtual depend upon each other for their existence. If Second Life's media practices operated simply and solely contrary to the principle of reality, their products would be nothing but pale imitations of real life, and the virtual world nothing but an imaginary illusion. As conventional realities Second Life and real life are dependent upon each other for their social existence. If Second Life exists, real life exists; if the virtual ceases to exist, the actual also ceases to exist. Obviously Second Life cannot exist on its own but is dependent on real life. Users never leave their chairs when they log on, and rather than going someplace "unreal," users actually just move pixels around on the screen. If all Linden Lab's servers were terminated, the virtual world would cease. In addition, avatars are contingent on actual people. Users cannot upload themselves to the cloud. Cyberspace does not allow users to discard bodies, as became apparent during my research team's fieldwork; users still need to eat, sleep, and use the bathroom. More subtly, Hoben would not be if residents had not built it; and it might not have been built at all, at least not in its present form. Had the residents come from a different society – if they had had different needs, values, or interests – they might well have built a different kind of thing, or built the present one differently, or not at all.

Less obvious, there would be no need for the concept of the actual if there were not a virtual; for "real life" to exist, there must be media practices that constitute it as Second Life's other. The virtual interpenetrates the actual. As the French philosopher Gilles Deleuze writes, "purely actual objects do not exist."[19] Because people have used media practices to create alternative fictions – from Paleolithic caves to movie theaters – in one sense people have always been virtual. Yet Second Life's dichotomy between the virtual and the actual has been shaped by digital media's late twentieth-century reception. Derived from cyberpunk novels, as the opposite of cyberspace, actual reality is often described as "meat space." For instance, the cyberpunk writer William Gibson's novels note the difference between the "Net of the console cowboys and the world of the meat outside." As *Cyber Zen* describes in chapter one, because of digital utopianism, the virtual has often been posited as a place of liberation and the free play of the imagination. As can be seen, even in early discussions such as the American pioneer of digital technology Ted Nelson's 1974 *Computer Lib/Dream Machines*, often cyberspace is imagined to hold "New Freedoms through Computer Screens."[20]

The creation of virtual and actual is not an abstract mysterious process but is produced by everyday media practices. To take one instance, *inworld* it was routine to mark a line of chat with "RL" (real life), which indicated that it referred to the meatspace of the actual world. In interviews over 13 percent of lines of chat were marked with "RL." For instance, I asked the resident, Twilight Language, "How would you compare your Avatar to your Real Life self?" She answered, "I've tried to make it parallel, I don't have as much grey in RL but it signals my age, clothing wise I dress very similar." Yet interviewing does not typify the way residents usually interact with each other, and our research questions seemed to generate more reference to the actual world. Still, an analysis of a random 1,000 lines of non-roleplay chat, indicated that "RL" marked speech acts accounted for 4.6 percent of all lines of text and tended to happen at the beginning and end of conversations. For instance, during the first Second Life Buddhist Council meeting, the Resident Zeus Ides interrupted, "sorry need to go phone in RL. Be right back."

Conventional/ultimate

What the gaps in Second Life revealed is that for many Buddhist practitioners, intertwined with the actual/virtual was a second band of reality, the conventional/ultimate. *Cyber Zen* contends that for convert Buddhists, the virtual/actual, as well as the ultimate/conventional, only exist in relation to each other. Obviously, because the virtual is dependent on the actual, Second Life boundaries are porous and not hermetically sealed behind the computer screen. Still, while there is ultimately no difference between on- and offline practices, there is nevertheless a conventional social difference, and this conventional difference is as real as other social practices that take place in the actual world. The horizon of these entwined realities – virtual/actual and ultimate/conventional – made Second Life's media practices spiritually significant to Zen practitioners. Yet, these realities did not exist as a preexisting underlying structure but emerged from the structured chaos of everyday media practices.

As a conventional reality, Second Life cannot exist on its own but is always dependent on human beings and their material systems of communication. For convert Buddhists, Second Life and real life were different but equally valid, and Second Life's empty nature illuminated the illusionary quality of the real life. They were obviously different because one was actual and the other virtual.

They were similar, in that both Second Life and real life were conditioned reality. Second Life differed in one other important manner, however. For people to recognize the truth about their desire, it needed to be given a face.[21] Practitioners need to become mindful of, as Human Riddle said, "What makes them tick." Second Life screened these desires, making them visible and conspicuous.

The very interdependence between the virtual/actual axis generated the relationship between conventional/ultimate axis. Convert Buddhists tended to approach both Second Life and real life through the lens of conventional reality which, as described in chapter five, was often glossed as "*samsāra.*" Samsara referred to lived fantasies, which for many were just as real on Second Life as in real life. As the resident Tripitaka Stormcloak's profile read, "This is samsara. Experience the world as a bubble, a wave, an illusion, a dream." As detailed in chapter two, fantasies are not artificial but authorize desire and play a part in determining lived reality. Conventional reality on Second Life had a family resemblance derived from Mahayana Buddhism where it indicates the socially conditioned lived world of everyday reality (*saṃvṛti-satya*). Samsara was theorized to be produced through codependent origination, a concept that argues that phenomena only arise in relation to other phenomena.[22] As touched upon in chapter five, Hoben's concept of samsara was also entangled with a general notion of networked systems, particularly Thích Nhất Hạnh's idea of "Interbeing," the state of the connectedness and interdependence of all phenomena.

Two truths

Cyber Zen argues that Hoben's ontology was a popularized version of the Mahāyāna Buddhist Two Realities Doctrine that claims that there are two types of reality, conventional and ultimate.[23] On the ultimate level there are simply aggregates – form, sensation, perception, mental formation, and consciousness – arising and passing away. The conventional notion of phenomena, on the other hand, arises in response to these aggregates. The Two Truths Doctrine makes a distinction between the constructed nature of everyday reality (*samsāra)* and the ultimate empty nature of the world (*nirvāna)*. As Nagarjuna writes, "The Buddha's teaching of the Dharma is based on two truths: A truth of worldly convention and an ultimate truth."[24]

Ultimately what was real for most Second Life Buddhist practitioners was emptiness (*śūnyatā*), the teaching that all phenomena lack independent essences and emerge into existence only in relationship to each other. As the classic Buddhist philosopher Nagarjuna writes in the *Fundamental Verses on the Middle Way* (*Mūlamadhyamakakārikā*), "whatever is dependently co-arisen, that is explained to be emptiness."[25] As described in chapter two, at Hoben "emptiness" did not mean that a phenomenon does not exist but that it has no static intrinsic essence. Emptiness is not a sui generis static void standing behind the veil of the illusion of conventional reality. Unlike the notion of a God, there is no Great

Emptiness out there somewhere to be found. Instead, as Human Riddle stated, "emptiness is right here, right now." Emptiness is simply the ontological condition (*pratyaya Thích*) of the world that everything is conventional, a vast network of interdependent and continuously changing phenomena. At Hoben emptiness is no different from conventional reality; emptiness indicates that conventional reality is conventional. In other words, emptiness is neither a thing nor a cause but rather a conditioned insight that phenomena are impermanent, that they lack intrinsic independent existence, and instead are dependently arisen.

Take, for example, the book you hold in your hands. Ultimately the book is "empty" because it holds no nonrelational self-intrinsic existence; one hundred years from now it will probably no longer exist as a physical object, and even now it depends upon human and nonhuman beings for its existence, as well as the material media practices through which it is disseminated. On a material level, this very book is conditioned by a network of people who made, wrote, and now read it using a semiotic system that evolved in a specific historical and cultural situation. Moreover, if a culture had not evolved "books," what appears to us as an obvious unity – a book – might appear as a flutter of pages or a good doorstop to the people of that culture. This book, like all conventional phenomena, as Jay Garfield writes in "Dependent Arising and the Emptiness of Emptiness," "is a purely arbitrary slice of space-time chosen by us as the referent of a single name, and not an entity demanding on its own, recognition and philosophical analysis to reveal its essence."[26]

What is key, for the Two Realities Doctrine, however, and what makes Second Life convert Zen Buddhist media practices spiritual, is that all these realities are true and actually required for liberation. As Nagarjuna writes, "The Buddha's teaching of the Dharma is based on two truths: A truth of worldly convention and an ultimate truth." The ultimate truth does not deny the reality of the conventional world, it simply reveals that it is empty. In other words, for most at Hoben reality is conventionally real but ultimately empty. All phenomena have both characteristics, and both characteristics are real. As Nagarjuna writes, "Everything is real and is not real, Both real and not real, Neither real nor not real. This is Lord Buddha's teaching." Just as a resident requires users and avatars, and Second Life requires both the virtual and the actual, an authentic online Buddhist practice needs an awareness of both conventional and ultimate realities. As Nagarjuna writes, "Without a foundation in the conventional truth the significance of the ultimate cannot be taught. Without understanding the significance of the ultimate, liberation is not achieved."[27]

Spiritual liberation

For those at Hoben, spiritual liberation does not indicate a state of mind but rather a media practice. For convert Buddhists on Second Life, the ontological orientation that afforded mindfulness proved similar to the Two Truths Doctrine that indicates that realities appear distinct while not being separate and affirms the understanding that while distinctions exist, dichotomies are ultimately an illusion. As I stated at the start of the chapter, on Friday, October 23, 2009, I asked BodhiDharma whether Second Life was real. Unsatisfied with his first answer, I asked him again (in all capitals, this time, to get his attention) "IS SECOND LIFE REAL?" There was a long pause, which often meant that he was searching the Web or his bookshelf. "There is no difference between samsara and nirvana. If you are mindful they are the same thing." And then laughed, "I don't know." There was another long pause. "Those who hold to things are dumb as cows. Those who hold to nirvana are even dumber."[28]

If one "minds the gap" and takes a clear look at Second Life and its relationship to real life, one sees that "reality" is not an essential state of being but a media practice. As discussed in chapter two, being mindful of media allowed Zen adherents an authentic spirituality that was neither the mimicking practices of fundamentalists nor the ludic imaginative play of New Agers. For convert Buddhist adherents, to be spiritual was to be "awake," which described media practices that were perceived not to transcend everyday reality but rather to make adherents mindful of the empty nature of everyday life. The aim of these media practices was an awareness of the practitioner's own desire. As the resident Tai Buckinghamshire said in an interview on April 4, 2009, "So basically, you are able to experience things here that you don't experience in real life. That sense of ★bare★ attention is so easy. It makes being here more 'real' than 'real life.'" Gaps did not clear practitioners' perception, opening a door to what lies outside of signification. Instead, by poking holes in the smooth transparent flow of media practices, gaps exposed their constructed nature, thus affording the insight that not only the virtual world, but also the actual world, is empty.

Spiritual liberation, as the resident Algama GossipGirl said, was "to be open to what the universe throws at you." A note card titled "Waking Up to What You Do" reads, "Enter Here — just this moment of openness, the truth of Just This. Just This is the gateway of transformation, when we can give over completely to our experience; it transforms into the peace and joy that comes with an open heart." The resident Ashley Lee, an avid gardener, described awakening in botanical terms. "It's like when a flower bursts open." Others, such as Rasa Vibration, described awakening in terms of bliss. When I asked her why she meditated, she answered, "I feel a creative boundless satisfaction. It's erotic, mystical, maybe even political." The meditation note card titled "A Wheel Out Of Kilter [Excerpt]" reads,

> The Buddha-dharma points the way to a similar, but more universal and profound, sense of "Aha!" It's not about pondering some vague, faraway realm. It's about here and now. About waking up to this moment, seeing this for what it is. This is called enlightenment, or awakening. This awakening is available to all of us, at every moment, without exception.[29]

To be awake was to be mindful of the world and oneself as being empty. As the resident Mystic Moon wrote on February 3, 2009, in a note card titled "Golden Sentence Awake," "One's awareness, to be awake, is to see through the clouds of the mind, breaking its chains to see and feel clearly oneness in many." For many at Hoben, the experience allows them to stop identifying with a narrow sense of ego and to start identifying, as the resident Human Riddle stated, "with the wider and more spacious context of awareness itself." As Yidam said in my interview, "Zen is about taking off the masks that we wear when we face the world. One day we can face the world as we are, not as we want the world to see us." Being awake was not insight into a transcendent realm but a mode of silent practice, which like lag, disrupted normal activities, thus generating a spiritual insight. As a spiritual media practice, being awake did not communicate new information but was rather perceived to bring about a shift in perception. As a note card titled "The Real Aim of Meditation" read, "Meditation is not about calming the emotions, it's about transforming the mind." Cyber Zen allowed Hoben's practitioners to assume a new relationship to conventional reality, which did not transcend it but allowed them to be nonattached.

The far shore

For those at Hoben, spiritual liberation meant to reach the far shore, to gain an awareness that although residents needed conventional norms in order to live and to know in what direction to transform their social world, that they were also constrained by media practices in ways that could not help but alienate. To cross over was to cease positing that something desired was lost and to accept that desires are posited by oneself as a means to compensate for the suffering inherent in human existence. Because Second Life allowed residents to give a face to their spiritual fantasies, Second Life Buddhism allowed residents to move from morals to ethics: from merely judging what is right and wrong, to creating alternative ways of being human. For Buddhists, Second Life's screening media practices are not merely a game of public fronts – because for the convert Buddhists there is no self (*anātman*) behind the mask. Instead, Second Life events such as online silent media practices embody Two Truths and are nondual. Through mindful media practices, convert Zen adherents engage the relationship between the virtual and actual to understand the gap between the conventional and ultimate. As BodhiDharma Rosebud said at the end of a long conversation, "There is no difference between samsara and nirvana. If you are mindful they are the same thing." As the Buddhist scholar Jay Garfield writes, in "Taking Conventional Truth Seriously: Authority Regarding Deceptive Reality," "The transcendence of ignorance is hence not the transcendence of *apprehension* of the conventional, but the transcendence of deception by it."[30]

In November 2009, near the end of our fieldwork, the resident Bodhi-Dharma vanished. His disappearance was not surprising. As a cloud community, groups whose media practices take place primarily online, Zen practitioners always seemed to be coming and going. Cloud communities often display a high "churn," the rate at which individuals flow into a community as compared with the rate at which they flow out. BodhiDharma's disappearance followed a typical pattern. He logged on less and less. Suddenly, he was online quite frequently to say farewell to his friends and to give away the objects in his inventory. My avatar still holds BodhiDharma's meditation bell and one of his robes. And finally he deleted his avatar. After he left, I emailed him and asked him why he had departed; he replied, "Second Life has been an adventure. Lots of good friends, _/!_. It has made me mindful of my practice but like a raft, it has taken me as far as it will go. Time to put it down."

To be spiritually liberated is to have crossed over, or traversed, to the other side of the fantasies that structure everyday life and to assume a new mindful position in relationship to them. To cross over is not to deny one's cravings but to stop being ceaselessly caught in their pull. As the resident Human Riddle said, "In Second Life I've seen a lot of aspects of reality I didn't realize existed. I've come away with an altered perspective. Maybe it takes a thing like this to break down the walls of the grove. My time here, the whole experiment, has been worth it." Often the Buddha's Four Noble Truths (*catvāri āryasatyāni*) were invoked to explain nonattachment and the notion that desire and craving could be extinguished. At Hoben nonattachment indicated not that one had separated from worldly concerns but rather that one was mindful of the emotions and desires that everyday life created. Nonattachment did not require that practitioners give up what they desired, but rather a new mindful perspective that created responsibility towards one's own desires and the suffering caused by them to oneself and others.

By making residents aware of their interconnectedness to both human and nonhuman elements, mindful nonattached awareness of their social responsibilities caused them to cease looking for the answer to one's desire but to accept that desire and suffering are part, as Human went on to say, "of just being a person." Users always reach out for what they desire. Many practitioners applied Buddhism's long complex history of addressing desire as a balm to the disease caused by Network Consumer Society. As a note card handed out on July 28, 2008, during a meditation session, titled "Life Comes Through" and attributed to Dzigar Kongtrul Rinpoche, read, "Imagine craving absolutely nothing from the world. Imagine cutting the invisible strings that so painfully bind us. What would that be like? Imagine the freedoms that come from the ability to enjoy things without having to acquire them, own them, and possess them."

Practitioners came to accept that suffering is not an event with a winner and a loser but a necessary part of the situation for human beings. As Georgina Florida said after an intense bout of contention in the community, to be mindful means giving up "settling the scores" of the resentful and the acquisitive project of trying to reclaim one's happiness from others. A note card that circulated at Hoben soon after, titled "Loss without Anger" and attributed to Georgina Florida, states,

> Understanding that life happens does not mean we will not be subject to sorrow. We are human. We have preferences. We are human Buddhas. Even Buddha preferred to teach what he had experienced rather than remain sitting under his tree. We would all prefer our loved ones not to die and we will all grieve their passing. We feel. It is what makes us human. it is what makes us Buddhas. Feel love, feel sorrow, feel joy, they go with life happening. _/ | _.

For many, crossing to the far shore was as a type of "dehypnosis." A note card handed out on April 24, 2008, titled "Sunset Boulevard" read, "I sometimes think of my Zen practice as a process of 'de-hypnosis,' reversing the developmentally necessary but contrary process – begun years ago by parents and teachers, schoolyard chums and siblings, screenwriters and advertising executives – of turning me into a conditioned good little American." "If you want to be free" as the resident Rasa Vibration said on May 23, 2009, "you need to wake up amidst the dreamlike illusion. You are able to witness it, if you are able to see it as it really is, if you are able to understand it as it really is, if you are able to work on it as it really is, you can use anything to attain the Way." A note card from October 10, 2009, titled "Open," reads, "Nirvana, or whatever you want to call it, means the complete deconstruction of all of our rigid mental patterns and habits as well as the deconstruction of all of our limiting beliefs. This deconstruction creates a space for true inquiry."[31]

Conclusion

In retrospect, BodhiDharma Rosebud's departure also marked the end of my research team's time on Second Life. We logged on less and less and finally found ourselves only going inworld reluctantly to check sources. What had been an enjoyable adventure and arena of discovery had simply become a chore. We also found that we tended to contact informants by email, skype, or telephone rather than meet them inworld "face to face." Leaving the field is common in ethnography and allowed us to ask again, with greater critical distance, the study's original question: "Why did BodhiDharma and other members of the Second Life's convert Zen community log on to the virtual world?"

Cyber Zen has illustrated that residents logged on to form community, fashion identity, build places, and engage in religious practice. The ultimate answer is that they sought spiritual liberation. Can digital media practices, however, lead to authentic Buddhism? For the vast majority of practitioners at Hoben, the ultimate point of cyber Zen was to end suffering (*duḥkha*). BodhiDharma Rosebud described suffering as "wheels out of kilter. Like when my truck is stuck in the mud." Mystic Moon described suffering as caused by "'brokenness,' an inability to effectively find good responses to situations because of interference caused by previously learned responses." When I was in a long conversation with Algama GossipGirl about suffering and Second Life, she went on to say that some used the virtual world as a way to end suffering but that others became addicted to the illusion and wanted to live as something that they could not in real life. "Second Life does not work for everyone. Some never see the point? Some can never overcome the learning curve. And like me, others get stuck, repeating and repeating the same, addictive actions over and over ★: (★."

Network Consumer Society makes it hard to be authentically human because it has dissolved many traditional communities, identities, locations, and practices, leaving many in contemporary society to perceive themselves as spiritually adrift. Online spiritual practice encourages users to keep alive the eternal human questions that testify to everyone's longing for authentic forms of life, which are truly worthy of being lived. Ultimately Hoben's spiritual practice was an ethical stance. To be nonattached and awake was perceived not to change oneself or one's social role. Residents needed social roles in order to live, but these could be inauthentic and cause suffering. Residents reported that attachment to their fantasies veiled them from the implication and responsibility for how they experienced the world. To be awake was to traverse the fantasy so as to reavow one's subjective responsibility. To be awakened in this context did not mean that one was "cured," however, only that one was mindful and aware of the systems that caused suffering and thus gave perspective and the ability to change, learn, and grow.

One might argue that convert Zen Buddhist practices merely habituate practitioners to a Network Consumer life – that online practice is a stress-relieving opiate that lessens the symptoms but does not cure the cause. Second Life Buddhism, however, also allowed residents to move from morals to ethics. If morals judge right from wrong, ethics puts these principles into practice. Both popular forms of spirituality and virtual worlds provide alternative models for people to deal with the reality in which they live. As Skeptical Starshine said in a May 23, 2009, interview, "Second Life also offers the opportunity to be things you want to be . . . or even don't want to be. To try things on, experiment. The pace of communications is significantly different and I think it enhances the ability to succeed in learning new life styles." The resident Algama GossipGirl said, "it leads to what Taoists call 'the way,' a full integration of Who You Are, embracing both the good and the bad, the strong and the weak, the masculine and the feminine . . . all polarities within you." Georgina Florida said, "Second Life is the greatest therapeutic role-playing tool ever created. As such, it can be used to grow as a person or to maintain and even deepen our real life problems."

Cyber Zen has illustrated that while Second Life may not have been perfect, adherents found it good enough for spiritual practice. During our research,

Hoben's adherents harnessed Second Life's potential to fantasize new ways of being in the world and prevented these emergent media from simply becoming a depersonalizing instrument monopolized by a powerful few. Media practices always exist in a tug-of-war between affordances and human agency, owners and users, and those who have and those who have not. All media are mercenary, a gun for hire, which are shaped by culture and the desires of those who use them. While people use media practices, they do not use them just as they please, and they do not use them under self-selected circumstances but rather under circumstances existing already, given and transmitted from the past.

The Second Life convert Zen Buddhist spiritual media practices were authentic neither because they created utopic locations completely separate from the actual world nor because Second Life could ever hope to be a perfect copy of real life. Instead, the spiritual practices were authentic because of the weird ambiguous gaps between the virtual and actual, between fantasy and fact, that illustrate that reality and identities are not fixed and do not determine who we are. In the gap between profane and divine, virtual and actual, as well as the real and imagined, residents such as BodhiDharma were always already outsiders. The gap characterizes the state between what is imagined and what is lived and creates a margin on which alternative visions can stand. This marginality, this zone of indeterminacy, is an ethical standpoint outside the norm from which artists, writers, and social critics have always been able to look past the status quo in order to see society from an alternative perspective. In these gaps, residents did not simply reflect on the meaning of reality but actively produced alternative media practices that resisted the monolithic dominance of Network Consumer Society. As Yidam Roads said in an interview from May 22, 2009, "You begin to pay attention to the things you manifest in Second Life, and they carry over into real life. Sort of like a sandbox, a safe way to play around with your concept of yourself and your world."

Notes

1 Jay Garfield, *The Fundamental Wisdom of the Middle Way: Nagarjuna's Mūlamadhyamakakārikā* (New York: Oxford University Press, 1995).
2 Pertti Alasuutari, *Social Theory and Human Reality* (London: Sage Publications, 2002).
3 Jeff Zaleski, *The Soul of Cyberspace: How Technology Is Changing Our Spiritual Lives* (San Francisco: HarperEdge, 1997), 28.
4 ". . . deconstruction doesn't consist in a set of theorems, axioms, tools, rules, techniques, methods . . . there is no deconstruction, deconstruction has no specific object . . ." (Jacques Derrida, "'As If I Were Dead': An Interview with Jacques Derrida," in *Applying: To Derrida*, eds. J. Brannigan, R. Robbins, and J. Wolfreys (London: Macmillan, 1996), 218. Cf. Martin Heidegger, *Basic Writings* (New York: Harper and Row, 1976), 22–27; Huber Dreyfus, *Being-in-the-World: A Commentary on Heidegger's Being and Time*, Division 1 (Cambridge, MA: MIT Press, 1991).
5 "Layman P'ang, Linji Yixuan, Hakuin Ekaku," Many Roads, http://bodhicharya.org/manyroads/layman-pang-linji-yixuan-hakuin-ekaku/ (accessed November 12, 2014).
6 "When we concern ourselves with something, the entities which are most closely ready-to-hand may be met as something unusable, not properly adapted for the use we have

decided upon . . . We discover its unusability, however, not by looking at it and establishing its properties, but rather by the circumspection of the dealings in which we use it" (Martin Heidegger, *Being in Time* [London: SCM Press, 1962], 102). Cf. "For example, if a carpenter, while doing some work, finds his Hatchet of excellent service, then this Hatchet has thereby attained its end and perfection; but if he should think: this Hatchet has rendered me such good service now, therefore I shall let it rest, and exact no further service from it, then precisely this Hatchet would fail of its end, and be a Hatchet no more" (Benedictus de Spinoza, *The Short Treatise on God, Man and His Well-Being* [New York: Russell & Russell, 1963], part II, chap. XVIII).

7 Thanissaro Bhikkhu, "Kama Sutta: Sensual Pleasure," Sutta Nipata 4.1, www.accessto insight.org/tipitaka/kn/snp/snp.4.01.than.htmlwww.accesstoinsight.org/tipitaka/kn/snp/snp.1.03.than.html (accessed November 12, 2015).
8 David Webster, *The Philosophy of Desire in the Buddhist Pali Canon* (Cambridge: Cambridge University Press, 2005), 22.
9 Christian Metz, "The Imaginary Signifier," in *Psychoanalysis and Cinema*, ed. Ann Kaplan (London/Basingstoke: MacMillan Press, 1982), 1–87.
10 Slavoj Žižek, *The Plague of Fantasies* (London/New York: Verso, 1997a), 60.
11 Charles L. Briggs, *Learning How to Ask: A Sociolinguistic Appraisal of the Role of the Interview in Social Science Research* (Cambridge: Cambridge University Press, 1986).
12 Daniel A. Getz, "Sentient Beings," in *Encyclopedia of Buddhism*, vol. 2, ed. Robert E. Buswell (New York: Macmillan Reference, 2004), 760.
13 Sally Haslanger, "Objective Reality, Male Reality, and Social Construction," in *Women, Knowledge and Reality*, eds. Ann Garry and Marilyn Pearsall (New York: Routledge, 1996), 84–108.
14 On the unconscious, see Sigmund Freud, *An Outline of Psychoanalysis* (New York: Norton, 1940). On historical materialism, see Frederick Engels, *Dialectics of Nature* (Moscow: Foreign Languages Publishing House, 1954). On truth and knowledge, see Friedrich W. Nietzsche, *Human, All Too Human: A Book for Free Spirits,* trans. Marion Faber, with Stephen Lehmann (Lincoln: University of Nebraska Press, 1984). On "cat state" of reality, see Erwin Schrödinger, "The Present Situation in Quantum Mechanics," www.tuhh.de/rzt/rzt/it/QM/cat.html (accessed November 12, 2015).
15 Robert Bellah, *Beyond Belief: Essays on Religion in a Post-Traditionalist World* (Berkeley, CA: University of California Press, 1970), 254.
16 James W. Carey, *Communication as Culture: Essays on Media and Society* (New York: Routledge, 1988), 25.
17 Peter Berger and Thomas Luckmann, *The Social Construction of Reality: A Treatise in the Sociology of Knowledge* (Garden City, NY: Anchor Books, 1966), 54.
18 John R. Searle, *The Construction of Social Reality* (New York: Penguin, 1996), 78.
19 Gilles Deleuze and Claire Parnet, *Dialogues* (New York: Columbia University Press, 1987), 148–53.
20 Theodor Nelson, *Computer Lib: You Can and Must Understand Computers Now/Dream Machines: New Freedoms through Computer Screens – A Minority Report* (Chicago: Hugo Book Service, 1974), DM cover (Nelson's book has two front convers. The flip side is Dream Machines here indicated by DM).
21 Emmanuel Lévinas, *Ethics and Infinity* (Pittsburg, PA: Duquesne University Press, 1985), 95, 98, 119.
22 Thanissaro Bhikkhu, "Paticca-samuppada-vibhanga Sutta: Analysis of Dependent Co-arising," www.accesstoinsight.org/tipitaka/sn/sn12/sn12.002.than.html (accessed November 12, 2015).
23 Jay Garfield, *Empty Words: Buddhist Philosophy and Cross-Cultural Interpretation* (Oxford: Oxford University Press, 2002), 24–45.
24 Garfield, *The Fundamental Wisdom of the Middle Way*, 68.
25 Garfield, *The Fundamental Wisdom of the Middle Way*, 69.

26 Garfield, *Empty Words*, 25.
27 Garfield, *The Fundamental Wisdom of the Middle Way*, 296, 298.
28 I could not locate the source of BodhiDharma's citation but believe it pertains to the Emperor Wu. See John McRae, *Seeing through Zen: Encounter, Transformation, and Genealogy in Chinese Chan Buddhism* (Berkeley: University of California Press, 2003), 22.
29 Steven Hagen, *Buddhism Plain and Simple* (North Clarendon, VT: Tuttle Publishing, 1997), 31.
30 Jay L. Garfield, "Taking Conventional Truth Seriously: Authority Regarding Deceptive Reality," *Philosophy East and West* 60, no. 3 (2010): 350.
31 Anam Thubten, "A Tomato Opened My Mind," *Tricycle*, www.tricycle.com/insights/how-tomato-opened-my-mind (accessed November 12, 2015).

Appendix I
Cyber Zen's theoretical tool box

This short alphabetical catalog lists *Cyber Zen*'s key theoretical tools. I constructed the toolbox for my use but felt that it might also be helpful to other readers. A few of the terms I coined specifically for this study, and some I borrowed from other scholars of religion and media or poached from other fields. Those interested in the sources of these theoretical terms should consult the book's index and bibliography.

Actual An etic term for the emic term real life.

Affordance The properties that shape how an object can be used, which block, increase, or decrease a particular action. For example, a doorknob affords the opening of a door. In media practices, it indicates how different communication media more easily transmit some types of content rather than others. Affordances include properties of the media, cultural and economic contexts, and social networks that link users together.

Alienation People's estrangement from their authentic ability to create and shape their selves, groups, and lived worlds.

Analog media See *digital media*.

Authenticity Two definitions of authenticity circulate: a mimicry to a source and an existential approach. If authenticity refers to fidelity to a source, then Second Life Buddhism has at best only a family resemblance to canonical Asian sources (see *transmission model of communication*). On the other hand, if authenticity refers to spiritual media practices that allow users to innovatively explore, create, and improvise lives out of a culture's flotsam and jetsam, then virtual world spiritual practice must be considered a genuine religious tool (see *cultural model of communication*). An existential approach explores how adherents frequently adopt, integrate, and adapt media practices in particular ways so that they fit more cohesively with the moral life and expectations of the communities with which they are affiliated.

Awake online The investigation's central concept. For convert Zen Second Life practitioners, to be awake online was to mind the gap between the real and the actual, so that one was mindful of the ultimate empty nature of existence. To be awake online was to use the obviously constructed nature of the virtual world to be mindful of the constructed nature of the actual world and to thus open up a glimpse into the ultimate empty nature of existence.

Churn   Attrition rate by which residents came and then left Second Life.

Cloud community   An online group that is temporary, flexible, and elastic. Members do not invest, rather they "rent" what community they need when they need it. Similar to the concept of a networked community, a term that describes groups that are bound by particular interests rather than notions of shared geography and familial ties. Yet different from networked communities because while networked communities often have a signifi-cant actual world presence as part of their makeup, a cloud community consists primarily, even consciously, of online digital media practices.

Community   Media practices that enable "communitas," those intense feel-ings of social togetherness and belonging, which are often afforded by reli-gious practice.

Computers   Electronic devices that automatically carry out logical procedures, have their practical roots in World War II, and are tied to a cybernetic ontology.

Conventional reality   Social reality whose structure is created through mutually constituted and historically contextualized material discourses, practices, and objects by which people construct, interpret, and manage their everyday lives. Conventional realities are constituted when people, systematically interacting over time, create trajectories of each other's actions and these concepts become habituated into reciprocal roles.

Conventional theory   Rather than seeing virtual worlds as containing ulti-mate essential differences, a conventional theory argues they constitute a distinct conventional social space, which offers new social fields with dif-fering social positions, lifestyles, values, and dispositions. A conventional theory suggests that to study Second Life investigators ought to use an ethnographic method consisting of "participant observation" and "thick description."

Convert Buddhism   Popular forms that focus on several facets of the Bud-dhist tradition: the therapeutic, the nonhierarchical, the nonviolent, the ecological, and, most importantly, the meditative. For the most part, convert Buddhists live in the West: North America, Europe, and other parts of the developed world.

Cosmologies   Spiritual media practices that turn space into place through the process of externalization, objectification, and internalization.

Cultural model of communication   A theory that models communica-tion as jointly constituted over time by people through media practices (see *transmission model of communication*).

Cyber   Referring to back to "cybernetics," indicates online social computer space – what is on the other side of the screen.

Cyberdelic   A movement advanced by the advocate of psychedelic drugs.

Cybernetic management A networked, entrepreneurial, noncentralized conception of personal interrelationships whose organizational style can be traced back to 1920 and Bell Laboratories (see *cybernetics*).

Cybernetics In the postwar period, an ontology that viewed the world as systems that contained individuals, societies, and ecosystems and was deeply influential in the creation of computers and digital media. The term "cybernetics" was coined in 1948 by the American mathematician and philosopher Norbert Wiener in his seminal work *Cybernetics: Or the Control of and Communication of Animal and Machine*. Wiener forged "cybernetics" from the Greek *kybernetes* (steersman) and defines it as "the entire field of control and communication theory, whether in the machine or animal" (New York: Technology Press, 1948, p. 11).

Cybersangha An online Buddhist group.

Cybersex The encounter between two or more residents in which they engage in mutual arousal through media practices that share sexual feelings and fantasies.

Cybersocial An entity that is created over time as the user interacts through his or her avatar with other residents and becomes an element in the social web of other residents.

Cyberspace The mediated social space created by interconnected electronic communications, cyberspace differs from telecommunication practices that have a sender and a receiver because it occurs in an imagined virtual social environment, in that space between screens. Derived from cyberpunk novels as the opposite of "meat space," cyberspace is often posed as a fantastic place of the imagination.

Cyborgs Hybrid systems of machine and biologic organisms, whose conception can be traced to postwar popular American culture.

Digital affordances The "affordances" of "digital media practices" that consist of the "spatial," "participatory," "encyclopedic," "and procedural."

Digital Dharma Buddhist teachings spread through computer-mediated communication.

Digital media As opposed to analog media such as newspapers, film, and vinyl discs that use a physical or chemical property to communicate, digital media practices consist of electronic technologies that are handled by computers as a series of numeric data. All digital media technologies are composed of programmable bits that can be used for semiotic manipulation and thus share common affordances.

Digital utopianism A historic movement that started in the early 1970s when counterculturists and technologists joined together using cybernetic models to imagine cyberspace as a place of personal liberation and for the building of alternative communities. Digital utopianism advances the conception that cybernetic practices will create a postpolitical, nonhierarchical society by freeing individuals' imaginations from the system of traditional legal, governmental, and social conditions.

Dwellers   See *fundamentalism.*

Dwelling   Indicates more than mere immersion, the perception that you are in a place; rather dwelling indicates that space has a deep lasting meaning that emerges from social interaction and embodied practices that make a world livable.

Emic   Insider's view. An analysis that takes into account categories that are determined by local custom, meaning, and belief and that make these intelligible to an outsider (see *etic*).

Encyclopedic affordance   Points to digital media's high capacity for storing information and retrieving data, as displayed by Google's or Second Life's search engine

Entanglement   See *social entanglement.*

Ethos   The often connoted tone and character of residents' lived worlds.

Etic   Outsider's view, the investigator's perspective.

Externalization   Residents acting upon and creating the virtual world.

Fantasies   Not opposed to real life, but those media practices that organize and give a face to users' desires.

Field site   The locations where an ethnographer's work is conducted; the natural nonlaboratory location where the activities in which researchers are interested to take place.

Frustration   Fantasies that stem from users being refused attention by other people.

Fundamentalism   A spiritual practice that holds fast to an imagined tradition and centers on a static essence as the spiritual force governing life. Fundamentalism tackles networked consumer anxiety by setting sharp boundaries through personal discipline, steadfastness, and regular engagement with authoritative scripture.

Heteronormativity   Media practices that divide people into complementary genders and assert heterosexuality as normative.

Human   The totality of living, conscious beings who are involved with the immediate world in which they live, able to become aware of the contingent element of that involvement and the evolving nature of the self and capable of imagining alternative ways of being.

Imagination   In the context of Second Life, the platform's creative software tools that enable resident fantasies, which are vital because they suture users into the virtual world.

Immersion   The experience of "being in" a virtual world; occurs when a user's awareness no longer focuses on real life but has moved inworld. Refers to media practices that generate a feeling of being in the virtual world; the actual world is sufficiently muted and the virtual world is sufficiently heightened, creating a feeling that one is no longer in the actual world.

Interactive affordance   Indicates how digital media invites users to manipulate the represented space and can consist of hyperlinks and/or textual fields or, as with an avatar, of maneuvering through a virtual environment.

Internalization The point at which the facticity of the world becomes subjectified and is apparent in virtual immersion; when users become so caught up in a world that it obliterates attention to the actual world.

Internet The "network of networks" that has its roots in the military-university research complex and arose as part of the Cold War fear of nuclear mutual assured destruction. The Internet began in 1969 with the launch of the U.S. Advanced Research Projects Agency (ARPA) and was based on a concept first published in 1967. At first the Net spread slowly and was limited to a small community of researchers. New types of media practices were quickly developed, however, because rather than being used as originally intended, as a space of research, it quickly became a place for social interaction.

Kybernetes (kybernētēs) A Greek term meaning "steersman, governor, pilot, or rudder"; the origin of the suffix "cyber" (see *cybernetics*).

Lived reality See *conventional reality*.

Meat space Indicates the "real life" social space of the actual world (see *cyberspace*).

The Media The diversified communication corporations that influence and even control most communication in a Network Consumer Society.

Media practice An activity such as reading a book; watching television or film; listening to the radio; or screening a computer, smart phone, or other digital device. Media practices do not merely transmit content but rather are the performance of embodied social activities that users execute with varying degrees of regularity, dexterity, and flair. Media practices emerge from a relationship between possible human action, on one hand, and systems of communication, on the other, and describe how social beings, with their diverse motives and their diverse intentions, tactically use the technologies of communication at hand to make and transform the realities in which they live.

Mediation Indicates how different media, such as print, broadcast, and digital, are not neutral conveyers of information; rather, through their affordances play a fundamental role in producing the message.

Metapragmatic When the effects and conditions of language use themselves as the objects of discourse (Example: "This is an example sentence.").

Mindfulness A nonjudgmental focus on the emotions, thoughts, and sensations occurring in the present moment. Derived from the Buddhist notion of *smṛti*; in contemporary convert practice the term is associated with "awakening" (*bodhi*), a clear and stable attention that affords a direct insight into the true nature of the world, self, and the relationship between the two.

Mobius effect A term that indicates that the reality of the binaries of virtual/actual and conventional/ultimate never exist on their own but only emerge in relationship to each other through media practices.

Network authority Describes consensual media interactions consisting of peer-to-peer egalitarian social ties.

Network Consumer Society   Late capitalistic forms of consumer-driven corporate free market economy that are intertwined with digital media practices. It is a cultural, social, and economic system that arose in the last quarter of the twentieth century and is defined by the fluidity of financial capital, an intensification of the free market, radical individualism, and interconnected globalization. Networked consumerism fosters a socioeconomic order based on the desire to purchase goods and services, which do not merely fulfill biological needs but cater to thirsts to have pleasurable experiences and to be separated from unpleasant ones.

New Age   A spiritual tactic that sees in the increasingly pluralistic religious setting the need to negotiate one's own spiritual path in the midst of endless alternatives. Seeks wholeness by overcoming the barriers that separate people from one another and emphasizes the feelings and experience in life more than a cognitive understanding. For New Agers, spirituality is negotiable; whatever you believe is true   at least for you.

Objectification   The point at which humanly constructed phenomena have taken on a social life of their own that shapes residents and channels their actions.

Online religion   Religious practices that occur in cyberspace and that tend to use spiritual tactics rather than religious strategies and tend to be more flexible and interactive rather than purely informational (see *network authority*).

Ontology   Pragmatic models of reality   not only how reality is discussed, but also the social procedures that generate everyday lived reality.

Orientalism   The network of media practices employed by European culture to divide the globe into two unequal halves, "East" and "West," employing this epistemological framework to dominate non-European people and places.

Participant observation   A qualitative method of data collection at the heart of ethnography in which a researcher gains intimate familiarity with a group's ethos and lived world by living for an extended period of time with that group.

Persistence   A virtual world locative property that relies on digital media's encyclopedic affordance to create relatively lasting media practices. Individual residents might come and go, but unlike a conference call that ends when everyone hangs up, a virtual world will continue to exist beyond one user logging off.

Physics   A virtual world locative property that creates a platform's "laws of nature," those underlying codes that dictate how automated rules simulate the laws of gravity, elasticity, and the conservation of momentum between colliding objects.

Practice   How people with diverse aims and desires, and in a dialectic between agency and social structure, make and transform their lived reality.

Privation   Fantasies that supply that which a user perceives him- or herself as lacking (but others as having) in real life.

Procedural affordance   Digital media's unique property that enables the ability to represent and execute conditioned behaviors. In a video game, when you shoot a zombie it dies; when a user clicks on a hyperlink on a webpage, it takes them to the location.

Procedural relationships   Social relationships afforded by Second Life's code itself (see *friend* and *partner* in Appendix 2).

Procedure   Like the code of a computer program, the term indicates a step-by-step practice that emerges from a set of rules for performing a particular operation.

Religion   As used by my research team, the category of religion describes the media practices by which Second Life groups engaged with what they perceived as ultimate reality. By giving a face to a group's ultimate reality, religious practice engages their authentic desires, those deeper existential needs that arise from the very social condition of being human. Our use of the word, however, was often at odds with most Second Life Buddhist practitioners, who often understood "religion" to indicate oppressive forms of organized institutions. Religion is authentic from a fidelity perspective and is best analyzed with a transmission communication approach (see *spirituality*).

Religious media practice   Indicates material systems by which people communicate ultimate reality and thus generate the moral economy of a lived religious world.

Scratch notes   When conducting ethnography research, I take "headnotes," which are mental pictures of a cultural practice, to include in later field notes; but more constructive are scratch notes, which are jottings of abbreviations of words and phrases.

Screening   The media practice by which users engage with their digital devices through a flat digital visual interface.

Seeker   See *New Age*.

Silence   Produced from specific media practices that have different connotations depending on their cultural context. It is not simply an absence of sound that somehow exists outside of language, nor does it have a universal meaning that conveys the same significance in different social settings.

Situation   Locations that gather together people's bodies, social roles, and cultural discourses into a coherent and effective practice.

Social entanglement   Epistemologically, entanglement has links to Buddhism and digital media. The concept of entanglement also stems from quantum physics, where it is used to describe pairs of particles that spookily interact in ways such that the state of each particle cannot be described independently. Instead, each variable must be analyzed as part of the system as a whole. In entangled systems, the behavior of the two is different from the juxtaposition of the behaviors of each considered alone.

Spatial affordance   Refers to how users, employing digital media, perceive of logging on and imagine navigating through cyberspaces such as web-pages as well as virtual worlds.

Spirituality   Often used by scholars to indicate popular forms of religious practice, spirituality was used by Second Life adherents to designate a deeply personal, unique, anti-institutional focus on personal exploration and spontaneity. Spiritual media practices often rewrote religion, tactically poaching from authoritative institutions and sources. Spirituality is authentic from an existential perspective and is best analyzed with a cultural communication approach (see *religion*).

Spiritual liberation   Often called being *awake*. For convert Zen Second Life practitioners, to be awake online was to mind the gap between the real and the virtual, so that one was mindful of the ultimate empty nature of existence. See also *awake online*.

Sticky   The ability of media practices to attract and keep a user's attention and engagement; the number of times people use a particular medium and the increased user retention and duration (see *churn*).

Strategy   An authoritative type of agency, such as the political, economic, scientific, and religious, that operates from a proper social location with standardized, even routinized, habitual forms of engagement (see *tactic*).

Symbolic castration   Media practices which are subject to the laws and conventions of the authoritarian social reality in which they are employed.

Tactic   A type of agency that operates from outside bases of established authority, is used by more marginalized individuals, and by necessity is more flexible and innovative (see *strategy*).

Thick description   An ethnographic method in which the researcher describes both a cultural phenomenon and the social context that gives that phenomenon meaning.

Transmission model of communication   Formed from a metaphor of transportation. In the transmission model, communication imparts, sends, and transmits information to others like water in a pipe or, better yet, like commodities along a factory's conveyer belt (see *cultural model of communication*).

Ultimate reality   Those ontological models that include both the content of what is ultimately real and what is not but also the larger cultural matrix that shapes the abstract idea of reality itself (see *conventional reality*).

User   Person behind the keyboard in the real world.

Virtual   The inside of cyberspace. The term does not take a position about real or unreal, authentic or inauthentic, but distinguishes a third thing, something powerful that differs from the ordinary everyday. The word "virtual," from a Latin word for power (*virtus*), identifies these powerful alternatives (see *actual* in Appendix 2).

Virtual world properties The digital media practices that transform the flat screen into a virtual world through the locative properties of physics and persistence as well as the social properties of avatars (see *avatar* in Appendix 2) and real-time interaction.

Workaround A computer science term describing a temporary fix that suggests that a final answer is still needed.

World In the context of Second Life, the term indicates the creation of an alternative conventional lived reality through immersive digital media practices, which are contextualized in the techno-fantasy of cyberspace.

Appendix 2
Second Life terms

;-)   An emoticon for "wink."

_/!_   An emoticon used in some Second Life Buddhist groups, which stands for the Japanese word *gasshō*, describing a gesture of palms together and fingers pointing upwards in prayer position.

Ageplay   Sexualized situations involving child avatars (see *edgeplay*).

Alt   Short for "alternate account," a different avatar that a user employs, usually for something other than her or his normal activity or to do things in privacy (such as building, scripting, or edgeplay).

Animation   A sequence of motions in which an avatar engages.

Animation override   A scripted attachment that adds animations to an avatar.

Attachments   An object that can be attached to an avatar.

Avatar   The on-screen representation of a user, which can be a three-dimensional model such as in Second Life, a two-dimensional icon as used in many chat forums, or a textual description as used in Multi User Dungeons (MUDs). Abbreviated as *av*.

Banning   Forbidding residents to enter a region.

Bot   Short for "robot," the term indicates an animated avatar that is controlled by computer code and not by a human operator.

Build   A structure that is put together in Second Life. Builds are the objects created by residents that compose the Second Life environment. The term usually refers to the architecture of buildings, but it can also be used to describe such things as art or vehicles. One who creates content is a *builder*; the act of creating content is *building*.

Builder   A resident who creates Second Life content and who, in particular, builds.

Building tools   Media practices that allow users to create and modify objects.

Cage   A trap that prevents avatars from moving (see *griefer*).

Campfire concerts   A common Second Life social activity; musical events and other such activities that occur around a virtual fire pit.

Characters   See *roleplay*.

Chat   See *public chat*.

Chat bubbles   Text that floats over an avatar's head, labeled with the avatar's name and a group title and displaying the text you type in open chat.

Chatroom   A social area in cyberspace that allows users to communicate, often about a single subject.

Clothes   In Second Life, skirts, pants, shirts, and jackets describe different layer-based, textured clothing that can be applied directly to a user's avatar.

Collar   A scripted object that allows the wearer to grant certain permissions to a third person, like animating their own avatar, limiting its mobility, or tracking whether the collar is worn or not.

Cross-posting   Posting messages to more than one groupchat.

Dance ball   An object that contains a dance animation file. When you click on it, your avatar's actions will be overridden to act out the animation.

Deformers   Used by griefers to alter the shape of an avatar as part of an attack (see *griefer*).

Dominant/submissive   A term describing resident-created relationships that involve the giving over of obedience and control of one person to another, usually in erotic roleplaying.

Drama   Relating to Second Life in such a way as to consistently overreact or exaggerate the importance of benign events so as to gain attention or make one's own life seem more exciting.

Drama-queen   A resident who engages in much drama.

Edgeplay   Resident behavior that pushes Second Life's conventions of safe and sane play.

Elder   The third stage in a resident's life cycle when a resident's creativity really begins. After feeling like they have made it, the question becomes what to do inworld. For many, this is the stage when the game truly begins because socializing and creating become the main focus.

Elder game   See *elder*.

Estate   A collection of regions that has tools available to help landowners manage multiple regions more easily.

Event   One of Second Life's search engine filters. Indicates a gathering of residents for a prearranged purpose. Events at Hoben included *campfire concerts*, dharma and book discussions, dharma talks and interviews, and more rarely weddings and memorials. By far the most prevalent and significant practice, however, was silent online meditation.

Flexi attachments   Prims (primitives) that are set to "flex" so that they mimic the physical movement of cloth, such as being blown in the wind.

Friend   A procedural relationship that forms the backbone of Second Life's social interaction. Residents add other residents as "friends" by choosing "Add Friend" from the pie menu or accepting their friend offer. Being a friend means that the other resident's name is listed in the friend's conversation menu, that friends can find each other on the world map, that friends will be notified when they log on, and that friends can see whether they are online by going to the Second Life website (see *partner*).

Full permission   Objects that are free to copy, modify, and transfer.

Furry   An avatar that looks like an anthropomorphic animal.

Grid   The software platform and hardware technology that runs Second Life. Usually capitalized, by convention. Collection of sims linked together. Several grids exist, including the Main Grid and Teen Grid in Second Life as well as non–Second Life Grids that use the OpenSim platform.

Griefer   An avatar who is harassing other avatars by using offensive language, bumping or generating garbage objects to leave on land, or any number of other activities that significantly disrupt another resident's inworld experience.

Group   One of Second Life's search engine filters. An official larger public association of at least two residents that is afforded by a function of the platform (see *relationship*).

Groupchat   Instant communication that can be sent to all members of a Second Life group (see *chat*).

Grouptitle   Also called a grouptag. The title of your role in your currently active group is shown by default above your display name inworld.

HUD   Heads-up display; attaches either directly to the avatar or to the Second Life program's screen.

InRealm   Used in role play to describe the region one is in.

Instant message (IM)   Private chat (see public *chat*).

Inventory   The collection of all the items that a resident owns or has access to in Second Life.

Inworld   Media practices and phenomena that take place inside the virtual environment. Example of usage: "Let's meet inworld."

Lag   Indicates the platform's slow reaction time, which can be caused by anything from inadequate Internet connection to residents' usage of too many scripts; the delay or interruption in a network or Internet connection caused by slow response time; or slow or jerky performance caused by an overworked processor, memory bandwidth, video card, or hard drive. Commonly referenced as "Boy, the lag is killing me today!"

Landmark   Shortcut to a place in Second Life stored in a resident's inventory.

Linden   Surname of an avatar that indicates a member of the Second Life company staff, which all use the surname "Linden." Also a unit of Second Life currency used for inworld transactions.

LSL (Linden Scripting Language)   A procedural scripting language that can be used to add interactivity to objects.

Middie   The middle stage of a resident's second life; no longer a nOOb, but not yet playing the elder game (cf. *noobie* and *elder*).

MMORPGs   Massively multiplayer online role-playing games.

Neko   Avatar that appears part cat, part human.

Noobie (also noob, nOOb)   A resident who is new to Second Life. This term can be meant as an insult depending upon the context (cf. *middie* and *elder*).

Notecard   An inventory item containing text and/or other embedded inventory items; it is a way to deliver more detailed information that will not fit into a single instant message.

Object   Indicates either a single prim or a collection of several linked prims that are created using Second Life building tools.

Partner   A procedural relationship. Partnering on Second Life is a way for residents to indicate in their public profiles that they have a serious relationship. As the resident Algama GossipGirl describes it, "partnering means you are going steady."

People   One of Second Life's search engine filters (see *resident*; see also *human* in Appendix 1).

Place   One of Second Life's search engine filters. The virtual environments built by residents in which avatars dwell (see *region*).

Poof   To suddenly teleport away; also used to describe when friends suddenly disappear and do not log back on to the virtual world.

Pose ball   An object that contains an animation file. By clicking on it, your avatar's actions will be overridden to act out the ball's animation.

Prim   Shorthand for "primitive;" refers to the three-dimensional shapes used to build objects in Second Life. The most basic building blocks on Second Life. Prims can be box, cylinder, and prism shaped, as well as sculpted (*sculpties*). Each prim's color, texture, bumpiness, shininess, and transparency can be adjusted, and images (textures) can be applied to each surface to change its appearance; mesh, textures for clothing or other objects, animations, and gestures can be created using external software and imported. A prim can also have a mass that corresponds to seven materials: stone, metal, glass, wood, flesh, plastic, and rubber.

Profile   A clickable statement that each avatar has that can be customized to share information about the user. Accessible to all residents. Displays information about each avatar's groups, favorite places, partners, and personal statements. The ultimate people-watching tool.

Public chat   Avatars can communicate via local chat, groupchat, global instant messaging (IM), and voice. Chatting is used for localized public conversations between two or more avatars, and it is visible to any avatar within a given distance. IMs are used for private conversations, either between two avatars or among the members of a group – or even between objects and avatars. Unlike chatting, IM communication does not depend on the participants being within a certain distance of each other.

Real life   The actual world, as opposed to the virtual world of Second Life (see *actual*).

Region   The virtual environments that constitute Second Life's land (see *sim*). A named area within Second Life, also commonly called a sim (simulator) or island.

Relationship   Smaller private unofficial social units whose media practices afford sociability between two or more residents (see *group*).

Residents   Second Life's cybersocial beings that are activated in the virtual world by the feedback between user and avatar. Those cybersocial entities created from digital media practices that entangle virtual avatars with their organic users. Residents constitute themselves and their world in a series of fantasy-driven media practices that are renewed, revised, and consolidated through time. Residents create the virtual world through chat, voice, building, gestures, and all manner of symbolic social sign. Yet they are also the object rather than just the subject of such constitutive acts. Being a resident is thus a media practice – a performance – but not one simply undertaken by a single subject. Being a resident is reiterative, it is marked by a repetition of media practices through which residents produce themselves and others. These practices lie in the gap between the voluntary and the determined.

Rez   "To materialize," poached from the science fiction film *Tron* (1982).

Roleplay   To act and communicate as if you are the avatar you are playing by changing behavior to fulfill a social role.

Roles   Different positions within a group of varying authority and abilities.

Ruthed   A term used for when your avatar erroneously takes the shape of the default female body type, named Ruth. This usually happens after a teleport.

Script   Refers to the Linden Scripting Language (LSL), which has a syntax similar to C and allows for the control of inworld objects.

Shape   The shape of your avatar's body. New shapes can be applied to change your appearance and even turn avatars into nonhumanoid things.

Sim   Short for "simulator." One of the host machines or physical servers that simulate regions in Second Life.

SLogosphere   As used in Second Life, the word indicates the blogs (short for web log) about the virtual worlds. The term emanated from a mashup between "SL" (Second Life) and "blog."

SLurl   Mashup of Second Life and Uniform Resource Locator. A hyperlink that connects users to the virtual world.

Snapshot   A screen image taken in Second Life. In the virtual world, a snapshot refers to a screenshot taken using a function built into the Second Life Viewer and retains the notion of an informal photograph taken in everyday life.

Teleport Instantaneous movement from one inworld location to another.

Texture An image used to cover the face of a prim, as a visual representation of the material an object is composed of.

Tiny An avatar in the form of a very cute animal that walks on its hind legs. There is an entire community of tinies in the Raglan Shire sim.

Voice (voice chat) A feature that lets residents speak to each other.

Appendix 3
Buddhist technical terms

In the study I have attempted to stay close to the emic use of terms by Second Life Buddhist residents. In a few cases, I found the need to refer back to more technical Buddhist terminology. For consistency, when possible *Cyber Zen* uses Sanskrit terms to describe these various Buddhist concepts.

Anapanasmrti (*ānāpānasmṛti*)   Mindfulness of breathing.

Anatman (*anātman*)   The concept of "no-self," which refers to the Buddhist concept that there is no permanent identity or soul.

Antarvasa (*antarvāsa*)   Lower covering of a monk robe.

Avidya (*avidyā*)   Delusion.

Bodhi (*bodhi*)   The understanding of an awakened being regarding the true empty nature of reality.

Bodhicittta (*bodhichitta*)   Striving for awakening.

Bodhisattva (*bodhisattva*)   "Awakened beings" who compassionately put helping others to be saved ahead of their own enlightenment.

Bushido (*bushido*)   Samurai moral values.

Chakai (*chakai*)   Japanese tea gathering.

Chawan (*chawan*)   Japanese tea bowl.

Chorten (*chörten*)   See *stūpa*.

Dana (*dāna*)   gift giving.

Dharma (*dharma*)   In Buddhism, when capitalized in English, the term refers to the Teachings of the Buddha. A key concept for Hinduism, Buddhism, Sikhism, and Jainism, which originated in South Asia and is derived from the Sanskrit root *dhṛ*, which means "to hold, maintain, and support." In the Second Life Buddhist community, Dharma tended to hold three meanings, as a respondent to our 2010 survey ($n=108$) answered: "the great teaching, the truth, [and] the way the universe functions."

Dharmachakra (*dharmachakra*)   Dharma wheel.

Dhyana (*dhyāna*)   Meditation practice.

Dokusan (*dokusan*)   Personal interview/instruction with a Zen teacher.

Duḥkha (duḥkha)   As the core of Buddhism, "suffering" is usually indicated as *duḥkha,* which literally means being stuck but is usually translated into English as anxiety, stress, unsatisfactoriness, or disease.

Five Precepts (pañca-śīlāni)   The basic core of Buddhist ethics, to abstain from harming living beings, stealing, sexual misconduct, lying, and intoxication.

Gassho (gasshō)   Buddhist gesture of pressing palms together as an act of piety. The gesture was translated into an important emoticon often used by Hoben practitioners: "_/!_."

Interbeing   A term coined by the Vietnamese monk Thích Nhất Hạnh to indicate the interconnectedness of human and nonhuman elements.

Karma (karma)   Translates from the Sanskrit as "action." At Hoben, karma was a spiritual concept reported to be deeply associated with the ethical implications of Buddhism because it denoted the moral consequences of one's engagement with the world.

Karuna (karuṇā)   Usually translated as "compassion," this is a key goal of Second Life Zen.

Kasaya (kāṣāya)   Buddhist monk robes.

Kesu (kesu)   Meditation bell.

Koan (kōan)   A record of a short dialogue or encounter between a student and teacher given by a teacher to help students go beyond discriminative, conceptual understanding to a more direct, experiential wisdom.

Mandala (maṇḍala)   An image that often represents the universe.

Mudra (mudra)   Hand gesture.

Paramartha-satya (paramārtha-satya)   Ultimate reality.

Pratityasmupada (pratītyasamutpāda)   Dependent origination, the Buddhist concept that things are intertwined and that nothing exists independently of other things.

Samghati (saṃghāti)   Outer robe.

Samsara (saṃsāra)   Cycle of life and death and also everyday lived reality.

Samvrti satya (saṃvṛti-satya)   Conventional reality.

Sangha (saṃgha)   The term originally connoted any group of people living together to pursue a unified purpose that ranged from trade guilds to political groups to religious orders. In Buddhism, it initially referred to the community of monks but came to denote the larger community that also includes lay practitioners and, in the most general sense, denotes the assembly of all beings on the path to awakening.

Shoshin (shōshin)   Beginner's mind.

Smrti (smṛti)   Often used to indicate remembrance, reminiscence, thinking of or upon, calling to mind. Posed by many at Hoben as the origins of mindfulness. Literally, "that which is remembered." In Buddhist scripture, it means awareness and is usually translated into English as "mindfulness."

Stupa (stūpa)   Mound-like or semi-spherical structure usually containing Buddhist relics.

Sunyata (śūnyatā)   Literally emptiness, but this does not mean that a phe-nomenon does not exist but that it has no static intrinsic essence. Emptiness is not a sui generis static void standing behind the veil of the illusion of conventional reality. There is no Great Emptiness out there somewhere to be found. Instead, as Human Riddle stated, "emptiness is right here, right now."

Tathata (tathatā)   The ultimate inexpressible reality.

Tathatgatagarh (tathāgatagarbha)   Bhudda-nature or, Buddha-Matrix within in all sentient creatures (lit. The womb of the thus-come-one).

Trsna (tṛṣṇā)   Desire; literally means "thirst" and defines an unquenchable craving that is the ultimate cause of suffering, anxiety, and dissatisfaction.

Upaya (upāya)   Expedient means.

Uttarsanga (uttarāsaṇga)   Upper covering of a monk's robe.

Zabutan (zabuton)   Large square, padded mat on which the zafu (medita-tion cushion) is placed.

Zafu (zafu)   Small circular cushion upon which practitioners sit when medi-tating. Typically a round shape about 15 inches across and packed tight with kapok, a silky fiber obtained from the fruit of the silk cotton tree. Meditation cushions are often placed on a zabuton.

Zazen (zazen)   Zen meditation. Literally "seated meditation"; a type of silent meditation often called "sitting" by Second Life practitioners. Dur-ing silent online meditation, residents rest their avatars on virtual cushions and remain inactive in front of their computer screens.

Zendo (zendo)   Zen meditation hall.

Bibliography

"1983 Apple Keynote – The '1984' Ad Introduction," YouTube Video, 6:41, posted by the Apple History Channel, April 1, 2006, www.youtube.com/watch?v=lSiQA6KKyJo.

Aarseth, Espen. *Cybertext: Perspectives on Ergodic Literature.* Baltimore: John Hopkins University Press, 1997.

"About Us," Barre Center for Buddhist Studies, www.bcbsdharma.org/about-us/.

"About Wisdom 2.0 Business," Wisdom 2.0: Living Mindfully in the Digital Age, www.wisdom2business.com/About.

Abu-Lughod, Lila. "Writing against Culture." In *Feminist Anthropology: A Reader*, edited by Ellen Lewin, 153–66. Malden, MA: Blackwell Publishing, 2006.

Addiss, Stephen, Stanley Lombardo, and Judith Roitman, eds. *Zen: Traditional Documents from China, Korea, and Japan.* Cambridge, MA: Hackett Publishing Company, 2008.

Admas, Vincanne. *Tigers of the Snow and Other Virtual Sherpas.* Princeton, NJ: Princeton University Press, 1995.

Adorno, Theodor. *The Jargon of Authenticity.* Evanston: Northwestern University Press, 1973.

Alasuutari, Pertti. *Social Theory and Human Reality.* London: Sage Publications, 2002.

Althusser, Louis. *Lenin and Philosophy and Other Essays.* London: Verso, 1970.

"American Anthropological Association Statement on Ethnography and Institutional Review Boards," Adopted by AAA Executive Board, June 4, 2004, website, www.aaanet.org/stmts/irb.htm.

Ames, Van Meter. "Current Western Interest in Zen." *Philosophy East and West* 10 (April–July 1960): 23–33.

Amit, Vered. *Constructing the Field: Ethnographic Fieldwork in the Contemporary World.* London: Routledge, 2000.

Anderson, Benedict. *Imagined Communities: Reflections on the Origin and Spread of Nationalism.* New York: Verso, 1983.

Arnould, Erik, and Craig Thompson. "Consumer Culture Theory (CCT): Twenty Years of Research." *Journal of Consumer Research* 3, no. 4 (2005): 868–82.

Au, James Wagner. *The Making of Second Life: Notes from the New World.* San Francisco: HarperCollins Publishers, 2008.

Ashby, Ross. *Design for a Brain.* London: Chapman & Hall, 1952.

———. *An Introduction to Cybernetics.* New York: Methuen, 1963.

Babb, Valerie. *Whiteness Visible: The Meaning of Whiteness.* New York: New York University Press, 1998.

Bainbridge, William Sims. *eGods: Faith Versus Fantasy in Computer Gaming.* Oxford University Press, 2013.

Balsamo, Anne. *Technologies of the Gendered Body*. Durham, NC: Duke University Press, 1996.

Barnes, Ruth, and Joanne B. Eicher. *Dress and Gender: Making and Meaning*. New York: Bloomsbury Academic, 1997.

Bartle, Richard. 2004. *Designing Virtual Worlds*. Berkeley: New Riders, 2004.

———. "Hearts, Clubs, Diamonds, Spades: Players Who Suit Muds," http://mud.co.uk/richard/hcds.htmhttp://mud.co.uk/richard/hcds.htm.

Basso, Keith. "'To Give Up on Words': Silence in Western Apache Culture." *Southwestern Journal of Anthropology* 23, no. 3 (1970): 213–30.

Baudrillard, Jean. *Simulacra and Simulation*. Ann Arbor, MI: University of Michigan Press, 1994.

Bauman, Richard. "Let Your Words Be Few: Speaking and Silence in Quaker Ideology." In *Let Your Words Be Few: Symbolism of Speaking and Silence among Seventeenth-Century Quakers*, 20–31. Cambridge: Cambridge University Press, 1983.

Beer, Stafford. *Cybernetics and Management*. London: English Universities Press, 1959.

———. "Cybernetics and the Knowledge of God." *Month* 34 (1965): 292.

———. *Brain of the Firm*. London: Penguin, 1972.

———. "The Impact of Cybernetics on the Concept of Industrial Organization." In *Proceedings of the First International Congress on Cybernetics*, edited by Namur, 26–29. June 1956. Paris: Gauthier-Villars. Reprinted in Beer, *How Many Grapes Went into the Wine? Stafford Beer on the Art and Science of Holistic Management*, 75–95. New York: Wiley, 1994.

———. "'What Is Cybernetics?' Acceptance Speech for an Honorary Degree at the University of Valladolid, Mexico, October 2001." *Kybernetes* 33 (2004): 853–63.

"The Beginning of Second Life," Second Life Wiki. http://wiki.secondlife.com/wiki/History_of_Second_Life.

Bell, Catherine. "The Ritual Body and the Dynamics of Ritual Power." *Journal of Ritual Studies* 4 (1990): 299–313.

———. *Ritual Theory/Ritual Practice*. Oxford: Oxford University Press, 1992.

———. "Performance." In *Critical Terms for Religious Studies*, edited by Mark C. Taylor, 204–24. Chicago: University of Chicago Press, 1998.

Bell, Daniel. *The Social Sciences since the Second World War*. New Brunswick, NJ: Transaction Publishers, 1981.

Bellah, Robert. *Beyond Belief: Essays on Religion in a Post-Traditionalist World*. Berkeley: University of California Press, 1970.

Benedict XVI. *Truth, Proclamation and Authenticity of Life in the Digital Age*. Vatican: The Holy See. For the 45th World Communications Day, June 5, 2011. http://w2.vatican.va/content/benedict-xvi/en/messages/communications/documents/hf_ben-xvi_mes_20110124_45th-world-communications-day.html.

Benedikt, Michael. *Cyberspace: First Steps*. Cambridge, MA: MIT Press, 1991.

Berger, Peter. *The Sacred Canopy: Elements of a Sociological Theory of Religion*. New York: Doubleday, 1967.

Berger, Peter, and Thomas Luckmann. *The Social Construction of Reality: A Treatise in the Sociology of Knowledge*. Garden City, NY: Anchor Books, 1966.

Bhikkhu, Thanissaro. "Kama Sutta: Sensual Pleasure," Sutta Nipata 4.1, www.accesstoinsight.org/tipitaka/kn/snp/snp.4.01.than.htmlwww.accesstoinsight.org/tipitaka/kn/snp/snp.1.03.than.html.

———. "Paticca-samuppada-vibhanga Sutta: Analysis of Dependent Co-arising," www.accesstoinsight.org/tipitaka/sn/sn12/sn12.002.than.html.

Bielefeldt, Carl, trans. *Dōgen's Manuals of Zen Meditation*. Berkeley: University of California Press, 1988.

Big Fish. "Zen Games," www.bigfishgames.com/download-games/1707/zen-games/index. html.

Blyth, R.H. *Zen in English Literature and Oriental Classics*. New York: Dutton, 1960.

Boellstorff, Tom. *Coming of Age in Second Life: An Anthropologist Explores the Virtually Human*. Princeton, NJ: Princeton University Press, 2008.

Boeree, George. "An Introduction to Buddhism," http://webspace.ship.edu/cgboer/ heartsutra.html.

Bogost, Ian. "Persuasive Games: Video Game Zen," *Gamasutra.com*. www.gamasutra.com/ view/feature/2585/persuasive_games_video_game_zen.php.

"Bragg v. Linden Research," www.paed.uscourts.gov/documents/opinions/07D0658P.pdf.

Brantley, Jeffrey. *Calming Your Anxious Mind: How Mindfulness and Compassion Can Free You from Anxiety, Fear and Panic*. Oakland, CA: New Harbinger Publications, 2007.

Brasher, Brenda. *Give Me that Online Religion*. San Francisco: Jossey-Bass, 2001.

Brautigan, Richard. *All Watched over by Machines of Loving Grace*. San Francisco: Communication Company, 1967.

Briggs, Charles L. *Learning How to Ask: A Sociolinguistic Appraisal of the Role of the Interview in Social Science Research*. Cambridge: Cambridge University Press, 1986.

Broughton, Jeffrey L. *The Bodhidharma Anthology: The Earliest Records of Zen*. Berkeley: University of California Press, 1999.

Browne, Ray. "Popular Culture as the New Humanities." *Journal of Popular Culture* 17, no. 4 (1984): 1.

Brownlee, John. "Kurt Vonnegut Interview in Second Life," www.wired.com/table_of_ malcontents/2007/04/kurt_vonnegut_i/.

Bruckman, Amy. "Gender Swapping on the Internet," Presented at the Internet Society, San Francisco, August 1993, www.cc.gatech.edu/~asb/papers/gender-swapping.txt.

———. "Ethical Guidelines for Research Online," April 4, 2002, website, www.cc.gatech. edu/~asb/ethics.

"TheBuddhaMachine – Computer.m4v," 5:58, posted by Gregory Price Grieve, May 4, 2010, www.youtube.com/watch?v=qAbxGCuv6-Q.

"The Buddhist Ethic and the Spirit of Global Capitalism," European Graduate School Video Lectures, YouTube Video, 1:09:56. October 2, 2012, www.youtube.com/ watch?v=qkTUQYxEUjs.

"Building Tools," http://wiki.secondlife.com/wiki/Edit_window#Edit_Tool.

Burman, Barbara. *Material Strategies: Dress and Gender in a Historical Perspective*. Malden, MA: Blackwell, Publishing, 2003.

Bush, Vannevar. "As We May Think." *Atlantic* (1945), www.theatlantic.com/magazine/ print/1969/12/as-we-may-think/3881/.

Bussabarger, Kara. "Go Ahead, Lose Your Mind – 'Monkey Mind' that Is." *BizJournal* (2008), www.bizjournals.com/louisville/stories/2008/03/17/story16.html.

Buswell, Robert E. *The Zen Monastic Experience*. Princeton, NJ: Princeton University Press, 1992.

Butler, Judith. *Gender Trouble: Feminism and the Subversion of Identity*. New York: Routledge, 1990.

———. *Bodies that Matter: On the Discursive Limits of "Sex"*. New York: Routledge, 1993.

———. *The Psychic Life of Power*. Stanford, CA: Stanford University Press, 1997.

———. *Precarious Life: The Powers of Mourning and Violence*. New York: Verso, 2004.

————. *Undoing Gender.* New York: Routledge, 2004.

————. *Giving an Account of Oneself.* New York: Fordham University Press, 2005.

Caillois, Roger. *Man, Play, Games.* New York: Glencoe, 1961.

————. *Man and the Sacred.* Urbana and Chicago: University of Illinois Press, 2001.

Campbell, Heidi. *Exploring Religious Community Online: We Are One in the Network.* Oxford: Peter Lang, 2005.

————. *When Religion Meets New Media.* New York: Routledge, 2010.

Campbell, John Edward. *Getting It On Online: Cyberspace, Gay Male Sexuality, and Embodied Identity.* New York: Harrington Park Press, 2004.

Carey, James W. *Communication as Culture: Essays on Media and Society.* New York: Routledge, 1988.

Carr, Michael. "'Mind-Monkey' Metaphors in Chinese and Japanese Dictionaries." *International Journal of Lexicography* 6, no. 3 (1993): 149–80.

Carroll, Lewis. *Alice's Adventures in Wonderland.* Toronto, Ontario: Broadview, 2011.

Castronova, Edward. *Synthetic Worlds: The Business and Culture of Online Games.* Chicago: University of Chicago Press, 2005.

"Category:Xstreet," http://wiki.secondlife.com/wiki/Category:Xstreet.

de Certeau, Michel. *The Practice of Everyday Life.* Berkeley: University of California Press, 1984.

Ceruzzi, Paul E. *A History of Modern Computing.* Boston: MIT Press, 2003.

Chakrabarty, Dipesh. *Provincializing Europe: Postcolonial Thought and Historical Difference.* Princeton, NJ: Princeton University Press, 2000.

Chidester, David. *Authentic Fakes: Religion and American Popular Culture.* Berkeley: University of California Press, 2005.

Chin, Justin. *Mongrel: Essays, Diatribes, + Pranks.* New York: Macmillan, 1999.

Ciolek, Matthew. "Asian Studies Online – A Timeline of Major Developments," www.ciolek.com/PAPERS/asian-studies-timeline.html.

Clifford, James. *Routes: Travel and Translation in the Late Twentieth Century.* Cambridge, MA: Harvard University Press, 1997.

Clifford, James, and George Marcus. *Writing Culture: The Poetics and Politics of Ethnography.* Berkeley: University of California Press, 1986.

Clynes, Manfred, and Nathan Kline. "Cyborgs and Space." *Astronautics* (September 1960), 26–27 and 74–76.

Coleman, William James. *The New Buddhism: The Western Transformation of an Ancient Tradition.* London: Oxford University Press, 2002.

"Collar," http://wiki.secondlife.com/wiki/Collar.

"Colossal Cave Adventure: The Original Text-Based Adventure Game," www.amc.com/shows/halt-and-catch-fire/colossal-cave-adventure/landing.

"Community Standards," https://secondlife.com/corporate/cs.php.

Conze, Edward. *Buddhism: A Short History.* London: Oneworld Publishing, 1980.

Copeland, Miller. "Edgeplay: The Dirty Little Secret of Second Life." *The Grid*, October 1, 2006, www.jasonpettus.com/inthegrid/itg01us.pdf.

Crawford-Mason, Clare. "If Japan Can . . . Why Can't We?" *NBC*, June 1980.

"CyberSangha Articles Available on the Web," https://groups.google.com/forum/#!topic/soc.religion.eastern/TMzWV9DBqKw.

Daniel, Valentine. *Fluid Signs: Being a Person the Tamil Way.* Berkeley: University of California Press, 1984.

Davis, Erik. *TechGnosis: Myth, Magic and Mysticism in the Age of Information.* London: Serpents Tail, 1998.

Davis, Fred. *Fashion Culture, and Identity*. Chicago: University of Chicago Press, 1992.

Dawson, Lorne. "Doing Religion in Cyberspace: The Promise and the Perils." *Council of Societies for the Study of Religion Bulletin* 30, no. 1 (2001): 8.

Dawson, Lorne, and Douglas Cowan, eds. *Religion Online: Finding Faith on the Internet*. New York: Routledge, 2004.

Delamont, S., P.A. Atkinson, and O. Parry. *The Doctoral Experience: Success and Failure in Graduate School*. London: Falmer, 2000.

Deleuze, Gilles, *Difference and Repetition*. New York: Columbia University Press, 1994.

Deleuze, Gilles, and Claire Parnet. *Dialogues*. New York: Columbia University Press, 1987.

DeLillo, Don. *White Noise*. New York: Viking Press, 1985.

Deming, Edward. *Elementary Principles of the Statistical Control of Quality*. Tokyo: Union of Japanese Scientists and Engineers, 1950.

Denyer, Nicholas. "Introduction." In *Alcibiades*, by Plato; edited by Nicholas Denyer, 1–26. Cambridge: Cambridge University Press, 2001.

"Dependent Co-Arising," Joanna Macy and Her Work, www.joannamacy.net/dependent-co-arising.html.

Derrida, Jacques. "'As If I Were Dead': An Interview with Jacques Derrida." In *Applying: To Derrida*, edited by J. Brannigan, R. Robbins, and J. Wolfreys, 212–27. London: Macmillan, 1996.

Desjarlais, Robert. *Body and Emotion: The Aesthetics of Illness and Healing in the Nepal Himalayas*. Philadelphia: University of Pennsylvania Press, 1992.

Detweiler, Craig, ed. *Halos and Avatars: Playing Video Games with God*. Louisville: Westminster John Knox Press, 2010.

Deuel, N.R. "Our Passionate Response to Virtual Reality." In *Computer-Mediated Communication: Linguistic, Social and Cross-Cultural Perspectives*, edited by S. Herring, 129–46. Amsterdam: John Benjamins Publishing Company, 1996.

Dibble, Julian. "A Rape in Cyberspace." *Village Voice* (December 21, 1993), 36–43.

———. *My Tiny Life: Crime and Passion in a Virtual World*. New York: An Owl Book, 1998.

———. *Play Money: Or, How I Quit My Day Job and Made Millions Trading Virtual Loot*. New York: Basic Books, 2006.

Dickstein, Morris. *Gates of Eden: American Culture in the Sixties*. New York: Basic Books, 1977.

"Disciplina Nomine Dharma," pieth.home.xs4all.nl/IPIR/philosophy/dharma/codex07.pdf.

Doctor Who, "The Tenth Planet," Television, BBC, 1966.

"Does Anyone Have Experience with the Adoption of a Child or Teenager?," http://community.secondlife.com/t5/General-Discussion-Forum/Does-anyone-have-experience-with-the-adoption-of-a-child-or/td-p/1451217.

"Don't Know What an Animation Override Is You Need to See this – Second Life Viewer 2.3 Beta Tutorial," www.youtube.com/watch?v=0ZmSmO2dhV8.

Downing, Michael. *Shoes Outside the Door: Desire, Devotion, and Excess at the San Francisco Zen Center*. Washington, DC: Counterpoint, 2001.

Dreyfus, Hubert. *Being-in-the-World: A Commentary on Heidegger's Being and Time, Division 1*. Cambridge, MA: MIT Press, 1991.

Ducheneaut, Nicolas, Nicholas Yee, Eric Nickell, and Robert J. Moore. "Virtual 'Third Places': A Case Study of Sociability in Massively Multiplayer Games." *Computer Supported Cooperative Work* 16, no. 1–2 (2007): 129–66.

Dumoulin, Heinrich. *Zen Enlightenment: Origins and Meaning*. Boston: Weatherhill, 1993.

———. *Zen Buddhism: A History, Volume 1: India and China.* New York: World Wisdom, 2005.

———. *Zen Buddhism: A History, Volume 2: Japan.* New York: World Wisdom, 2005.

Dundes, Alan. "From Etic to Emic Units in the Structural Study of Folktales." *Journal of American Folklore* 75, no. 1 (1962): 95–105.

Eliade, Mircea. *Cosmos and History: The Myth of the Eternal Return.* Princeton, NJ: Princeton University Press, 1954.

———. *The Sacred and the Profane: The Nature of Religion.* New York: Harvest/HBJ Publishers, 1957.

———. *Patterns in Comparative Religion.* London: Sheed and Ward, 1958.

Engels, Frederick. *Dialects of Nature.* Moscow: Foreign Languages Publishing House, 1954.

Eskelinen, Markku. "The Gaming Situation." *Game Studies* 1, no. 1 (2001), www.gamestudies.org/0101/eskelinen/.

Evans-Pritchard, Edward Evan. *The Nuer, a Description of the Modes of Livelihood and Political Institutions of a Nilotic People.* Oxford: Clarendon Press, 1940.

Faure, Bernard. *The Rhetoric of Immediacy: A Cultural Critique of Chan/Zen Buddhism.* Princeton, NJ: Princeton University Press, 1991.

———. *Chan Insights and Oversights: An Epistemological Critique of the Chan Tradition.* Princeton, NJ: Princeton University Press, 1993.

———. "Quand l'habit fait le moine: The Symbolism of the Kāsāya in Sōtō Zen." *Cahiers d'Extrême-Asie* 8, no. 3 (1995): 335–96.

———. *Double Exposure: Cutting across Buddhist and Western Discourses.* Translated by Janet Lloyd. Stanford: Stanford University Press, 2004.

———. *Unmasking Buddhism.* New York: Blackwell, 2007.

"Featured Events," http://secondlife.com/destinations/events.

Fink, Bruce. *The Lacanian Subject: Between Language and Jouissance.* Princeton, NJ: Princeton University Press, 1995.

Foucault, Michel. "Nietzsche, Genealogy, History." In *The Foucault Reader*, edited by Paul Rabinow, 76–100. New York, NY: Pantheon, 1984.

———. *The Hermeneutics of the Subject: Lectures at the Collège de France*, 1981–1982. New York: Picador, 2005.

Frakes, Jonathan. *Star Trek: First Contact*, Paramount Pictures, 1996.

Freud, Sigmund. *An Outline of Psychoanalysis.* New York: Norton, 1940.

"Friends and Partnering," https://community.secondlife.com/t5/English-Knowledge-Base/Friends-and-partnering/ta-p/700067.

"Friends in Second Life," http://wiki.secondlife.com/wiki/Friends_in_Second_Life.

Fromm, Erich. *Escape from Freedom.* New York: Farrar and Rinehart, 1941.

Frow, John. "Michel de Certeau and the Practice of Representation." *Cultural Studies* 5, no. 1 (1991): 52–60.

Fuller, Robert. *Spiritual, but Not Religious.* Oxford: Oxford University Press, 2001.

Galloway, Alexander. *Gaming: Essays on Algorithmic Culture.* Minneapolis: University of Minnesota Press, 2006.

Ganz, Lowell and Babaloo Mandell. *Gung Ho*, Paramount Pictures, 1986.

Garfield, Jay. *The Fundamental Wisdom of the Middle Way: Nagarjuna's Mūlamadhyamakakārikā.* New York: Oxford University Press, 1995.

———. *Empty Words: Buddhist Philosophy and Cross-Cultural Interpretation.* Oxford: Oxford University Press, 2002.

———. "Taking Conventional Truth Seriously: Authority Regarding Deceptive Reality." *Philosophy East and West* 60, no. 3 (2010): 341–54.

Garmon, Meredith. "The New Buddhism," www.uufg.org/ . . . /397/2006-August13-The-New-Buddhism-Garmon.pdf.

Geertz, Clifford. *The Interpretation of Cultures.* New York: Basic Books, 1973.

———. *Local Knowledge: Further Essays in Interpretive Anthropology.* New York: Basic Books, 1983.

George, Frank Honywill. *The Brain as a Computer.* Oxford: Pergamon Press, 1961.

Gertner, Jon. *The Idea Factory: Bell Labs and the Great Age of American Innovation.* New York: Penguin Press, 2012.

Getz, Daniel A. "Sentient Beings." In *Encyclopedia of Buddhism*, volume 2, edited by Robert E. Buswell, 760. New York: Macmillan Reference USA, 2004.

"Gibson Island Second Life!—Home of Gibson Guitar Corp." YouTube Video, 4:35, posted by Earth Primbee, www.youtube.com/watch?v=8hnOd2ZsIxA.

Golub, Alex. "Being in the World (of Warcraft): Raiding, Realism, and Knowledge Production in a Massively Multiplayer Online Game." *Anthropological Quarterly* 83 (2010): 17–46.

Gombrich, Richard. "The Consecration of a Buddhist Image." *Journal of Asian Studies* 26, no. 1 (1966): 23–36.

"Gorean Roleplay in Second Life," Second Life Adventures, www.second-life-adventures.com/gorean-roleplay-in-second-life/.

Grieve, Gregory, P. "Imagining a Virtual Religious Community: Neo-Pagans on the Internet." *Chicago Anthropology Exchange* 7 (1995): 98–132.

———. "Signs of Tradition: Compiling a History of Development, Politics, and Tourism in Bhaktapur, Nepal." *Studies in Nepalese History and Society* 7 (2003): 281–307.

———. "Symbol, Idol and *Murti*: Hindu God-images and the Politics of Mediation." *Culture, Theory and Critique* 44 (2003): 57–72.

———. "One and Three Bhairavas: The Hypocrisy of Iconographic Mediation." *Revista de Estudos da Religião* 4 (2005), www.pucsp.br/rever/rv4_2005/p_grieve.pdf.

———. *Retheorizing Religion in Nepal.* New York: Palgrave Macmillan, 2006.

———. "There Is No Spoon? *The Matrix*, Ideology, and the Spiritual Logic of Late Capital." In *Teaching Religion and Film*, edited by Greg Watkins, 189–207. American Academy of Religion's Religious Studies Teaching Series. Oxford: Oxford University Press, 2009.

———. "Virtually Embodying the Field: Silent Online Buddhist Meditation, Immersion, and the Cardean Ethnographic Method." *Online – Heidelberg Journal of Religions on the Internet* 4, no. 1 (2010), www.online.uni-hd.de/.

———. "Do Human Rights Need a Self? A Skillful Reading of Engaged Buddhism, Literature and the Heroic Compassion of the Samsaric Subject." In *Human Rights and Literature*, edited by Elizabeth Swanson Goldberg and Alexandra Schultheis, 247–61. Philadelphia: University of Pennsylvania Press, 2011.

———. "Religion." In *Digital Religion: Understanding Religious Practice in New Media Worlds*, edited by Heidi Campbell, 104–19. New York: Routledge, 2012.

———. "The Formation of a Virtual Ethnographic Method: The Theory, Practice and Ethics of Researching Second Life's Buddhist Community." In *The Pixel in the Lotus: Buddhism, the Internet and Digital Media*, edited by Gregory Price Grieve and Daniel Veidlinger, 23–40. New York: Routledge, 2014.

———. "Studying Religion in Digital Gaming: A Critical Review of an Emerging Field." *Online – Heidelberg Journal of Religions on the Internet* 5, no. 1 (2014), www.online.uni-hd.de/.

Grieve, Gregory, P. and Daniel Veidlinger. *The Pixel in the Lotus: Buddhism, the Internet and Digital Media.* New York: Routledge, 2014.

"Group," http://wiki.secondlife.com/wiki/Group.

Gruber, Jacob. "Ethnographic Salvage and the Shaping of Anthropology." *American Anthropologist, New Series* 72, no. 6 (1970): 1289–99.

Gupta, Akhil, and James Ferguson. "Discipline and Practice: 'The Field' as Site, Method, and Location in Anthropology." In *Anthropological Locations: Boundaries and Grounds of a Field Science,* edited by A. Gupta and J. Ferguson, 1–46. Berkeley: University of California Press, 1997.

Hagen, Steven. *Buddhism Plain and Simple.* North Clarendon, VT: Tuttle Publishing, 1997.

Hahn, Harley. *The Internet Complete Reference.* New York: Osborne McGraw-Hill, 1996.

Halacy, Daniel Stephen. *Cyborg: Evolution of the Superman.* New York: Harper and Row, 1965.

Hạnh, Thích Nhất. *Zen Keys.* New York: Random House, 1974.

———. *Love in Action: Writings on Nonviolent Social Change.* Berkeley: Parallax Press, 1993.

———. *Going Home: Jesus and Buddha as Brothers.* New York: Riverhead Trade, 2000.

———. *The Blooming of a Lotus: Guided Meditation for Achieving the Miracle of Mindfulness.* Boston: Beacon Press, 2009.

Hansen, Mark. *Bodies in Code: Interfaces with Digital Media.* New York: Routledge, 2006.

Haraway, Donna. "A Cyborg Manifesto: Science, Technology, and Socialist-Feminism in the Late Twentieth Century." In *Simians, Cyborgs and Women: The Reinvention of Nature,* 149–83. New York: Routledge, 1994.

Harvey, David. *A Brief History of Neoliberalism.* Oxford: Oxford University Press, 2005.

Haslanger, Sally. "Objective Reality, Male Reality, and Social Construction." In *Women, Knowledge and Reality,* edited by Ann Garry and Marilyn Pearsall, 84–108. New York: Routledge, 1996.

Hayles, Katherine. *How We Became Posthuman: Virtual Bodies in Cybernetics, Literature, and Informatics.* Chicago: University of Chicago Press, 1999.

Heidegger, Martin. *Being and Time.* London: SCM Press, 1962.

———. "A Dialogue on Language between a Japanese and an Inquirer." In *On the Way to Language.* New York: Harper & Row, 1971.

———. *Poetry, Language, Thought.* New York: Harper and Row, 1971.

———. *Basic Writings.* New York: Harper and Row, 1976.

Heims, Steve. *The Cybernetics Group.* Cambridge MA: MIT Press, 1991.

Hein, Steven, and Dale Wright, eds. *The Zen Canon: Understanding The Classic Texts.* Oxford: Oxford University Press, 2004.

Helland, Christopher. "Religion Online/Online Religion and Virtual Communitas." In *Religion on the Internet: Research Prospects and Promises,* edited by Jeffery K. Hadden and Douglas E. Cowan, 205–24. London: JAI Press/Elsevier, 2000.

———. "Online Religion as Lived Religion. Methodological Issues in the Study of Religious Participation on the Internet." *Online – Heidelberg Journal of Religions on the Internet* 1, no. 1 (2005), www.ub.uni-heidelberg.de/archiv/5823.

"Hello Avatar – Second Life Wiki," Wiki.secondlife.com.

Hine, Christine. *Virtual Ethnography.* London: Sage Publications, 2000.

Hoover, Stewart. "The Cultural Construction of Religion and Media." In *Practicing Religion in the Age of the Media: Explorations in Media, Religion and Culture,* edited by Stewart Hoover and Lynn Schofield Clark, 1–6. New York: Columbia University Press, 2002.

Hoover, Stewart, and Knut Lundby. *Rethinking Media, Religion and Culture.* London: Sage, 1997.

Hoover, S.M., L.S. Clark, and L. Rainie. "Faith Online: 64% of Wired Americans Have Used the Internet for Spiritual or Religious Information," 2004, www.pewInternet.org/reports/toc.asp?Report.119.

Hoover, Stewart, and Nabil Echchaibi. "Media Theory and the Third Spaces of Digital Religion," Center for Media, Religion, and Culture, University of Boulder, 2014.

Hori, Victor Sogen. *Zen Sand: The Book of Capping Phrases for Kōan Practice.* Honolulu: University of Hawaii Press, 2003.

Horn, Vincent. "Two-Player Meditation," Buddhistgeeks lab, www.buddhistgeeks.com/2011/03/two-player-meditation/.

Hubbard, Jamie. "Introduction." In *Pruning the Bodhi Tree: The Storm over Critical Buddhism,* edited by Jamie Hubbard and Paul Swanson, vii–xxii. Honolulu: University of Hawai'i Press, 1997.

Hubbard, Jamie, and Paul Swanson. *Pruning the Bodhi Tree: The Storm over Critical Buddhism.* Honolulu: University of Hawai'i Press, 1997.

Huhtamo, Erkki. "Screen Tests: Why Do We Need an Archaeology of the Screen." *Cinema Journal* 51, no. 2 (2012): 144–48.

Huizinga, Johan. *Homo Ludens: A Study of the Play-Element in Culture.* Boston: Beacon Press, 1950.

Iwamura, Jane Naomi. *Virtual Orientalism: Asian Religions and American Popular Culture.* Oxford: Oxford University Press, 2011.

James, William. *The Principles of Psychology.* New York: Henry Holt and Company, 1890.

Japan: The Electronic Tribe, Television, PBS, 1988.

Jenkins, Henry. "*Star Trek* Rerun, Reread, Rewritten: Fan Writing as Textual Poaching." *Critical Studies in Mass Communication* 5, no. 2 (1988): 85–107.

Josephson, Jason Ānanda. "When Buddhism Became a 'Religion': Religion and Superstition in the Writings of Inoue Enryō." *Japanese Journal of Religious Studies* 33, no. 1 (2006): 143–68.

Kageki, Norri. "An Uncanny Mind: Masahiro Mori on the Uncanny Valley and beyond." *IEEE Spectrum,* June 12, 2012, http://spectrum.ieee.org/automaton/robotics/humanoids/an-uncanny-mind-masahiro-mori-on-the-uncanny-valley.

Karaflogka, Anastasia. *E-Religion: A Critical Appraisal of Religious Discourse on the World Wide Web.* London: Equinox, 2006.

Kelty, Christopher. *Two Bits: The Cultural Significance of Free Software.* Durham, NC: Duke University Press, 2008.

Kendall, Lori. *Hanging Out in the Virtual Pub: Masculinities and Relationships Online.* Berkeley: University of California Press, 2002.

Kerouac, Jack. *The Dharma Bums.* New York: Penguin, 1958.

Kierkegaard, Søren. *Concluding Unscientific Postscript to the Philosophical Crumbs.* Cambridge: Cambridge University Press, 2009.

Kimura, Kiyotaka. "The Self in Medieval Japanese Buddhism: Focusing on Dogen." *Philosophy East and West* 41, no. 3 (1991): 327–40.

King, Richard. "Spirituality and the Privatisation of Asian Wisdom Traditions." In *Selling Spirituality the Silent Takeover of Religion,* edited by Jeremy Carrette and Richard King, 87–123. London: Routledge, 2005.

Kohn, Tamara. "She Came Out of the Field and into My Home." In *Questions of Consciousness,* edited by A.P. Cohen and N. Rappaport, 41–59. London: Routledge, 1995.

Koman, Richard. *Congress Goes Virtual in Online World Hearing by Mike Musgrove,* April 2, 2008, www.cio-today.com/article/index.php?story_id=0220020SF4V8.

Kononenko, Igor. *Teachers of Wisdom*. Pittsburgh, PA: RoseDog Books, 2010.

Krueger, Myron. *Artificial Reality 2*. Reading, MA: Addison-Wesley Professional, 1991.

Lacan, Jacques. *The Ethics of Psychoanalysis: The Seminar of Jacques Lacan Book VII*. New York: Norton Company, 1986.

————. *The Seminar of Jaques Lacan: On Feminine Sexuality, the Limits of Love and Knowledge. Boox XX Encore 1972–1973*. New York: W.W. Norton & Company, 1988.

"LambdaMOO," www.moo.mud.org/.

"Land," http://wiki.secondlife.com/wiki/Land.

"Layman P'ang, Linji Yixuan, Hakuin Ekaku," Many Roads, http://bodhicharya.org/manyroads/layman-pang-linji-yixuan-hakuin-ekaku/.

Leary, Timothy. *Chaos and Cyber Culture*. San Francisco: Ronin Publishing, 1994.

Lessig, Lawrence. *Free Culture: How Big Media Uses Technology and the Law to Lock Down Culture and Control Creativity*. New York: Penguin Press, 2004.

Lévinas, Emmanuel. *Ethics and Infinity*. Pittsburg, PA: Duquesne University Press, 1985.

Levine, Noah. *Dharma Punx*. New York: Harpercollins, 2009.

Levy, David. "No Time to Think: Reflections on Information Technology and Contemplative Scholarship." *Ethics and Information Technology* 9, no. 4 (2007): 237–49.

Levy, Steven. *In the Plex: How Google Thinks, Works, and Shapes Our Lives*. New York: Simon and Schuster, 2011.

"License for Press Use of the Second Life Eye-in-Hand Logo," The Second Life® Brand Center, https://secondlife.com/corporate/brand/trademark/press.php.

Linden, Brett. "Introducing the Sandbox, the Official Second Life Newsletter," http://community.secondlife.com/t5/Community-General/Introducing-The-Sandbox-the-Official-Second-Life-Newsletter/ba-p/661318.

Linden Lab. "Press Room," http://lindenlab.com/press_2.php.

"Linden Lab Official: Bot Policy," http://wiki.secondlife.com/wiki/Linden_Lab_Official:Bot_policy.

"Linden Lab Official: Clarification of Policy Disallowing," ageplayLinden_Lab_Official:Clarification_of_policy_disallowing_ageplay.

"Linden Lab Official: Terms of Service Archive," http://wiki.secondlife.com/wiki/Linden_Lab_Official:Terms_of_Service_Archive.

"Linden World," http://secondlife.wikia.com/wiki/Linden_World.

Lisberger, Steven. "Tron," Buena Vista, 1982.

Lokos, Allan. "By Working with the Lay Precept on Speech, We Can Learn to Say the Right Thing at the Right Time," *Tricycle*, www.tricycle.com/precepts/skillful-speech.

Lopez, David. *Buddhist Hermeneutics*. Honolulu: University of Hawaii Press, 1988.

————. *The Heart Sutra Explained*. Albany: State University of New York Press, 1988.

————, ed. *Buddhism in Practice*. Princeton, NJ: Princeton University Press, 1995.

————. *Curators of the Buddha: The Study of Buddhism under Colonialism*. Chicago: University of Chicago Press, 1995.

————. *Elaborations on Emptiness: Uses of the Heart Sutra*. Princeton, NJ: Princeton University Press, 1996.

————. *Prisoners of Shangri-La*. Princeton, NJ: Princeton University Press, 1997.

————. *A Modern Buddhist Bible: Essential Readings from East and West*. Boston: Beacon Press, 2002.

Lovink, Geert. *Zero Comments: Blogging and Critical Internet Culture*. New York: Routledge, 2008.

"LSL Protocol/Restrained Love Relay/Introduction," http://wiki.secondlife.com/wiki/LSL_Protocol/Restrained_Love_Relay/Introduction.

Ludlow, Peter, and Mark Wallace. *The Second Life Herald: The Virtual Tabloid that Witnessed the Dawn of the Metaverse.* Cambridge, MA: MIT Press, 2007.

Macy, Joanna. *Mutual Causality in Buddhism and General Systems Theory.* Albany: State University of New York Press, 1991.

Magid, Barry. *Ending the Pursuit of Happiness: A Zen Guide.* Bloomington, MA: Wisdom Publications, 2008.

Mahoney, Stephen. "The Prevalence of Zen." *Nation* (November 1, 1958), 11.

Malaby, Thomas. "Beyond Play: A New Approach to Games." *Games and Culture* 2, no. 2 (2007): 95–113.

———. *Making Virtual Worlds: Linden Lab and Second Life.* Ithaca, NY: Cornell University Press, 2009.

Malinowski, Bronislaw. *The Sexual Life of Savages in North-Western Melanesia: An Ethnographic Account of Courtship, Marriage and Family Life among the Natives of the Trobriand Islands, British New Guinea.* New York: Halcyon House, 1929.

———. *Argonauts of the Western Pacific.* New York: E. P. Dutton, 1961.

———. *Magic, Science and Religion.* Prospect Heights, IL: Waveland Press, 1992.

Mander, Jerry. *Four Arguments for the Elimination of Television.* New York: Morrow Quill Paperbacks, 1978.

———. "Six Grave Doubts about Computers." *Whole Earth Review* (January 1985), 17–18.

———. *In the Absence of the Sacred: The Failure of Technology and the Survival of the Indian Nations.* San Francisco: Sierra Club Books, 1991.

Markham, Annette, and Elizabeth Buchanan. "Ethical Decision-Making and Internet Research (2.0)," Portable Document Format, 2012, http://aoir.org/reports/ethics2.pdf.

Markoff, John. *What the Doormouse Said.* New York: Penguin, 2005.

Marx, Karl. *The German Ideology.* London: Lawrence & Wishart, 1965.

"Mass Lab," Second Life Wiki, http://wiki.secondlife.com/wiki/Mass_Lab.

McCloud, Sean. *Making the American Religious Fringe: Exotics, Subversives, and Journalists, 1955–1993.* Chapel Hill, NC: University of North Carolina Press, 2004.

McLuhan, Marshall. *Understanding Media: The Extensions of Man.* New York: McGraw-Hill, 1964.

McMahan, David. *The Making of Buddhist Modernism.* Oxford: Oxford University Press, 2008.

McRae, John. *Seeing through Zen: Encounter, Transformation, and Genealogy in Chinese Chan Buddhism.* Berkeley: University of California Press, 2003.

Mead, Margaret. *Coming of Age in Samoa: A Psychological Study of Primitive Youth for Western Civilisation.* New York: William Morrow, 1928.

"Meditation/Mindfulness Apps for Smart Phones," WE MEDITATE, http://wemeditate.weebly.com/apps.html.

"Meet Mozilla FireFox," Mozilla Foundation, www.mozilla.org/en-US/firefox/central/.

Mehlman, Jeffrey. *The "Floating Signifier": From Lévi-Strauss to Lacan.* New Haven, CT: Yale University Press, 1972.

"MentalPlex," https://archive.google.com/mentalplex/.

Merleau-Ponty, Maurice. "Eye and Mind." In *The Primacy of Perception,* edited by James E. Edie, 159–90. Evanston, IL: Northwestern University Press, 1964.

Metz, Christian. "The Imaginary Signifier." In *The Imaginary Signifier: Psychoanalysis and Cinema,* 1–87. London/Basingstoke: MacMillan Press, 1982.

Micklethwait, John, and Adrian Wooldridge. *The Witch Doctors: Making Sense of the Management Gurus.* New York: Random House, 1996.

Mindell, David. *Between Human and Machine.* Baltimore: John Hopkins University Press, 2002.

"Mindfulness Meditation," Mental Workout, www.mentalworkout.com/store/programs/mindfulness-meditation/.

"The Mission of Linden Lab," Philip Rosedale, https://community.secondlife.com/t5/Features/The-Mission-of-Linden-Lab/ba-p/533170.

"Monier-Williams Sanskrit-English Dictionary," 1899, www.sanskrit-lexicon.uni-koeln.de/scans/MWScan/2014/web/webtc/indexcaller.php.

Moore, Laurence. *Religious Outsiders and the Making of Americans*. Oxford: Oxford University Press, 1986.

———. *Selling God: American Religion in the Marketplace of Culture*. Oxford: Oxford University Press, 1994.

Mori, Masahiro. "The Uncanny Valley." *Energy* 7, no. 4 (1970): 33–35.

Morningstar, Chip, and Randall Farmer. "The Lessons of Lucasfilm's Habitat." In *Cyberspace: First Steps*, edited by Michael Benedikt. Cambridge, MA: MIT Press, 1991.

Mumford, Lewis. *The Myth of the Machine: Technics and Human Development*. New York: Harvest/HBJ Book, 1979.

Murray, Janet H. *Hamlet on the Holodeck*. Cambridge, MA: MIT Press, 1999.

Murray, Janet. *Inventing the Medium: Principles of Interaction Design as a Cultural Practice*. Cambridge, MA: MIT Press, 2011.

"Myron Krueger – Videoplace, Responsive Environment, 1972–1990s," YouTube Video, 7:35, posted by "MediaArtTube," www.youtube.com/watch?v=dmmxVA5xhuo.

Negroponte, Nicholas. *Being Digital*. New York: Alfred Knopf, 1995.

Nelson, Theodor. *Computer Lib: You Can and Must Understand Computers Now/Dream Machines: New Freedoms through Computer Screens – A Minority Report*. Chicago: Hugo Book Service, 1974.

Ney, David. *American Technological Sublime*. Boston: MIT Press, 1994.

Nietzsche, Friedrich. *Human, All Too Human: A Book for Free Spirits*. Lincoln, NB: University of Nebraska Press, 1984.

Noriaki, Hakamaya. "Scholarship as Criticism." In *Pruning the Bodhi Tree: The Storm over Critical Buddhism*, edited by Jamie Hubbard and Paul Loren Swanson, 113–37. Honolulu, HI: University of Hawai'i Press, 1997.

North, Edmund. *The Day the Earth Stood Still*. Motion Picture, 20th Century Fox, 1951.

Novak, Philip. "The Buddha and the Computer: Meditation in an Age of Information." *Journal of Religion and Health* 25, no. 2 (1986): 188–92.

"The Office: Second Life Is the Same," YouTube Video, 0:25, posted by yoyomaster, October 31, 2007, www.youtube.com/watch?v=U3d_fqDcN1s.

Oldenburg, Ray. *The Great Good Place: Cafes, Coffee Shops, Community Centers, Beauty Parlors, General Stores, Bars, Hangouts, and How They Get You through the Day*. New York: Paragon House, 1989.

"Orientation to Zen 01 – Zazen (Zen Meditation)," YouTube Video, 24:29, posted by Eshu Martin, April 30, 2012. https://www.youtube.com/watch?v=1_djWyC1-_4

"ORIGINAL EDISON 1877 TIN FOIL RECORDING," YouTube Video, 1:17, posted by THEVICTROLAGUY, Dec 2, 2012, www.youtube.com/watch?v=g3qPT30LejM.

"'An Owner's Manual' for Google's Shareholders," 2004 Founders' IPO Letter, https://investor.google.com/corporate/2004/ipo-founders-letter.html.

Paccagnella, Luciano. "Getting the Seats of Your Pants Dirty: Strategies for Ethnographic Research on Virtual Communities." *Journal of Computer Mediated Communication* 3, no. 1 (1997), 1–10.

Pascale, Richard. "Zen and the Art of Management: A Different Approach to Management for the 'Cards-on-the-Table' Executive, Which Works." *Harvard Business Review*, March 1978, br.org/1978/03/zen-and-the-art-of-management/ar/1.

———. "Intentional Breakdowns and Conflict by Design." *Planning Review* 22, no. 3 (1994): 12–19.

———. *Surfing the Edge of Chaos: The Laws of Nature and the New Laws of Business*. New York: Crown Business; Reprint edition, 2001.

"Pew Forum on Religion and Public Life," 2008, www.pewforum.org/files/2013/05/report-religious-landscape-study-full.pdf.

Pew Internet Project. "Wired Churches, Wired Temples: Taking Congregations and Missions into Cyberspace," December 20, 2000, www.pewinternet.org/reports/toc.asp?Report.28.

———. "Cyberfaith: How Americans Pursue Religion Online," 2001, www.pewinternet.org/reports/reports asp?Report.53&Section.ReportLevel1&Field.Level1ID&ID.229.

———. "Search Engines," 2002, www.pewinternet.org/reports/toc.asp?Reports.64.

———. "America's Online Pursuits: The Changing Picture of Who's Online and What They Do," 2003, www.pewinternet.org/reports/toc.asp?Report.106.

Pew Research Center. "64% of Online Americans Have Used the Internet for Religious or Spiritual Purposes," www.pewinternet.org/2004/04/07/64-of-online-americans-have-used-the-internet-for-religious-or-spiritual-purposes/.

Pickering, Andrew. "The Science of the Unknowable: Stafford Beer's Cybernetic Informatics." In *The History and Heritage of Scientific and Technological Information Systems*, edited by W. Boyd Rayward and Mary Ellen Bowden, 29–38. Medford, NJ: Information Today, 2004.

Pirsig, Robert. *Zen and the Art of Motorcycle Maintenance: An Inquiry into Values*. New York: Bantam Books, 1974.

Prebish, Charles. *American Buddhism*. North Scituate, MA: Duxbury Press, 1979.

———. *Luminous Passage: The Practice of and Study of Buddhism in America*. Berkley: University of California Press, 1999.

———. "Online Peer-Reviewed Journals in Buddhism: The Birth of the Journals of Buddhist Ethics and Global Buddhism." In *Buddhism, the Internet, and Digital Media: The Pixel in the Lotus*, edited by Gregory P. Grieve and Daniel Veidlinger, 79–92. New York: Routledge, 2015.

Prebish, Charles, and Kenneth Tanaka. *The Faces of Buddhism in America*. Berkeley: University of California Press, 1998.

"Recognizing the Suffering in Your Own Life – Chapter 4," Dharma Wisdom, http://dharmawisdom.org/books-phillip-moffitt/dancing-life/excerpt-dancing-life#sthash.kfvAx7H6.dpuf.

Reps, Paul. *Zen Flesh, Zen Bones*. New York: Charles E. Tuttle, 1957.

"Resident," http://wiki.secondlife.com/wiki/Resident.

Rheingold, Howard. *The Virtual Community: Homesteading on the Electronic Frontier*. Reading, MA: Addison-Wesley Publications, 1993.

Rimpoche, Gelek. "The Four Noble Truths," Jewel Heart Publication, www.jewelheart.org/digital-dharma/four-noble-truths-transcript/.

Roddenberry, Gene. *Star Trek: The Next Generation*, "Q Who?," CBS Television Distribution, 1989.

"Role Play," http://wiki.secondlife.com/wiki/Role_play.

Rosedale, Philip. "Life in Second Life," TED, www.ted.com/talks/the_inspiration_of_second_life?language=en.

Roszak, Theodore. *The Making of a Counter Culture: Reflections on the Technocratic Society and Its Youthful Opposition*. New York: Doubleday Books, 1968.

———. *From Satori to Silicon Valley*. San Francisco: Don't Call It Frisco Press, 1986.

Rymaszewski, Michael. *Second Life: The Official Guide*. Hoboken, NJ: John Wiley & Sons, 2007.

"S-1/A 1 ds1a.htm AMENDMENT NO. 9 TO FORM S-1," www.sec.gov/Archives/edgar/data/1288776/000119312504142742/ds1a.htm.

Said, Edward. *Orientalism*. New York: Vintage, 1979.

Schilt, Kristen. "Doing Gender, Doing Heteronormativity: 'Gender Normals,' Transgender People, and the Social Maintenance of Heterosexuality." *Gender and Society* 23, no. 4 (2009): 440–64.

Schlütter, Morten. *How Zen Became Zen: The Dispute over Enlightenment and the Formation of Chan Buddhism during the Song Dynasty China*. Honolulu: University of Hawai'i Press, 2008.

Schrödinger, Erwin. "The Present Situation in Quantum Mechanics," www.tuhh.de/rzt/rzt/it/QM/cat.html.

Schrödinger, Erwin, and M. Born. "Discussion of Probability Relations between Separated Systems." *Mathematical Proceedings of the Cambridge Philosophical Society* 31, no. 4 (1935): 555–63.

Searle, John. *The Construction of Social Reality*. New York: Penguin, 1996.

"Second Life," http://secondlife.com/.

"Second Life in 2002/News," http://wiki.secondlife.com/wiki/Second_Life_in_2002/News.

"Second Life Community," http://secondlife.com/community/.

"Second Life Grid Survey – Region Database," www.gridsurvey.com/.

"Second Life Havok 4 – No Lag with 2000–3400 Physical Prims," www.youtube.com/watch?v=t5_Lzxvuizg.

"A Second Life Holiday," Gratuitous.com, March 6, 2007, www.youtube.com/watch?v=EgtGcTHL2dI.

"Second Life Marketplace," https://marketplace.secondlife.com/?lang=en-US.

"Second Life Search," http://search.secondlife.com/.

Shannon, Claude. "A Mathematical Theory of Communication. Part I." *Bell Systems Technical Journal* 27 (1948): 379–423.

Shannon, Claude E., and Warren Weaver. *A Mathematical Model of Communication*. Urbana, IL: University of Illinois Press, 1949.

Shapiro, Elmer. "Computer Network Meeting of October 9–10, 1967," November 1967, http://web.stanford.edu/dept/SUL/library/extra4/sloan/mousesite/Archive/Post68/ARPANETMeeting1167.html.

Sharf, Robert H. "Modernism and the Rhetoric of Meditative Experience." *Numen* 42 (1995): 228–83.

Sharf, Robert. "The Zen of Japanese Nationalism." In *Curators of the Buddha: The Study of Buddhism under Colonialism*, edited by Donald Lopez, 107–61. Chicago: University of Chicago Press, 1995.

Silverman, Kaja. *The Subject of Semiotics*. New York: Oxford University Press, 1983.

———. *Male Subjectivity at the Margins*. New York: Routledge, 1992.

Silverstein, Michael. "Shifters, Linguistic Categories, and Cultural Description." In *Meaning in Anthropology*, edited by Keith Basso and Henry A. Selby, 11–55. Albuquerque, NM: University of New Mexico Press, 1976.

————. "Metapragmatic Discourse and Metapragmatic Function." In *Reflexive Language*, edited by J. Lucy, 32–58. New York: Cambridge University Press, 1993.

Smith, David. "The Authenticity of Alan Watts." In *American Buddhism as a Way of Life*, edited by Gary Storhoff and John Whalen-Bridge, 13–39. Albany: SUNY Press, 2010.

Smith, J.Z. *Map Is Not Territory: Studies in the History of Religions.* Chicago: University of Chicago Press, 1978.

————. *Imagining Religion: From Babylon to Jonestown.* Chicago: University of Chicago Press, 1982.

————. "Constructing a Small Place." In *Sacred Space: Shrine, City, Land*, edited by Benjamin Z. Kedar, R. J. Zwi Werblowsky, 19–31. New York: New York University Press, 1998.

Snodgrass, Judith. *Presenting Japanese Buddhism to the West.* Chapel Hill, NC: University of North Carolina Press, 2003.

Soeng, Mu. *Diamond Sutra: Transforming the Way We Perceive the World.* Somerville, MA: Wisdom Publications, 2000.

Soja, Edward. *Thirdspace: Journeys to Los Angeles and Other Real-and-Imagined Places.* Oxford: Basil Blackwell, 1996.

Spencer, Robert. "Social Structure of a Contemporary Japanese-American Buddhist Church." *Social Forces* 26, no. 3 (1948): 281–87.

de Spinoza, Benedictus. *The Short Treatise on God, Man and His Well-Being.* New York: Russell & Russell, 1963.

Snyder, Gary. *Earth House Hold: Technical Notes & Queries to Fellow Dharma Revolutionaries.* San Francisco: New Directions Book, 1957.

Staff, Mindful. "Can I Be Honest with You?" *Mindful*, August 25, 2010, www.mindful.org/can-i-be-honest-with-you/.

Steingrubner, J.H. "Cybersangha: Building Buddhist Community Online." *Cybersangha: The Buddhist Alternative Journal*, www.newciv.org/CyberSangha/stein95.htm.

Suwattano, Bikkhu. "Mindfulness and Insight on the Internet," www.budsas.org/ebud/ebmed008.htm.

Talamasca, Akela. "Second Life Ranked 8th Most Effective Placement on TV in 2007," December 30, 2007, http://massively.joystiq.com/2007/12/30/second-life-ranked-8th-most-effective-placements-on-tv-in-2007.

Taylor, Charles. *Sources of the Self: The Making of the Modern Identity.* Cambridge, MA: Harvard University Press, 1989.

"Terms of Service," Linden Lab, www.lindenlab.com/tos.

Thompson, James, and Jacek Koronacki. *Statistical Process Control: The Deming Paradigm and Beyond.* London: Chapman & Hall, 2002.

Thubten, Anam. "A Tomato Opened My Mind," *Tricycle*, www.tricycle.com/insights/how-tomato-opened-my-mind.

"Tibetan Buddhism 48 First Noble Truth from the Four Points," Jewel Heart Channel, YouTube Video, 13:27, www.youtube.com/watch?v=PG8LSJmUVGU.

Tönnies, Ferdinand. *Gemeinschaft und Gesellschaft – Abhandlung des Communismus und des Sozialismus als empirischer Kulturforment.* Leipzig: Fues's Verlag, 1887.

Turkle, Sherry. *The Second Self: Computers and the Human Spirit.* New York: Simon and Schuster, 1984.

————. *Life on the Screen: Identity in the Age of the Internet.* New York: Simon and Schuster, 1995.

————. *Alone Together: Why We Expect More from Technology and Less from Each Other.* New York: Basic Books, 2011.

Turner, Edith. *Communitas: The Anthropology of Collective Joy*. New York: Palgrave Macmillan, 2012.

Turner, Fred. *From Counterculture to Cyberculture*. Chicago: University of Chicago Press, 2006.

Tweed, Thomas. *The American Encounter with Buddhism: 1844–1912*. Chapel Hill, NC: The University of North Carolina Press, 1992.

Tworkov, Helen. "Many Is More." *Tricycle* 1, no. 2 (1999), www.tricycle.com/new-buddhism/buddhism/many-more.

Uchiyama, Kosho. *Opening the Hand of Thought: Foundations of Zen Buddhist Practice*. Delhi: Wisdom Publications, 1993.

Vargas, Jose Antonio. "The Face of Facebook." *The New Yorker*, September 2010, www.newyorker.com/magazine/2010/09/20/the-face-of-facebook.

Veidlinger, Daniel. "From Indra's Net to Internet: Communication, Technology and the Evolution of Buddhism," Draft, California State University, Chico, 2015.

Victoria, Daizen. *Zen at War*. New York: Routledge, 1997.

von Bertalanffy, Ludwig. *General System Theory: Foundations, Development, Applications*. New York: George Braziller, 1968.

von Foerster, Heinz. *Observing Systems*. Seaside, CA: Intersystems Publications, 1981.

Wagner, Rachel. "The Importance of Playing in Earnest." In *Playing with Religion in Digital Games*, edited by Heidi Campbell and Gregory Price Grieve, 192–213. Bloomington, IN: Indiana University Press, 2014.

Wallace, Sam Littlefair. "Mark Zuckerberg Says 'Buddhism Is an Amazing Religion'." *Lion's Roar: Buddhist Wisdom for Our Time*, October 27, 2015, www.lionsroar.com/mark-zuckerberg-says-buddhism-is-an-amazing-religion/.

Watts, Alan. *The Wisdom of Insecurity: A Message for an Age of Anxiety*. New York: Pantheon Books, 1951.

———. *The Way of Zen*. New York: Pantheon, 1958.

———. *Psychotherapy, East and West*. New York: New American Library, 1961.

———. *The Tao of Philosophy*. London: Tuttle Publishing, 2002.

Webster, David. *The Philosophy of Desire in the Buddhist Pali Canon*. Cambridge: Cambridge University Press, 2005.

Weinberger, Sharon. "Congress Freaks Out over Second Life Terrorism," March 4, 2008, www.wired.com/2008/04/second-life/.

"Welcome to the Bartle Test," http://4you2learn.com/bartle/.

Welter, Albert. "Mahākāśyapa's Smile: Silent Transmission and the Kung-an (Kōan) Tradition." In *The Kōan: Texts and Contexts in Zen Buddhism*, edited by Steven Heine and Dale S. Wright, 75–109. Oxford/New York: Oxford University Press, 2000.

"What Is Second Life?," http://secondlife.com/whatis/.

"Who Coined the Term 'Resident'," Second Life Forums Archive, http://forums-archive.secondlife.com/139/e9/125712/1.html.

Wiener, Norbert. *Cybernetics, or Control and Communication in the Animal and the Machine*. New York: Technology Press, 1948.

———. *Human Use of Human Beings*. New York: Houghton Mifflin, 1950.

———. *I Am a Mathematician: The Later Life of a Prodigy*. Cambridge, MA: MIT Press, 1964.

Williams, John. "Techne-Zen and the Spiritual Quality of Global Capitalism." *Critical Inquiry* 37, no. 1 (2011): 18–70.

Wilson, Jeff. *Dixie Dharma*. Chapel Hill, NC: University of North Carolina Press, 2012.

Winnicott, Donald Wood. *Playing and Reality*. London: Tavistock, 1971.

Wuthnow, Robert. *After Heaven: Spirituality in America since the 1950's*. Berkeley: University of California Press, 1998.

"X4 Female Starter Pack," www.getxcite.com/item_v2.php?product=2288.

Yampolsky, Philip, trans. *The Platform Sutra of the Sixth Patriarch*. New York: Columbia University Press, 1996.

Young, Charles M. "Plato and Computer Dating." *Oxford Studies in Ancient Philosophy* 12 (1994): 227–50.

Young, Iris Marion. *On Female Body Experience: "Throwing Like a Girl" and Other Essays*. Oxford: Oxford University Press, 2005.

Zaleski, Jeff. *The Soul of Cyberspace: How Technology Is Changing Our Spiritual Lives*. San Francisco: HarperEdge, 1997.

Žižek, Slavoj. *Tarrying with the Negative: Kant, Hegel, and the Critique of Ideology*. Durham, NC: Duke University Press, 1993.

———. *For They Know Not What They Do: Enjoyment as a Political Factor*. New York: Verso, 1994.

———, ed. *Mapping Ideology*. New York: Verso, 1994.

———. "From Virtual Reality to the Virtualization of Reality." In *Electronic Culture: Technology and Visual Representation*, edited by Timothy Drucjery, 290–95. New York: Aperture, 1996.

———. "Cyberspace, Or, the Unbearable Closure of Being." In *The Plague of Fantasies*, 127–59. London: Verso, 1997.

———. *The Plague of Fantasies*. London/New York: Verso, 1997.

———. *The Ticklish Subject: The Absent Centre of Political Ontology*. New York: Verso, 2000.

———. *Welcome to the Desert of the Real*. New York: Verso, 2002.

———. *The Puppet and the Dwarf: The Perverse Core of Christianity*. Cambridge: MIT Press, 2003.

———. *The Sublime Object of Ideology*. London: Verso, 2008.

Zukin, Sharon. *Point of Purchase: How Shopping Changed American Culture*. New York: Routledge, 2004.

Index

140; endless 55, 62, 83; fantasy 47, 218;
fashion 133, 147; gender 142; ideology
47; knowledge 10; media practice 132;
network consumer society 47, 61, 219;
relationships 10; screening 198–9; Second
Life 55; shopping 62; spirituality 55
Dharma [in tool box 230] 1–3, 5, 6–16, 22,
33, 38, 74, 85, 87–9, 94–5, 114–15, 120–2,
126–7, 134, 149, 151, 156, 160, 171, 179,
182, 187, 197, 205–6, 207, 217, 225, 230;
digital (see digital Dharma); discussion 7,
8; without dogma 121; emic definition
6–7, 38; emptiness 8; etic definition 6;
mindfulness 8; spreading inworld 4–6,
15–19, 85–7, 94, 104, 112, 116, 217;
transhistorical 14; see also digital dharma
Dharma talks 7, 33, 120, 126, 149, 156,
179–80; definition 179–80
Dharma teachers 3, 6, 86, 89, 90, 103, 111,
118, 120–2, 180, 183, 185, 210; Cassius
Lawndale 120; Zazen as only true 103,
121, 185
digital Dharma [in tool box 217] 1, 3, 6–10,
11–14, 19, 22, 72–4, 87, 94; critics 12, 22,
95–6; definition 1–2, 6–8; empowering
12; evolving 22; history 74; liberating
12; recycle media practices 87; silence
72; symptom network consumer society
14; theorization 9–10; usual academic
understanding 11, 22
digital media [in tool box 217] 19, 23,
47–50, 64, 72; affordances 48–50; appeal
47; definition 48–9; vs. mindfulness 71;
network consumer society 61; renovation
everyday life 23
digital religion 23, 33, 47; leaves no mystery
71; mirrors broad cultural change 23;
on-offline 33
digital technology see digital media
digital utopianism [in tool box 217] 19,
47, 52, 54, 56–61, 64, 90, 117, 204, 123,
217; authority 117; community 123;
counterculture 64, 117; cybernetics 56;
definition 47, 56, 90; Google and 124–5;
history 126; ideology 56; imagination 52,
56; network consumer society 64, 90–1;
Zen 90–1
disabled 2, 5, 138
dominant/Submissive [in tool box 225] 5,
108, 109, 225; collar 108; definition 108;
Goreans 108; Hoben 109; see also resident
created relationships

drama [in tool box 225] 5, 9, 38, 103, 120,
225; defined 103
dress see fashion
Dr. Evol 106, 108, 144; cybersex 106;
partnered 108
Duhkha (duḥkha) [in tool box 231]
see suffering
dweller [in tool box 218] 79–81, 218;
definition 80; see also fundamentalist
dwelling [in tool box 218] 81, 91, 145,
156–61, 167, 172, 196; theorized 161; see
also immersion

Eden, Fae 1, 7, 45, 53; see also Mystic Moon
edgeplay [in tool box 225] 5, 48, 55, 224,
225; definition 55
Emerita rathbunae see Fred Young
emic [in tool box 218] 8, 19, 24, 32, 40, 76–7,
86, 169, 176; definition 8, 76, 86; Second
Life terms 24–5; Zen 76; see also etic
emptiness 6–8, 20, 47, 72–7, 85–6, 93,
105, 133, 147, 151, 156, 165, 170, 172,
175, 177, 180–1, 188, 190–1, 194,
202–8, 215–16, 222, 232; codependence
133; cushion 165; definition 85, 133;
impermanence 85, 133; robes 133;
self-fashioning 133, 146–9; ultimate
reality 76
entanglement see social entanglement
Epps, Sabrina ix, 34, 36; see also team
ethics 6, 12, 21, 24, 32–3, 37–8, 61, 86, 93,
110, 208, 211, 231; ethnography 37–8;
Institutional Review Board 32, 38, 40;
karma 86, 231; terms of service 32;
see also compassion; moral economy
ethnography 19, 29–30, 31–9; description
32; effectiveness 19, 39; empty your
cup 31–3, 35, 36, 38–9; ethics 37–8;
exploration 39; interpretation 32,
33; middle-way 39; theorizing 32–3;
transformation of researchers 39, 41;
unknown unknowns 39; virtual 33–5;
virtual tourism 39, 66; see also participant
observation; thick description
ethos [in tool box 218] 33, 90, 93, 112–13,
126, 162, 218, 220; definition 112–13
etic [in tool box 218] 26, 32, 38, 218; see
also emic
event [in tool box 225] 1, 5, 7, 19, 21,
22, 31, 65, 85, 92–3, 95, 118, 120, 172,
175–91, 209, 225; definition 21; online
meditation 175–91; tea ceremony 31

191, 194, 205, 217, 220; computers 72; cybernetics 17, 51, 87, 91, 124; cyberspace 51; definition 112–13, 194; procedure 17; Zen 112–13, 115, 203
orientalism [in tool box 220] 13–14, 20, 28, 74–5, 95, 104, 166, 220; definition 13; network consumer society 13–16; virtual 13–16
owner 2, 20, 46, 119, 120, 136, 147, 166, 179, 212, 225; authority 119

pagan 5, 19, 110, 113, 121, 126, 146–7, 160, 162, 166, 179; groups 110; music 126
paramartha-satya (paramārtha-satya) [in tool box 231] see ultimate reality
participant observation [in tool box 220] 19, 33–4, 36–7; description 34; theorization 34–5; virtual 34
partner [in tool box 227] 5, 7, 45, 53, 105, 107–8, 109, 118, 221, 227; definition 107; marriage 108
PDCA (plan-do-check-act) wheel [figure 2.2] 73–4, 93–4; see also Edwards Deming
people [in tool box 227] see resident
personal 6, 8, 35, 56–7, 63, 77–81, 90, 120–3, 133, 144, 148, 181, 218, 222
personal relationship see relationship
physics (virtual) [in tool box 221] 50, 53, 119, 141, 221
Pirsig, Robert 16, 65, 75, 91–3, 123, 189; corporate management 91; cybernetics 91; see also quality; Zen and the Art of Motorcycle Maintenance
place [in tool box 227] 5, 8, 12, 20–1, 39, 48, 50–2, 56, 65, 71, 79–81, 90, 95, 110, 115–16, 122, 144, 147, 156–73, 182, 204, 210, 216, 218, 226; authentic 12, 161; cosmology 166–8; definition 21, 157, 160–1; explorer 39; fantasy 51; fundamentalist 160; imagination 46, 51, 52, 217; mindful 160; New Age 160; pseudonyms 25; ruins 166; spirituality 56–7, 90, 144, 147, 166–7, 182, 204; utopia 20, 212; see also third place
platform 12, 15, 19, 23, 32, 45, 53–4, 64, 78, 80, 87, 107–8, 110, 115, 119–20, 132, 135–6, 143–6, 151, 158–60, 165–6, 168, 170, 178, 194, 197–202, 218, 220, 226; grid 226; group 226; imagination 218; lag 226; see also Second Life viewer
play 5, 53, 109, 116–17, 119, 124, 132, 139, 143–5, 150–1, 168–9, 183, 196, 204, 207, 212; authority 117; gamist 53; google

124–5; life-style play 139–40; magic circle 169; mindfulness 212; religion 169; see also role play; self-play
poach 5, 12, 16, 18, 20, 26, 73, 79, 82, 95, 135, 153, 189, 215, 222, 228
poaching 5, 12, 16, 20, 25, 73, 79, 135, 153, 189; definition 26, 153; spiritual 79
popular culture 3, 5, 11–24, 29–30, 46–7, 52, 56–7, 63, 65, 72, 75, 82, 87, 89, 91–5, 105–6, 110–11, 121, 126, 131, 134, 140–5, 153, 158, 169, 176, 178, 181, 189, 196, 205, 211, 216–17, 222; America 13, 57, 87, 89, 93, 95, 178; cyborg 131, 140–1; relation to network consumer society 72
postwar 16–17, 20, 63–5, 72–5, 87–9, 92, 95, 123, 131, 140, 189, 200, 217; cyborg 131, 140–1; network consumer society 133
practice [spiritual] 6, 7, 8, 14, 15, 20, 69, 72, 71–9, 80–99; authentic 74; belief 81; community 126; cushion 164; fashion 134; fundamentalist 83; path 72; personal effort 81; robes 134; seeker 81; spirituality 77–8; statistics 81; Zen 74, 76
practice [theoretical term] [in tool box 221] see media practice
practice-oriented spirituality 20, 81–3, 94, 121, 145, 152; cushion 164; cybernetics 87–8; self 147–9; see also tactic
practitioners 6, 8, 11, 12, 15, 72; Laity 76
Pratityasmupada (pratītyasamutpāda) [in tool box 231] see dependent arising
Prebish, Charles 8, 25, 28, 74
prims [in tool box 227] 52, 67, 134, 158, 162, 227; definition 158; robes 134
procedural relationship [in tool box 221] 107, 221, 225–7; see also friend; partner; relationship
procedure [in tool box 221] 16, 21, 32–3, 39, 49, 51, 65, 75, 93, 143, 165, 177, 180–7, 189, 202, 211, 221; affordance 49; cybernetics 21; definition 177; ritual 21, 175–7; silence 32, 180–7

quality 73, 91; cybernetics 93; defined 91, 93; Deming 73, 93; information 92; mindfulness 83, 91; Pirsig 91; steersman 92; system 73, 91

reality 6, 8, 11–15, 17–18, 21–4, 25, 27, 34, 39, 46–8, 50–1, 53–4, 61–2, 67, 71–2, 76, 79, 80, 82, 112, 120, 122, 129, 132–25, 139, 145, 147–8, 150, 151, 153, 161–2,

sandbox: definition 10, 22, 53–4, 60, 106, 132, 143–5, 160, 175, 212; definition 10, 132; mindfulness 212; Second Life as 53; self 132, 143–4

sangha (*saṅgha*) [in tool box 231] *see* community

screening *see* screens

screens [in tool box 221] 3–4, 8, 19–12, 21–4, 31, 34, 47, 54–6, 71, 117, 133, 136–9, 157, 161, 175–7, 182, 186, 190, 194, 198–205, 208, 221; body 138; desire 55, 198–205; filter 21; imagination 21; pixels on 19, 21; spiritual 21; Zen 71

search engine 20, 49, 75, 125, 129, 135, 161; Google 124–5

Second Life 6, 15, 19, 20, 32–3, 45–70, 72, 74–82, 86–7, 90, 94–5, 98, 100; alienation 60–1; alternative reality 132, 142; authority 117–25; body 138; boundary 139; chore 141; conventional level 4; corporate use 105; deconstructing 195; definition xi, 1, 45, 53; description 45–6, 52; *vs.* email and chat 138; experience 65; fantasy 46, 62; gender axes 143; god-like 54; hard to use 55; heteronormative 142–3, 149–50; historical context 46, 47; imagination 47, 53; koan 120; media practice 46; MMORPGs 1, 53; music 126; naming 64; network consumer society 61, 133; not game, xi, 12, 53; online religion 2; real life 15; samsara 170–1; shopping 62; socializing 5; spiritual journey 12; statistics 77; theorization ethnographic field 34; *vs.* real life 46; *see also* virtual world

Second Life viewer 21, 55, 64; definition 64; description 64–5

seeker [in tool box 221] 77, 79–81, 124; definition 80; letting go 80; theorizing 80

self 5, 8, 17–18, 27, 29, 38, 50, 55, 63, 67, 76, 80–1, 83, 84, 89–90, 108, 115, 129, 131–5, 139, 140–9, 151, 168–9, 171, 180, 187–9, 204, 218, 219; alternative 29, 55, 142; authentic 151, 168; awareness 17, 67, 76, 82–3, 89, 187–9; compassion 84; cybernetics 90, 171, 189; cyborg 131, 140; decentering 27; essential 141, 152; fantasy 139; fashion 134; feedback 89–90; fluid 144; human 218; loss 129; mindfulness 129, 132–3, 219; modernist 129, 135; myself 1, 38, 103, 115, 175, 195; play 144; post-modern 135; real

life 38, 146–9, 204; roles 135; sandbox 132, 143–4; steerman 87; template 135; theorized 135; therapy 6, 68, 83, 144, 180; transparency 18; utopic 129; who are you 134; zazen 80; *see also* identity; no-self; self-fashioning; steersman

self-fashioning 17, 67, 80, 108, 132–4, 141–2, 145; agency 132, 151–2; consumerism 134; description 137, 141–2; desire 142; fantasy 142; gender 132, 142; sanbox 143–4; spirituality 132, 145–9; virtual worlds 134

self-play 5, 109, 116–17, 139, 143–5, 150–1, 168–9, 196, 212; *see also* role play; self-fashioning

sex *see* cybersex

shape [in tool box 228] 12, 52, 137, 139, 142, 228; caboose 142; *see also* avatar; body

shopping 1, 48, 53, 60, 62, 112, 141, 147, 200; agency 62; American society 62, 65; authenticity 147; avatar 141, 147; community 62; digital technology 63; identity 62; ideology 63; real affect 62; relationships 62; self-liberation 63; social relations 63; statistics 62

silence [in tool box 221] 9–10, 20–1, 31–2, 72, 76–7, 118, 162, 163, 164, 167, 167, 172–8, 180–91, 196, 221; critical 72; definition 10; gaps 21; interpretation 76, 181–2; justification 181; media practices 32, 72, 176, 180–1; mediated by digital technology 72; mindfulness 10; not outside language 72; ritual 164; sign 72 [see figure 2.1]; theorizing 10, 32

sitting *see* zazen

situation [in tool box 221] 75, 90, 135, 136, 139, 157, 167, 175–7, 178, 180–1, 190, 209–11, 221; definition 176

skillful means 72–3, 85, 93, 182; digital media 85; engagement 85; silence 182

skin 52, 132, 137–41, 189; *see also* avatar; body

smrti (*smṛti*) [in tool box 231] 6, 21, 82, 177, 219, 231; *see also* anapanasmrti; mindfulness

social construction 26, 29, 72, 75, 76; authenticity 72, 75; religion 75; religious studies 76; zen 75

social entanglement [in tool box 221] 16–18, 124, 171, 189, 218, 221; system 221; theorizing 18

socializing 38, 52; statistics 52, 103

Milton Keynes UK
Ingram Content Group UK Ltd.
UKHW031537071024
449327UK00024B/1869

9 780415 628730